Dancing in the English style

MANCHEStER
1824

Manchester University Press

STUDIES IN POPULAR CULTURE

General editor: Professor Jeffrey Richards

Already published

Dancing in the English style

Consumption, Americanisation and national identity in Britain, 1918–50

ALLISON ABRA

Manchester University Press

Published by Manchester University Press
Altrincham Street, Manchester M1 7JA, UK
www.manchesteruniversitypress.co.uk

British Library Cataloguing-in-Publication Data is available

ISBN 978 1 7849 9433 4 hardback
ISBN 978 1 5261 4262 7 paperback

First published by Manchester University Press in hardback 2017

This edition first published 2019

Typeset by Toppan Best-set Premedia Limited

STUDIES IN POPULAR CULTURE

There has in recent years been an explosion of interest in culture and cultural studies. The impetus has come from two directions and out of two different traditions. On the one hand, cultural history has grown out of social history to become a distinct and identifiable school of historical investigation. On the other hand, cultural studies has grown out of English literature and has concerned itself to a large extent with contemporary issues. Nevertheless, there is a shared project, its aim, to elucidate the meanings and values implicit and explicit in the art, literature, learning, institutions and everyday behaviour within a given society. Both the cultural historian and the cultural studies scholar seek to explore the ways in which a culture is imagined, represented and received, how it interacts with social processes, how it contributes to individual and collective identities and world views, to stability and change, to social, political and economic activities and programmes. This series aims to provide an arena for the cross-fertilisation of the discipline, so that the work of the cultural historian can take advantage of the most useful and illuminating of the theoretical developments and the cultural studies scholars can extend the purely historical underpinnings of their investigations. The ultimate objective of the series is to provide a range of books which will explain in a readable and accessible way where we are now socially and culturally and how we got to where we are. This should enable people to be better informed, promote an interdisciplinary approach to cultural issues and encourage deeper thought about the issues, attitudes and institutions of popular culture.

Jeffrey Richards

For my parents, Douglas and Glennis Abra

Contents

Illustrations

Acknowledgements

In the years I have been working on this book, people have often asked how I got interested in studying dancing – especially since I am not a dancer myself. The project had several different starting points – a faded photograph of my grandfather, Lieutenant-Colonel Jack Abra, in uniform at a tea dance in London during the Second World War; a favourite movie where characters danced the Lambeth Walk; a conversation in a graduate seminar on wartime women at Queen's University about the curious lack of research on the dance hall. In different ways, I have been thinking about dancing for a long time, and have accrued a great number of debts along the way.

The formal research and writing of this book began at the University of Michigan, and whatever strengths it possesses are in large part owing to its genesis within that engaged community of scholars. I am particularly indebted to Kali Israel, Sonya Rose and Jay Cook for their time, guidance and ongoing support. Each of them has influenced the development of this project in countless ways, and provided me with stellar examples of how to be both a scholar and a teacher. I am forever grateful for the wonderful colleagues and good friends that I met at Michigan, and on whom I continue to rely long after we left Ann Arbor. I especially want to thank Angela Thompsell, Will Mackintosh, Sara Babcox First, Josh First, Dan Livesay, Mary Livesay, Holly Maples, Diana Mankowski, Sara Lampert, Jonathan Eacott, Alex Lovit, Liz Hudson, LaKisha Simmons, Laura Hilburn, Victoria Castillo and Kara French. I am also appreciative of the assistance and guidance I have received from friends, mentors and colleagues at the other institutions I have been privileged to move through as either a student or teacher. My sincere gratitude goes to Chris Trott, Adele Perry, Gerry Friesen, Francis Carroll and John Wortley at the University of Manitoba, and to Bob Malcolmson and Sandra den Otter at Queen's University.

As I dived into the most intense period of writing and revision, I was lucky to land in the History Department at the University of Southern Mississippi, a rare gem where colleagiality, intellectual exchange and true friendships are fostered in equal measures. I am grateful to all of my colleagues at Southern Miss for their encouragement and support, but special thanks go to Kevin Greene for our many chats about jazz; to my faculty mentor, Andrew Haley, for all of his advice and challenging (in the best way) questions about my work; to our administrative assistant, Cindy Warren; and to my co-fellows in the Dale Center for the Study of War & Society – Kyle Zelner, Susannah Ural, Heather Stur, Ken Swope, Douglas Bristol and Andrew Wiest – for too many things to list, so let's start with all the fun lunches? Another big thank you goes to the members of the History Department's junior faculty writing group – Andrew Ross, Matt Casey, Courtney Luckhardt and Rebecca Tuuri – for their helpful comments on different chapters over coffee and wine. Thank you also to the other generous and thoughtful readers at Southern Miss and elsewhere who read sections of or the entirety of the manuscript: Kevin Greene, Sara Babcox First, Andrew Haley, Heather Stur, Kyle Zelner, Bob Malcolmson and especially Amy Milne-Smith (my dear friend and 'history partner in crime' of long standing). My time at Southern Miss has also been greatly enriched by my friendships across the disciplines with the Reserve crew and the English ladies. Thank you to Rebecca Morgan Frank and Alexandra Valint for being such lovely friends and colleagues even though we get off the elevator on different floors of the Liberal Arts Building. I should probably also thank T-Bones Records & Café in Hattiesburg for allowing Alex, Morgan, and I to sit there for hours on Writing Wednesdays.

A number of institutions have supported the research and writing of this book at different stages of its evolution. Thank you to the Council on Library and Information Resources in Washington, DC, as well as to the University of Michigan's Department of History, Rackham Graduate School, International Institute, Institute for Research on Women and Gender, and Eisenberg Institute for Historical Studies. Generous support also came from the History Department, College of Arts & Letters, Office of the Provost, Office of the Vice President-Research, and the Dale Center for the Study of War & Society, at the University of Southern Mississippi. I am also grateful for all of the advice and assistance provided by archivists and librarians as I conducted the research for this book at the Mass Observation Archive, the British Library, the British Newspaper Library, the National Archives, the National Archives of Scotland, the National Library of Scotland, the BBC Written Archives Centre, the Imperial War

Museum, the London Metropolitan Archives, the Women's Library, the Liverpool Record Office, the Museum of Liverpool Life, the Hammersmith Borough Archives, the Theatre Museum and the Royal Opera House, Covent Garden. Thank you to the Trustees of the Mass Observation Archive for permission to quote from the collection, and to the British Library Board for permission to reproduce the cover and interior images.

As this project has entered its final stages, I have been grateful to everyone at Manchester University Press for their help in shepherding the book through the publication process, as well as for their patience with a first-time author's many questions. Thank you to my anonymous readers and to the series editor, Jeffrey Richards, for their careful reading and thoughtful comments on the proposal and manuscript; to Holly Maples for taking on an ad hoc assemblage of research tasks in London so that I could finalise notes and images; and to Matt Abra for last minute technical support. An earlier version of Chapter 6 was published as 'Doing the Lambeth Walk: novelty dances and the British nation', *Twentieth-Century British History* 20:3 (2009), 346–69. Portions of Chapters 1 and 2 previously appeared as 'Dancing in the English style: professionalisation, public preference, and the evolution of popular dance in 1920s Britain', in Brett Bebber (ed.), *Leisure and Cultural Conflict in Twentieth-Century Britain* (Manchester: Manchester University Press, 2012), pp. 41–62.

Last, but definitely not least, I want to thank my friends and family. For over twenty years, Andrea Murray, Margo Granda and Jen Smith have been my closest confidantes, fiercest allies, and greatest cheerleaders. David Meade, and Mary and Neil Griffiths have consistently housed and fed me – and been enthusiastic and patient tour guides – during many research trips to Britain. Thank you most of all to my parents, Doug and Glennis Abra; my sister and brothers, Katherine Abra, Matt Abra and Scott Janke; my grandparents, Jim and Shirley Williamson, Jack and Marion Abra and Flic Trott; and more recently and delightfully my nephew, Teddy Janke. Without their unwavering love and encouragement, this book would not exist.

Abbreviations

AIR	Records of the Air Ministry and Royal Air Force
BBC	British Broadcasting Corporation
CO	Records of the Colonial Office
HO	Records of the Home Office
ISTD	Imperial Society of Teachers of Dancing
IWM	Imperial War Museum
LAB	Records of departments responsible for labour and employment matters
MEPO	Records of the Metropolitan Police Office
MOA	Mass Observation Archive
NAS	National Archives of Scotland
NVA	National Vigilance Association
PMC	Public Morality Council
TNA	The National Archives

General editor's foreword

The end of the First World War signalled the start of the dance craze as the young in particular celebrated their liberation from the shadow of destruction that had hung over them since 1914. From 1919 onwards public dance halls sprang up all over the country with the result that from the 1920s to the 1950s dancing came to be second only to cinema-going as a major form of popular culture. Allison Abra's book charts the evolution of this cultural form as experienced by dance professionals, the dance hall industry and the consumers. She shows how the dance professionals, comprising dance teachers, exhibition and competition dancers, and dance magazine writers, shaped the development of modern ballroom dancing in a standardised style that was proclaimed distinctively English in its restraint, refinement and gracefulness, purged of the wild abandon associated with Latin and black American music. She links this with the emergence of the dance hall industry, which provided the space for the expression of the new style. She analyses the criticisms of the dance halls as leading to sexual immorality, the undermining of respectable models of masculinity and femininity and the Americanisation of British society. But she also examines the arguments advanced in favour of dancing, which was said to promote health, fitness, beauty and youthfulness. Dance band music was not confined to dance halls and could be heard on the wireless and seen in musical films both British and American. Hollywood films in particular familiarised British audiences with American dance styles which they were only too keen to imitate. There was another dance boom during the Second World War when the dance hall was seen as a positive expression of 'The People's War'. This leads to two fascinating case studies. Allison Abra explores the popularity of the 'Lambeth Walk', purportedly a typical cockney movement, as the anthem of cross-class community solidarity in the lead-up to and early years of the Second World War. The same war witnessed an invasion of American

GIs and the popularisation of the jitterbug with its associated discourses of sex and race. The popularity of the jitterbug and later the jive paved the way for the rock'n'roll revolution and signalled the end of the dance hall era. Throughout her book, Allison Abra demonstrates that through dance the consumers were enabled to negotiate their way through gender relations, class tensions, foreign influences, issues of national identity and the impact of war. In so doing, she confirms the role of dancing and dance halls as an essential part of the cultural and social identity of the nation over four decades.

Jeffrey Richards

Introduction

In the spring of 1922, British dance teacher Alec Mackenzie embarked on a trip to Paris. Over the course of several evenings, he toured through many of the city's vibrant public ballrooms, where, to lively and carefree music, dancers performed energetic foxtrots, tangos and one-steps. Mackenzie occasionally joined in, but he also just observed: he was keen to see what was new in French dancing. It was common practice for dance professionals like Mackenzie to visit the Continent, especially when the British dancing season went on hiatus for the summer: they toured as exhibition dancers, participated in competitions and taught classes in places such as the French Riviera. Since the long-ago days when the waltz had been imported to Britain from Vienna, first scandalising but ultimately captivating Regency society, British dancers had also looked to Europe for inspiration and innovation – although by the time Mackenzie visited Paris, both Britain and the Continent had grown increasingly enthralled by the American music and dances of the Jazz Age. Indeed, in one Parisian ballroom, Mackenzie observed the impact that a crowd of American tourists had on the dancing, when they introduced a new variation of the foxtrot from their own country and it was eagerly taken up by their French hosts. Mackenzie later reflected on these events in the British dance profession's premier periodical, the *Dancing Times*: 'in London this could not have happened. Here the dancing is an absolutely national development, extremely characteristic of the national temperament, and very suited to it'. He went on to assert that whereas dancing in France was 'cosmopolitan' and reflected a 'melting-pot' of foreign styles, British dance was 'concrete' and resistant to outside influences.[1]

This moment on a dance floor in Paris, and one British teacher's reaction to what transpired, reveal a great deal about the national and international contexts within which British popular dance operated during the first half of the twentieth century. Owing to expanding global networks of popular cultural exchange, representatives of Britain, France and the United States were all familiar with the same dance: the foxtrot. Where the dance had originated was also reflective of the growing influence of American culture abroad in this period, although it is significant that the foxtrot continued to be performed in different ways in discrete national settings. What had happened that night in Paris was in fact one example of how transatlantic cultural transmissions occurred, when visitors from America – whether they were performers, teachers or simply tourists – shared dance steps and figures, and helped to modify European dancing. While these exchanges occurred in the opposite direction as well, the flow of American cultural forms to Europe had grown disproportionately strong, a reality that was embraced by some and prompted concerns about Americanisation in others. These patterns were as real for Britain as they were for France, which is what makes Mackenzie's statement that his country was resistant to foreign influence so striking and incongruous. He was not alone in making these types of claims, however: though very few of the dances Britons enjoyed in this period were home-grown, the teachers and entrepreneurs who controlled commercial dancing regularly claimed that Britain had a style of dance that was all its own, and which was expressive of British national identity. This book is in large part about the origins and impacts of that conviction.

Popular dance in Britain fundamentally transformed in the early 1920s. The end of the First World War witnessed what contemporaries referred to as a dancing 'craze' or 'boom', as war-weary men and women of all classes took to the dance floor in an effort to celebrate their victory and forget their traumas. But importantly, *where* and *what* Britons danced was also changing. In 1919, the Hammersmith Palais de Danse opened in west London, inaugurating a new era in British leisure as many more purpose-built and affordable public dance halls began to crop up around the country. Within their often luxurious confines, patrons participated in a wide array of new dances. Building on dramatic changes to dancing styles that had commenced even before the war, the first years of the peace saw the social ascendency of the foxtrot, one-step and other so-called 'modern' ballroom dances. These dances and the public spaces where they were performed both provoked controversy. Modern dances were criticised for being overtly sexual in their movements, and those that were imported from the United States were subject to racist attacks and condemned as examples of American cultural encroachment. Public dance halls, or palais (from the French 'palais de danse'), also waged a continuing battle for respectability, and in some quarters, dancing became synonymous with a controversial culture of excessive pleasure-seeking, particularly by young women.

Dancing in the English style takes this moment of transformation and disorder at the end of the First World War as its point of departure, and explores the development, experience and cultural representation of popular dance in Britain during the first half of the twentieth century. The specific focus is on two distinct yet occasionally overlapping commercial producers – the dance profession and the dance hall industry – which both emerged in the 1920s to seize control of and restore order to the new dancing juggernaut. I argue that these producers, motivated by interests that were both artistic and financial, negotiated the creation of a national dancing style, and its many attendant cultural meanings, with the consumers who composed the 'dancing public'. In making the case for a 'national' dancing style, I am not suggesting that the steps or experience of British dancing were universal or monolithic. Rather, I am arguing that producers and consumers of dance each contributed – sometimes in collaboration, sometimes in conflict – to deliberations over what would be danced in Britain, how and where it would be danced, and what meanings the national style would create, circulate, and embody. In a period of intense social upheaval and warfare, gender, class, sexuality, and race all intersected and were contested through popular dance. In particular, the strong foreign – and increasingly American – influences on dancing directly connected this cultural form with questions about the autonomy and identity of the British nation. Consequently, as much as this book is a history of dancing and dance culture, it also uses dancing as a lens through which to better understand broader historical processes of popular cultural production and consumption, and national identity construction.

The first part of the book focuses on the efforts of dancing's producers to construct a standardised style and experience for British dancing, and the response to those efforts by consumers. These interactions determined which dances would find success in Britain, and how and where they would be performed. It was usually the dance profession and the dance hall industry that introduced new dances to Britain, and they were driven by sizeable financial interests: new dances boosted enrolments in dancing schools and kept people interested in an evening out at the palais. Yet the dancing public also strongly influenced the development of popular dance. They made choices determined by their age, sex, geographic region, personal preferences and, of course, degree of interest in dancing, which significantly individualised their own, and by extension, the nation's collective experience and style. There were dances that the profession sought to promote, like the tango, which the public resisted, and others that the dancing public continued to perform – such as the Charleston or the jitterbug – regardless of professional ambivalence. In addition, despite the efforts of dance hall chains to construct a standardised experience throughout the British Isles, the ways that people used dancing spaces frequently defied industry intentions. Some patrons were keen amateur dancers, while others came to hear the music of the band, and still others were most interested in socialisation and romance. Through these interactions, the nation's dance culture was created, and revealed for its uniformity and its diversity.

Part two of the book demonstrates how these interactions between dancing's producers and consumers constructed, circulated, embodied – but also commodified – ideologies of gender, class, race and nation. The performance of modern ballroom dances and the goings-on within the plethora of new public dancing spaces fostered debates about sexual behaviour and respectability, and were central to contemporary deliberations over femininity and masculinity. At the same time, within the context of broader societal debates about the impacts of Americanisation, the dance profession and dance hall industry reacted to expanding foreign influence by attempting to 'Anglicise' the nation's popular dancing. The dance profession transformed the steps and figures of foreign dances like the foxtrot and tango into what became known as the 'English style' of ballroom dancing, while the dance hall industry launched a series of novelty dances that were celebrated for their British origins and character, and marketed the wartime dance floor as a site of patriotism and resistance. Through the effort to imbue or legitimate something 'British' in popular dance, this leisure form become an important means through which ideas about what it meant to be British were created, contested and embodied.

Historians of Britain have frequently pointed to the connections between popular culture and national identity construction.[2] Like film, music hall or football, dancing produced and circulated ideologies of nation. This book will show that at different moments popular dance evoked the reserve, refinement and discipline of the national character; nostalgically celebrated Britain's natural beauty and folk tradition; and championed democracy, courage under fire and national unity in wartime. However, I argue that within popular dance national identity also became something that could be sold. I define this phenomenon as *commercial nationalism*. Commercial nationalism was the cultural interaction through which the producers of dance created and marketed a national dancing style and culture, and the dancing public accepted, resisted or transformed the visions of the nation articulated and physically embodied through dance to varying degrees.[3]

There were a variety of ways in which the dance profession and dance hall industry commodified national identity: paid dance instruction presented a correct British way to dance, certain dances were marketed for their explicit (although often manufactured) Britishness, and during the Second World War Britons were assured that they could do their 'bit' for the war effort and reinforce democracy through a visit to the local palais. Yet Britons were not simply passive recipients of the nationalist impulses promoted through commercial dance culture; they were savvy consumers, generally prioritising a dance's quality or entertainment value over its national origins. In addition, as the American influence on British culture grew as the nation entered the Second World War and re-built in its aftermath, many Britons chose to dance American imports in their original, un-Anglicised forms, expressing alternative national imaginaries. The national identity that was produced through popular dance was thus in a constant state of flux, negotiated and re-negotiated by the British people, often right on the dance floor with their dancing bodies.

The vision of the nation that was produced and circulated by popular dance also illuminates the contested underpinnings of British national identity in this period. First, with the appellation of the 'English style' of ballroom dance serving as the most flagrant example, popular dance often expressed a nationalism that was more English than it was British. Specific idioms of Englishness rather than Britishness were also invoked by dancing's commercial producers when creating the English style or marketing novelty dances. This can in part be explained by what Kenneth Lunn has called the 'series of assumptions about the natural right of England to speak for Britain', which existed long before and continued to be manifested long after the early twentieth century.[4] Peter Mandler has also observed that the England/Britain 'semantic confusion' was never greater than it was during the interwar years (the period upon which much of this book is focused) owing to imperial decline, Irish home rule debates and Celtic nationalism, and the inward turn represented by Little Englandism.[5]

Yet despite its clear reflection of these Anglo-centric tendencies, the popular dance culture produced by the dance profession and dance hall industry was unquestionably meant to be truly national in scope. The dances that comprised the English style were performed throughout the country, some professionals did in fact refer to a 'British style' and regularly called for the English style to be re-named, and dance hall chains extended into all regions. Particularly

Scottish professionals, entrepreneurs, and dancers found important ways to interact with and shape the nation's dancing. Therefore, throughout the book I employ the language of the sources, which generally means referring to the national style or describing certain idioms as 'English'. However, I am concerned with the experience and meanings constructed by popular dance throughout the whole of Britain, and use 'British' to describe the broader dance culture that was created in this period, especially pertaining to its operation in international contexts.

Second, British popular dance constructed national identity in relation to foreign others, including continental Europeans, Latin Americans and especially Americans. It is a central contention of this book that Britain's relationship with the United States and interaction with American cultural products were fundamental to the production and circulation of ideologies of nation in this period. While the importance of the Empire to constructing these idioms has been well established by historians, popular dance helps us to see that the impact of other international influences were also profound by the first half of the twentieth century. As Andrew Thompson has noted, 'the empire [was] not the only frame of reference for national imagining'.[6] At the same time, the 'local' is still a critical element in this study, and the different ways that popular dance was created and experienced not just nationally, but regionally, within the British Isles, clarify its complicated impact on the national culture. In a crucial historical period that witnessed the expansion of commercial leisure, a redefinition of gender roles and significant changes to the racial make-up of the nation – as well as two world wars, new challenges to British imperial hegemony, and the growing global dominance of the United States – an everyday practice like dancing provided a way for Britons to make sense of and to test the social boundaries of their world.

History, theory and 'popular' dance

Dancing was rivalled only by the cinema as the most widespread and favoured leisure activity in Britain during the first half of the twentieth century, and yet it has only recently begun to receive significant attention from historians. Previous scholars have examined dancing as part of broader historical studies about expanding leisure practices, or the class and youth cultures of the interwar years.[7] In this context, there has been especially important scholarship on dancing and women and gender, by historians such as Claire Langhamer, Judith Walkowitz, Melanie Tebbutt and Lucy Bland.[8] The importance of jazz and its attendant dances to modernist literature has also received attention from literary critics such as Rishona Zimring and Genevieve Abravanel, and dance scholar Theresa Jill Buckland has provided a thorough analysis of British ballroom dancing in the years immediately preceding the period covered here.[9] The most extensive historical work on this topic has been that of James Nott, who in two books has explored dancing's expansion in tandem with the interwar popular music industry, as well as the development and social experience of the dance hall business.[10] This book builds upon and is indebted to all of this work.

However, my approach is distinguished from the existing scholarship on dancing in several key respects. First, I closely examine the origins and evolution, as well as the social and cultural impacts, of what was the nation's primary popular dance style in the first half of the twentieth century: modern ballroom dancing. Second, I emphasise the critical importance of not only the dance hall industry, but also the dance profession, to the commercial production and consumption of popular dance. Finally, I disentangle dancing from its customary associations with women and the young – showing that it shaped the lives and experiences of Britons of all ages and both sexes – and explore the manifold ways that popular dance operated within British society beyond the social practice of visiting the palais. Outside the walls of the public ballroom, thousands of dancing schools were in operation around the country, and dance culture was circulated through both the popular press and a voluminous dance-themed print culture, as well as via the burgeoning entertainment industries that surrounded music, radio, theatre and film. I argue that in all of these realms, dancing provided a vehicle through which Britons grappled with some of the most critical issues of the day, including the instability of gender relations, class tensions and respectability, race relations and the encroachment of foreign culture, international diplomacy and war, and their very self-understanding as Britons. In these ways, popular dance constructed cultural meanings and had social effects even for those people who never danced a day in their lives.

Crucially, while highlighting the complex mechanisms and impacts of the domestic cultural production of popular dance, this book also situates these processes within global networks of exchange. Prior to this period, Britain already had a long history of importing dances: both the waltz and the polka, introduced from the European continent, were among the most important ballroom dances of the Victorian period. By the early 1900s, the Continental influence on British dancing was still strong, though growing more complicated. Dances that were imported from Paris, notably the tango and the Boston, had actually begun life in Argentina and the United States respectively. Direct cultural influence from the Americas was also on the rise. From the 1840s onward, with the first British tours of blackface minstrel troupes, which were soon followed by Wild West shows and Hollywood films, Britain was inundated with more and more performers and popular cultural forms from across the pond. As Victoria DeGrazia has shown, in the twentieth century, Britain and the rest of Europe were profoundly shaped not only by cultural imports, but by the broader production and consumption practices of America's 'market empire'.[11] In this context, there were already potent anxieties about Americanisation in Britain by the interwar period.

However, this book joins with historical scholarship that has complicated the picture of unrelenting and straightforward American cultural encroachment in the twentieth century.[12] Instead, I show that 'Americanisation' was a complex, messy and ongoing process of cultural appropriation, modification and resistance, which produced new cultural forms and multiple meanings. As Alec Mackenzie's experience on a Parisian dance floor exposed, American culture was not understood or experienced in identical ways in different national contexts. While the music and dances of the Jazz Age were a driving engine of Americanisation in this period, recent scholarship has shown that Europe, Africa, the Caribbean and Latin America did not simply receive and absorb these American cultural products. Rather, they were places where music and dances were created or reimagined, and then sent out into the world, even reciprocally influencing the culture of the United States.[13] As Robin D. G. Kelley has summed up this state of affairs, we can 'no longer speak so confidently about jazz as an *American* art form'.[14]

This book seeks to more firmly place Britain into this story of transnational cultural exchange during the Jazz Age.[15] The popular dances that achieved success in Britain during this period – everything from the foxtrot and the tango to the jitterbug – were hybrid, transatlantic creations that incorporated African, North and South American, and European cultural influences. However, more often than not, Britons demonstrated little awareness of these complex origins and responded to them according to broad understandings of cultural, national and racial differences. With motivations that were nationalistic, artistic – but also economic – commercial producers took up foreign dances and recreated them as British. This intrinsically British dancing style – emblemised in the syllabus of English style ballroom dance steps and popular novelties like the Lambeth Walk – was then regularly exported abroad to Europe, the Empire and North America. In these ways, I argue, British dancers, teachers and entrepreneurs were active participants in the global system of cultural production and consumption that defined this period, helping to shape popular dance both within and beyond the British Isles.

The book's focus on the critical relationship between the producers and consumers of dancing – in both national and international contexts – accounts for why I employ the term 'popular' rather than 'social' dance as the primary analytical framework. In so doing, my understanding of how dance operates within societies is strongly indebted to scholarship in both dance studies and cultural studies – although it should be noted at the outset that the analyses and perspectives contained herein are very much those of an historian. Dance, as a participatory experience or viewed performance, can have dramatic social and cultural effects. In the words of dance scholar Julie Malnig, 'social and popular dance reflects and absorbs daily life as well as shapes, informs, and influences social patterns and behaviors'.[16] Scholars of dance have also long shown that the physical performance of dancing can construct, embody, and express meaning. As Jane Desmond observes, dance, 'as an embodied social practice and highly visual aesthetic form, powerfully melds considerations of materiality and representation together'.[17] In particular, according to Danielle Robinson, dancing creates 'a powerful space for body-based articulations of identities', wherein race, class, gender, or nation can be physically enacted.[18] In early twentieth-century Britain, an embodied expression of national identity was at the heart of efforts by the dance profession and dance hall industry to construct a British dancing style. Crucial cultural meanings were also produced at what Malnig has called the 'moment of dance', when Britons stepped onto the dance floor and with their moving bodies were able to reinforce or transform the vision of the nation being expressed.[19] These embodied negotiations between the producers and consumers of dance produced cultural meanings and shaped the national style. It was in this reciprocal process, I argue, that social dance became *popular* dance.

In keeping with theories from cultural studies, I mobilise the 'popular' in order to invoke the processes of a culture industry, wherein a dominant culture is produced through practices of commercial production and consumption, and possesses powers of manipulation and social control. Yet, as a number of historians and theorists have shown, within these processes consumers are often able to identify, suppress, and resist the domination of the producer, and to construct their own individual and collective meanings.[20] The analysis which follows will demonstrate that there were many occasions when the dancing public consumed and readily reinforced the style of dance and the meanings about gender, class, race and nation that were produced by the profession and the industry. But at other times, dancers chose to perform a jitterbug when a quickstep was played, walked off the floor because they were intimidated by the tango, or flatly rejected dances – even 'British' dances – that were marketed to them by producers. There were also important moments when the dancing public was able to discern the motivations at work in the actions of the commercial producers of dance. Peter Bailey has called this awareness 'knowingness' within the context of the Victorian music hall, while James W. Cook, drawing on some of the later writings of Theodor Adorno, has described the ability of consumers to perceive and critically evaluate cultural products – to be 'at once shaped by culture industry formulas and conscious of the shaping' – as ' "split" consumer consciousness'.[21] The phrase 'popular dance' is thus meant to invoke the many nuances, complexities and contradictions of the dialectical relationship between dancing's producers (the dance profession and dance hall industry) and its consumers (the dancing public), through which British dancing and dance culture were forged.

The producers and consumers of popular dance

The first commercial producer analysed here is the dance profession. The profession emerged as increasingly formal ties developed between dancing teachers, exhibition and competition dancers, and writers of dance-themed books and magazines, starting around 1920. It was the profession that was most influential in shaping the evolution of modern ballroom dancing, and which had strong concerns about the reputation and artistic integrity of this style as it achieved popular ascendancy in the 1910s and 1920s. However, dance professionals were also businesspeople – invested in keeping their schools at peak enrolment, selling books and magazines, and commanding impressive salaries for public performances – all of which shaped their activities and interactions with the dancing public. Additionally, what I am calling the dance profession was constituted by a vast group of professionals and semi-professionals, with varying skill levels and qualifications, who were engaged in the wide array of employment opportunities – performance, instruction, and writing – connected with popular dance. The profession included everyone from the men and women selling dances at the palais for six pence each, to the dancers like Victor Silvester or Santos Casani who achieved global fame and celebrity.

Many dance professionals also worked for or alongside the second major producer responsible for commercialising popular dance in this period: the dance hall industry. Following the opening of the Hammersmith Palais, the 1920s and 1930s saw the rise of a large number of public dance halls all over the country, which gradually consolidated into chains of halls, the most influential and renowned of which was the circuit controlled by the Mecca organisation. At the same time, other types of dance establishments continued to thrive – from nightclubs to independent dance halls – and promoters operated dances in rented spaces such as town and institutional halls, public baths, parks, churches and many other locations. The dance hall industry is therefore defined in this book as the whole and wide-ranging array of opportunities for dancing outside of the home, as well as many associated enterprises – from dance creation and music publishing, to dance band management and print media.

Finally, the consumers of popular dance, defined here and by many contemporary Britons as the 'dancing public', also contained a diverse group of people, engaged in dancing to widely varying degrees. In a primary respect, the dancing public was the dancers who frequented dance classes and dance halls, and engaged in the performance of dancing. However, Britons consumed popular dance in a multitude of ways beyond physical practice. Some people patronised dancing spaces, but never took a turn on the floor. There were also significant numbers of Britons who rarely or never went to a public ballroom, but who experienced dance music or the performance of dancing via the radio or cinema. Even those Britons who espoused no personal interest in dancing at all were exposed to it through advertising, fiction or newspaper articles. Popular dance was almost ubiquitous within British society – as a social practice but also as a cultural representation – providing numerous ways in which it was consumed. To unpack this complexity, I rely on a wide array of different sources including the popular press; dance-themed print culture; personal diaries and memoirs; the extensive research undertaken into 'music, dancing and jazz' by the social research organisation Mass Observation; published and recorded music; short stories and novels; films; police reports; and government and institutional documents. Indeed, that Britons consumed – and left traces of the impacts of dancing – via this plethora of material, makes clear both that the dancing public was not a monolithic entity, and that popular dance had dramatic historical effects.

Periodisation and book structure

The book's periodisation is based on the rise and then decline of modern ballroom dancing as Britain's predominant popular dance style. In the early

1910s, the arrival of the tango from Argentina (by way of continental Europe) and ragtime dances from the United States propelled British dancing into a self-consciously modern era. It was only after the First World War that the full impact of the new dances was felt, however, as processes of professionalisation and commercialisation led to the emergence of two producers of popular dance: the dance profession and dance hall industry. The early chapters of the book describe these events, as well as the profession and industry's efforts to standardise the steps and public experience of dancing, and the mechanisms of their relationships with the dancing public. The second half of the book then turns to how the popular dance culture produced by the profession and the industry – in conjunction with the dancing public – fostered redefinitions of gender, class, race and nation throughout the interwar years and during the Second World War. The book concludes in the early 1950s, when ballroom dancing was increasingly marginalised in favour of the more improvisational, independent and Americanised styles of dance epitomised in the jive.

Chapter 1 traces the early development of modern ballroom dancing in Britain, from its origins in the ragtime era prior to the First World War through the dance craze that came with the peace. It provides a history for the major dances that would predominate in Britain from the 1920s through the 1950s, particularly the so-called 'standard four' – the foxtrot, the modern waltz, the tango and the one-step (which was later replaced by the quickstep). The chapter also considers the social and cultural response to the new dances in Britain – particularly their perceived modernity – which was celebrated by some, but condemned by others. It explores some of the ongoing controversies that surrounded popular dance, and the active defence mounted by its proponents, who touted dancing's value for the cultivation of good health and beauty, among numerous other advantages.

Chapter 2 describes the standardisation of the English style of ballroom dance and the professionalisation of the dance community, showing that these processes were inextricably connected. The catalyst to the dance profession's consolidation was a series of conferences convened in the 1920s by prominent teachers who sought to standardise the steps of new ballroom dances arriving in Britain from the United States and continental Europe. From these events emerged the rudimentary English style, which the profession then passed on to the dancing public via dancing schools, exhibition dancing, dance competitions and print culture. However, the chapter also argues that the success – and even the steps and figures – of a dance were not determined entirely by this top-down process. Not only did a significant segment of the dancing public eschew instruction, and remain largely oblivious to professional activities, but the two groups were not always aligned in their dancing preferences. The result was that questions about which dances would be danced in Britain, how they would be performed, and what the gradually evolving national style would look like, were continually negotiated between producers and consumers of popular dance.

Chapter 3 describes the evolution of the dance hall industry – the second major cultural producer that shaped the commercialisation and experience of popular dance in Britain during the interwar and wartime periods. The new purpose-built dancing spaces that began to emerge after the war were affordable to Britons of almost every class, and many adopted a standard layout and format, providing an increasing uniformity of experience throughout the nation. A standard dancing experience was in fact a major objective of figures such as Carl L. Heimann, managing director of Mecca, Britain's largest chain of dance halls, and a figure so influential that social research organisation Mass Observation called him one of the 'cultural directors' of the nation.[22] However, despite this commercial might and cultural authority, the chapter shows that patrons entered into negotiations with the dance hall industry just as they did with the dance profession. A great disparity remained in terms of the access to and quality of public dancing spaces for Britons of different regions and classes, but most significantly, the dancing public made important choices as to where, how, and why they consumed dancing. This served to individualise their experience and kept going to the palais from becoming a wholly homogenised experience.

Chapter 4 explores how the social perception and cultural representation of dancing – especially its chief enthusiasts, professionals and the public venues where it took place – were shaped by contemporary anxieties about gender, class and sexuality. It examines the controversies that surrounded the 'dancing girl' (also called the flapper or modern woman), as well as the male 'lounge lizard' or 'dancing dandy', within the context of the gender upheavals that occurred during and immediately after the First World War. The chapter also considers the negative assumptions about particular public dancing spaces, as well as the paid dance partners who were employed within them, showing that these were underpinned by class prejudice and anxieties about crime and sexual immorality. However, the chapter argues that social concerns about dancing were strongly contested from the very start of the modern dance era, and that this leisure form became progressively more respectable and integrated into the national culture as professionalisation and commercialisation processes progressed throughout the interwar years.

Chapter 5 is the first of three that examine the creation and commodification of national identity within popular dance. The discussion returns to the efforts on the part of the dance profession to standardise the steps of the English style, and demonstrates that there was far more invested in that process than simply establishing a formal set of steps and figures. Within the context of broader fears about Americanisation, dance professionals sought to transform foreign dances like the foxtrot and tango in a way that made them more suitable to the national character or temperament. This vision of the nation was explicitly articulated in opposition to foreign and racial others, and emphasised English virtues like reserve and refinement. With its specific syllabus of standard steps and figures, the English style also became a marketable commodity which was sold at home as well as abroad. Yet the chapter shows that, in keeping with the dialectical nature of commercial nationalism, the profession's efforts to craft a national dancing style were greeted with mixed responses from the British dancing public. While dance enthusiasts were eager to perfect the English style's standard versions of dances such as the foxtrot, they showed little interest in the home-grown dances developed by the profession, such as the five-step and the trebla, which were marketed as explicit bulwarks against Americanisation. Instead, they retained a strong interest in foreign dances like the rumba and truckin', especially as they began to view the English style technique as stagnant and excessively regimented by the 1930s.

Chapter 6 demonstrates that the commercial nationalism that characterised the efforts of the dance profession to Anglicise dancing in the 1920s reached its apogee in the late 1930s, as the dance hall industry even more overtly commodified the nation as a way of encouraging more Britons to dance. It uses as a case study the series of novelty dances produced by the Mecca chain starting in 1938: the Lambeth Walk, the Chestnut Tree, the Park Parade, the Handsome Territorial, and Knees Up, Mother Brown. These were deliberately simply sequence dances, which Mecca director Heimann hoped would bring more patrons into his company's dance halls, particularly those who were untutored in ballroom dancing. While the marketing campaign for the dances stressed their ease and accessibility, another major focus was on the dances' British origin and character. The first Mecca novelty dance, the Lambeth Walk, was a staggering success, both at home and abroad, and was embraced by the dancing public for its connections to British culture. However, the chapter shows that the other four Mecca novelty dances which followed the Lambeth Walk met with a mixed response, and argues that their success or failure was largely owing to their quality as dances rather than their national origins.

Chapters 7 and 8 each focus on different aspects of dancing during the Second World War. Chapter 7 demonstrates that the mechanisms of commercial nationalism contained within popular dance carried into the war years, though the meanings shifted to comply with hegemonic visions of the nation at war. Popular dance provided a potent means for producers and consumers alike to express and embody many of the ideals associated with the 'people's war', such as cheerful endurance, grace under fire, and social and imperial unity. At the same time, both commercial producers – but especially the dance hall industry – repackaged patriotism as a way of staying in business, utilising war-themed promotions and causes to attract patrons, or advertising their ballrooms as bomb shelters. As Chapter 8 reveals, the dance profession and dance hall industry also shifted tactics with respect to American culture, choosing to embrace the latest dance import, the jitterbug – albeit in a toned down Anglicised form. Indeed, questions about American culture achieved a new magnitude in wartime, owing to the physical presence in Britain of large numbers of American troops beginning in 1942. As part of their ongoing negotiations with producers, the dancing public expressed greater interest in the 'authentic', American jitterbug than the Anglicised versions presented to them by the profession and industry, in ways that reflected contemporary deliberations over racial difference. As a dance, the jitterbug also heralded a critical shift away from modern ballroom dancing as the nation's favoured style.

Finally, the epilogue reflects on popular dance in the post-war years. After the war, going to the palais remained as popular as ever, but the dances performed within the dance halls continued their long evolution. Following on some of the individualised and independent movements introduced by the jitterbug, modern ballroom dancing slowly began to give way to new dances which could be performed without a partner, or which better accompanied rock 'n' roll and later disco. Owing to their particular focus on ballroom dance, the dance profession began the modern dance era with arguably more cultural influence than the dance hall industry, but those positions had clearly undergone a switch by the 1950s. Ballroom dancing eventually became a niche professional art form, while many of the 1920s dance halls continued to operate for decades after their establishment, even as they faced new challenges of their own. In fact, while it went through many incarnations, the Hammersmith Palais only closed its doors for a final time in 2007, before being demolished in 2012, perhaps heralding an official end to Britain's dance hall days.

Notes

1 Alec Mackenzie, 'Dancing in Paris and London', *Dancing Times* (June 1922), pp. 777–9.
2 This represents a vast literature, on a multitude of cultural forms. For recent examples, see Brett Bebber (ed.), *Leisure and Cultural Conflict in Twentieth-Century Britain* (Manchester: Manchester University Press, 2012).
3 Mica Nava has identified a similar phenomenon that she calls 'commercial orientalism', wherein generic Eastern motifs were present in the commodity culture of the Edwardian department store Selfridges, and predominately female consumers were able to use these products as a means of self-expression and in the quest for political emancipation. See Mica Nava, *Visceral Cosmopolitanism: Gender, Culture, and the Normalisation of Difference* (Oxford: Berg, 2007), p. 34.
4 Kenneth Lunn, 'Reconsidering "Britishness:" the construction and significance of national identity in twentieth-century Britain', in Brian Jenkins and Spyros A. Sofos (eds), *Nation & Identity in Contemporary Europe* (London: Routledge, 1997), p. 87.
5 Peter Mandler, *The English National Character: The History of an Idea from Edmund Burke to Tony Blair* (New Haven, CT: Yale University Press, 2006), p. 148.
6 Andrew Thompson, *The Empire Strikes Back? The Impact of Imperialism on Britain from the Mid-Nineteenth Century* (Harlow: Pearson Education, 2005), p. 200.
7 See Ross McKibbin, *Classes and Cultures: England, 1918–1951* (Oxford: Oxford University Press, 1998); Martin Pugh, *'We Danced All Night:' A Social History of Britain Between the Wars* (London: Bodley Head, 2008); David Fowler, *The First Teenagers: The Lifestyle of Young Wage-earners in Interwar Britain* (London: Woburn Press, 1995); Dan Laughey, *Music and Youth Culture* (Edinburgh: Edinburgh University Press, 2006).
8 On women, gender, and dancing, see Claire Langhamer, *Women's Leisure in England, 1920–60* (Manchester: Manchester University Press, 2000); Selina Todd, *Young Women, Work, and Family in England, 1918–1950* (Oxford: Oxford University Press, 2005); Judith Walkowitz, *Nights Out: Life in Cosmopolitan London* (New Haven, CT: Yale University Press, 2012); Melanie Tebbutt, *Being Boys: Youth, Leisure and Identity in the Inter-War Years* (Manchester: Manchester University Press, 2012); Lucy Bland, *Modern Women on Trial: Sexual Transgression in the Age of the Flapper* (Manchester: Manchester University Press, 2013).
9 Genevieve Abravanel, *Americanizing Britain: The Rise of Modernism in the Age of the Entertainment Empire* (Oxford: Oxford University Press, 2012); Rishona Zimring, *Social Dance and the Modernist Imagination in Interwar Britain* (Farnham: Ashgate, 2013); Theresa Jill Buckland, *Society Dancing: Fashionable Bodies in England, 1870–1920* (Basingstoke: Palgrave Macmillan, 2011).

10 James Nott, *Music for the People: Popular Music and Dance in Interwar Britain* (Oxford: Oxford University Press, 2002); James Nott, *Going to the Palais: A Social and Cultural History of Dancing and Dance Halls in Britain, 1918–1960* (Oxford: Oxford University Press, 2015). See also Allison Abra, 'Doing the Lambeth Walk: novelty dances and the British nation', *Twentieth-Century British History* 20:3 (2009), pp. 346–69; Allison Abra, 'On with the Dance: Nation, Culture, and Popular Dancing in Britain, 1918–1945' (PhD dissertation: University of Michigan, 2009); Allison Abra, 'Dancing in the English style: professionalisation, public preference, and the evolution of popular dance in 1920s Britain', in Brett Bebber (ed.), *Leisure and Cultural Conflict in Twentieth-Century Britain* (Manchester: Manchester University Press, 2012), pp. 41–62.

11 Victoria De Grazia, *Irresistible Empire: America's Advance through Twentieth-Century Europe* (Cambridge, MA: Harvard University Press, 2005).

12 Select examples include R. Kroes, R. W. Rydell and D. F. J. Bosscher (eds), *Cultural Transmissions and Receptions: American Mass Culture in Europe* (Amsterdam: VU University Press, 1993); Robert Rydell and Rob Kroes, *Buffalo Bill in Bologna: The Americanization of the World, 1869–1922* (Chicago, IL: Chicago University Press, 2005); Sarah Meer, *Uncle Tom Mania: Slavery, Minstrelsy and Transatlantic Culture in the 1850s* (Athens, GA: University of Georgia Press, 2005); Adrian Horn, *Juke Box Britain: Americanisation and Youth Culture, 1945–1960* (Manchester: Manchester University Press, 2010); Mark Glancy, *Hollywood and the Americanization of Britain: From the 1920s to the Present* (London: I.B. Tauris, 2013); Kelly Boyd, 'Early British television: the allure and threat of America', in Erika Rappaport, Sandra Trudgen Dawson and Mark J. Crowley (eds), *Consuming Behaviours: Identity, Politics and Pleasure in Twentieth-Century Britain* (London: Bloomsbury Academic, 2015), pp. 253–68.

13 Robin D.G. Kelley, *Africa Speaks, America Answers: Modern Jazz in Revolutionary Times* (Cambridge, MA: Harvard University Press, 2012); Jeffrey H. Jackson, *Making Jazz French: Music and Modern Life in Interwar Paris* (Durham, NC: Duke University Press, 2003); Lara Putnam, *Radical Moves: Caribbean Migrants and the Politics of Race in the Jazz Age* (Chapel Hill, NC: University of North Carolina Press, 2013); Christina D. Abreu, *Rhythms of Race: Cuban Musicians and the Making of Latino New York City and Miami, 1940–1960* (Chapel Hill, NC: University of North Carolina Press, 2015); Marc Matera, *Black London: The Imperial Metropolis and Decolonization in the Twentieth Century* (Oakland, CA: University of California Press, 2015).

14 Kelley, *Africa Speaks, America Answers*, p. 10, original emphasis.

15 See also Peter Bailey, 'Fats Waller meets Harry Champion: Americanisation, national identity, and sexual politics in inter-war British music hall', *Cultural and Social History* 4:4 (2007), 495–509; Peter Bailey, ' "Hullo, ragtime!" West End revue and the Americanisation of popular culture in pre-1914 London', in Len Platt, Tobias Becker and David Linton (eds), *Popular Musical Theatre in London and Berlin, 1890–1939* (Cambridge: Cambridge University Press, 2014); Abravanel, *Americanizing Britain*.

16 Julie Malnig (ed.), introduction to *Ballroom Boogie, Shimmy Sham, Shake: A Social and Popular Dance Reader* (Urbana, IL: University of Illinois Press, 2009), p. 6.

17 Jane C. Desmond (ed.), introduction to *Meaning in Motion: New Cultural Studies of Dance* (Durham, NC: Duke University Press, 1997), p. 2.

18 See Danielle Robinson, preface to *Modern Moves: Dancing Race during the Ragtime and Jazz Eras* (New York: Oxford University Press, 2015), p. xii. See also Ann Cooper Albright, *Choreographing Difference: The Body and Identity in Contemporary Dance* (Middletown, CT: Wesleyan University Press, 1997); Beth Genné, ' "Freedom incarnate:" Jerome Robbins, Gene Kelly, and the dancing sailor as an icon of American values in World War II', *Dance Chronicle* 24:1 (2001), 83–103; Desmond, (ed.), *Meaning in Motion*.

19 Julie Malnig, 'Women, dance, and New York nightlife', in Julie Malnig (ed.) *Ballroom Boogie, Shimmy Sham, Shake: A Social and Popular Dance Reader* (Urbana, IL: University of Illinois Press, 2009), p. 82.

20 For an excellent overview of how the study of culture industries has evolved in history and cultural studies, see James W. Cook, 'The Return of the Culture Industry', in James W. Cook, Lawrence Glickman and Michael O'Malley (eds), *The Cultural Turn in U.S. History: Past, Present, and Future* (Chicago, IL: University of Chicago Press, 2008).

21 Peter Bailey, 'Music hall and the knowingness of popular culture', in *Popular Culture and Performance in the Victorian City* (Cambridge: Cambridge University Press, 1998); Cook, 'The Return of the Culture Industry', p. 307.

22 Tom Harrisson and Charles Madge, *Britain by Mass-Observation* (London: Harmondsworth, 1939), p. 141.

Dancing mad!
The modernisation
of popular dance

In October 1919 the *Daily Express* proclaimed that the British nation was 'Dancing mad!'. London, the newspaper elaborated, 'is stricken with the craze, and so also are the great towns throughout the country. The adult population of London at the present time can be roughly divided into three classes – those who are dancing, those who are learning, and those who want to do both.'[1] A few months earlier, the *Daily Mail* had similarly commented that dancing was 'the mania of the moment', and even more strongly conveyed a democratic impulse behind the phenomenon: 'Society men and girls dance, business men and girls dance, working girls and men dance, every sort and kind of girl and boy dance; all have been caught up in the enveloping wave of dancing which is sweeping over the country.'[2] Accounts such as these abounded in the months after the end of the First World War, as the euphoric British nation entered into a frenzy of celebration and pleasure-seeking, chiefly expressed in a craze for dancing. Press reports described how businessmen left their offices in the middle of the day for a brief turn around the floor, and that women stopped in for a quick dance in the midst of a shopping trip.[3] Another article revealed that a London dance studio was providing special classes to instruct disabled war veterans how to dance with artificial limbs, while a letter to the editor of a national daily expressed annoyance that authorities appeared to be prioritising the building of dance halls over regular waste disposal.[4] The *Dancing Times*, the nation's premier dance-themed magazine, naturally took note of the upswing, observing in November 1919, 'The population of the dancing public was probably never greater than it is at the present moment. Hundreds of dancers in the Metropolis are so fond of it that they are not content unless they can go to a dance two or three times a week.'[5] As Philip J. S. Richardson, the editor of the *Dancing Times* and one of Britain's leading dance aficionados in the first half of the twentieth century, would later recall, following the Armistice Britain was seized by a 'perfect orgy' of dancing.[6]

Much of the coverage of the dance craze suggested that it was a natural by-product of the end of a long and devastating war. A London-area newspaper, upon announcing weekly dances at the local masonic hall, remarked that 'never in history has dancing been indulged in to the extent it is this season, doubtless the re-action after the dreary days of the past five years, has something to do with this'.[7] Cecil Sharp, a founder of the early twentieth-century British folklore revival, similarly speculated in a 1920 speech that 'the popularity of dancing to-day is due to the post-war tendency to exercise some form of expression', while in another piece, the *Daily Mail* proclaimed, 'People are dancing as they have never danced before, in a happy rebound from the austerities of the war.'[8] Modern scholars have also ascribed the dance craze to the effects of the war. Literary critic Genevieve Abravanel notes that many social pleasures had been 'stifled in wartime', and argues that the nation was 'haunted by terrible loss and eager to forget it in a frenzy of music and dance'.[9] Juliet Nicolson likewise observes that music and dance provided a 'release of emotion' after the war, while Rishona Zimring calls dancing in this context 'a form of celebration, a symptom of trauma, and an expression of longing'.[10]

Post-war euphoria unquestionably lent fuel to the nation's desire to dance, but these assumptions obscured the fact that the dance craze was part of a much broader transformation and restructuring of dancing as a cultural form. As the first part of this chapter will show, a revolution in popular dance had in fact been in progress since before the war. In the 1910s, via expanding conduits of international popular cultural exchange, the Argentinian tango and American ragtime dances arrived in Britain and propelled dancing into the modern era. As the country endured the war and transitioned to the peace, these new dances of the Jazz Age forever altered the style, practice and meanings of British dancing. Importantly, this was a transformative moment of which contemporaries were aware. The second half of the chapter will discuss the ways in which British popular dance was self-consciously modern in this period, provoking strong admiration in some and condemnation in others. While 'modern dance' and modernist bodily expression tend to be most strongly associated with the concert dance of Isadora Duncan, Maud Allen and Martha Graham, social or popular dance is increasingly being acknowledged as another important manifestation of modernity.[11] As dancing styles modernised, their movements and meanings helped Britons to grapple with who they were and who they wanted to become.

Ragtime, the tango and the origins of modern ballroom dancing

It is commonly held that the arrival of the American Expeditionary Forces in 1917–18 flung Europe into the Jazz Age. However, even before the First World War British popular dance entered the modern era, owing to the transformative effects of cultural imports from throughout the Atlantic world. All of the dances performed at the height of the dance craze, and which would continue to predominate in dancing classes and public ballrooms well into the 1920s – most notably the foxtrot, tango, one-step and modern waltz – had Edwardian antecedents. All of these dances also originated beyond the borders of the British Isles. In the 1910s, the Argentinian tango and American ragtime dances arrived in Britain at virtually the same moment (often by way of the European continent), highlighting the complex and multitudinous foreign influences on British dancing. Gradually the influence of the United States began to outstrip that of the Continent and everywhere else, but in the years before and immediately following the war, British popular dance modernised owing to imports from all directions. Popular dance was broad-based and cosmopolitan, simultaneously encapsulating what were understood to be European, American (particularly African American) and Latin American cultural traditions.

There were many pathways for the transmission of popular dances across international borders in this period. Professional dancers travelled frequently between cities such as New York, London and Paris, providing instruction in dancing schools and performing exhibitions at hotels, restaurants, nightclubs and in theatrical musical revues.[12] In these ways, they shared dances and figures native to their own countries, and accrued knowledge about the latest trends elsewhere. Musicians and tourists also played a part in transporting dances in their travels, while print culture and the emerging music publishing, record and film industries were increasingly crucial to the circulation of dance culture. Britain was part of a transatlantic network of popular cultural production and consumption, aided by a burgeoning commercial entertainment economy, which would grow only more formidable as the years passed.

In his 1946 book *A History of English Ballroom Dancing*, Philip J. S. Richardson – by then the long-time editor of the *Dancing Times* – pointed to an evolution of the waltz as the first major event in the modernisation of popular dance. Though Victorian dance programmes featured the odd two-step, lancers or quadrille – and the 1840s had seen a brief furore for the polka – the waltz had been the 'unchallenged queen of the ballroom' for over a century.[13] The dance had also failed to evolve in significant ways after the mid-1800s, promoting a belief by the first years of the twentieth century that ballroom dancing was growing stagnant. It was in this context that a new version of the waltz, known as the Boston, arrived in Europe from the United States, finding success in Paris before it made its way to London. Most likely named for the city in which it originated, the dance was eagerly embraced by scores of younger dancers, for, much to their relief and glee, it bore little resemblance to the waltz their parents danced other than it was performed to waltz music. Most notably, the Boston differed from its Victorian predecessor by being performed with a flat-footed, parallel walking motion – rather than turned out on the tips of the toes – movements that were to become the hallmark of modern ballroom dancing.

Like most dances from this period, the Boston was not standardised. It was generally characterised by a close, hip-to-hip hold between partners, but possessed many variations in the United States and Europe. According to Richardson, the Boston that flourished in Britain called for three steps of equal time value (rather than the 'long, short, short' speed of the traditional waltz), and was a progressive rather than rotary dance; men led their partners by taking six steps across the floor and then turning according to a zig-zag pattern. It first appeared in Britain as early as 1903, but only found widespread success amid a 'blaze of publicity' for a brief period starting around 1910.[14] As a travelling dance, the Boston required a great deal of space to be performed correctly, which, given the increasingly crowded dance floors of the Edwardian period, spelled its inevitable doom. Nonetheless, while the Boston had all but faded out by the eve of the war, some of its elements lived on in further evolutions of the waltz.[15] The 'hesitation waltz' restored the traditional hold of the Victorian dance, and compensated for the faster tempos of waltz music by requiring dancers to turn and take a step with every three beats of music, rather than for each one; during one step of the three they would 'hesitate', suspending a foot in the air or dragging it on the ground.[16] After the war, the dance settled into a form known simply as the 'modern waltz', which was also defined by its simple, progressive movements on the balls of the feet, rather than in the tip-toed, rotary motions of the 'old-time' version of the dance.[17]

Though Richardson remembered the Boston as Britain's introduction to modern dance styles, in fact it came to prominence alongside a plethora of American dances typically associated with the new musical form known as ragtime. Ragtime music evolved in the United States in the final decades of the nineteenth century, from a creolisation of African, African-American and

European traditions. Incorporating the irregular rhythms of African music with the exceptionally popular military marches of figures like John Philip Sousa, ragtime was characterised by syncopation, meaning to break or 'rag' the beat. The music first developed within African American communities in cities such as St. Louis, and was popularised by pianists such as Scott Joplin. Particularly appealing to the younger generation for its energy, vitality and dramatic challenge to musical conventions, ragtime became the predominant popular music of the decade leading up to the First World War, spreading across the United States and eventually to Europe.[18]

Dancing was an integral part of ragtime from its first emergence. One of the first dances to be linked to the new music was the cakewalk, which was born on the plantations of the American south as a slave parody of European dancing; later it was caricatured in turn by blackface minstrel performers. In the 1890s, the cakewalk resurfaced as a couples' dance, in which partners stood side-by-side, linked elbows, leaned back, and strutted across the floor in a high-stepping motion, 'with ample licence for comic improvisation'.[19] Then, in the first years of the twentieth century, a whole host of 'rag' dances began to develop in working-class dance halls across the northern United States, but often based on steps first devised in 'juke joints' – the African-American music and dancing establishments scattered throughout the rural south.[20] In ragtime dancing, partners maintained close bodily contact – cheek-to-cheek, chest-to-chest and hip-to-hip – and mimicked the rag of the music through angular movements, dramatic pauses and direction·changes. Improvisation was encouraged, and many dancers inserted dips, kicks, hops, foot stomps and drags, grinding, hip shaking and spontaneous gestures of various kinds. These tendencies were typified in the so-called 'animal dances', such as the bunny hug, monkey glide, grizzly bear, dog trot and the turkey trot. Each of these was supposed to depict the movements of the animal for which it was named, leading dancers to dramatically 'flap' their elbows, or outstretch their 'paws' and 'claws'.[21]

Ragtime's British debut is usually dated to the arrival of Irving Berlin's extraordinarily successful song 'Alexander's Ragtime Band' in 1911, although the cakewalk and other heralds of ragtime had reached Britain before then. 'Alexander's Ragtime Band' was a global phenomenon, selling two million sheet music copies in its first year alone, and in 1913, Irving Berlin himself appeared in the musical revue *Hullo, Ragtime!* at the London Hippodrome.[22] The animal dances began to appear on the floors of West End dance clubs, and received considerable publicity. For the British, however, the most durable of the ragtime dances was the one-step, in which dancers moved around the floor in imaginative patterns, taking one stiff step to coincide with each beat of the music, while shifting their weight from foot to foot.[23] The one-step was little more than a rhythmic walk, easy to master and appealing to dancers who felt self-conscious performing the animal dances. Of this dance, famed dancer Vernon Castle proclaimed, 'The Waltz is beautiful, the Tango is graceful, the Brazilian Maxixe is unique … but when a good orchestra plays a "rag" one has simply *got* to move. The One Step is the dance for rag-time music.'[24]

In these comments Castle also referenced the third critical innovation in popular dance prior to the war – the tango – which arrived in Britain amid the flurry of American waltzes and one-steps, but from the opposite direction. The tango's precise origins are murky, but undoubtedly stretch back well into the nineteenth century, when it developed in impoverished neighbourhoods of Buenos Aires from a fusion of dance traditions belonging to inhabitants of European, creole Argentinian and African descent. By 1900 the tango had worked its way into middle- and upper-class Argentine society by way of the stage, as well as through elite men's visits to the clubs and bordellos associated with the dance in popular memory. In the first years of the twentieth century, these same upper-class men ventured forth to Europe on the Grand Tour, bringing the tango with them, particularly to the cafés and cabarets of Montmartre and the wider Parisian demi-monde.[25]

Consequently, though occasionally billed as the 'Argentine' tango, the dance that enthralled Britain during the last two dancing seasons prior to the outbreak of war actually came from Paris. Like the Boston and ragtime dances before it, there was as yet no standard version of the tango, and some dancers complained of feeling confused over the profusion of possible steps. However, the dance was generally characterised by a tight hold between dancers and close, sensual movements. In its original form from Buenos Aires, it involved *el corte* – or cuts – wherein the male lead made a sudden movement backward against the flow of dance. As with the waltz, there were subsequently efforts to eliminate these cuts owing to the chaos they created in crowded ballrooms.[26] Taken up by the British dance teachers who spent much time in the French capital and in the resort towns along the Riviera, the tango initially appeared in Britain as an exhibition dance on the stage, as well as in hotels, restaurants and department stores. One in particular, Selfridges, helped spur on the craze for the dance by marketing a range of tango-themed commodities, such as dresses, hats, cosmetics and cigarette holders.[27] Meanwhile, those members of elite society who had witnessed or participated in the dance during their own continental travels began to request it back home. It soon reigned supreme at

London's premier dancing schools, and at the 'tango teas' first hosted at the Savoy hotel, but which were quickly replicated by a multitude of other hotels and restaurants. The tango also sparked the interest of the lower ranks of society, who, though lacking the purpose-built dance halls that would appear after the war, experimented with the tango in the streets and in the dancing rooms attached to pubs. As Richardson recalled, 'London in common with the other great cities of Europe went tango mad.'[28]

At the same time, despite the widespread fervour for the dance at home and abroad, the tango spurred considerable outcry over its 'imagined indelicacies'.[29] Indeed, throughout the transatlantic network in which the tango evolved and circulated – from South and North America, and across Europe – criticisms of the dance abounded. It called for close bodily contact between dancing couples, and suggestive, sexualised movements; rightly or wrongly, the tango was associated with disreputable social spaces, and was said to promote bad behaviour in its practitioners – particularly young women – or to place dancers in danger of physical injury.[30] Ragtime dances suffered similar censure, for being silly and grotesque in appearance and, like the tango, prompted accusations of obscenity owing to their close holds and overtly suggestive movements of grinding, wiggling and shaking. In addition, the European/African-American cultural hybridity that scholars have subsequently identified in ragtime was not something of which contemporaries were generally aware.[31] Critics and proponents on both sides of the Atlantic thus reflexively identified ragtime music and dances as black, which prompted a racist backlash in addition to the other objections described above.

In 1914 the Vatican flatly denounced the turkey trot and the tango, and around the same time, the Dancing Teachers Association of America instituted a policy whereby it refused to provide instruction in any syncopated dance.[32] As this would imply, dance professionals were themselves initially divided on the new dances – Edward Scott was a particularly vocal critic among British teachers – but the most vociferous complaints came from 'nondancing moralists', such as clergy and conservative newspapers.[33] In Britain, critics of modern dancing also began to advance the commentary that would surround popular dance imports for the next three decades: that they were at odds with the national character or temperament. As *The Times* lamented in 1914:

> With a hundred dances that grew out of the English temperament, and the English soil … we toil wearily round our ball-rooms in lumpish imitations of modes of self-expression that are not, and never can be, our own. Whether we like it or not, we are English.[34]

Yet these denunciations existed in tension with the rampant enthusiasm for modern dancing expressed elsewhere, especially among the young. There was a clear generational divide between youthful one-step and tango enthusiasts and older dancers nostalgic for the dances of their own early lives. In particular, modern dancing's celebration of close physical contact provided young women with a means of sexual self-expression, and – in an historical moment that witnessed the ascent of the New Woman and emergence of the militant suffrage campaign – a way to make claims for independence by dramatically displaying and extending their bodies across public spaces.[35] In addition, for many Britons, the foreign origins of these dances made them all the more exotic, appealing and modern. Effectively, all of the reasons the Boston, tango and ragtime dances were decried by some, were the very reasons they were embraced by others. This was a pattern that would repeat itself again and again in the history of British popular dance.

It was the intercession of one couple that helped to ease, if not quite eliminate, the anxieties about modern dancing on both sides of the Atlantic. Vernon and Irene Castle were a married dance team who found international fame for their sophisticated and graceful renderings of the new dance styles. The Castles were the most prominent among a larger group of dance professionals in the United States and Europe who took up the dances associated with African-American and working-class immigrant social practices, and modified them in ways that made them more palatable to white, middle-class society.[36] In their 1914 instruction manual, *Modern Dancing*, the Castles argued that it was not the dances themselves that were inappropriate but the way they were performed by some segments of the public. Their aim was to 'uplift dancing, purify it, and place it before the public in its proper light. When this has been done, we feel convinced that no objection can possibly be urged against it on the grounds of impropriety'.[37] To fulfil this mandate, they developed the 'Castle Walk', a simple set of dance steps that could be applied to most of the popular dances of the day, and advised their readers, students and audiences to eliminate entirely the dramatic gesturing, stomping and kicking associated with particularly with the animal dances. Significantly, these were also the movements most closely linked to African-American dancing and, as will be discussed further in Chapter 5, these efforts by the Castles and other professionals began a long tradition of whitening black dances for mass consumption on both sides of the Atlantic.

As a married couple, and through the displays of 'skill, elegance, and propriety' in their dancing, the Castles appealed to and appeased middle-class moralists.[38]

At the same time, they embodied all that was modern, and were also admired by those who did not need to be convinced as to the virtues of the new dance styles. First attaining success in Paris, they performed all over the world, opened a dancing school that bore their name, and were one of the first teams to dance on film. Irene sported bobbed hair and became a style icon, lending her name to a wide array of cosmetics, fashions and other commodities marketed to women. Their band, led by famed bandleader James Reese Europe, was African American, and their female manager was in a long-term same-sex relationship, imbuing the Castles with an aura of racial and sexual transgressiveness.[39] With their widespread foreign travels – and through their very union – they embodied the transatlantic production of popular dance in this period, in that Vernon was British while Irene was American.

Most associated with dances like the tango and the one-step, the Castles also played a crucial role in popularising what would become – for the British – the most enduringly successful of the new dances to emerge from this period: the foxtrot. Contemporary sources and scholarly writing provide a number of different histories for this dance. Possibly simply another animal dance, based on the 'sly running of a fox', the origins of the foxtrot were also associated with American vaudeville performer Harry Fox.[40] The foxtrot's movements have additionally been linked by dance scholars to the slow drag, a dance prevalent within African-American migrant communities in early twentieth-century New York.[41] In its rudimentary form, the foxtrot was little more than 'walking round the room in time to fast music'.[42] Even for those who attempted a more sophisticated rendering than this would imply, there were no standard steps and many variations of the dance. However, borrowing elements from both the one-step and the waltz, the foxtrot was another natural dance based on a walking step (initially a trot, and later a glide), set in 4/4 time, rather than the 3/4 employed by the waltz; later in its evolution dancers moved across the floor taking steps in a slow-slow-quick-quick-slow sequence.

In the summer of 1914, as the country edged towards war, British dancers were introduced to the first foxtrot songs at London dance clubs. Around the same time, a Scottish teacher exhibited the foxtrot, having witnessed the dance on a recent trip to the United States to meet with American professionals. Special foxtrot balls soon followed in cities such as London and Liverpool, and like the tango and ragtime dances before it, the foxtrot was given 'a big fillip' through exhibitions on the stage.[43] When the war began, dancing soon emerged, according to Richardson, as 'the most popular form of relaxation for men on leave'.[44] Owing to its simplicity, the foxtrot proved a particularly accessible and pleasing dance for those with little dancing experience, and no prior knowledge of the steps of the waltz or tango. Popular dance had an erratic wartime history, as the desire to provide servicemen and war workers with forms of recreation and relaxation did battle with increasing restrictions on leisure in association with the Defence of the Realm Act 1914, and a brief military ban on officers dancing in uniform. Nonetheless the foxtrot, in its multitude of variations, endured, and proved to be the dance that bridged the ragtime era to the next dramatic moment of cultural transformation for Britain: the coming of jazz.

The definitions and meanings of jazz have been mutable and much debated by musicians, fans and scholars alike. Throughout the first half of the twentieth century, this musical form was continually re-shaped by the movements of people and the incorporation of influences from across the United States, as well as the Caribbean, Africa and Europe. However, in arguably its earliest incarnation, jazz came from early 1900s New Orleans. It developed from a fusion of ragtime and the blues – the music born within African-American communities in the Mississippi Delta in the years after the Civil War – which made its way down the river to New Orleans with migrant workers. Distinctive for its greater use of brass and wind instruments, such as trumpets, clarinets, saxophones and cornets, to produce syncopation, jazz began to spread across the United States via travelling musicians like Jelly Roll Morton, Sidney Bechet and Louis Armstrong, as well as the thousands of African Americans who moved north to Chicago, New York and other cities as part of the Great Migration.[45]

By the time the United States entered the war in 1917, jazz had been recorded for the first time in New York City by the Original Dixieland Jazz Band (an all-white band from New Orleans), and was beginning to supplant ragtime as the popular music favoured by the American servicemen embarking for Europe. Military jazz bands, such as the 'Hellfighters' led by the Castles' former bandleader, James Reese Europe, were soon formed to entertain and maintain the morale of the troops. Touring across France and performing for audiences composed of French, American and British soldiers, Europe played a major role in introducing jazz to the continent that shared his name.[46] Meanwhile, American servicemen travelling through Britain to the Western Front, or visiting the country on leave, triggered an interest in jazz among the civilian population as well. As the war drew to a close, British curiosity about jazz was enhanced by press reports and gramophone recordings, so much so that when the Original Dixieland Jazz Band embarked on a London tour in the spring of 1919, they were an instant sensation – though subject to some condemnation from musical purists.[47] The band performed in various London theatres before moving into a nine-month residence at the brand new Hammersmith Palais de Danse.

For Britons, the meanings of 'jazz' went well beyond the music, as the word was employed in multiple ways to encapsulate the whole of the frenzied culture of pleasure-seeking that defined the first months of the peace. Virtually any band performing music for dancing was known as a 'jazz band'.[48] Dance enthusiasts spoke of 'jazzing', while professionals promoted a new step, the 'jazz roll' – three steps forward or backward, with a slight crossing of the feet, which became most associated with the one-step. However, generally what British dancers performed in this new musical era were the same foxtrots and one-steps, and to a lesser degree the tangos and waltzes, of the pre-war and wartime years; there was as yet little to no cohesion or consistency to their steps, which, as will be shown Chapter 2, was a state of affairs that professional dancers would soon seek to rectify. Indeed, the sheer volume of new dances that had characterised the Edwardian years had by this time begun to lessen, as teachers on both sides of the Atlantic worked to purge their art of those dances and dance steps which provoked the most controversy in favour of the toned-down style increasingly known as 'modern ballroom dancing'. As Britain transitioned from war to peace, this explicitly modern style of popular dance helped those who loved and hated it alike to make sense of the modern age.

Dancing modernity after the First World War

In January 1920, the urban district council of Leyton, in Essex, attempted to ban the 'jazz' and one-step from dances held at the municipal hall and town baths on the grounds that they were 'morally bad'.[49] The move inspired an angry response from the independent promoter who oversaw the dances at the baths, and he tried to get out of his contract owing to the new prohibition. When this request was refused, the promoter sent local jazz enthusiasts sympathetic to his position two hundred free tickets to the next dance. They turned up in droves and energetically performed the banned dances – some of them in hobnail boots in order to assure maximum destruction of the venue. Meanwhile, the *Daily Express*, in reporting on the incident, decried the move by Leyton's council in no uncertain terms:

> If the dissecting glass of suspicion be once applied, immorality – a fine, comprehensive, and vague sort of word – may be found in all sorts of attractive and, as we think, harmless pleasures … This sort of inquest leads to lunacy. Leyton will not achieve a higher virtue by losing its jazz.[50]

The Leyton incident is strongly illustrative of the contestations over popular dance that occurred as Britain entered the interwar period. Government officials, the popular press, as well as commercial dance providers, dance professionals and the dancing public, all entered into negotiations over the state of dancing in the country – negotiations that were sometimes heated, and occasionally conducted with their dancing bodies. While the events in Leyton demonstrated that criticisms of modern ballroom dances persisted throughout the post-war craze and beyond, proponents also found a variety of ways to defend and promote their favoured pastime. Amid ongoing critiques, modern ballroom dancing was touted for its ease and simplicity, its benefits to health and beauty, and above all, its ability to express modern life. As Martin Daunton and Bernhard Reiger note, from the 1870s through to the 1940s, 'Britons repeatedly resorted to the semantics of modernity to make sense of changes in their society.'[51] This was no less true of the discourses that surrounded popular dance in the 1920s, within which a language of modernity was central – a fact perhaps made most apparent by the very appellation 'modern' ballroom dancing. In the aftermath of the First World War popular dances were seen as expressions of the changing conventions of the age that had produced them, and were understood in terms of the political, social and cultural changes that this new era had wrought.

After the war, lingering condemnations of modern ballroom dances echoed those that had been levelled against ragtime dances or the rudimentary tango – that they were ridiculous, ugly, promoters of immorality and simply un-British. In 1919, a writer for the *Daily Express* provided a vivid description of his objections to the new dancing style: 'Personally I object to being forced against my will to cut absurd and fantastic capers in a ball-room, to slide and slither, and slide again, like a drunken sailor; to perform an involuntary treadmill exercise for three hours on end; to twinkle my toes and dip my knees and make myself look thoroughly ridiculous – in fact, to jazz.'[52] A similar condemnation of modern ballroom dancing as silly and unattractive came some time later in the *Daily Mail* from a critic calling himself 'An Old Stager'. Titling his piece 'Dances I Dislike', Old Stager recounted his experience at a recent dance in the Midlands, and lamented the stark changes to what was being performed in the ballroom since his own dancing days in the 1880s: 'For a man who used to be fond of dancing to sit and look on at the ungraceful contortions of the fox-trot is about as amusing as a devotee of Bridge being compelled to watch people playing beggar-my-neighbour or snap.' He decried the vulgarity of American dances in particular, and described retiring out of earshot of the jazz-filled ballroom in order to let his memory 'drift back to the perfect dancing and lovely music of forty years ago … dream-like waltzes, the dignified Lancers, the jolly, rollicking polkas'.[53]

Yet even in condemning jazz and modern ballroom dancing, both of these writers understood that they occupied an increasingly minority opinion. The correspondent for the *Daily Express* referred to himself as a '*rara avis*', and pronounced that his dislike of jazz dancing had made him 'a pariah outcast from society; voted generally a bore and a thoroughly dull fellow'.[54] Many letters to the editor in the following days confirmed this supposition, basically advising the man to stop whining and join in the fun. Old Stager similarly reported that he had been declared 'a dear old crank' by his hostess, and once again correspondence to the newspaper in the wake of the article largely endorsed this view.[55] One writer who signed himself 'Another Old Stager' reminded the original author that the dancing of the 1880s was 'Gone forever like the 8d. income tax. Young people want to enjoy themselves in their own way, which, naturally, in 1926, is different than that of 1886.'[56] Another letter from a forty-year-old woman also proclaimed that modern dances were more appropriate to the current time period, and in fact were an improvement on the ' "jolly" polka' and ' "dignified" lancers' Old Stager recalled so fondly: 'Compared with the smooth, cool, easy rhythm of the modern young dancers, these bygone performers seem as children gamboling noisily beside their quietly progressing elders.'[57]

This conception that the current popular dances best expressed the modern age was one continually asserted after the war. Modern ballroom dances, such as the foxtrot and one-step, represented a critical rupture with styles of the past – like the quadrille, the polka or the Victorian waltz – which collectively became known as 'old-time' dances. The latter were said to belong to a bygone era, and were often compared to other relics from the past. In 1922, editor Richardson proclaimed in the *Dancing Times*, 'I am not going to suggest that the modern foxtrot is more beautiful than the old minuet, but it is more in harmony with the times, just as the modern Rolls-Royce is more suitable to-day than the more beautiful coach and four of one hundred years ago.'[58] Stage dancer Ethel Levey used another form of transportation to make a similar comparison about the old and the new. Contrasting modern music and dances to minuets and gavottes, she remarked, 'it would be just as easy to compare the beauty of a sailing ship with the beauty of an Atlantic liner'.[59]

Similar arguments were advanced in rebuttal to efforts in this period to revive English folk dancing. At the head of this campaign was Cecil Sharp, who, as director of the English Folk Dances Society, was an enthusiastic preserver of British folklore, and open critic of jazz and modern ballroom dancing.[60] However, once again many dance professionals and writers for the popular press suggested that these efforts were misguided. In a 1919 speech to the Arts League of Service, concert dancer Margaret Morris argued that folk dancing could never be successfully revived since 'the spirit of the times has changed'.[61] A writer for the *Dancing Times* similarly declared, 'The old dances expressed the spirit of the age during which they were performed, but that age is long dead. The new dances express the spirit of the day, and they are therefore suited to and popular with the people of the day.'[62] Other observers went even further, suggesting that jazz dancing *was* the folk dancing of the modern age. As the *Daily Express* proclaimed in 1920, 'Many experts consider that the jazz is the folk-dancing of to-day, and that the folk-dancing in which Mr. Sharp … is so interested, is the folk-dancing of yesterday and has no place in swift modern life.'[63]

The claims for modern ballroom dancing's modernity were based not only in its moment of origin, but in its movements. Unlike Victorian ballroom dances, which were founded on the five turned-out positions of the feet as in ballet, dances such as the foxtrot, one-step and modern waltz were based on natural walking movements. They were heralded as simple and free, easy to learn and a welcome change from the structure and regimentation of the past. As Richardson informed the *Daily Mail*, 'the up-to-date dances are the antithesis of the mechanical, rule-bound movements insisted upon by the dancing masters of the late Victorian period'. His comments were foregrounded by an argument that dancing, like all art forms, was affected by the 'trend of modern thought', which had been shown in the recent world war to be a 'revolt against despotic autocracy'.[64] As will be shown in Chapter 2, Richardson and other professionals often praised the dancing public for casting off the shackles of the autocratic Victorian dancing master, and for directing the evolution of dancing style themselves. These dance professionals also clearly believed that this was something that could only have happened in the wake of the changes that came with the war. As renowned teacher and bandleader Victor Silvester would later recall, 'The coming of the First World War, when old institutions went by the board … there was introduced by the dancers themselves – not the teachers, mark you – a free and easy go-as-you please style based more or less on the natural movements used in walking.'[65]

Silvester's comments encapsulated much about how modern ballroom dancing was understood in the early 1920s; it was uncomplicated, easily mastered and expressive of changes that had come from the war. As Richardson's references to revolts against autocracy attest, one of the social and political transformations the new dances were said to reflect was Britain's expanding democracy. Though strong social divisions persisted throughout the interwar years – some in fact exacerbated by popular dance, as will be shown in subsequent chapters – the shared victory in the war also cultivated a sense of collective will and a belief national unity. At the same time, the Representation of the People Act 1918 provided for universal manhood suffrage for the first time in British history, reinforcing that at least in political terms all (male) citizens were equal. In this context, simple dances that anyone could learn and perform had a natural appeal and symbolic resonance. Writing a month after the Armistice in 1918, Richardson reassured readers of the *Daily Mail* that anyone could participate in the new dances:

> A number of people who have not danced for years feel they would like to commence again, but they are deterred because they cannot do the 'complicated modern dances'. Let me assure them the modern dances are not complicated, and if they can do the old valse well they need never dread adventuring in the modern ballroom.[66]

Another professional dancer believed that the simplicity of modern ballroom dances was in fact the reason for the dance craze, asserting in a letter to the editor of *Daily Express* that 'The reason why the present dances, fox-trot, one-step, and waltz, are so popular is because they are … very simple to learn.'[67] The ease and accessibility of modern ballroom dancing was thus widely proclaimed, particularly by professional dancers seeking to draw new devotees to this leisure form. One teacher guaranteed he 'could teach anybody in two lessons'.[68] A common mantra asserted, 'if you can walk, you can dance'.

At the same time, in another gesture towards democracy, the fervour for modern ballroom dancing was held to be a phenomenon that transcended social hierarchies. A *Daily Express* headline from October 1919 observed that in London, 'all classes [were] affected by the craze'.[69] A month later, the *Dancing Times* reported that in Leeds 'everybody, without distinction of class or age, is dancing'.[70] There were even those who suggested that this shared love of dance promoted social and national unity. As the *Daily Express* further proclaimed, 'never before has dancing played the part it now plays as a social equaliser; never has its influence penetrated to the heart of a people as it has done to the heart of the British public to-day'.[71] Modern ballroom dancing was thus represented as a shared national experience, a stimulant of cross-class unity, and a symbol of democracy – an ideal cultural expression of the more progressive society that some Britons hoped the war had created.

Dancing was associated with other social and cultural changes as well. Notably, the modern dance styles reflected and reinforced a perceived breakdown in formality and social convention. As a 1924 article in *Popular Music and Dancing Weekly* declared, 'All that I can see in the change of dances during the centuries is that they signalised the change in conventions, and if the modern dances show nothing else, they certainly depict a greater freedom of movement.'[72] This release from restraint and escape from tradition was also believed to extend to the public spaces where the new dances were performed. Ballrooms were said to be less formal than they had been before the war, with more of a feeling of gaiety and fewer restrictions on behaviour. A writer for the *Daily Express* observed, 'Not only is the public taste in dancing in process of evolution, but also the manners and customs relating to the art are changing. It is refreshing to note the atmosphere of freedom and goodwill which permeates our ball-rooms.'[73] Gone were the pre-war conventions – at least at middle- and upper-class dances – of formal invitations, dance cards and chaperones.

This liberty from protocol in the ballroom, and the sense of freedom expressed through the natural movements of modern ballroom dances, were especially connected with questions about the status of women after the war. As Britain moved into the 1920s, uncertainty lingered as to what would be the long-term social effects of women's direct participation in the war effort as munitions workers, nurses and ambulance drivers, and auxiliary servicewomen, and their assumption of a wide variety of typically masculine roles. For those who desired the 'modern woman' to retain greater levels of autonomy and independence, 'modern dancing' in a less formal ballroom was an ideal form of expression. As the *Daily Mail* reflected, 'there is a free-and-easy air about dances, the result no doubt of the emancipation of the young girl which has been brought about by war conditions'.[74] Another article in *Popular Music and Dancing Weekly* linked the specific movements of modern ballroom dancing to women's emancipation, proclaiming that 'the lack of conventional restraint [in the dances] points to the fact that woman is taking her right place in the world'.[75] As will be shown in Chapter 4, the diminished inhibitions at public dances and the independence expressed by women who enjoyed dancing contributed to some of the strongest objections to this leisure form. But for enthusiasts, the performance of a smooth and simple foxtrot or one-step – in a lively and carefree ballroom – represented freedom from convention and regulation, and a very modern escape from tradition.

Indeed, modern ballroom dancing's modernity and suitability to the moment was often employed as specific defence against its critics. One oft-repeated counterargument to attacks on the new dances was that historically all new styles were poorly received upon their first introduction. As a writer for *Popular Music and Dancing Weekly* pointed out, 'it is not without interest to realise that once a ban was put upon the waltz'.[76] Richardson made the same point even more forcefully in the *Dancing Times* in 1922:

> Will those who take delight in belittling our modern dances remember that they are the creations of the age? and will those who cry for the return of the dances of our grandparents and great-grandparents remember that they are crying for an anachronism? and will they also remember that one hundred years ago, when the valse was first introduced, folks held up their hands in horror, and begged for a return to the minuet and the country dance, just as in all probability one hundred years hence there will be those who belittle the dance then in vogue, and beg for a return of the stately foxtrot of their ancestors?[77]

Similar statements abounded in the writings of professional dancers throughout the 1920s, many of which drew particular attention to the poor public reception of the waltz in the early nineteenth century. The parallels were in fact given further credence by the fact that the tango was ultimately granted a boost in respectability much as the waltz once was: after the waltz was included in the programme of a dance hosted by the Prince Regent in 1816 it attained widespread social acceptance, and the same fate resulted for the tango once Queen Mary had witnessed an exhibition of the dance at a ball and pronounced it 'charming'.[78]

Pointing out the historical parallels between the now respectable waltz and the still questionable foxtrot or tango was part of a much broader effort by dance enthusiasts to rehabilitate the reputation of modern ballroom dances, and to silence their critics. One of the primary ways in which this was undertaken was through the standardisation of the foxtrot, one-step, tango and modern waltz, a process which is the subject of Chapter 2. Another was to espouse the many advantages and benefits of dancing. This began during the earliest days of the dance craze, and continued throughout the interwar period. For instance, dance enthusiasts repeatedly praised dancing's value as a form of exercise and benefits to physical health. As the *Daily Mail* observed in 1920, 'Dancing is to be something more than the joyous amusement of gay and giddy youth. It is being taken up quite solemnly as a form of indoor exercise by the serious. Our books on sports and pastimes will be out of date until a new chapter gives dancing its honoured place.'[79] Santos Casani likewise observed in a long treatise on the benefits of dancing in one of his dance instruction manuals, 'I have come to the conclusion that there is only one way to keep fit, and that is, to keep dancing.' Casani continued, 'If "dancing for health" was advertised as loudly as patent medicines, and folks danced instead of taking drugs and pills, we would have a healthy race.'[80] In the popular press, physical recreation guides, and dance magazines and instruction manuals, dancing was offered as a cure or preventative for conditions ranging from depression, to indigestion, flat feet and poor blood; dancing and dance music were even put forward as a means of restoring the health of war veterans.[81] In any number of contexts, Britons were assured that they could 'dance [their] way to health'.[82]

Additionally, while many of the testaments to dancing's health benefits were rather general, others drew on the specificities of this art form to explain its curative properties. To be a good dancer required a mastery of rhythm, and this was explicitly connected with its value to good health, in a way that distinguished it from other forms of physical recreation. As one doctor wrote in a dance magazine,

> [Dancing's] supreme value lies in the fact that it is rhythmic. Few people realise that the human body is, first and foremost, a rhythmic machine. Every organ, every pulse, has its rhythm. In health it never departs from that 'ebb and flow'. Thus the heart, the most vital organ of all, does all its work to dance music.[83]

Another report claimed that an official from Guy's Hospital in London had endorsed dancing as a cure for stammering. The hospital allegedly gave as an example 'the case of a twenty-year-old girl whose stammering was due to lack of rhythm and who was completely cured by dancing'.[84]

Beyond physical health, dancing was also touted as a means of retaining a youthful look and demeanour, and for cultivating grace and physical beauty. As one writer noted, 'Doctors say dancing is one of the finest exercises in the world, as it does not over-develop your muscles, but just keeps you young.'[85] The *Dancing Times* declared that dancing was 'the secret of youth',[86] while one London dance hall advised its patrons to 'Dance and Keep Young!'[87] Not only was dancing said to be an ideal means through which to maintain one's youth, other commentators suggested that it could also be advantageous to the development of those who still were young. As the *Edinburgh Evening News* proclaimed, 'Shy and awkward children have been transformed into models of natural ease and grace by learning to dance.'[88] Casani likewise argued that 'Dancing cultivates physical grace', before suggesting it could also boost physical attractiveness: 'Beauty specialists can do much to make a woman attractive, but unless there is poetry in her movements she fails to be wholly alluring.'[89] A writer for *Popular Music and Dancing Weekly* echoed this sentiment, commenting that 'Dancing and beauty go hand in hand', and that it provided the ideal exercise for 'maintaining slender hips, slim ankles, and graceful arms and wrists'.[90] In these ways, dancing was strongly embedded within a contemporary interest in regimens geared towards the cultivation of beauty, health and fitness, that which Ina Zweiniger-Bargielowska has termed 'body management'.[91]

According to commentators, dancing had any number of more abstract powers as well, and offered a means of assessing a person's personality, temperament or character. As Casani put it, 'dancing helps to express personality … In a real sense dancing may be called the personality of motion'.[92] Another writer suggested, in dancing 'we give expression to whatever is foremost in our character. Temperament always comes to the surface in the ballroom'.[93] Accordingly, *Popular Music and Dancing Weekly* advised women that they could learn something about a man's character by the way that he danced. As celebrity writer Nelly Wigley wrote, 'dancing is the sincerest and most ancient form of self-expression, and a dancer's worst faults, as well as his best qualities, come to the surface as soon as his foot touches the floor'.[94] According to Wigley, the way in which a man behaved in the ballroom could reveal a range of traits, including timidity, aggression and vanity. On the opposite side of the gender line, the *Daily Express* similarly advised male readers that 'A woman reveals her temperament by the way she responds to her dancing partner.'[95] The article went on to suggest that a man could be assured that a woman who surrendered herself to her partner, and did not attempt to lead on the dance floor, would likely make an admirable and compliant wife. Finally, dancing was promoted for its ability to cultivate 'social success',[96] and for manifold virtues that ranged from limiting social unrest and preventing labour strikes, to improving one's tennis game. Casani perhaps best summed up the many advantages of dancing as a sport and art in his *Home Teacher*, when he wrote, 'Dancing is the highroad to happiness. It is more than mere pleasure; it is a subtle combination of art and exercise which blends the mind and body into perfect harmony.'[97]

The concerted effort to promote dancing's advantages to health, beauty and a wide range of other aspects of modern life are evidence of lingering concerns among dance enthusiasts that their favoured activity remained suspect to many people and was in need of an active and ongoing defence. As will be shown in subsequent chapters, though condemnations of jazz and modern ballroom dances, such as the foxtrot, one-step, tango and modern waltz, were marginalised relatively quickly after the war, conservative and often racist polemics against dancing recurred throughout the interwar period upon the introduction of new dances ranging from the Charleston to the jitterbug. Moreover, controversies surrounding the 'modern' women who were among dancing's greatest devotees, and the perceived links between some public dancing spaces and sexual immorality and deviant or even criminal behaviour, continued to shape social perceptions of dancing as a whole. However, the fact that the most vehement avowals of dancing's many virtues came from professional dancers was also reflective of the significant financial motives these men and women possessed to maintain the public's interest in popular dance. This will be explored further in Chapter 2, but it is worth noting here that by 1929, dance professionals were collectively and officially espousing 'Dancing for Health' as a useful slogan that might be 'the means of filling our ballrooms and our classrooms'.[98] These efforts were also clearly successful. In a survey conducted by the social research organisation Mass Observation at a south London dancing school in the late 1930s, 'exercise' and 'to keep fit or slim' were respectively the second and third most common reasons given by those present for why they took lessons, even trumping 'to dance' as a motivation.[99]

Earlier in the interwar period, not everyone was convinced that modern ballroom dancing would enjoy such longevity within British culture. As the dance craze of the post-war years proceeded, there were already those speculating on its inevitable end. These commentators believed that the enthusiasm for jazz and its attendant dances was ephemeral, and likely to fade away like so many previous social trends. As early as 1919 the *Daily Express* printed an article entitled 'Jazzed out', in which the author argued that people were bored with modern ballroom dancing, and longing for a return to the days of the mazurka and minuet. Describing the scene at a recent dance, he wrote, 'After midnight the juveniles performed prodigies of pedal exertion, but they looked just a little bored. That beginning of boredom means the end of jazz.'[100] A month later, a letter to the editor of the same newspaper concurred that the pleasure-seeking culture embodied in the dance craze was just a 'passing phase', and that soon those currently enjoying playing outside the home would choose to return to the quietude of card-playing and chats by the fireside. He concluded by prophesising that, 'The slogan, for the next few years at any rate, will be, I surmise: "After the ball was over."'[101]

Yet other observers had a different view of the state of popular dance as Britain progressed through the 1920s. While acknowledging that the 'mania' and 'madness' for dancing would inevitably decrease, they claimed that modern ballroom dancing represented an important shift in Britain's social and cultural life, and an enduring one. As the *Dancing Times* declared in 1922, 'There is nothing ephemeral about the interest which the public takes in dancing to-day. It has become an integral part of our social life, and a dance follows dinner as naturally as does the black coffee.'[102] A writer for *Popular Music and Dancing Weekly* similarly observed, 'The craze for dancing no longer exists. Instead, dancing has become an established form of amusement and recreation. Dancing is an institution – as much an accepted item of life's curriculum as the Sunday joint or the breakfast eggs and bacon.'[103] Dancing was compared to aspects of everyday life by another commentator as well, who proclaimed it to be 'almost as much a part of our lives as getting up or going to bed!'[104]

It is not insignificant that just like the attestations about dancing's health and beauty benefits many of these comments originated with writers and teachers who had a vested financial interest in promoting dancing's durability within society. However, they were not wrong that a dramatic and permanent alteration to British popular dance had occurred. Whatever nostalgia some may have felt for the traditional waltz or the minuet, or whatever scorn others heaped upon modern styles, the years that followed showed that there was simply no going back. Even before the war, modern dances – with their simple, natural movements and diverse, cosmopolitan origins – were those seen to best express the modern age. After the war, they helped Britons to make sense of a world that was forever altered, and, as the interwar period progressed, popular dance continued to provide Britons with a vehicle through which to grapple with issues of race, gender, class and sexuality, as well as foreign influence and national identity. Dancing became ever more embedded within the national culture, and, as the next two chapters will show, two commercial producers were at the forefront of these developments: the dance profession and the dance hall industry.

Notes

1 'London's Orgy of Dancing', *Daily Express* (30 October 1919), p. 7.

2 'The Mania of the Moment', *Daily Mail* (8 January 1919), p. 7.

3 'Tea-dancing', *Daily Mail* (27 January 1919), p. 4.

4 'One-legged dancers', *Daily Express* (22 December 1919), p. 6; S.A.M., Letter to the Editor, *Daily Express* (31 January 1920), p. 4.

5 Sitter Out, *Dancing Times* (November 1919), p. 79. Note: The 'Sitter Out' was a *nom de plume* for *Dancing Times* editor Philip J. S. Richardson.

6 Philip J. S. Richardson, *A History of English Ballroom Dancing* (London: Herbert Jenkins, 1946), p. 37.

7 'Select Dances', *Eastern Mercury* (21 October 1919), p. 4.

8 'Tea Table Talk', *Daily Express* (5 January 1920), p. 3; *Daily Mail* quotation from Robert Graves and Alan Hodge, *The Long Week-End: A Social History of Great Britain, 1918–1939* (New York: W.W. Norton & Company, 1940, 1994), p. 28.

9 Genevieve Abravanel, *Americanizing Britain: The Rise of Modernism in the Age of the Entertainment Empire* (Oxford: Oxford University Press, 2012), p. 53.

10 Juliet Nicolson, *The Great Silence, 1918–1920: Living in the Shadow of the Great War* (Toronto: McArthur & Company, 2009), p. 151; Rishona Zimring, *Social Dance and the Modernist Imagination in Interwar Britain* (Farnham: Ashgate, 2013), p. 4.

11 See Zimring, *Social Dance and the Modernist Imagination;* Theresa Jill Buckland, *Society Dancing: Fashionable Bodies in England, 1870–1920* (Basingstoke: Palgrave Macmillan, 2011); Danielle Robinson, *Modern Moves: Dancing Race during the Ragtime and Jazz Eras* (New York: Oxford University Press, 2015).

12 On Edwardian musical theatre, see Peter Bailey, 'Hullo, Ragtime! West End revue and the Americanisation of popular culture in pre-1914 London', in Len Platt, Tobias Becker and David Linton (eds), *Popular Musical Theatre in London and Berlin* (Cambridge: Cambridge University Press, 2014).

13 Richardson, *A History of English Ballroom Dancing*, p. 18.

14 Richardson, *A History of English Ballroom Dancing*, pp. 19–21.

15 Victor Silvester, *Modern Ballroom Dancing* (London: Stanley Paul, 1977, 1990), p. 22.

16 Jo Baim, *Tango: Creation of a Cultural Icon* (Bloomington, IN: Indiana University Press, 2007), p. 50.

17 Santos Casani, *Casani's Self-Tutor of Ballroom Dancing* (London: Cassell, 1927), p. 31.

18 Bailey, 'Hullo Ragtime!', pp. 142–3. See also Nadine George-Graves, 'Primitivity and ragtime dance', in Julie Malnig (ed.), *Ballroom Boogie, Shimmy Sham, Shake: A Social and Popular Dance Reader* (Urbana, IL: University of Illinois Press, 2009).

19 Bailey, 'Hullo Ragtime!', p. 140.

20 For more on juke joints, see William Barlow, *Looking Up at Down: The Emergence of Blues Culture*, (Philadelphia, PA: Temple University Press, 1989), pp. 29–30.

21 On ragtime dancing, see Kathy Peiss, *Cheap Amusements: Working Women and Leisure in Turn-of-the-Century New York* (Philadelphia, PA: Temple University Press, 1986); Ann Wagner, *Adversaries of Dance* (Urbana, IL: University of Illinois Press, 1997); Julie Malnig, 'Women, dance, and New York nightlife', in Julie Malnig (ed.), *Ballroom Boogie, Shimmy Sham, Shake: A Social and Popular Dance Reader* (Urbana, IL: University of Illinois Press, 2009); George-Graves, 'Primitivity and Ragtime Dance'; Bailey, 'Hello Ragtime!'; Robinson, *Modern Moves*.

22 Bailey, 'Hullo Ragtime!', p. 142.

23 Robinson, *Modern Moves*, p. 90. On the one-step, see also Baim, *Tango*, p. 50; Buckland, *Society Dancing*, pp. 161–2.

24 Quoted in A. H. Franks, *Social Dance: A Short History* (London: Routledge & Kegan Paul, 1963), p. 176.

25 Baim, *Tango*, pp. 13–84.

26 Christine Denniston, *The Meaning of Tango: The Story of the Argentinian Dance* (London: Portico Books, 2007), p. 70.

27 Mica Nava, *Visceral Cosmopolitanism: Gender, Culture, and the Normalisation of Difference* (Oxford: Berg, 2007), p. 34.

28 Richardson, *A History of English Ballroom Dancing*, p. 25.

29 Richardson, *A History of English Ballroom Dancing*, p. 25.

30 Baim, *Tango*, pp. 55–66.

31 Robinson, *Modern Moves*, pp. 64–9.

32 Ian Driver, *A Century of Dance: A Hundred Years of Musical Movement, from Waltz to Hip Hop* (London: Hamlyn, 2000), p. 33.

33 Baim, *Tango*, p. 77.

34 'The Cult of the Tango', *The Times* (15 December 1913).

35 Peiss, *Cheap Amusements*, p. 102. See also Holly Maples, 'Embodying resistance: gendering public space in ragtime social dance', *New Theatre Quarterly*, 28:3 (August 2012), 243–59.

36 Robinson, *Modern Moves*, pp. 83–99.

37 Vernon and Irene Castle, forward to *Modern Dancing* (New York: Harper & Bros., 1914).

38 Wagner, *Adversaries of Dance*, p. 255.

39 For more on the Castles, see Eve Golden, *Vernon and Irene Castle's Ragtime Revolution* (Lexington, KT: University of Kentucky Press, 2007).

40 Liverpool Record Office, Liverpool Libraries, Hq79333GRA, *Grafton Rooms: Souvenir Brochure on the Occasion of our Silver Jubilee, 1924–1949* (1949), p. 30.

41 Robinson, *Modern Moves*, p. 55.

42 Denniston, *The Meaning of Tango*, p. 84.

43 Richardson, *A History of English Ballroom Dancing*, p. 34.

44 Richardson, *A History of English Ballroom Dancing*, p. 33.

45 For more on the history of jazz, see Ted Gioia, *The History of Jazz* (New York: Oxford University Press, 2011).

46 Jeffrey H. Jackson, *Making Jazz French: Music and Modern Life in Interwar Paris* (Durham, NC: Duke University Press, 2003), pp. 16–20.

47 James Nott, *Music for the People: Popular Music and Dance in Interwar Britain* (Oxford: Oxford University Press, 2002), p. 128; see also Jim Godbolt, *A History of Jazz in Britain, 1919–1950* (London: Northway Publications, 2010).

48 Nott, *Music for the People*, p. 129.

49 'Banned Dances at the Baths', *Daily Express* (2 January 1920), p. 1.

50 'Chadband at the Dance', *Daily Express* (2 January 1920), p. 4.

51 Martin Daunton and Bernhard Reiger, introduction to *Meanings of Modernity: Britain from the Late-Victorians Era to World War II* (Oxford: Berg, 2001), p. 15.

52 E.C.M., 'Nightmares of the Ball-room', *Daily Express* (22 November 1919), p. 4.

53 An Old Stager, 'Dances I Dislike', *Daily Mail* (9 March 1926), p. 8.

54 E.C.M., 'Nightmares of the Ball-room', p. 4.

55 An Old Stager, 'Dances I Dislike', p. 8.

56 Another Old Stager 'Over Sixty', Letter to the Editor, *Daily Mail* (11 March 1926), p. 8.

57 Letter to the Editor, *Daily Mail* (13 March 1926).

58 The Sitter Out, 'In the Ballroom', *Dancing Times* (January 1922), p. 338.

59 Ethel Levey, 'Has our music improved?', *Popular Music and Dancing Weekly* (8 November 1924), p. 47.

60 Bailey, 'Hullo Ragtime!', p. 144

61 'Tea Table Talk', *Daily Express* (14 November 1919), p. 3.

62 G. E. Fussell, 'Modern Folk and Their Dances', *Dancing Times* (March 1920), p. 442.

63 'Tea Table Talk', *Daily Express* (5 January 1920), p. 3.

64 Philip J. S. Richardson, 'Everybody Dancing Now', *Daily Mail* (14 December 1918), p. 4.

65 Silvester, *Modern Ballroom Dancing*, p. 15.

66 Richardson, 'Everybody Dancing Now', p. 4.

67 Bernard G. Carrington, Letter to the Editor, *Daily Express* (3 February 1920), p. 4.

68 'The Spirit of the Dance', *Daily Mail* (23 January 1919), p. 7.

69 'London's Orgy of Dancing', p. 7.

70 'Provincial Notes – Leeds', *Dancing Times* (November 1919), p. 135.

71 Geoffrey D'Egville, 'Present Taste for Dancing', *Daily Express* (21 November 1919), p. 3.

72 Ella Retford, 'From Minuet to Fox Trot', *Popular Music and Dancing Weekly* (21 June 1924), p. 164.

73 D'Egville, 'Present Taste for Dancing', p. 3.

74 'How We Dance', *Daily Mail* (15 January 1919), p. 4.

75 Retford, 'From Minuet to Fox Trot', p. 164.

76 Ratford, 'From Minuet to Fox Trot', p. 164.

77 The Sitter Out, 'In the Ballroom', *Dancing Times* (October 1922), p. 23.

78 Richardson, *A History of English Ballroom Dancing*, pp. 25–6.

79 'Serious Dancing', *Daily Mail* (10 February 1920), p. 6.

80 Santos Casani, *Casani's Home Teacher: Ballroom Dancing Made Easy* (London: Heath Cranton, 1936), pp. 36–9.

81 E. J. Wass, 'Music that Heals', *Popular Music and Dancing Weekly* (8 May 1926), p. 56.

82 A Doctor, 'Dance Your Way to Health', *Popular Music and Dancing Weekly* (16 August 1924), p. 78.

83 A Doctor, 'Dance Your Way to Health', p. 78.

84 'Around the Dance and Music Hall', *Popular Music and Dancing Weekly* (13 February 1926), back cover.

85 Molly Carmichael, 'Watch Your Step', *Daily Mirror* (9 November 1935), p. 23.

86 'Provincial News, Leeds', *Dancing Times* (November 1919), p. 135.

87 MOA: TC 38/1/F, Peckham Pavilion: Literature (1939).

88 'Dance This Winter: and Be Happy and Healthy', *Edinburgh Evening News* (28 December 1933), p. 3.

89 Casani, *Casani's Home Teacher*, pp. 38–42.

90 Margaret Black, 'Graceful Health', *Popular Music and Dancing Weekly* (6 December 1924), p. 138.

91 Ina Zweiniger-Bargielowska, *Managing the Body: Beauty, Health, and Fitness in Britain, 1880–1939* (Oxford: Oxford University Press, 2011).

92 Casani, *Casani's Home Teacher*, p. 34.

93 Maggie Dickenson, 'Should Husbands and Wives Be Dancing Partners?' *Popular Music and Dancing Weekly* (28 November 1925), p. 110.

94 Nelly Wigley, 'Dancing and Character', *Popular Music and Dancing Weekly* (14 February 1925), p. 73.

95 'Types of Dancers. Character Revealed in the Ballroom', *Daily Express* (9 October 1919), p. 3.

96 Vesta, 'The Social Value of Dancing', *Popular Music and Dancing Weekly* (18 October 1924), p. 249.

97 Casani, *Casani's Home Teacher*, p. 47.

98 'Report', *Dancing Times* (August 1929), p. 451.

99 MOA: TC 38/1/A, M-O Enquiry at Locarno School of Dancing, June 1939.

100 Gerald Denston, 'Jazzed Out', *Daily Express* (28 October 1919), p. 6.

101 M. L. Trunket, Letter to the Editor, *Daily Express* (27 November 1919), p. 6.

102 The Sitter Out, 'In the Ballroom', *Dancing Times* (October 1922), p. 21.

103 Franklyn Graham, 'Things Every Dancer Should Know', *Popular Music and Dancing Weekly* (20 September 1924), p. 173.

104 Mona Vivian, 'Has the Dance "Craze" Come to Stay?' *Popular Music and Dancing Weekly* (10 January 1925), p. 229.

2

Who makes new dances? The dance profession and the evolution of style

In 1920, from the pages of the *Dancing Times*, editor Philip J. S. Richardson praised the dancing public for having cast off the shackles of the tyrannical Victorian dance teacher, and for embracing the simple modern styles that allowed them to reclaim control over their dancing experience. He even compared this rebellion to the events of the recent war: 'The modern ballroom dancer has revolted against the despotism of the Victorian dancing master ... in the same way that in the great world of which the dancing world is but a microcosm, the free nations have revolted against the military autocracy of the Teutonic peoples.'[1] Two years later, he reflected on lingering resistance to modern ballroom dances among an older generation of teachers, observing,

> I think if we were to ask what is the real objection that these old teachers have ... we should find that it is because fifty years ago the teachers ruled the ballroom, whereas to-day the dancers themselves rule it. They are the most autocratic people on earth, these Victorian dancing masters.[2]

Nor was Richardson the only one to identify dictatorial tendencies in his professional forebears. In an article on dance pedagogy, another prominent teacher, Eve Tynegate-Smith, also recalled 'the old days when the Dancing Master was a Mussolini and said exactly how and when and where the pupils – mere marionettes – were to move'.[3]

Hyperbole aside, what these comments reflected was a belief among dance professionals in the 1920s that modern ballroom dancing's greatest charm was its simple and natural movements – which made it easier to learn, but which also put popular dance under the control of dancers rather than their teachers, by making them less reliant on instruction. However, these comments were made during the very period in which the emerging profession that surrounded ballroom dancing attained a critical influence over how and what the British people danced. As popular dance entered the modern era, some fundamental questions emerged about how Britons performed new dances, such as the foxtrot and one-step. At the forefront of this debate was a group of dancing teachers, performers and writers who sought to seize control of popular dance and guide its continued development. Starting in 1920, these aficionados held a series of meetings and purpose-driven dances at which they deliberated over what was being danced in Britain, and how these dances were being executed and taught. They also diversified their activities, growing the number of dance exhibitions and competitions, and producing an extensive dance-themed print culture. This chapter will demonstrate that the results of these processes were two-fold: the professionalisation of ballroom dance and standardisation of what became known as the 'English style' of ballroom dancing.

As its name suggests, the new dancing style was meant to reflect the will and tastes of the British people. Throughout the process of standardising the steps of the foxtrot, one-step, tango and modern waltz, the dance profession consistently asserted that decisions concerning the content and appearance of the national style should remain in the hands of the British dancing public. However, despite these avowals, dance professionals wielded considerable authority over the establishment of the English style, and had significant financial motives for continuing to intervene in popular dance. As prominent teacher Victor Silvester observed in a letter to the editor of the *Dancing Times*, 'From a business point of view we are all dependent on the popularity of Ballroom Dancing.'[4] These pecuniary concerns inevitably shaped how the dance profession interacted with the dancing public, and – as a close examination of dances such as the foxtrot, tango, blues, Charleston and quickstep in the second half of this chapter will show – the preferences and agendas of the producers and consumers often diverged. What became the national dancing style was thus forged through ongoing negotiations between the profession and the public, which played out in dancing schools, at dance competitions, in print culture and on the floors of the nation's ballrooms.

The professionalisation and standardisation of modern ballroom dancing

The period that followed the end of the First World War was a chaotic one for British popular dance: in the midst of the dance craze, public dance halls opened by the dozen, and new variations of modern ballroom dances appeared every day, with little to no cohesion as to how they were performed. Leaders within the dancing community looked upon the untamed and mutable British dancing scene with no small degree of trepidation. Foremost among those seeking to intervene was Richardson, editor of the *Dancing Times*, and one of the most prominent figures in British dancing. The son of a maltster from Nottinghamshire, Richardson combined training in journalism with a keen interest in many different styles of dance, when he took over and re-launched the *Dancing Times* in 1910. He remained in that position until 1957, and in the interim played a pivotal role in both the development of British ballet, and the professionalisation and standardisation of modern ballroom dancing.

These intertwined processes began when Richardson – in dialogue with other leading professionals – began to voice concerns about the undisciplined and untutored manner in which many Britons danced. As he later recalled, the quick tempos of jazz, combined with the constant emergence of wild new steps and figures during the heady days of the dance craze, placed 'the smooth foxtrot which had been slowly developing in grave peril. There was much freak dancing to be seen and freak variations.'[5] Richardson did not place the blame for 'freak' steps solely on the dancers, however; he was also concerned about how Britons were being *taught* to dance. Post-war enthusiasm for the activity had seen dancing schools crop up by the hundreds, as eager Britons sought tutelage in the modern styles. As the *Daily Express* remarked in October 1919, 'Teachers of dancing are having the harvest of their lives.' The newspaper further observed that 'Any person who claims to be able to teach the newest form of hesitation waltz or jazz can find and easy and remunerative form of livelihood.'[6] With respect to the number of schools in the city of Leeds, the *Dancing Times* expounded, 'Classes are springing up in nearly every street, and municipal authorities will seriously have to consider the advisability of opening up new streets to enable teachers to have one each.'[7] But while dancing schools existed in abundance, there was little regulation over who was teaching the classes, or consistency as to how the dances were being taught. Richardson opined about this state of affairs from his editorial perch in 1920: 'I should dearly like it to be possible for the teachers to close up their ranks so that no new-comer could pose as a teacher unless she had first demonstrated that she was qualified to teach.'[8] Shortly thereafter, Richardson and others embarked on a quest to restore order to ballroom dance pedagogy by creating a proper system of accreditation for teachers and, most importantly, by standardising the steps of the dances they were teaching.

In addition to restoring order to chaotic ballrooms and the unregulated provision of instruction, Richardson had another reason to standardise ballroom dance steps: in order to deflect public criticism away from the modern styles. As was shown in Chapter 1, dance professionals made strong efforts to reinforce the timeliness and benefits of modern ballroom dances as a counterweight to the lingering controversies that swirled around them. However, the catalyst to standardisation efforts was actually not criticism at home, but abroad. Throughout 1919 and 1920 Richardson and other dance professionals followed with perturbation the attempts by Catholic Church authorities in France to stamp out dances like the foxtrot and the tango. Cardinal Amette, Archbishop of Paris, and Bordeaux's Cardinal Andrieux, among others, condemned the dances for their perceived indecency, frivolity and 'unseemly gyrations'.[9] At the behest of the Church, the Marquise de Monstier produced a report that decreed modern ballroom dances 'ugly and indecent', and there were attempts in Paris to establish a dance censorship board, which would evaluate new dances much in the same way that films underwent review.[10] There was no similar campaign in Britain, but from the pages of the *Dancing Times* Richardson expressed considerable concern about the possibility that one could emerge. As he wrote to his readers in May 1920, 'you and I know that these dances are perfectly clean, but unless we make a little counter-attack the very large number of people who do not dance will begin to pay attention to the other side'.[11] A few months later, he similarly cautioned, 'They have not seriously attacked dancing in England yet … Believe me, it is a very serious danger if allowed to develop.'[12]

While Richardson was no doubt sincere, he and other dance professionals had another, less overt motive for seeking to standardise the instruction and steps of modern ballroom dancing. Richardson decried what he called 'freak' variations as a threat to the aesthetics, integrity and reputation of ballroom dance, yet these movements also represented improvisation and originality on the part of dancers. A lack of standardisation, or of a 'correct' way to dance, posed a considerable economic threat to those who earned their income as dance instructors. As dance scholar Juliet McMains has noted, 'if dancing became a free-form frenzy with no standards or techniques, dance teachers would soon be out of jobs'.[13] Importantly, while the criticisms of modern ballroom dances were never as vociferous in Britain as they were in France and elsewhere, some teachers were not above fomenting the belief that dancing was under public scrutiny and attack in order to fill their classes. For instance, one advertisement for the Méthode Sielle School of Dancing featured a heading that screamed 'Vulgarity in the Ballroom!' before the text went on to assert that such claims were buoyed by those who refused to learn proper technique:

> Ballroom dancing is brought into disrepute by people of unimpeachable character who would be most insulted if told of their responsibility. Their well-meaning but untutored movements are nine-tenths of the cause of the present absurd outcry in the Daily Press, in which one sees dancing described as negroid, indecent and vulgar. It is because many dancers do not know how to hold themselves that their dancing calls forth this strong condemnation.[14]

The idea that dancing – especially when it was improperly performed – was a source of controversy provided dancing teachers with a justification for their profession's continued existence. The teachers' professed concerns about the reputation and aesthetic value of their art existed alongside their status as businesspeople, and their need to maintain a reason for Britons to continue attending dance classes. As will be shown, this need also existed in tension with the burgeoning profession's continually avowed desire that the dancers – and not the teachers – should be the ones to direct the future of British dancing.

Early in 1920, therefore, with a variety of motives both declared and undeclared, Richardson and other teachers began to discuss the need for a meeting that would assess the state of ballroom dancing in Britain. Accordingly, the first 'Informal Conference of Teachers of Ballroom Dancing' was convened on 12 May of that year. Organised under the auspices of the *Dancing Times*, and chaired by Richardson, the conference brought together about two hundred teachers and members of the press at the Grafton Galleries, a dance club located underground in Piccadilly, London. Over the course of the afternoon, the teachers debated what should be the standard steps and figures of the foxtrot, one-step and modern waltz, and an exhibition of the three dances was performed by famed dancers Monsieur Maurice and Leonora Hughes.

Summing up the meeting after the fact, Richardson wrote in the *Dancing Times*: 'The business of the recent conference may be put under two headings. Firstly, to eliminate what is bad. Secondly, to put what is good on a firm basis.'[15] A number of resolutions were passed in order to accomplish these somewhat ambiguous goals. In the quest to eliminate what was 'bad', all the teachers present avowed 'to do their very best to stamp out freak steps'.[16] These specifically referred to movements that produced havoc in crowded ballrooms, such as an over-pronounced pause in the hesitation waltz, or side and backward steps in the foxtrot, as well as the kicks, hops, stomps and dramatic gestures that were remnants from ragtime dancing. Freak steps also included lifts and dips, which the teachers believed were attractive enough as part of exhibition dances, but which were usually poorly performed by ordinary dancers. As will be discussed in Chapter 5, references to 'freak' steps were also racially encoded, as dance teachers attempted to replace what were perceived to be black movements with those that were reserved, graceful, civilised and, allegedly, more British; there were also gender and class implications to this quest for 'refinement'. While the conference of teachers was quite sure as to what constituted bad dancing, there was little consensus as to what was acceptable or good. The decision was thus taken to form a smaller committee responsible for determining what should be the recognised steps of the major modern ballroom dances, and which would report back to the larger group later that year.

The first informal conference had two major impacts on British popular dance: it began the process of standardising the English style of ballroom dance, which was to become the nation's primary dancing style, and it accelerated the professionalisation of the British dance community. Over the next few years both of these processes continued in a variety of ways. The small committee formed at the first meeting of dancing teachers issued a preliminary report, and further conferences were convened at public dancing spaces around London. Richardson and the *Dancing Times* also began organising special dances at which teachers could practise and confer about the steps of specific ballroom dances, such as the 'Tango Ball' in May 1922, or the 'Blues Ball' held in the fall of 1923. In this way the steps of the foxtrot, one-step, tango and modern waltz were gradually standardised. These dances, known as 'standard four', formed the rudimentary version of the English style of ballroom dancing, but its continued evolution was also profoundly shaped by the expansion and diversification of activities among professional dancers.

At the most basic level, the men and women who formed the ballroom dance profession were teachers. As the number of dancing schools around the country exploded in the early 1920s, so too did the number of people working as dance instructors. Schools ranged in scale from small, one-room studios to large commercial chains; some teachers, such as Silvester, Santos Casani, and Belle Harding, eventually achieved such fame and success that schools throughout the country and occasionally even on the Continent, bore their names. Men, but also a large number of women, served as the heads of dance studios, while several were controlled jointly by married couples. Most schools offered instruction not only in ballroom dance, but also ballet, operatic, stage and Greek dancing. A single lesson generally cost two to three shillings, and prices rose depending on the nature of instruction, with group lessons being less expensive than private sessions. Students included those seeking to improve their dancing for social reasons, but also men and women who had professional aspirations of their own. Eventually a standard syllabus of ballroom dances was created by the profession, and a series of 'medal tests' were devised through which students progressed to demonstrate their growing skills and qualifications.

When their studios were not being used for lessons, many schools hosted open practice dances, or 'assemblies', which made them an important space for public dancing as well. In this way, dancing schools were to some degree in commercial competition with the dance halls, particularly since the latter also provided instruction, generally via the presence of professional dance partners who could be hired for a small fee. These so-called 'six-penny partners' were usually procured for one dance, in order to provide a partner for those men and women without one, but also to help clients improve their dancing. This represented a cheaper and arguably more convenient form of instruction for many within the dancing public, so much so that the *Dancing Times* discouraged the hiring of six-penny partners in 1926 owing to the negative impact it could have on enrolments at dancing schools. As the dance hall industry expanded, the magazine also expressed concern about the effect the growing number of venues for public dancing was having on practice dances, which especially provincial teachers relied on for additional income.[17] However, the lines between the dance profession and dance hall industry were not as rigidly maintained as these disputes would imply, and became increasingly blurred as the interwar period progressed. In particular, the expansion of public dance halls provided additional employment opportunities to professional dancers: as dance partners, demonstrators and as instructors in the schools that opened in conjunction with many of the larger halls, restaurants and hotels.

As these varied employment opportunities make apparent, teaching was only one part of the job description for many professional dancers. Exhibition dancing, which by the simplest definition was dancing performed before an audience, also formed a significant portion of their work. This was a practice that had really taken off after the introduction of the tango to Britain, when many purveyors of dancing engaged an experienced couple to provide a demonstration to others eager to learn the dance.[18] By the 1920s, ballroom dance, like ballet, remained a popular concert style in music halls, theatres and even department stores; many professionals were also trained in various dance forms, and might teach by day and perform theatrically by night. Exhibitions were also frequently used to fill the interval between shows at the cinema, and there was a period of disquietude among professionals that the advent of 'talkies' might eliminate this practice known as the 'dancing turn'. However, in the end, the introduction of sound to motion pictures, and especially the rising popularity of the musical film, actually increased the employment opportunities for professional dancers, as many found additional work on the silver screen.[19]

Exhibition dances were also an important part of the programme in public dance halls, and were commonly featured during the cabaret, when a break would be taken in the general dancing for some type of entertainment. The larger halls employed on-staff professionals to both serve as six-penny partners and provide exhibitions, though special dance teams were occasionally engaged on a temporary basis. Certain teams achieved a considerable degree of celebrity – often by winning championships, or appearing on film or in print – and dance hall proprietors knew that the chance to see a famous couple perform would attract more people to their halls. They were therefore willing to invest considerable sums of money in procuring popular acts; during a week-long engagement at the Glasgow Norwood Ballroom, for example, Casani and Jose Lennard were purportedly paid a hundred pounds per day to perform exhibition dances.[20] Celebrity ballroom dancers also frequently undertook national and even international tours to display their talents. In 1929, the *Dancing Times* reported on the world tour of exhibition team Gerardo and Enid Adair, which included stops in the United States, South Africa and Australia.[21]

Exhibition teams were also fixtures on the dance competition circuit, another aspect of professional and popular dance that grew by leaps and bounds during the interwar period, and which was influential in shaping the national style. As the *Dancing Times* observed in 1930, competitions 'have made modern English ballroom dancing what it is to-day: they have crystallised into concrete form the suggestions of teachers, conferences and expert dancers'.[22] The first competitions were rather informal affairs, usually arranged under the auspices of a dancing club or newspaper. However, in 1921 the *Daily Sketch* announced a national foxtrot and waltz competition, which introduced a new level in competition dancing to Britain. Local heats were held throughout the country, with a grand finale at the Queen's Hall in London in February 1922. Competitions such as this one also had a significant impact on how the English style evolved. Authorities such as Richardson argued that the *Daily Sketch*'s decision to include the waltz in its first nationwide competition, for instance, was an important factor in bringing the dance back to public favour after interest had waned in the Boston and hesitation.

Eventually specific definitions of professional, amateur and novice arose in connection with competition dancing. Prominent British dancers also participated in international contests; one annual event saw some of Britain's best ballroom dancers face off against the most talented dancers from Denmark. However, the annual Blackpool Dance Festival was far and away the nation's premier competition event. Debuting around 1920, during the 1930–31 season Blackpool became the location for the British Professional and British Amateur Dance Championships. Often referred to as ballroom dancing's version of the Wimbledon tennis tournament, Blackpool was also highly revered within the international dance community, and by the late 1930s the championship attracted spectators in the tens of thousands. Finally, it should be noted that the growth of professional competition dancing did not prevent the continuance of less formal affairs for the dancing public, which many dance halls hosted on a weekly basis or as one-night only special events.

The expansion of dance instruction, competitions and exhibitions required some degree of regulation, and the interwar period saw the growth of large numbers of associations and societies dedicated to ballroom dancing, which further contributed to the process of professionalisation. Professional dancing associations had in fact been developing since the early years of the twentieth century. The Imperial Society of Dance Teachers – re-named the Imperial Society of Teachers of Dancing (ISTD) in the mid-1920s – had been created in 1904, while the National Association of Teachers of Dancing appeared in 1907. For most of the period under review the ISTD was headed by Cecil H. Taylor, who was commonly referred to as 'Major', and who was the last in a long line of dancing masters in his family from the city of Leeds. Under Taylor, the ISTD was the most prominent of the various professional societies that accredited teachers and governed the affairs of all styles of dancing in Britain. From the 1920s onward, the ISTD contained specific branches dedicated to ballet, stage and operatic dancing, and the rising importance of ballroom dancing was marked with the creation of a 'Ballroom Branch' in 1924.[23] The bureaucratisation of ballroom dancing continued with the creation of the Official Board of Ballroom Dancing in 1929, and by the late 1930s such a significant number of amateur and professional bodies had emerged that occasional conflicts arose among them. For example, in 1938, the National Society of Amateur Dancers got into a dispute with the Official Board over the management of competitions and eventually resigned from the umbrella organisation.

Finally, another critical way in which professional dancers made connections with one another and with the dancing public was through print culture. An abundance of dance-themed magazines and newspapers emerged in the interwar years, and became a chief vehicle through which discussions about new dances – or alterations to existing ones – took place. Members of the profession wrote articles or made contributions through letters to the editor, collaborating on the development of ballroom dancing. While a number of periodicals devoted to dancing came and went throughout this period, the *Dancing Times* was far and away the most influential. First introduced in 1894 as the house magazine for a London dance club, the magazine went defunct for a year before being re-launched in 1910 by Richardson and publisher T. M. Middleton in the midst of the dramatic transformations to popular dance that occurred with the ascendance of the Boston, tango and ragtime dances. It was from the pages of the *Dancing Times* that Richardson guided the dance profession, and organised events such as the informal conferences. This magazine and others provided an organ of communication for dance professionals around the country, helping to maintain consistency in instruction, and conformity in style and technique. Less prominent teachers, or those unable to attend the conferences and other gatherings, were able to maintain contact with leaders in the profession through print, and keep up-to-date with news and trends. As one teacher in 'an out of the way corner of England' noted in a letter to the editor, without the *Dancing Times* 'it would be quite impossible for those away from the "heart of things" to keep in touch with what is going on in the dancing world'.[24] However, the magazine also reflected its editor's belief that professionals should largely be at the service of the dancing public: dozens of pages were dedicated to advertising dancing schools, and many of the articles provided 'how-to' information about specific dances, as well as discussion of public dancing spaces throughout the country.

With the dancing public in mind, professionals also wrote a voluminous number of instruction manuals. One of the most successful was Silvester's *Modern Ballroom Dancing*, which was first published in 1927, and eventually reproduced in dozens of printings and editions; Richardson estimated that over a million copies of Silvester's work had been sold by 1945, and it continued to be reprinted for decades afterward.[25] However, dozens of other professionals also produced their own instructional works, which enjoyed a widespread readership of other professionals and members of the dancing public. The manuals generally included a few introductory pages of biographical information on the author, outlining their credentials and providing testimonials as to their expertise from the press and other professionals. Early chapters contained general comments on correct hold, balance and positions for modern ballroom dancing, and later chapters were dedicated to the performance of specific dances, with diagrams and detailed instructions (see Figure 2.1). Some manuals also featured additional content, such as short histories of ballroom dancing; suggestions on how to host a dance; advice on succeeding in dance competitions and getting accredited as a teacher; or the advantages of dancing to good health, beauty or social life. The manuals were designed to be widely accessible – of use to both beginner and more advanced dancers – though with slightly more emphasis on the former. As Casani noted in the opening pages of one of his books,

> I shall proceed as if the reader knows nothing at all about the subject. I want to make the "Self-Tutor" justify its description, and take my invisible pupil from the kindergarten stage, step by step, to that perfection which can only come with well-grounded knowledge.[26]

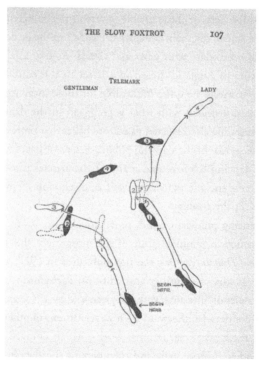

2.1   A typical diagram from a dance instruction manual.

As teachers, performers, competitors and authors, members of the dance profession often wore numerous professional hats – simultaneously, or at different points in their career. A striking example resides in the career of Silvester, who was at various times a paid dance partner, champion competitor, teacher, writer, bandleader, and radio and television personality. According to his autobiography, Silvester began his career in the heady days of the post-war dance craze.[27] Following a period of distinguished wartime service while still only a teenager, he enthusiastically embraced the modern dance styles and found he had a talent for them. Silvester obtained employment as a professional dance partner at the Empress Rooms in London, under one of the period's most formidable teachers and entrepreneurs, Belle Harding. His work at the Empress Rooms was only supposed to be for the summer before he resumed his military career by enrolling at Sandhurst; however, after only a few weeks at the military academy he ran away and returned to his dancing career. In 1922, with his partner Phyllis Clarke, he won the World Championship of Ballroom Dancing, and then began to teach dancing alongside his wife, Dorothy Newton. By the late 1920s Silvester was regarded as one of Britain's foremost authorities on modern ballroom dancing, serving on the Official Board and publishing the first of the many subsequent editions of his seminal *Modern Ballroom Dancing*. He later moved his teaching beyond the studio and onto the airwaves with the BBC Dancing Club, which began on the radio and later progressed to television. At the same time he worked as a bandleader, forming his own orchestra and becoming one of the pioneers of strict tempo dance music.

Many professionals began their careers in a similar manner to Silvester; they were swept up in the new craze for ballroom dancing either before or after the war, involved themselves in teaching, competitions and performance, and slowly built their professional lives. A few prominent teachers – like the head of the ISTD, Taylor – came from a long line of dance teachers, but others were 'first generation'. They were born into a range of social and regional backgrounds – Silvester was the son of a Wembley vicar; Josephine Bradley was from a large Catholic family in Dublin; Casani was of Italian heritage and born in South Africa. Those professionals who attained the greatest success were generally based in London – in addition to classes, competitions and exhibitions, and writing, their celebrity and influence was enhanced by endorsements and film appearances. Led by Richardson, it was leading professionals like Silvester, Bradley, Murial Simmons, Tynegate-Smith, Lisle Humphreys, Casani and Lennard, and other famous teams such as Maxwell Stewart and Pat Sykes, and Alex Moore and Pat Kilpatrick, among others – who guided the standardisation of the English style.[28] However, hundreds of other dance professionals also plied their trade around the country, advertising their ability to teach on the basis of their credentials, as well as their success in national and international dance competitions. They forged connections through their professional activities and writings, and helped to collaborate on the evolution of the national dancing style.

As much as exhibitions, competitions and print culture linked members of the dance profession, they also provided a vital connection between professionals and the rest of British society – and a way to teach dancing beyond the studio. The instructional benefits of dance manuals and magazines are likely self-evident, but the profession felt that the dancing public could also learn a great deal from witnessing an exhibition or competition, and by following the extensive coverage the major events received in both the dance and popular press. Professionals sought to use these forums to educate dancers as to correct steps and figures, to introduce a new dance, or alert them to the latest trends. But critically, there was debate within the profession and the dancing public as to how effective these measures actually were in guiding how the average Briton danced.

There is strong evidence for public interest in the dictates of the dance profession. Thousands of dancing schools were sustained in London and throughout the country. The market for instruction manuals also continually expanded, and their readership was in fact substantial enough that some teachers feared they were cutting into their business by eliminating the need for face-to-face lessons.[29] The *Dancing Times* also had a significant circulation among interested members of the dancing public, one of whom heralded the magazine for

> [passing] on to a grateful public all that the best brains in the profession have to offer … [The] press has done a great deal to raise the standard of dancing among the public, who have neither the time, money, nor inclination to visit teachers, but welcome an authoritative paper where the latest phase in dancing is expressed in simple language.[30]

The creation of Silvester's BBC Dancing Club was likewise a testament to public interest in dance instruction, and he was only one of several teachers to provide lessons over the radio and later television. Instruction, as well as the latest news from the professional world – such as the steps of a new dance, or the winners of a competition – was also presented to cinema audiences in the form of short films and newsreels.

Additionally, many dancers followed dance competitions and professional exhibitions with a close eye. As was noted above, the most accomplished exhibition dancers could command impressive salaries, and demonstrations were a regular feature on dance hall programmes throughout the country. Serious dancers welcomed the opportunity to watch and learn from professionals. For instance, one enthusiast was very pleased when his military service during the Second World War brought him to London and enabled him to visit the Hammersmith Palais, as he recorded in his diary: 'Had a most enjoyable afternoon here spent mostly watching the professional couples practising new steps.'[31] Dance competitions also drew large crowds, and generated extensive press coverage. As one spectator wrote in a letter to the editor of *Modern Dance*, 'As a keen amateur dancer, whenever I can get the opportunity I never miss seeing our leading professionals, and have attended the finals in Blackpool for the last four years, and seen most of them dancing at the Astoria, Hammersmith, and other London dance places.'[32] Interest in competition dancing's premier event was in fact sufficiently high that in the 1930s Richardson began providing radio coverage of the event to listeners throughout the country. Local heats and regional finals of dance competitions also helped considerably in elevating the standard of British dancing outside the capital. In 1927, Richardson stated in the *Dancing Times* that competitions 'have been undoubtedly one of the principal causes of the excellence of English dancing, which has reached so high a standard that the "English style" is the ambition of all continental dancers'.[33] Beyond enrolling in dancing classes, therefore, there were many ways Britons could access and take advantage of the tutelage of the dance profession.

Nonetheless, there is also evidence that the public frequently ignored or remained oblivious to the guidance and innovations of the profession, and that professional activities were not all geared towards tutoring the public in correct dancing. Some professionals felt that exhibition dances and even competitions should really be focused on providing entertainment rather than instruction. Instead of performing the standardised, simplified versions of the four dances of the English style, these teams chose to exhibit more complex figures or different dances. As exhibition dancers Marjorie and Georges Fontana explained, 'the audience at most modern dances can do the ballroom dances now in vogue quite well themselves, and ... they would prefer to see an exhibition couple do something that they cannot do ... We make a point therefore of giving dances of a far more elaborate nature'.[34] Conversely, other professionals feared that the 'superlative excellence' of those who performed in competitions and exhibitions set too intimidating a standard and ultimately 'frightened thousands of the general public from the ballroom'.[35] Still other teachers felt that many within the dancing public were neither intimidated nor inspired by exhibitions or competitions, but simply found them to be an annoying interruption to the evening's dancing rather than a source of entertainment or instruction. In an interview with Mass Observation, Taylor acknowledged the tedium with which many dance hall patrons greeted exhibitions and questioned their instructional value; he believed competitions were a more useful teaching tool, but conceded that the 'mass don't want competitions'.[36]

The reality of the dancing public's interest in exhibitions and competitions appears to have resided somewhere between these divergent professional opinions. In the 1930s, the *Dancing Times* began asking dance hall managers throughout the country to provide reports as to the goings-on in their respective halls, and their responses revealed a decidedly mixed reception to exhibitions and competitions. For instance, the manager of the Plaza dance hall in Glasgow reported that patrons 'never seem to tire of watching demonstrations'. Further south in Brighton, in contrast, an exhibition needed to be given by dancers 'of repute' or they were of 'no attraction'.[37] Meanwhile, in Birmingham, demonstrations were 'not given, as the public does not seem to have a great interest in this type of entertainment'.[38] Contradictory comments such as these abound in the correspondence from dance hall managers: certain patrons loved exhibitions, while others did not. Some enjoyed them only if a famous dance team was performing, if they were done only occasionally, or if the demonstration was to introduce a new dance. Views on competitions were similarly divided, though generally appealed most strongly to patrons who were serious about their dancing. As one manager from Liverpool reported, 'When a competition is put on it is usually the same crowd entering.'[39]

The varying reactions to exhibitions and competitions, and the willingness of some Britons but not others to seek out dance instruction, are explained by the simple fact that the dancing public was constituted by a diverse group of people with distinct preferences, aptitudes and backgrounds. To begin with, the degree to which dancers sought professional guidance or formal instruction was underpinned by economic circumstances and class. Dance magazines and instruction manuals could be as inexpensive as a few pence, and so were within reach of the average working-class Briton. Formal lessons, in contrast, could vary widely. While many classes remained affordable, there was no consistent price scheme, causing one angry correspondent to the *Dancing Times* to complain, 'few people can pay 7/6 per half-hour'.[40] In addition to economic disparities, individual dancers diverged significantly in their level of interest in perfecting their technique. In 1929, Tynegate-Smith observed that she and her colleagues had to contend with 'at least two distinct sets of dancers, both of which consist of prospective pupils'. Some students, she wrote, were 'generally satisfied to learn just sufficient to enable them to progress round the ballroom without looking conspicuous', whereas another set of students had reached a high enough level of skill that they were 'keen on competition[s] and on dancing chiefly ... where the better professionals can be encountered'.[41] However, to this list other professionals believed a third category of dancer must be added: those who were uninterested in instruction of any kind. As one writer who shared this view declared in *Modern Dance*, 'only a small percentage of dancers are really serious over technique'. Everyone else, he proclaimed, were simply 'weekend dancers'.[42]

Indeed, much to the chagrin of the dance profession, it is clear that many Britons went dancing without ever having taken a lesson, attended a competition, or read a dance manual. As will be discussed further in Chapter 3, dance halls and other public ballrooms were important spaces for socialisation and romance, food and drink, and enjoying the music and, for some patrons, the actual dancing was a negligible aspect of the overall experience. As the manager of the Cricklewood dance hall in London told the *Dancing Times*, 'it is noticeable that the public seem to regard dancing as a social entertainment and an amusing pastime and not with any great enthusiasm for the actual dances'.[43] Some dance hall attendees, assuming they danced at all, did so merely by emulating others on the floor. Professionals and enthusiastic amateur dancers often referred to this group as 'walkers', in that they simply ambled about the dance floor with little to no concern about technique. As one letter to the editor of the *Dancing Times* lamented, 'From the point of view of the girl or man who can dance, it is very disappointing to be obliged to revert to "walking" with a partner who knows nothing.'[44] Another 'novice' dancer complained to the magazine that he had taken the opportunity to improve his dancing through lessons in advance of a cruise, but found the technique he had perfected to be of little to no value among the 'walkers' on board ship, or in the hotel ballrooms he had frequented since his return.[45]

Importantly, this correspondent, and a number of others who communicated with the *Dancing Times*, identified a frustrating disjuncture between the technique espoused by the profession, and the level of dancing that was realistic in public ballrooms, which were often crowded and full of poorly trained dancers. As one 'average dancer' complained in an article for the magazine, too many teachers insisted on providing instruction in intricate steps and figures which were of 'no practical use'. Teachers, this writer advised, needed to appreciate that most dancers were not concerned with proper technique, but simply 'want to learn enough to enjoy dancing with the partners we meet in the ballrooms where we dance'.[46] As early as 1922, another observer of popular dance had recognised the unresolvable tension that would persist between the profession and the public. According to this writer, most dancers craved simplicity in technique, because they 'do not want their pleasure to become a difficult task, something to be painfully learned'. However, he argued that professionals – for all that they praised the simplicity of modern ballroom dancing and the agency of the dancing public in directing the evolution of the national style – always had important financial concerns: 'From a business point of view they would like to introduce and popularise something that is much more difficult to learn. It would be good business for them.'[47]

The intricacies of the relationship between the dance profession and dancing public were prominently displayed at what became known as the 'Great Conference', another meeting of leading professionals held at the Princes Galleries on 14 April 1929. Nearly a decade of discussion and debate over the content and specific steps of the English style culminated in this event, at which the dance profession agreed on two primary points. First, the Great Conference saw the establishment of the Official Board of Ballroom Dancing, the committee which would consider all major issues of concern to professionals, and the general state of ballroom dancing in Britain. With this move the teachers affirmed their continued relevance, and their intention to continue intervening in the development of British ballroom dancing for the foreseeable future. They also acknowledged and protected their ongoing business interests by agreeing to coordinate each season on which new dances to 'push' on the public; to continue advocating the health advantages of dancing; and to 'co-operate in obtaining publicity for dancing both in the newspapers and on the films'. However, secondly, the profession used the Great Conference to formally mandate that in teaching and modifying modern ballroom dancing their focus should be on the dancing public, rather than on professionals such as themselves. As the *Dancing Times* described it a month after the conference, 'The first aim of the profession should be to cater for the general dancer and not the "super-dancer," and to attract the man who does not dance to-day.'[48] To achieve these ends, the professionals at the meeting resolved to keep the steps of the four standard dances, and any new dances they might create or adapt, as simple as possible.

This had been the professional mantra throughout the 1920s: that the development of dancing should be controlled by the aptitudes and preferences of the dancing public, rather than by the directives of the profession. Yet there can be little question that through its series of conferences and other events, dance competitions and exhibitions, and the voluminous production of dance manuals and periodicals, the profession had sought and achieved a critical influence over the evolution of the English style, and popular dance more generally. The profession also clearly had motivations above and beyond the public interest, seeking out new ways to fill dancing classes and maintain its *raison d'être*. The profession therefore responded to the dancing public, but also undeniably sought to guide it as to what dances should be included in the national dancing style, how they were performed, and what cultural meanings were attached to them. This becomes acutely apparent through a closer examination of some of the most – and least – successful popular dances of the 1920s.

Negotiating a national dancing style

In 1921, renowned teacher Monsieur Pierre wrote an article for the *Dancing Times* that posed a question in its title: 'Who makes new dances?' In the opening lines of the piece, Pierre immediately answered his own query by categorically stating that it was 'not the teachers'. According to Pierre, new dances, as well as variations on established ones, were introduced into Britain's public ballrooms each day, but he proclaimed that this phenomenon was directed entirely by the dancers themselves, rather than teachers like him. While Pierre appeared to lament the manner in which 'teachers, powerless to exercise any control, have had no alternative but to follow the lead of the very people they had once hoped to govern', his concerns were not universal among his colleagues.[49] As has been shown, most British dance teachers believed, and would eventually codify as best practice at the Great Conference, that the dancing public should remain in control of popular dance, and that the profession should respond accordingly.

Yet whatever ideals these teachers professed over adhering to public preferences, there is little question that they consistently and powerfully intervened in the continued development of popular dance. The profession was a primary conduit through which new dances were introduced to Britain, and its members actively attempted to guide public tastes. Moreover, the stated desire of dance professionals that the public should control the development of popular dance in Britain had to be continually negotiated in terms of their own business interests. However, as influential as professionals were, they found that they could not always predict or govern the tastes or actions of their students, and especially of those dancers who ignored or remained oblivious to their dictates. Specifically, professionals aggressively promoted dances such as the tango and the blues, but resisted others, notably the Charleston, which the public embraced and performed in a manner beyond their control. Adding further nuance to these negotiations was the influence of other parties – notably the dance bands and music publishers – who interacted with the dance profession and dancing public to shape the progression of popular dance.

The negotiations between the dance profession and dancing public were strongly apparent even in the case of a dance they both admired: the foxtrot. Throughout the 1920s, as the steps of the standard four were formalised by the dance profession and even as new dances were consistently introduced each season, the foxtrot remained the favourite dance with the dancing public. As the manager of the Hammersmith Palais told *Popular Music and Dancing Weekly* in 1924, 'We find that the fox trot is the most popular dance, then the waltz and the one-step, and finally the Blues and the tango.'[50] A dance bandleader likewise observed that no dance 'so far has been invented to assail the popularity of the foxtrot … People will go on fox trotting till the cows come home, and then some'.[51] There were a number of reasons for this pre-dominance, which were cyclical and self-perpetuating. Public enthusiasm for the dance meant that music composers and publishers produced far more foxtrot songs than any others, which then became the most commonly played songs by the dance bands in public ballrooms. The effect of this abundance of foxtrots was that the public continued to perform the dance the most frequently, and remained more comfortable with it than with any other dance. Many Britons also seemed to favour the foxtrot simply owing to its attractive appearance and relative lack of complexity. As one professional dancer observed in 1925, the enduring appeal of the foxtrot was easily accounted for because 'it is an easy, healthy and natural dance, combining a pleasing rhythm with an ease of accomplishment which is greater than that found in any other dance'.[52]

As this comment attests, the dance profession also valued the foxtrot, and recognised it as the staple dance of the English style. However, the state of foxtrot, and the question of whether or not any dance could seriously challenge its supremacy, was also a topic of incessant discussion among professionals. In fact, despite its acknowledgment of the foxtrot's attributes, the profession increasingly lamented the dance's pre-eminence. Pointing to the influence of dance bands in maintaining the foxtrot's ubiquity, teacher Casani complained,

> Because nine out of ten dances that are played are fox trots … consequently dancers have every opportunity of becoming proficient. If only dance-hall bands would play different dances in turn, and so give dancers an opportunity of practising other steps, the fox trot would soon topple from its pedestal and fall into line with the other dances.[53]

From the pages of the dance press, many other professionals similarly expressed boredom with the dance, and began to suggest that this boredom was shared by the public. As early as 1922, the *Dancing Times* reported that '[the foxtrot] has almost become stereotyped, and dancers feel that they want something a little different in this present winter from the foxtrot of a year ago.'[54] By 1926, the magazine had decreed that the dance had been in a 'rut' for some time.[55]

Given the profession's control over much of the dance press, it is difficult to discern from these sources whether or not the dancing public actually shared the profession's tedium with the foxtrot or not. What is certain is that just as it had been to the professionals' advantage to suggest that dancing was being attacked by social purists, it was also to their advantage to suggest that interest in the foxtrot was waning and that Britain needed a new dance, or at least a new variation. The foxtrot's continued supremacy meant that once dancing enthusiasts had perfected it they might cease taking lessons, which represented a significant threat to a profession dominated by teachers of dancing. The *Dancing Times* acknowledged this reality at the start of the 1921 dancing season, noting that with no new dance on the horizon, 'a number of teachers will complain that this absence … is very bad for business'.[56] The result was that despite its avowal that the dancers and not the teachers should shape the development of the national style, the profession regularly intervened in its development. In particular, the profession was constantly on the lookout for new dances that it could use to draw Britons into dancing classes.

One of the profession's major efforts in this respect involved not a new dance, but an established one: the tango. While the dance remained fashionable in Paris after the war, it never replicated the success it had enjoyed in Britain during the 1912–13 season. In a 1920 letter to the editor of the *Dancing Times*, teacher and exhibition dancer Robert Sielle bemoaned this fact: 'Although we now have a tango remarkable for its beauty, simplicity, and general suitability to the requirements of ballroom dancing, we are still faced with the difficulty of overcoming the public timidity which invariably heralds the opening bars of tango music. No one seems to care to be the first to get up and dance.'[57] Other professionals clearly shared Sielle's concerns, and there were persistent attempts by the dance profession to modify and publicise the dance in ways that would make it more palatable to the public. New variations of the tango were frequently introduced, and it was central to the deliberations over the standardisation of the English style. The tango was also frequently displayed through competitions and exhibitions, and at the start of each new dancing season professionals declared in the dance press that the tango would almost certainly be back in vogue in the coming year. In the fall of 1924, for example, *Popular Music and Dancing Weekly* proclaimed, 'There is much talk of a revival of that exotic Southern dance.'[58] Two years later, the same periodical again asserted, 'I hear that the Tango is going to be a definite feature of the new season's dances. This is as it should be.'[59]

Yet simply stating that the tango would rally could not make it so, and many within the dancing public were wary of the dance. At the root of this reticence appears to have been a belief that the tango was more difficult than the other standard dances of the English style. As the 'novice' who had undertaken dance lessons in advance of a cruise told the *Dancing Times*, 'When I asked if the Tango were danced [on board ship], everyone spoke of it as a very difficult dance.'[60] In 1926, a writer for *Popular Music and Dancing Weekly* similarly recounted that when she conducted a study of the tango problem at a London dance hall, she overheard one dancer proclaim, ' "Tango music is sweet and I like listening to it, but the dance looks as if only an expert should attempt it." ' The result, the author noted, was that 'when a tango tune was played a few couples with a conscious air of bravery left the crowded floor-side to attempt the tango – lonely souls in a vast Sahara!'[61]

Dance professionals worked hard to overcome these qualms and embolden Britons to experiment with the tango. Following a tour of a few public ballrooms, one columnist for *Popular Music and Dancing Weekly* wrote encouragingly to his readers:

> I noticed that nearly all the dance halls include a tango in their programmes, but – I also noticed – that at such times there was more than a plentiful supply of space on the dance floor. I wonder if any of you have ever tried the tango, or if you realise how very fascinating a dance it really is?[62]

However, significantly, the same columnist speculated in another issue that the perception that the tango was difficult – and the public's reluctance to attempt it – was in large part owing to the profession's preoccupation with the dance. As he wrote then, 'The tango died almost before it was born, the result, I am convinced, of so many teachers trying to improve it by introducing their own steps.'[63] In an attempt to perfect, and perhaps renew public interest in the tango, the profession may well have scared casual dancers away from the dance.

Throughout the 1920s, therefore, the tango remained a topic of considerable interest to professional dancers, and a staple of competitions and exhibitions, but not a prominent element of popular dance. This disunity between the producers and consumers of ballroom dance was replicated repeatedly as the dance profession introduced (or reintroduced) a series of dances to the dancing public. The quest to locate 'standard five', a fifth dance that could enter into the English style canon, was decidedly on. In seeking out this fifth dance, professionals turned once again to the Continent and United States for possible imports, but also devised new dances of their own. They were motivated by the sincere desire to elevate the art, as well as the need to maintain enrolments in dancing classes. But whatever their basis, these efforts by the profession generally resulted in failure.

For instance, in 1923 the dance profession was extremely enthusiastic about the 'blues', another new dance imported from America. As Richardson proclaimed in the *Dancing Times* in August of that year, 'A new dance at last. We shall all be dancing "Blues" this autumn.'[64] The blues originated from an effort to adapt the various partner dances performed to African-American blues music for the ballroom; like the foxtrot, the dance was performed in 4/4 time, but at a slower tempo. It appeared at a moment when foxtrot tempos began to speed up in public ballrooms, culminating in the development of the quickstep, so it was perhaps not surprising that the blues never achieved great success with the dancing public. As one dance bandleader described it in 1924, he would witness 'the floor empty when we play the opening bars of a blues number'.[65] The dance profession continued to engage with the blues for a number of years, both in print and at conferences and special dances, but the public did not embrace the dance. Richardson himself later admitted that while the blues intrigued professionals, except 'among the best dancers this dance was never popular'.[66] Like the tango, the blues was a dance that the profession saw as possessing great potential, but to which the public remained indifferent; professional zeal was simply not enough to ensure a dance's success. And significantly, another dance was about to demonstrate that professional ambivalence was also not enough to ensure a dance's failure.

In 1925, a new American dance called the Charleston was introduced to Britain through the musical revue *Midnight Follies*. It was not until later that year, however, when dance professionals Sielle and Annette Mills witnessed an exhibition of the ballroom version in New York, that the dance found a route to Britain's dance floors. In July, in conjunction with the *Dancing Times*, Sielle and Mills staged a 'Charleston tea' at a Soho dance club in order to experiment with the dance and introduce it to other professionals. As Bradley, who was present at the event later recalled, 'Questions, comment, argument, discussion went on for hours. Oh, yes, the Charleston had hit London with a resounding thud.'[67] The dance was quick-tempoed and energetic; just as there had been no standard steps to the rudimentary foxtrot and tango, the Charleston encouraged improvisation – dramatic gestures, stomping and especially vigorous kicking. After the Charleston tea, teachers across the country immediately began offering lessons in the dance, and the demand was great. Silvester recalled in his autobiography that he and his wife taught thirteen hours a day at a profit of a hundred pounds per week – a number he felt they could have doubled with a larger studio.[68]

However, despite the boon to the dancing schools brought about by the Charleston, when the new season commenced that fall, yet more Britons chose to attempt the wild new dance without instruction. Two professional dancers described the situation in the *Dancing Times*: 'Hundreds of wild youths endeavoured to copy [the] kicking and stamping steps and to adapt them to the ballroom, with disastrous results. It was positively unsafe to go within two yards of any couple performing these ridiculous antics.'[69] In the aftermath of such scenes, some professionals turned on the Charleston; they decried it for reintroducing wildness and 'freak' steps to the ballroom, and condemned it as a threat to serious dancing. In an article in *Popular Music and Dancing Weekly*, one writer dismissed the dance altogether in a summary of the new season: 'So far I have intentionally omitted the Charleston because no one seems to have taken it seriously.'[70] Other professionals acknowledged the dance's popularity, but also its perceived deficiencies and liabilities. In May 1926 the *Dancing Times* observed, 'First, a very large section of the dancing public wish to dance the Charleston. Secondly, the majority of those who do Charleston are not only a nuisance but even a source of danger to other dancers.'[71]

Meanwhile, it was not only dance professionals who objected to the Charleston. Dance hall proprietors were greatly concerned about the effect of the dance's wild steps on their wooden dance floors, and the general disruption it caused in the ballroom. Some dancing spaces banned the dance outright, while others displayed signs with the letters 'P.C.Q.' for 'Please Charleston Quietly'. For a time the Charleston was denounced regularly in the pages of the popular press; it was deemed vulgar and coarse, ridiculous and a 'nuisance' to other dancers.[72] Some newspapers even suggested it was dangerous, and could cause permanent damage to the ankles or paralysis-inducing shocks to the body.[73] Much of the criticism of the dance was also strongly racialised, given the dance's perceived African-American origins. One aristocratic critic of the Charleston, for instance, declared that watching a couple perform the dance was like watching 'two Christy Minstrels on the beach', in reference to a famous group of Victorian blackface minstrel performers.[74]

Condemnations of the Charleston from the dance profession and elsewhere did little to diminish widespread enthusiasm for the dance, however. As Silvester later recalled,

> Wherever you went people seemed to be practising the Charleston – in bus queues, in Tube stations waiting for a train, at street corners, in shops; even policemen on point duty were seen doing the steps – because in practically every ballroom in London every second dance was the Charleston, although ministers fulminated against it from their pulpits, schools banned it, and various cultural societies staged protest marches.[75]

Interest in the Charleston was also deliberately stoked. The popular press, despite being one of the primary sources of Charleston criticisms, provided widespread reporting on and helped to perpetuate the dance's success. National dailies fulminated against the Charleston on one page, but on the next would discuss its influence on fashion, or report that the Prince of Wales was a keen enthusiast of the dance.

Confronted with intense public ardour for the Charleston, the dance profession saw that action had to be taken. In October 1926, Richardson acknowledged that the juggernaut could not be stopped: 'The rhythm and beat of [Charleston] music has obtained too firm a hold upon the popular imagination for any official "bannings" or attacks by disgruntled correspondents in the daily Press to stop it.' As the editor went on to counsel, 'those halls which attempt to "bar" the Charleston would be doing good dancing a far greater service if, instead of telling their patrons they must not do it, they would help them to dance it in a quiet and simple manner'.[76] In the months that followed, Richardson and other professionals sought to make reality the second part of this assessment of the Charleston situation, by developing a 'quiet and simple' form of the dance. Known as the 'flat progressive Charleston', it was a milder, smoother,

How the Charleston was " Tamed "

2.2   The modification of the Charleston (bottom) into the 'flat progressive' Charleston (top).

more subdued version of the original that eliminated the violent side-kicks (see Figure 2.2). To generate publicity for the new dance, Casani and Lennard famously performed it on top of a taxi cab, to highlight how little floor space was required in comparison to the original Charleston. Deemed more refined and graceful – and designed to reduce chaos in the ballroom – the transformation of the Charleston was in keeping with broader professional efforts to standardise the foxtrot, tango, waltz and one-step as the English style of ballroom dance.

The Charleston craze reached its zenith in December 1926 with the star-studded 'Charleston Ball' at the Royal Albert Hall, which featured a cabaret, competition and general dancing, and which was attended by many of the leading dance professionals and celebrities of the day. Arguably, the event marked the Charleston's achievement of general social acceptance, but soon afterward the craze for the dance began to dissipate: respectability and professional sanction seemingly made it far less interesting to the dancing public. But while the fervour for the Charleston was short-lived in the final analysis, it was illustrative about the processes of cultural negotiation that occurred between the dance profession and dancing public when it came to the introduction of a new dance, and to the evolution of the national style.

In its continued quest to locate 'standard five' – both for its own sake, and to keep people attending dancing classes – the profession latched on to the Charleston as a new dance to introduce to the dancing public. However, some professionals soon came to regret this move, since the dance proved to inspire the very experimentation and improvisation that represented such a threat to 'correct' dancing and to their own expertise and *raison d'être*. Others also despised the dance for its wild appearance and for the rough element that it reintroduced to the ballroom, which stood in direct contrast to the graceful elegance professionals had tried to inculcate into the English style. But despite these concerns, most within the dance profession decided they could not – and would not – reject the Charleston out of hand. In fact, the *Dancing Times* espoused the opposite, labelling calls in the popular press for the abolition of the dance as 'ridiculous' and 'harmful'.[77] Even those professionals who were wary of the Charleston recognised that it had to be embraced for two primary reasons. First, public enthusiasm for the dance brought many new students to classes, which was clearly to the dancing teachers' economic advantage. Second, the profession's persistent belief, and the one eventually codified at the Great Conference in 1929, was that the public should largely determine the direction that popular dance in Britain would take. In embracing the Charleston, or in rejecting other dances like the tango or the blues, the public played an important role in shaping the national dancing style simply by determining which dances would be successful. In order to remain relevant, the dance profession was required, and indeed expressed their desire, to respond accordingly. As Bradley later recalled,

> [The Charleston] illustrated a viewpoint that I have always had that in reality the public lead the teachers in dancing taste and fashions... You cannot foist a new dance arbitrarily upon the general public ... New dances have been put forth as the latest fashion – and what has happened to them? They have quietly faded away in a few weeks.[78]

Though the dance profession sought to acknowledge and even promote the agency of the dancing public, this power of the people to shape the nation's dancing should not be overstated. First of all, the channels through which the dancing public was exposed to new dances – dancing classes, exhibitions, competitions and print – were strongly mediated by the profession; even the

Charleston had, after all, been introduced to Britain by two professional dancers. The dance profession also continued to exert a strong influence over how a dance would evolve once the dancing public had embraced it, as was made evident in the creation and dissemination of the flat progressive Charleston. In this case, the profession once again took up a dance that it found objectionable and contrary to how the British were 'supposed' to dance, and transformed it into something more aligned with the graceful elegance of the English style. So while the dancing public helped to influence which dances would find success in Britain, throughout the 1920s it was predominately the profession that continued to determine which dances the public would be exposed to, and how they would develop once they had been publicly accepted.

The Charleston did have one final impact, which was to influence the evolution of the quickstep, another innovation that added even more nuance to the complex relationship between the producers and consumers of popular dance. Alongside and in interaction with the dance profession and dancing public were still other entities that helped to shape the national style. As the previous discussion of the tango and foxtrot highlighted, one of these institutions was the dance bands, which also exerted influence over what was danced in the public ballroom, and how dancers moved about the floor. In the mid-1920s, the dance profession and dancing public began to notice, and in many cases condemned, the fact that the bands were playing foxtrot music at a much faster tempo than before. As the *Daily Express* noted, 'Foxtrots are quicker. In almost every big ballroom where a star dance band makes the music you notice this now. Three years ago the foxtrot speed was about 46 bars a minute. Now it is nearer 54 and sometimes as high as 58.'[79] A number of possible explanations for the faster tempos were speculated upon in both the dance and popular press. A common belief was that the large number of American bands working in Britain was the root cause, since foxtrot music was typically played faster in the United States. Another theory was that composers were now writing foxtrot songs in a faster-paced rhythm, and that the bands were simply following the music. There was also a suggestion that the bands were not shaping developments in quick-time dancing at all, but rather that it was the other way around; ballrooms were generally so crowded that dancers were forced to take shorter steps while performing the foxtrot, and the bands were thus attempting to keep pace with the people on the floor. The *Daily Express*'s dancing correspondent, Patrick Chalmers, further theorised that dancers were embracing, and perhaps fomenting, the change in tempo because they were desperate for a little variety in their foxtrotting, which would seem to confirm the profession's belief that the dance was in a bit of a 'rut' by the mid-1920s.[80]

The dance profession began to engage with the quick-time foxtrot issue late in 1924. In October Richardson and the *Dancing Times* convened a Dancer's Circle Dinner at the Hotel Cecil in London, during which it was determined that the slower and faster versions of the foxtrot should be regarded as two distinct dances. It was also likely at this meeting that the name 'quickstep' first emerged, suggested by Florence Purcell as a possible appellation for the faster dance.[81] The name did not come into general usage for several years, however; instead, the dance was referred to as the 'quick-time foxtrot', or even more cumbersomely as the 'quick-time foxtrot and Charleston'. The new dance received further sanction in 1927, when the 'quick-time foxtrot and Charleston' replaced the one-step as a competition event at the annual *Star* Dance Championship. Then, in 1929, the quickstep officially replaced the one-step as one the standard four dances of the English style in discussions at the Great Conference, and in the ensuing report by the Official Board of Ballroom Dancing. This professional recognition symbolised the quickstep's acceptance into the British ballroom dancing canon, but perhaps even more significant was the dancing public's zeal for the dance. The quickstep eventually eclipsed the foxtrot as the nation's favourite ballroom dance.

The part played by the dance bands in the foxtrot's evolution into the quickstep was a herald of things to come. By the end of the 1920s the dance profession faced growing competition from public dance halls, as well as the entertainment industries surrounding music, radio and film, as a source for new popular dances, and even with respect to the provision of instruction. From the time of the Great Conference onward, there was much internal discussion about how the profession could better market its wares, and the start of the Depression affected dance teachers as much as other businesspeople; in the face of the economic downturn, attendance in dance classes slumped and many schools closed their doors. Further signs of professional anxiety came in 1932, when the *Dancing Times* instigated a series of meetings between teachers and marketing consultants, while at the same time the Official Board endorsed pithy slogans such as 'Try Dancing' to entice more people to classes.[82] Professional leaders also attempted to foster more cooperation with the dance hall industry by inaugurating an annual meeting with its representatives.

Increasing financial pressures, as well as artistic differences, created new tensions and divisions within the profession. One of the major impetuses for the Great Conference was in fact a growing realisation among leading professionals that their pursuit of standardisation and conformity in instruction had not been as effective as they had hoped. In particular, individual efforts to identify a dance that could be standard five had run seriously amuck by the late 1920s. Many teachers, in cooperation with a willing and eager popular press, introduced a series of new dances imported from abroad or created at home. These included the 'black bottom', the 'five-step', the 'trebla', the 'Yale blues', the 'heebie jeebies', the 'Baltimore', the 'six-eight', the 'midway rhythm' and the 'moochi' – to name only a few – most of which were composed of what were decried in one letter to the editor as 'foolish and unintelligent steps'.[83] None was a major success, and many professionals feared that the incessant flurry of silly new dances threatened their artistic integrity, and undermined their authority with the dancing public. It was for this reason that one of the main resolutions passed at the Great Conference was that the teachers must coordinate their efforts in selecting a new dance to 'push' each season. As the *Dancing Times* report on the conference put it, 'We don't want any more "freak" dances exploited by individuals for the sake of personal publicity. They confuse the public.'[84]

It does appear that the dancing public was confused – and increasingly disgruntled – though not entirely for the reasons that many within the profession assumed. There certainly was some disillusionment among casual dancers over the profusion of new dances, and yet, as the *Dancing Times* noted in an article entitled 'Pity the Poor Teacher', there was also a converse frustration among students that there was nothing new in dancing.[85] However, if dancers complained of 'stagnation in the ballroom' as this article suggested, it had more to do with the state of modern ballroom dancing in general than the lack of a new dance they enjoyed as much as the foxtrot. Though a primary goal of the standardisation of the English style had been to simplify dancing, it also inevitably created a 'correct' way to dance that had to be mastered through instruction and all of the other modes of transmission that had evolved between the profession and public. Ongoing professional efforts to tweak the steps, or to introduce new variations of the standard four dances, were perhaps necessary for boosting dance class enrolments and selling instruction manuals, but they also added more complexity to dancing in the eyes of those Britons who were uninterested in formal instruction. In these ways, modern ballroom dancing in Britain did begin to feel stale or even repressive to some within the dancing public by the 1930s. In fact, although modern ballroom dancing teachers had always openly abhorred and rejected the behaviour of dictatorial dancing masters in the Victorian period, they were themselves good-naturedly described in a 1935 *Popular Music and Dancing Weekly* article as the 'Dictators of Dancing'.[86]

Meanwhile, for innovations in popular dance, the dancing public was increasingly able to turn away from the teachers and towards other sources, including dance hall proprietors; the popular press; radio, television, and film; as well as foreign musicians, performers, and visitors. As will be shown in subsequent chapters, some of these innovations, such as novelty dances, were exceedingly simple, or, in the case of new American imports such as truckin' and the jitterbug, encouraged improvisation. The impact of these alternative sources and styles was not immediately apparent, but ever so slowly public interest in the English style and the dictates of the dance profession began to wane. The professionals who embraced the new dances, or opted to work in tangent with the other forces shaping British dancing, often survived and thrived. For others, their influence on popular dance would continue to decrease, and they began to embody the title first suggested by the *Dancing Times* in 1931: 'pity the poor teacher'.

Notes

1 The Sitter Out, *Dancing Times* (May 1920), p. 606.
2 The Sitter Out, 'In the Ballroom', *Dancing Times* (January 1922), pp. 337–8.
3 Eve Tynegate-Smith, 'The Art of Teaching Ballroom Dancing', *Dancing Times* (February 1931), p. 590.
4 Victor Silvester, Letter to the Editor, *Dancing Times* (May 1931), p. 106.
5 Philip J. S. Richardson, *A History of English Ballroom Dancing* (London: Herbert Jenkins, 1946), p. 39.
6 'London's Orgy of Dancing', *Daily Express* (30 October 1919), p. 7.
7 Provincial Notes, *Dancing Times* (November 1919), p. 135.
8 The Sitter Out, *Dancing Times* (May 1920), p. 607.
9 'Seven Sinful Dances', *Daily Express* (18 December 1919), p. 1.
10 'Dances to Prelates', *Daily Express* (8 March 1920), p. 1; 'Tango Without the Tang', *Daily Express* (26 January 1920), p. 5.
11 The Sitter Out, *Dancing Times* (May 1920), p. 606.
12 The Sitter Out, *Dancing Times* (November 1920), p. 84.
13 Juliet McMains, *Glamour Addiction: Inside the American Ballroom Dance Industry* (Middletown, CT: Wesleyan University Press, 2006), p. 80.
14 'Vulgarity in the Ballroom!' *Dancing Times* (January 1921).
15 The Sitter Out, *Dancing Times* (June 1920), p. 687.
16 Richardson, *A History of English Ballroom Dancing*, p. 44.

17 'The Palais de Danse and the Profession: A Suggestion', *Dancing Times* (February 1926), p. 558.

18 Marjorie and Georges Fontana, 'Ballroom and Exhibition Dancing', *Dancing Times* (December 1920), p. 176.

19 See *Dancing Times*, 1934–1935.

20 Elizabeth Casciani, *Oh, How we Danced! The History of Ballroom Dancing in Scotland* (Edinburgh: Mercat Press, 1994), p. 49.

21 'Exhibition Dancing', *Dancing Times* (August 1929), p. 433.

22 The Sitter Out, *Dancing Times* (December 1930), p. 290.

23 A. H. Franks, *Social Dance: A Short History* (London: Routledge & Kegan Paul, 1963), p. 171.

24 Cumberland, Letter to the Editor, *Dancing Times* (October 1930), p. 30.

25 Richardson, *A History of English Ballroom Dancing*, p. 70.

26 Santos Casani, *Casani's Self-Tutor of Ballroom Dancing* (London: Cassell and Company, 1927), p. 6.

27 See Victor Silvester, *Dancing is My Life* (London: William Heinemann, 1958).

28 Richardson, *A History of English Ballroom Dancing*, pp. 59–60.

29 A. H. Franks, 'Fact and Fallacy', *Modern Dance* (October 1937), p. 1.

30 Letter to the Editor, *Dancing Times* (January 1928), p. 544.

31 IWM: Documents.6498, Private Papers of Captain J. S. Gray (20 October 1943).

32 Richard S. Gray, Letter to the Editor, *Modern Dance* (October 1936), pp. 13–14.

33 'Our Novices' Competition', *Dancing Times* (February 1927), p. 586.

34 Marjorie and Georges Fontana, 'Ballroom and Exhibition Dancing', *Dancing Times* (December 1920), p. 176.

35 The Sitter Out, *Dancing Times* (December 1930), p. 290.

36 MOA: TC 38/6/G, The Imperial Society of Teachers of Dancing (19 June 1939), p. 3.

37 'How the Season is Shaping', *Dancing Times* (November 1931), p. 159.

38 'The Coming Ballroom Season', *Dancing Times* (October 1933), p. 29.

39 'The Coming Ballroom Season', *Dancing Times* (October 1932), p. 45.

40 A. M. Gordon, Letter to the Editor, *Dancing Times* (October 1932), p. 38.

41 Eve Tynegate-Smith, 'Ballroom Dancing Simplified', *Dancing Times* (January 1929), p. 532.

42 Harry Kahn, 'Swing', *Modern Dance* (February 1938), p. 13.

43 'The Present Ballroom Season', *Dancing Times* (November 1935), p. 211.

44 Ena M. Bartley, Letter to the Editor, *Dancing Times* (October 1932), p. 38.

45 Novice, Letter to the Editor, *Dancing Times* (September 1932), p. 518.

46 An Average Dancer, 'Controlling our Ballroom Dancing', *Dancing Times* (May 1928), p. 143.

47 G. E. Fussell, 'New Steps and the Dancer', *Dancing Times* (February 1922), p. 483.

48 'The Informal Conference', *Dancing Times* (May 1929), p. 126.

49 Monsieur Pierre, 'Who Makes New Dances?' *Dancing Times* (December 1921), p. 299.

50 Draycot Dell, 'Dance Halls of To-Day', *Popular Music and Dancing Weekly* (29 March 1924), p. 194.

51 Alfredo, 'Confessions of a Dance Band Leader', *Popular Music and Dancing Weekly* (2 August 1924), p. 38.

52 Isobel Elsom, 'After the Fox Trot – the Fox Trot', *Popular Music and Dancing Weekly* (18 July 1925), p. 246.

53 Santos Casani, 'The Dances of To-morrow', *Popular Music and Dancing Weekly* (31 May 1924), p. 112.

54 The Sitter Out, 'In the Ballroom', *Dancing Times* (October 1922), p. 23.

55 'Are Ballroom Dancers too Conservative?' *Dancing Times* (September 1926), p. 530.

56 The Sitter Out, *Dancing Times* (January 1921), p. 306.

57 Robert Sielle, Letter to the Editor, *Dancing Times* (November 1920), p. 95.

58 Around the Dance Halls, *Popular Music and Dancing Weekly* (13 September 1924), p. 157.

59 Around the Dance Halls, *Popular Music and Dancing Weekly* (23 October 1926), p. iii.

60 Novice, Letter to the Editor, *Dancing Times* (September 1932), p. 518.

61 June, 'Dancing in 1926', *Popular Music and Dancing Weekly* (9 January 1926), p. 232.

62 Around the Dance Halls, *Popular Music and Dancing Weekly* (8 November 1924), p. 53.

63 Around the Dance Halls, *Popular Music and Dancing Weekly* (15 March 1924), p. 148.

64 Philip J. S. Richardson, 'A New Dance At Last', *Dancing Times* (August 1923), p. 1061.

65 Alfredo, 'Confessions of a Dance Band Leader', p. 38.

66 Richardson, *A History of English Ballroom Dancing*, p. 57.

67 Josephine Bradley, 'My "Cavalcade" of Dancing', *Popular Music and Dancing Weekly* (27 October 1934), p. 3.

68 Silvester, *Dancing is My Life*, pp. 88–9.

69 Phyllis Haylor and Alec H. Miller, 'Taming the Charleston', *Dancing Times* (October 1926), p. 9.

70 June, 'Dancing in 1926', p. 232.

71 The Sitter Out, 'Some Thoughts on the Present Situation', *Dancing Times* (May 1926), p. 255.

72 Molly Ashley, Letter to the Editor, *Daily Mail* (28 April 1926), p. 7.

73 Casciani, *Oh, How We Danced!*, p. 52.

74 'A Vulgar Dance', *Daily Mail* (27 April 1926), p. 7.

75 Silvester, *Dancing is My Life*, p. 88.

76 The Sitter Out, 'Ballroom Notes', *Dancing Times* (October 1926), p. 35.

77 The Sitter Out, 'Some Thoughts on the Present Situation', p. 255.

78 Bradley, 'My "Cavalcade" of Dancing', p. 3.

79 Patrick Chalmers, 'Quicker Foxtrots', *Daily Express* (15 February 1926), p. 8.

80 Chalmers, 'Quicker Foxtrots', p. 8.

81 'The Quick-Step', *Dancing Times* (November 1924), p. 143. See also Richardson, *A History of English Ballroom Dancing*, p. 58.

82 'Publicity for Dancing', *Dancing Times* (January 1932), p. 422.

83 'What Our Readers Say', *Dancing Times* (December 1929), p. 341.

84 'The Informal Conference', *Dancing Times* (May 1929), p. 126.

85 'Pity the Poor Teacher', *Dancing Times* (March 1931), p. 670.

86 John K. Newnham, 'Dictators of Dancing', *Popular Music and Dancing Weekly* (16 March, 1935), p. 20.

3

At the palais: the dance hall industry and the standardisation of experience

In a 1939 interview with Mass Observation, Major Cecil Taylor, renowned teacher and long-time president of the Imperial Society of Teachers of Dancing, remarked, 'I don't see what we could do without the palais now ... They are a [part] of our life and are essential to our being.'[1] He pointed to the affordability, high quality dance floors, excellent bands, general cleanliness and efficient staff as all of the reasons why the 'palais de danse' had become such an intrinsic and valued part of the national culture. Yet remarkably, the leisure spaces that Taylor described had not existed only twenty years before. It was only in 1919, in the midst of the post-war dance craze, that the first purpose-built spaces for public dancing began to open throughout the country. From the first dance hall – or palais – at Hammersmith in west London, a whole industry was born, and public dancing became one of the cornerstones of commercial leisure in the middle part of the twentieth century.

This chapter will discuss how the experience of going out dancing changed as Britain entered the interwar period, looking at the advent of the public dance hall and considering other opportunities for dancing outside of the home. It explores the emergence and expansion of the dance hall industry, arguing that one by-product of this development was the cultivation of an increasingly standard dancing experience for Britons, regardless of where they lived in the country. The standardisation of public dancing was in fact a specific goal of developing dance hall chains such as the one controlled by the Mecca organisation, and Britons did gradually come to know what to expect from an evening at the palais. However the second part of the chapter will show that uniformity of experience was never an entirely fulfilled project, since, despite the best efforts of companies such as Mecca, there remained distinct differences between the opportunities available for public dancing among Britons of different regions and classes. At the same time, patrons influenced their own consumption of dance hall culture: they ventured out to dance for different reasons, chose where to go based on different criteria, and enjoyed different aspects of the public dancing experience. With the expansion of the popular music, radio and film industries, there were also a multitude of ways beyond physically entering a ballroom that Britons could participate in what occurred within them. Just like the dance profession, the dance hall industry wielded formidable influence in the evolution of British popular dance. However, members of the dancing public found ways to interact with this commercial producer to shape their individual and by extension the nation's collective dancing experience.

Where Britain danced

Along with the emergence of modern styles and the professionalisation of ballroom dancing, the introduction of thousands of new commercial spaces for public dancing was the third critical aspect of the major transformations to popular dance that occurred after the First World War. In October 1919, the Hammersmith Palais de Danse opened in west London, inaugurating a new era in British leisure as hundreds of dance halls began to spring up around the country. While dancing outside of the home had a long and established history in Britain, what distinguished the new venues was that they were created entirely for the purpose of dancing. They were spacious, with high quality dance floors, and talented bands playing the latest jazz hits. They were also inexpensive enough to be accessible to Britons of all classes. As the *Dancing Times* observed in 1926, the growing number of public dance halls around the country fulfilled 'a long felt want'.[2]

The options for public dancing in Britain before 1919 were disparate and strongly reflective of social hierarchies, with the middle and upper classes having access to the most wide-ranging opportunities for dancing outside of the home. Dances were an inherent part of both country and city life for those Britons who composed the upper social echelon known as Society, and were also a prominent feature of an evening out at the various hotels, restaurants and nightclubs frequented by the elite. The Edwardian period also saw the development of both subscription dances and dance clubs, which further expanded the public dancing options for middle and upper class enthusiasts. Subscription dances were often held in conjunction with social organisations, generally organised by the dancers themselves, with attendees paying a fee that went to cover expenses including the venue, music and refreshments. Dance clubs were similarly composed of groups of people who paid a membership fee that went to hosting dinner-dances. Unlike subscription dances, however, which were held throughout the country, dance clubs were more a phenomenon of urban centres, especially associated with the West End of London. Initially dance clubs had no fixed premises, but in the last years before the war, when the tango and ragtime heralded the transition to the modern era of popular dance, some clubs began to establish permanent venues, with some of the most renowned being Murray's, Ciro's, the Embassy, the Café de Paris and the Grafton Galleries.

The West End dance clubs charged as much as ten to fifteen shillings for their dinner-dances, putting them out of reach for most of the lower middle and working classes. These Britons were able to take part in the dances that were occasionally held at assembly or municipal halls, and many urban working-class neighbourhoods featured public 'dancing rooms', often attached to public houses. At a shilling or less, the assemblies hosted by dancing schools were also generally affordable, and starting around the turn of the century, there were several relatively inexpensive public dance halls in seaside towns such as Brighton, Margate and Douglas, designed to cater to holiday-makers. Most notable of the holiday dancing centres was Blackpool, which featured both the Tower Ballroom and the Empress Ballroom in the Winter Gardens, establishing the town early as the ballroom dancing centre that it would become with the expansion of competition dancing. However, until the interwar period trips to the seaside were still largely the purview of the middle and upper classes.[3] Therefore, as Britain entered the post-war dance craze, there were mounting calls for the establishment of more widespread and affordable options for public dancing. Commentators pointed to the plethora of public dance halls in the United States and on the European continent as models for what Britain should put into place, and argued that the creation of respectable ballrooms would do much to diminish the controversies that swirled around dancing in that period. As the *Daily Mail* suggested in January 1919, public dance halls would provide those young men and women still residing in towns far from home due to military service or war work with the opportunity to mix and mingle 'under the best and healthiest circumstances'.[4]

The desire for more dedicated public dancing options was profound enough that when the Hammersmith Palais finally opened its doors on 28 October 1919, the event received a great deal of attention and an effusive response. As the *Daily Express* enthused, 'This new super-palace of jazz and other dances of the day is declared to be without its equal as a dancing hall anywhere in

Europe. Everything about it is in the superlative degree.' The newspaper further declared that with the coming of the Palais, 'Popular dancing [has] reached its climax.'[5] Thousands of tickets were sold for its grand opening, and a few weeks later a columnist for the *Dancing Times* declared the Palais was still 'the talk of the town'.[6] As this enthusiastic response attested, the amenities provided by the Hammersmith Palais exceeded anything the nation had previously experienced in public dancing. Covering a space of over 2,500 square metres the Palais boasted an immense dance floor capable of accommodating a thousand dancers, and a general capacity of a thousand more. The hall also featured a café and restaurant, sumptuous and ornate Asian-themed décor, and, for the first nine months of its existence, the musical stylings of the Original Dixieland Jazz Band from the United States.

As the first and among the most luxurious to open in Britain, the Hammersmith Palais always retained a fame and mystique above and beyond the average dance hall. As *Popular Music and Dancing Weekly* pronounced in 1924, the hall was 'almost as much London's home of dancing as the Law Courts is London's home of legal activity'.[7] The Palais was the only public dance hall to feature a royal box, and it would go on to witness a number of famous patrons take a turn on the dance floor, including the Duke of York and actress Mary Pickford. The hall's amenities and renown also meant that it drew dancers from well beyond west London, but from all over the capital and beyond, and possessed a reputation as a cross-class ballroom and social leveller.[8] In 1987, when the hall underwent renovations, a former dance bandleader described this social mixing in the *London Daily News*: 'The Palais was always a real meeting-place, a melting-pot. When they were dancing, you couldn't tell the daughter of a duchess from an ordinary working class girl.'[9] While the reality of the social make-up of the Hammersmith Palais was undoubtedly more complex than this remembrance implied, it stands as a testament to the enduring myth and fame that surrounded the nation's first dance hall.

Yet the Hammersmith Palais's greatest legacy was the new era in public dancing that its opening helped to launch. The success of the Palais led to the creation of more and more purpose-built dance establishments throughout Britain, with one estimate suggesting that 11,000 dance halls and nightclubs opened around the country in the first six years after the war.[10] As the *Dancing Times* remarked in that year, 'That the "Palais de Danse" has come to stay is very evident ... in a short time there will be few towns of any size which do not boast their big dance hall.' The magazine went on to assert that most of these halls were thronged nightly by large crowds, which was a testament to

South London's Magnificent New Palais.

The Locarno dance hall in Streatham Hill, shortly after it opened in 1929.   **3.1**

public enthusiasm for dancing, and quite understandable given that the '[the palais] are generally bright, cheery places with spacious dance floors, very fair bands and moderate charges'.[11] This comment underscored that while there continued to be considerable distinctions between public dance spaces throughout the country, a basic dance hall model had begun to emerge (see Figure 3.1).

Most dance halls featured a large 'sprung' dance floor of maple or oak, which accommodated anywhere from a few hundred to a few thousand dancers. The dance floor was typically surrounded by clothed tables and chairs from which patrons could enjoy refreshments and observe the dancing, and in some halls further viewing spaces were provided via balconies, or promenades, that overlooked the ballroom. A band performed from a stage or raised dais, or occasionally a revolving bandstand, and the larger halls engaged two bands simultaneously, which would alternate playing so that there was never a break in the music. Dance halls also often possessed attached dining and drinking spaces, in the form of cafés, restaurants, snack or refreshment stands, lounges and bars. The remaining space was filled out by cloak rooms, separate rest areas for men and women, and frequently grand entrance areas, staffed by uniformed ushers and usherettes. The other staff on hand generally included a master of ceremonies who led the dancing, various managerial personnel, cloak and rest room attendants, serving staff, and professional partners who could be hired for six pence a dance, and occupied an area of the ballroom dubbed the 'pen'. The halls were designed and decorated in a manner meant to signify luxury and comfort, and dancers helped to reproduce the glamour of the palais by investing considerable energy and expense in dressing up for their visit; evening dress was commonly worn, and even required at some of the larger dance halls.[12]

Indeed, many dance halls were ornate and ostentatious in their décor, with proprietors employing elaborate decorative features as a means of distinguishing their hall from the competition.[13] As one writer for *Popular Music and Dancing Weekly* mused in 1925, 'Almost every month sees the opening of a new dancing hall – some gorgeous new temple erected to the shrine of Terpsichore and rivalling in splendour and glittering magnificence the palaces of the East.' She went on to marvel at the modern dancing palace's 'beautifully panelled walls, marble columns, perfect glass-like floor, coloured lighting effects, jazz orchestras and so on'.[14] The sumptuousness of many establishments was also commented on by another writer conducting a survey of the nation's dancing spaces for the same periodical: 'Since I first began writing about some of the popular dance-halls in London and the provinces, I have found that, unless one has a wide range of descriptive words at one's command, it is impossible to do full justice to the splendour of the modern ballroom.'[15] But while this decorative 'splendour' was a common feature of the palais, how this was achieved, and what meanings the décor may have conveyed to patrons, varied considerably.

Some dance halls sought to highlight their status as thoroughly modern leisure spaces through the use of elaborate and dramatic lighting displays, as well as striking decorative pieces. The Plaza dance hall in Glasgow, for example, featured a sunken floor illuminated by coloured footlights, at the centre of which was a fountain decorated in flowers and containing real goldfish.[16] Fountains were a common feature at a number of other dance halls as well, and the one at the Palais de Danse in Nottingham was given vivid description by a contemporary writer: 'The water rises to a height of twenty feet, and is illuminated by a rainbow lighting system, so that it constantly changes colour.'[17] Another notable adornment of the Nottingham Palais was the large illuminated globe that graced its entrance, and many other halls also possessed dramatic exterior lighting, such as the famed Barrowlands in Glasgow. As James Nott notes, the use of water and bright lights in these venues, as well as loud colours, chrome and geometric shapes, promoted a self-consciously modernist aesthetic.[18] Contemporary commentators found the modern décor to be particularly in step with the equally modern music and dances that predominated within the halls. As one writer remarked about the Regent dance hall in Brighton, 'Dazzling colour schemes carried out in fantasies so bizarre as to suggest the incarnation of jazzdom give the Regent a most modern note.'[19]

However, even as they provided spaces for modern dancing, other dance halls eschewed modernity, at least as a decorative style, in favour of more classical or exotic themes. One London hall was described upon its opening in 1920 as positively 'Neroesque' by the *Daily Express*. According to the newspaper, through the venue's marble columns and Roman-style courtyard, 'The classical idea has been carefully adhered to, and the chaste, cool design of a palace of ancient Rome lifts the place high above the status of the ordinary dancing hall.'[20] The use of elaborate columns, carpeting, and painted murals was common in public dance halls, in some cases to highlight a classical motif such as the one previously described, or to convey foreign, often 'eastern' themes. Many halls, including the Hammersmith Palais, featured Chinese or Japanese lanterns and incorporated what was purported to be Asian-inspired architectural elements into their décor. As the *Dancing Times* described the Hammersmith Palais, 'That which has been a vast barn has been transformed by the wand of a magician into an Aladdin's fairy palace, which sparkled with a thousand lights reflecting all the colours of the Orient.'[21] Meanwhile, the Wimbledon Palais was in possession of a 'Japanese tea room', as well as an 'Egyptian alcove', while Nottingham's New Victoria hall was adorned in wall paintings of 'waving palms and oases'.[22] One hall in Birmingham was decorated as a mosque, with prayer mats hanging from the walls, and contained two lounges respectively dubbed the 'Alcazar' and the 'Baghdad'.[23] Other dancing spaces that were not specifically decorated with foreign motifs often had special theme nights in which these elements were promoted; 'Oriental' nights were common, when patrons were required to wear 'Eastern costume'.[24] As Nott points out, the very names commonly bestowed upon dance halls, including 'Rialto', 'Lido', 'Ritz', and 'Plaza', conveyed 'sophistication and foreignness'.[25] A continental influence was also strongly reinforced by the widespread use of the French 'palais de danse', usually shortened simply to the 'palais'.

A wide range of meanings would thus have been conveyed to the dancers taking a turn in the ballroom. Many halls represented what Mica Nava has identified as 'commercial orientalism', wherein cultural difference and the allure of the exotic were produced and consumed in the decorative features of cinemas and department stores, or through fashion, concert dance and film.[26] Nava's study focused on a slightly earlier period, but it is clear that the impetus to market an orientalist aesthetic carried over into the design of public dance halls in the interwar years. Yet even orientalism does not quite encompass the breadth of foreign influences represented in the décor or cultural practices present in dance hall culture, which were, as was described above, equally inspired by a modernist aesthetic and continental Europe. The cultural influence of the Americas was also visible through special theme nights in dancing spaces. Amid the 'Oriental' nights, there were also 'Argentine' and 'Plantation' dances, at which some patrons even sported blackface; by the 1930s many dance halls began hosting 'Harlem' or 'American' theme nights. In these events, further evidence is provided as to Britain's expanding cultural exchange with America, through which Britons engaged with and negotiated their understandings of cultural and racial difference.

Britain's status as an imperial power also influenced public dancing spaces. In fact, popular dance was fused directly to imperial culture when a dance hall became one of the main attractions at the British Empire Exhibition at Wembley in 1924. The hall was built directly within the exhibition grounds, in the shadow of the domed Indian Pavilion, and the event also inspired a new dance tune, the 'Wembley, Wibbly, Wobbly Dance', which was performed as a one-step. The lyrics to the song commanded Britons to come to Wembley, to choose to see the exhibition and learn the new Wembley dance rather than to seek out recreation elsewhere in Britain, or in France or the United States.[27] The imperial theme was further adhered to through the hosting of special 'Dominion Balls', on the respective Dominion Days of Canada, Australia and New Zealand, and in general the ballroom proved to be enough of a success that another dance hall was featured at the 1938 imperial exhibition in Glasgow. However, rather than highlighting specific British colonies through its design motifs, the Wembley hall was decorated in a mishmash of the same 'eastern' and 'oriental' themes present in many of the dance venues described above. According to one contemporary report, the exterior was 'gaily decorated in Oriental fashion', and the interior was adorned in red, panel-painted walls, 'orange gauzy hangings', as well as a balcony that contained palm trees beneath which refreshments were served.[28]

The public ballrooms in which Britons danced, therefore, reflected Britain's position within imperial but also global networks of cultural exchange. Much like the dances that were performed within them, dance venues presented – but also marketed – cultural and racial difference as part of the dancing experience. As they danced steps that had originated in Europe, Latin America or the United States, dancers were surrounded by and negotiated with a cosmopolitan mélange of decorative features and special events that commodified these same regions, as well as a nebulous and exoticised 'east'. But diverse though they may have been, the fixtures and décor of every public ballroom did have one important thing in common: they were used to get people in the door. Just as the dance profession sought to standardise ballroom dance steps in order to make popular dance accessible and acceptable to the majority of Britons, the emerging dance hall industry sought to construct an experience of public dancing that would have mass appeal.

There were thus standard elements to the experience provided by public dance halls throughout the country. Many halls featured both an afternoon and evening session, of approximately three to four hours – or thirty to fifty dances – in length. With reduced rates for the afternoon session and slightly higher prices at the weekend, admission to the larger halls cost anywhere from a shilling to five shillings, though the standard price tended to be two shillings, six pence. Bands would play from a programme of songs written to accompany the range of English style ballroom dances, namely the foxtrot, modern waltz, tango, one-step or quickstep, and whatever other dances might currently be in favour. In many cases, the type of dance being performed was signified by different colour lights descending upon the floor, such as blue for a foxtrot, red for a waltz and full light for a quickstep, with an encore if the dance was proven a success by the level of applause.[29] Another customary feature of the dance programme was the cabaret, during which time a break would be taken in the dancing for some form of entertainment or special activity. Exhibition dances were common during the cabaret, as were acrobats, jugglers, singers, magicians and other variety acts; additional diversions included treasure hunts, costume contests and of course dance competitions. Some halls were more successful in these endeavours than others. In 1924, *Popular Music and Dancing Weekly* noted that the female manager of the Wimbledon Palais possessed 'a genius for special nights. She has had "coiffure" competitions, fancy dress balls, surprise nights, prettiest dress competitions – indeed, every type of competition that can add to the general interest'.[30]

In these ways, Britons gradually came to know what to expect from an evening's dancing at the palais. As greater numbers of dance halls opened throughout the 1920s, the experience became to some extent as standardised as the steps of the foxtrot, notwithstanding the competing decorative features and the creative strategies of dance hall managers. This uniformity of experience was further cultivated by the consolidation of popular dance as a business, and the emergence of corporate chains of dance halls. In the late 1920s, a number of companies that were primarily concerned with cinemas witnessed the popularity of dancing and saw the advantage of diversifying; large conglomerates such as General Theatres Ltd., Gaumont British and Odeon therefore began buying up independent or small chains of dance halls.[31] In some cases, these companies merged their combined interests, producing large-scale entertainment complexes featuring a cinema, dance hall and places to eat on one site, in a number of urban areas. The Blackpool Palace for example, contained not only a dance hall, but a cinema and a variety theatre. However, the greatest of the dance hall chains had no connection to the cinema at all, but instead focused entirely on dance halls and dancing-related concerns. This was the Mecca circuit of dance halls, the company most responsible for commercialising popular dance by the outbreak of the Second World War.

Mecca consolidated under the leadership of one man, Carl L. Heimann, whose influence on British dancing came to be so significant that in 1938 Mass Observation referred to him as one of the 'cultural directors of the nation'.[32] Born in Denmark, Heimann arrived in Britain in 1912 while still a teenager, having decided, as he told a biographer, 'that feeding and entertaining people would be my business in life'.[33] In the mid-1920s, he took a job with a firm called Ye Mecca Cafés, which provided catering services to a number of dance venues including the Royal Opera House and the Café de Paris. Perceptive to the growing opportunities connected with commercial dancing, Heimann convinced Mecca to purchase another of its catering clients, Sherry's dance hall in Brighton (then owned by the circus company Bertram Mills), and to name him as the manager of the new enterprise. He quickly made a number of changes at Sherry's that later become standard in many dance halls, including opening up the balcony to non-dancing viewers, and the creation of new staff like usherettes.[34] Indeed, a decade later, while interviewing Heimann for Mass Observation, Tom Harrisson recorded the impression that the Mecca manager was 'on the look out for ideas every minute'.[35] It is perhaps not surprising then that the Brighton hall proved to be an immense success, and Mecca soon expanded its interests in dancing; by 1933, the company had taken control of the Ritz in Manchester, the Locarno in Streatham (south London) and the Lido in Croydon.[36]

Soon thereafter Heimann was named the head of Mecca Dancing, a subsidiary of Mecca Cafés, but the company then decided to halt its foray into dancing when the Lido proved to be Heimann's first real failure. Undeterred, Heimann persuaded Mecca to let him continue pursuing (and financing) the dance hall expansion on his own, but still under the company name. In 1935, he partnered with a Scottish amusements entrepreneur, Alan Fairley, and starting with the Locarno dance hall in Glasgow, the two began buying up halls around the country at a rapid pace. By 1938, in addition to its existent halls, Mecca controlled dance halls in Edinburgh, Leeds, Sheffield, Nottingham, Bradford, Birmingham, as well as London's Tottenham, Paramount and Wimbledon dance halls. During the Second World War, the company also took over the management of the Royal Opera House in Covent Garden, which was transformed into a dance hall for the duration. According to his interview with Mass Observation, Heimann prided himself on taking halls that were 'white elephants' and turning them a 'healthy pink'.[37]

At the same time, Mecca had expanded into almost all other aspects of the dance business, including catering, construction projects such as the laying of dance floors and building of bandstands, managing and supplying bands and cabaret acts, accounting and publicity services, and employing professional dancers. With respect to the last, the company retained professionals, often of considerable renown, as dance partners to fill the halls' 'pens', as exhibition acts, and as teachers for its dancing schools, the most notable of which was Adele England's school, connected to the Streatham Locarno. Mecca also developed a significant publishing arm, under the auspices of its Danceland Publications, which printed dance-themed newspapers, pamphlets and books. All of these publications were used to promote Mecca halls, the special events and competitions that occurred within them, and the original dances that the company began to produce and market.

The creation of dance hall chains like Mecca was one of the critical factors in the rapid and pervasive commercialisation of public dancing, and to the evolution of a standard dance experience throughout the nation. Mecca deliberately targeted a working-class clientele by keeping its halls affordable, but at the same time, and as will be discussed at more length in Chapter 4, sought to appeal to middle and upper class patrons through the institution of policies designed to elevate the palais's respectability. While seeking to draw in a truly cross-class and nationwide clientele, companies like Mecca sought to make an evening's dancing uniform regardless of where one was in the country. 'Dancing the Mecca Way' was the company's slogan, advancing the notion that the Mecca dancing experience was a standard one that patrons increasingly understood and relied upon. The company also implemented promotional campaigns and special events specifically designed to promote feelings of community and simultaneity within the national dancing experience;

a notable example were the nationwide launches of Mecca's original dances, when each new dance was introduced at every hall in the chain on the very same evening. Mecca halls also sponsored preliminary rounds of national dance competitions, engaging Britons throughout the country in the same series of events. A big part of the Mecca experience in fact was a seemingly endless series of promotions, giveaways, and special events, about which a writer for the *Dancing Times* observed in the summer of 1939, 'Mecca Cafés are a most enterprising firm, you never know what they may produce for you.'[38]

Mecca's business model was clearly effective, for many within the dancing public came to see the company's dances halls as a step above the rest. The responses to a questionnaire about public dancing circulated by Mass Observation are telling in this respect. One woman observed that she appreciated 'that EXTRA SOMETHING that only Mecca Halls provide. I dance at the "Royal" regularly two and three nights each week and know that I get value for money and an enjoyable time.' A Scottish man who frequented the Edinburgh Palais concurred with this assessment, declaring, 'I have been to other dance halls, but it is the up-to-date methods, tunes, cabarets and style that puts this Mecca Hall in a class far superior to anything else in Edinburgh.' Other respondents also offered laundry lists of the advantages at Mecca halls over others, including the non-stop dancing, the quality of the bands, the refreshments, the cabarets and especially the price, which was inexpensive, but as one writer noted, still offered an 'atmosphere of luxury'. Significantly, one respondent to the question-naire even used Mecca's own promotional language to explain his or her prefer-ences for one of the chain's halls: 'There are probably few pastimes more agreeable in London, than to dance the Mecca Way at the Paramount.'[39]

These comments are evidence of an unmistakeable response to Mecca's marketing efforts on the part of patrons, and they illustrate the strong influence of the dance hall industry as a commercial producer within British society. As Mecca continued to expand, the dance hall experience that the company and its closest competitors provided was an increasingly standard one – from the spatial organisation, to the song and dance sequence, to the fun activities and special events on offer – all of which shaped the dancing public's needs and expectations for a visit to the palais. However, within these structures, patrons made choices that shaped the experience of the public ballroom, and with which dance hall proprietors were required to negotiate. As the next section will show, while the commercial might and cultural influence of the dance hall industry was real, how Britons used public dancing spaces could complicate or defy industry intentions.

How Britain danced

By 1938, according to one estimate, approximately two million Britons went dancing each week, or a hundred million annually.[40] As the previous section has shown, there were increasing universals to this experience, in terms of the layout, programme organisation, and dances performed in Britain's public dancing spaces. Prominent companies, such as Mecca, perfected a dance hall model that other corporate chains or independent proprietors sought to emulate, and which influenced the dancing's public's preferences and expectations for a visit to the palais. However, significant differences persisted as to the types of spaces in which Britons danced, as well as with respect to when, why, and how they used them. Additionally, in various ways the commercialisation of public dancing in the interwar years transcended the ballroom itself, enabling even greater diversity as to how popular dance was consumed and experienced.

Providing an important glimpse into the dynamics at play during an afternoon or evening session at a public dance hall is the data that was compiled by Mass Observation as part of a dedicated study undertaken by the social research organisation into 'music, dancing, and jazz' in Britain during the final years of the 1930s. Founded in 1937 by Harrisson and Charles Madge, Mass Observation's stated objectives were to document everyday life in Britain, and to conduct anthropological research in order to produce a 'science of ourselves'.[41] Within this mandate, Mass Observation had plans for a whole book on the subjects of popular music and dance, and the research it conducted was extensive. The investigation included interviews with key figures in the dance hall industry and dance profession; a questionnaire administered via the Mecca periodical *Danceland*; a collection of dance hall industry promotional materials; and reports by observers as to the goings-on at a variety of dance halls around the country (though mainly in London and Bolton). Data collection for the dancing project largely fell to one investigator, Alec Hughes, who conducted a tour of many of London's large commercial dance halls throughout 1938 and 1939. Hughes provided a consistent if mediated perspective on goings-on at the palais, and, owing to his mother having been a dance teacher, was knowledgeable about ballroom dancing. Most importantly, Hughes produced observations of, and interviews with, dance hall staff and management *and* their patrons, and his materials often capture the complex interactions between the producers and consumers of popular dance. This section therefore uses Mass Observation's materials, alongside diaries, memoirs and contemporary print culture, to explore the cultural mechanics of the dance hall experience.

There were any number of factors that influenced an individual's decision to frequent one dance hall over another. As the attestations of Mecca clientele described above make plain, the perceived superiority of one hall (or chain of halls) over others was certainly a factor: there was a wide spectrum of dance halls, and their respective décor, facilities and special events were taken note of by potential patrons. Mass Observation's Hughes remarked in several reports about the care and attention to detail taken at Mecca halls, seemingly much impressed by the free shoe shine and shaving kits on offer in the men's lavatory; he also noted somewhat derisively upon a visit to the illustrious Hammersmith Palais that even it was 'not so well kept as Mecca'.[42] Many other patrons also expressed preferences for one palais over another according to their relative comfort levels, amenities and intangible factors, such as 'atmosphere'. However, other reasons for selecting a specific hall tended to be more practical in nature; someone venturing out for an evening's dancing often found it most convenient to visit the palais in their own neighbourhood, in order to avoid incurring the time and expense involved in travelling farther afield. In these ways, dance halls became part of the fabric of the community – a place where someone might pop in in the midst of their day or at the spur of the moment. One of Hughes's dance partners, for example, described her decision to visit the Streatham Locarno in south London, like this: 'I live quite close and as it was raining I came in.'[43]

Certain halls were also known for being 'better' on different nights, in which case patrons might make their choice about which hall to visit based simply on the day of the week, even if it meant travelling significant distances. One man stated in a Mass Observation questionnaire that he often journeyed more than an hour each way to visit specific Mecca halls, while another of Hughes's partners at the Locarno reported that she had come all the way to Streatham from north London, planned to dance in the morning session, have lunch and return for the afternoon's dancing.[44] Conversely, for some avid dancers, the popularity of a certain night was cause *not* to visit the palais then, since crowded floors made it much more difficult to dance correctly. As one woman observed to Hughes about the Locarno, 'Don't come at the weekends unless you enjoy a crush.'[45]

In choosing a palais, dance enthusiasts were also influenced by a hall's reputation for the quality – or 'standard' – of dancing, or which was their favourite dance to perform. Some halls were acknowledged as venues for those people who took dancing more seriously. Upon a visit to the Hammersmith Palais during a military posting during the Second World War, Captain J. S. Gray, a keen ballroom dancer then serving in uniform, recorded in his diary an admiration for the 'seriousness of the floor'.[46] When one mass observer admitted to being an inexperienced dancer to a potential partner at the Streatham Locarno, the young woman told him: 'If you want to learn this isn't a very good place. There are lots of snobs here who turn their noses up and won't dance if they see you aren't very good.'[47] Hughes, who spent more time at the Locarno than anywhere else, noted upon a visit to another hall – the Paramount – that the 'Dancing is always more showy here than other Mecca places.'[48] Certain halls also became more associated than others with specific dances from the English style canon. As one writer for *Popular Music and Dancing Weekly* observed in 1924, 'in my peregrinations over London … I had discovered that … whereas at some halls fox trots are all the rage, at others, not many miles distant, the one step or the blues held sway'.[49] Correspondence between the *Dancing Times* and dance hall proprietors throughout the 1930s further confirmed this state of affairs. Different managers from around the country mentioned every one of the standard four as the preferred dance in their establishment; while the foxtrot, quickstep and waltz were the most commonly referenced, other halls catered to the smaller number of tango enthusiasts or to those who favoured 'old-time' dancing.[50] A related concern was the style of music played in one hall over another. Depending on their preferences, patrons selected a ballroom based on the band's tendency to play 'hot' jazz or strict tempo dance music; since many bands had permanent gigs at specific dance halls, choices were also influenced by the quality or fame of the musicians. Therefore, despite the efforts of companies like Mecca to create a standard experience at all their halls, Britons made clear choices in determining which hall to patronise based on a wide variety of considerations.

The frequency with which people visited a public dancing space was also strongly variable. Enthusiastic dance hall patrons such as the woman described above, who was keen to dance during two sessions in the same day, were not uncommon. Another woman Hughes questioned reported she 'Goes dancing every night in the week. [I ask] her if she doesn't get fed up with it. She seems surprised and says no!'[51] Still another partner, now thirty years of age, reported that when she was a bit younger she 'used to practically live here', and 'never missed a Saturday night unless [she] was ill in bed'.[52] However, the men and women reflected in the Mass Observation reports represented a wide range between those who danced regularly and those who danced almost never. At a special morning dance held on Easter Monday 1939, for example, Hughes wrote this of his various partners: 'Three … report being frequent dancers;

one tends to watch from café; one does not comment; one says she does not dance very much.'[53]

As the second partner on that list reveals, some visitors to dance halls were not there to dance at all, or at least not solely to dance. This fact is borne out by the reduced entry fee many halls provided for those who simply wanted access to the balcony rather than to enter the ballroom proper. These non-dancers enjoyed observing the general dancing (which some saw as a way to improve their own skills), watching the cabaret and exhibitions, and listening to the music of the band. In fact, at dance halls that featured musicians of considerable renown, jazz enthusiasts who cared little for dancing might be drawn to the palais entirely for the purpose of enjoying the music. In his autobiography, historian Eric Hobsbawm described the experience of visiting a dance hall in order to hear Duke Ellington play, where he and his companion '[nursed] single beers in the gallery as we despised the slowly heaving mass of South London dancers below, who were concentrating on their partners and not on the wonderful noises'.[54] In addition, there were naturally those who visited the palais with minimal interest in any of the entertainments provided: these were sites for the enjoyment of food and drink, socialising with friends, and pursuing romantic interests, and the decision to visit the dance hall, or to choose one ballroom over another, was influenced by all of these factors.

Indeed, for many Britons their knowledge of the other patrons strongly affected their choice of venue, and this fact was utilised by management to attract the clientele they preferred or from whom they would most benefit financially. People were more likely to visit a hall at which they had friends and acquaintances, a reality which caused the enterprising manager of the Aberdeen Palais to implement a policy whereby patrons arriving within the first fifteen minutes after the hall opened could bring one friend in for free.[55] This tendency to seek out or bring friends along when dancing contributed to a contemporary belief that dance halls were often 'cliquey'. The Mass Observation reports reveal that Hughes experienced this cliquey-ness often enough himself, turned down for dances by women who preferred to stick with their friends. Certain halls also catered to different social, ethnic or racial groups. The Royal dance hall in north London was known as a 'Jewish hall', and, as Judith Walkowitz has shown, the Astoria on Charing Cross Road, was also popular with young women from the Jewish community.[56] The Paramount dance hall on Tottenham Court Road typically attracted a more racially diverse clientele than any other, and age also had an impact on dance hall clientele.

As an article about dancing in Birmingham featured in *Popular Music and Dancing Weekly* attested, Tony's Ballroom attracted people of all ages – though the writer noted that the 'grey-haired' patrons were typically more interested in listening to the music than dancing – while another of Birmingham's halls, the West End dance hall, was dominated by the young. These distinctions could be influenced by decisions of the management, as was the case with the West End hall, whose manager specifically told the author, 'We do not cater here for anyone but young people'.[57]

Of all demographic and social factors, the ones that shaped dance hall patronage the most were region and class. Despite companies like Mecca's quest for a national dancing experience, there were inevitable disparities in terms of access to high quality dancing facilities for Britons of distinct geographic areas and social positions. The commercial dance hall chains were mainly confined to large urban centres like Glasgow, Manchester, Newcastle, Birmingham, Liverpool, Cardiff, Edinburgh and, of course London, as well as popular holiday destinations like Brighton and Blackpool. In terms of class, in a reversal of the usual mechanisms of social hierarchies, it was actually the upper classes that were at a disadvantage in terms of access to quality dancing facilities. It was not until the mid to late 1930s that public dance halls like Mecca's began successfully drawing in a more cross-class clientele, and the palais, with its superior facilities for dancing, was largely patronised by the working and lower middle classes. So while the expansion of the dance hall industry was critical to the creation of a standardised public dancing experience, it was never a wholly completed project; there remained numerous other types of spaces and opportunities for dancing outside of the home.

Though small town Britons did not have access to the multiple public dancing options presented to city-dwellers, most medium-sized towns and cities did maintain at least one dance hall. Dancing was also held in a number of public spaces beyond the palais in both urban and rural areas alike, including dancing schools, municipal and institutional halls, public houses, baths and swimming pools, churches, hotels, restaurants, and in outdoor spaces, such as parks. Dances of this variety were more likely to be patronised by a locale clientele – those based in the same neighbourhood, village or surrounding area. Many villages staged a weekly dance, usually on Saturday night, which drew heavily from local populations with far fewer leisure opportunities than urban Britons. Village dances therefore fulfilled the needs of dancing enthusiasts, but also served an important community function, bringing together local dancers and non-dancers alike in a social setting.

The nature of the facilities provided for dancing in spaces beyond the purpose-built palais was naturally extremely varied. Often there was no live band, but rather music provided by a piano or gramophone. The dance floor was also likely to be far inferior to the palais's wood-sprung splendour. For example, upon attending a dance at the Forester's Hall in Canterbury, an observer for Mass Observation noticed that the floor on which attendees danced was still marked out as a badminton court.[58] Gray's wartime diary described a village dance in Church Stretton, at which the hall was illuminated only by oil lamps.[59] Dances of this type were often very crowded, and very hot. Yet whatever their limitations, dances held beyond the purpose-built palais were also increasingly commercialised as the interwar period progressed, usually operated by independent promoters. These entrepreneurs rented out spaces in which to provide dances, used the entry fees to cover costs, and then pocketed the difference. Interviews conducted by Mass Observation in the late 1930s revealed that many dance promoters, particularly in cities, were working-class men who held other jobs during the day, and ran dances in the evenings as a way of making a little extra money.[60] Their dances largely catered to a clientele from the same social class, and with entry fees of sometimes as little as three or six pence, they were an even cheaper option for dancing than the palais.

At the other end of the urban social spectrum were the hotels, restaurants, and nightclubs which formed the primary dancing opportunities for the elite. While dancing was a main feature of these establishments, it was not the primary focus that it was in the palais. Restaurants and hotels tended to provide meals as well as dancing; nightclubs often featured some sort of cabaret entertainment.[61] These ballrooms were generally far inferior to the palais in terms of the facilities that they could provide for dancing. As Cecil Taylor told Mass Observation,

> In restaurant and hotel dances one seldom looks or expects to find good dancing. The floors are too small and are always crowded. They all look alike because they are brought down to what we call "crush" that is [when the] dancers have to crush their steps into a small space.[62]

A writer for the *Daily Mirror* noted similarly in 1935 that particularly the West End hotels and restaurants were poorly equipped for 'real dancing', remarking that 'Hammersmith and Cricklewood could teach Mayfair a thing or two'.[63]

As these comments underlined, many contemporaries, particularly within the dance profession, were highly derisive of both the facilities and the standard of the dancing in upper-class venues, and reserved far more praise for the dancers who frequented the palais. As Josephine Bradley observed in 1935, 'it is good to see how the big public dance places have grown all over the country, for that is where you will always see the best ball-room dancing, not in the smart places of the West End of London'.[64] Significantly, while the upper-class dance clubs had been the centre of British popular dance in the period before the First World War, the advent of the public dance hall era transferred the greatest degree of influence to palais patrons, despite their lower status within the social hierarchy. These lower and middle class Britons played a pivotal role in shaping the national dancing style – so much so that amateur dancers seeking to perfect their skills, even from higher up the social ladder increasingly turned to the palais as the interwar period progressed. Resistance to cross-class moves of this type remained. The novice dancer, described in the previous chapter, who wrote to the *Dancing Times* to complain about the quality of dancing on cruises and other ballrooms he frequented, was advised by other correspondents to seek out the palais as an alternative. However, in another letter, he was clearly disinclined to this notion: 'I don't much like the idea of giving up the comforts of good hotels and restaurants, and the society of my friends, to discard my usual evening dress for [an] old suit of clothes … and go out in search of unknown partners at the cheaper type of ballrooms, however excellent these places may be.'[65] But regardless of classist concerns such as these, by the late 1930s, it was the predominately at the palais where new dances were demonstrated, trends took hold, competitions were hosted, and the highest standard of dancing was seen.

It was therefore also in the dance halls where critical negotiations over the national style and experience of popular dance occurred between the dancing public, dance profession and dance hall industry. How patrons consumed the dancing and other entertainments provided by the dance hall was wide-ranging, and suggestive about their divergent concerns. As was shown in Chapter 2, the dance profession's activities were guided by what it perceived to be the marked preferences and disinclinations exhibited by the dancing public when it came to the standard dances of the English style of ballroom dance. Professionals believed casual dancers tended to favour the foxtrot and quickstep, were relatively comfortable with the waltz, and spurned or feared the tango and the blues. For the most part, the evidence for the goings-on in public dance halls bears out the perceptions of the profession as to the preferred dances. One report for Mass Observation recounted that when 'the lights go up for a Quickstep' there was 'a great surge onto the floor'.[66] On another occasion Hughes observed that the 'floor crowded immediately' for every quickstep, foxtrot and waltz. And equally, when the band shifted from playing a foxtrot or quickstep to a tango, there was typically a significant exodus from the dance floor.[67] Dance hall managers clearly responded to the widespread anxieties about the tango by instructing their bands to play fewer of them; Hughes's notes suggest that on a typical evening at a Mecca hall, there would be only four tangoes for every dozen quicksteps.

Yet the Mass Observation materials also give voice to the segment of the dancing public that sincerely enjoyed the more challenging dances, and worked hard to perfect their nuances. As one avid dancer wrote, 'one special feature which attracts me [to Mecca halls] is that you include in your Dance Programmes, plenty of Tangos, some "Blues" ... and after all the keen dancer <u>does</u> like plenty of Tangos and blues, as a change from the round of Quicksteps, Foxtrots and so on'.[68] Hughes also noted in one report that although the tango brought fewer couples to the floor, for those present the 'Standard of dancing [was] high and all have different forms of the dance.'[69] Importantly, in these observations the complexity of the public reception of the tango specifically, and popular dance more generally, are exposed. While the majority of British dancers did not possess the time or inclination to learn more complicated dances like the tango, the dancing public was constituted of a diverse group; it was composed of those happy to do a passable shuffle across the floor, and those very interested in perfecting their dance skills, and everything in between.

In Hughes's observations as to the variety of tango steps, the public ballroom is also revealed to be a space of innovation, creativity, and self-expression for many within the dancing public. More so than arguably anywhere else in Europe or North America during this period, by the late 1930s there was a correct way to dance in Britain; this had been promulgated and reinforced by the standardisation of steps by the dance profession, and disseminated to the public via dancing classes, exhibitions, competitions, and print culture. But in the Mass Observation reports there is strong evidence of British dancers operating beyond these parameters. They experimented with new steps and figures, and even chose to dance something different than what was being played by the band. In the face of the dreaded tango, for example, dancers might leave the floor, or they might simply perform a foxtrot to a tango tune. As the swing variety of jazz was popularised in the 1930s, dancers began incorporating some of its associated dance steps, such as 'Suzie-B' or 'truckin', into their ballroom dancing. Hughes observed on one occasion at the Locarno,

> [It is] interesting to watch the dancing styles. A quickstep was in progress. About 250 couples on the floor – band playing fairly hot rhythm. There is a great variety of steps … In this dance noticed two couples which indulged in hot-rhythm – man and woman breaking away from each other [and] doing a sort of truckin' cum Charleston.[70]

This type of experimentation occurred in direct opposition to the standard steps advocated by dance professionals, but also to dance hall proprietors and their bands, who chose the sequence and frequency of the different dances that would be featured on the programme.

British dancers challenged the experience being produced for them by dance hall industry in other ways as well. Regarding the cabaret, exhibitions and other diversions on offer during an evening at the palais, patrons were most discerning. As one of the proprietors of Tony's ballroom in Birmingham told the *Dancing Times* in 1934, 'It is … essential at the present time to offer outstanding attractions, of which the present generation of the dancing public are more than exacting.'[71] On an earlier occasion the magazine had itself observed, 'Young and enthusiastic dancers begrudge the time given over to Cabaret – sometimes they even resent the short five minutes devoted to an exhibition couple.'[72] As was shown in Chapter 2, beyond entertainment, exhibitions were designed to help the members of the audience improve their dancing, and typically featured the hall's staff of professionals performing a demonstration of one of the standard four. While some patrons enjoyed exhibitions, particularly if a renowned dance team performed, others were ambivalent about or even hostile to these intervals. Those who were serious about dancing resented the interruption to their practice time, while other patrons who were less interested in perfecting their technique preferred to focus on the other attractions that brought them to the palais.

As the dance hall industry consolidated, proprietors also used demonstrations to introduce new dances. By the late 1930s, Mecca in particular used its stable of dance teachers to continually create (or adapt) and then present original dances to patrons of their halls. The primary goal of these initiatives was to enliven the proceedings, sustain interest in dancing (especially at Mecca halls), and to market sheet music, instructional materials, and a range of other products associated with the new dance. Significantly, dance hall staff and management expressed every confidence in their ability to sway the public as to the merits of a new dance, in a way that demonstrated their awareness and deployment of their influence as a commercial producer. Charles Chaperlin, the manager of the Locarno, told Hughes in an interview that there was an 'art' to getting people to dance, based on the 'atmosphere' of the hall, and energy of the band. As Chaperlin contended, 'It is the way that a bandleader puts his stuff across that makes the dance successful. If they do it properly the people have no option about dancing. They can't resist it.'[73] Even the cloakroom attendant at one of the Mecca halls expressed the belief that the public could be persuaded to attempt any dance by management and the professional dancers: 'Oh they'll do anything. If you give them [a] cannibal costume and asked them to do a cannibal dance they'd do it.'[74]

Yet once again the observer reports reveal that the reception of a new dance was not always so straightforward. Despite the Mecca staff's conviction that they could convince their patrons to perform anything, the response to new dances was strongly variable. It also varied from night to night, hall to hall: in one place a new dance might be a roaring success, while in another it might fall flat. Very often the crowd on the floor was happy to join in after professionals exhibited a new dance, or try it out once the general dancing had recommenced. In one instance, following a demonstration of the new American dance, the jitterbug, at the Locarno in January 1939, Hughes noted, 'Later when the dancing started again [I] noticed in a [quickstep] at least 3 couples trying some of the steps.'[75] Other times, however, dance hall patrons responded with ambivalence or open defiance to the demonstration of a new dance. Hughes's description of the premiere of a dance called the yam to the crowd at the Streatham Locarno in February 1939 is illustrative. On that occasion, after the formal demonstration of the dance by Mecca professionals, 'There was then an attempt to get the public to attempt the 'Yam', and three minutes of empty floor followed.' Despite this failure, manager Chaperlin remained confident in his general ability to put a dance over, telling Hughes that his mistake on the occasion of the yam debut had been not taking the microphone and leading the demonstration himself: 'I could kick myself for not having taken it. You can make them do anything if you get them the right way.'[76]

In such cases, the dancing's public's resistance to new offerings arose from any number of sources. The yam, for instance, was fairly complicated; only a small number of patrons felt comfortable attempting it in the immediate aftermath of the demonstration, although Hughes did witness a few more experimenting with the dance during the next foxtrot that was played. As will be shown in more detail through an analysis of Mecca's novelty dances in Chapter 6, the reasons for the success or failure of a dance introduced at the palais were wide-ranging and unpredictable. Just like the dance profession, the dance hall industry continually presented the dancing public with new options, but it then fell to their patrons to determine whether a dance would be successful; some new dances they embraced, while others they rejected, while still others they reimagined and reshaped on the ballroom floor in the moment of dance. This varied reception of new dances, along with all other aspects of the dance hall experience – from the songs played by the band, to the dances on the programme, to the cabaret or other special events – reveal a dynamic and interactive relationship between the dance hall industry and dancing public.

Within these interactions, the dance hall industry retained – as the dance profession did – significant cultural power. So much of popular dance was mediated by commercial producers before ever reaching the dancing public. Yet critically, this influence was something of which contemporary dancers occasionally expressed awareness. For instance, when asked by Mecca, in coordination with Mass Observation, what improvements could be made to the experience of their dance halls, one respondent suggested that new dances such as the carioca and swing step might be played more often since 'the mecca agency is large enough to make or break any dance'.[77] As this comment revealed, in the face of a dominant commercial leisure entity, such as Mecca, British dancers were often able to discern the company's motivations and manipulations in introducing new dances or determining the programme; they operated within these structures, according to their distinct preferences, priorities and reasons for visiting the palais.

Adding even more nuance to this picture is the fact that the experience of a public ballroom was also one that could be glimpsed and participated in from a distance. Even those Britons who never visited a dance hall were exposed to the goings-on within them via other cultural forms. Naturally dance-themed print culture, but also the popular press paid considerable attention to what transpired in ballrooms around the country. Readers of the *Dancing Times* encountered numerous articles and columns about events at different venues, while *Popular Music and Dancing Weekly* likewise featured a column entitled 'Around the Dance Halls' in every issue, and regularly undertook focused research into the nation's different dance halls. Mecca's Danceland Publications also produced a number of newspapers, magazines and pamphlets which provided thorough accounts of all of the events occurring in Mecca halls. Yet while the dance press enjoyed a significant readership, it did not have the widespread reach possessed by the popular press (especially among non-dancers), and the latter was also an important vehicle for disseminating knowledge of dance hall culture. Every type of newspaper from small locals to national dailies featured content about popular dance, often with specific coverage of events in public ballrooms. By way of example, the *Liverpool Echo* featured such a column entitled 'Dancing Time on Merseyside', while the *Daily Sketch* and *The Star* were important sponsors of prominent dance competitions.

Another critical vehicle for the dissemination of dance hall knowledge was the popular music industry, which, as Nott has shown, successfully marketed the same dance music enjoyed in public dancing spaces to Britons of all classes and regions.[78] The rapid growth of music publishing and record production, and the mass-marketing of gramophones and sheet music during the interwar years enabled even those Britons who never stepped foot in a public ballroom to stay abreast of what was currently in favour. Dance music was also disseminated to non-dancers via the radio. The expansion of the 'wireless' into the homes of Britons was accomplished at a frantic pace in the interwar years; by 1939, there were over nine million BBC licence-holders, and radio listeners, according to Asa Briggs, 'constituted a representative cross-section of the British public'.[79] Dance music was a staple part of the programming at the BBC and at competing commercial radio stations on the Continent, and the radio became another critical conduit for the circulation of popular dance to listening Britons. The plethora of dance songs heard over the radio helped to increase public interest in the dances that could be performed to them, and also allowed listeners to stay current as to the most popular ballroom dance music, even if they rarely went dancing themselves. As *Popular Music and Dancing Weekly* noted in 1926, '[Dance music] is a very popular part of the broadcasting programmes, because even those people who do not dance – a very small number nowadays – enjoy listening to the rhythmic, time-perfect syncopation to which few can resist tapping out the beats with their feet.'[80] The influence of the radio in spreading music and dance to the nation was perhaps best illustrated in the case of the Lambeth Walk, the greatest song and dance phenomenon of the late 1930s; in a survey conducted by Mass Observation, almost half of those queried indicated that they had first heard about the Lambeth Walk over the radio, not in the dance hall.[81]

However, it was not only dance music that could be brought to Britons via the radio, but the whole experience of an evening's dancing. Much of the music heard on the BBC was not transmitted from a studio, but from a public ballroom in which one of Britain's many famous dance bands played for actual dancers. In the 1920s, dance bands were typically based in a London hotel ballroom. Henry Hall played the Gleneagles Hotel Ballroom, while Jack Payne was at the Hotel Cecil; there were also two bands in residence at the Savoy hotel – the Savoy Orpheans and the Savoy Havana bands. With the continued development of the dance hall industry, even more musicians began broadcasting from public ballrooms, such as Joe Loss's band, which performed from the Astoria dance hall on Charing Cross Road. The widespread popularity of these broadcasts was put on vivid display in 1926, when the BBC made plans to halt the transmission of the various Savoy bands, but backed down in the face of huge public outcry. As the *Daily Mail* reported, the hotel and BBC reopened negotiations entirely 'owing to the wishes of a large number of listeners that the bands should continue to broadcast'.[82]

More than merely offering entertainment, these broadcasts provided listeners at home with knowledge of public dancing spaces that they might never visit personally. They could hear the applause of the dancers, and imagine them moving about the floor, joining in from their own sitting room if they so chose. As one woman recalled in her memoir, 'I have memories of trying to teach my brother to dance by guiding him around the living room floor to the strains of Victor Sylvester's [sic] orchestra issuing from the old wireless set and to the detriment of my toes, but we managed a passable waltz.'[83] The *Dancing Times* also attested to the widespread reach of the ballroom broadcasts, observing that 'these orchestras, when broadcasting, are playing to thousands upon thousands of the British public, and not only the few hundred revellers at ultra fashionable hotels and clubs in the heart of the West End of London'.[84] Broadcasts of dance orchestras thus provided a shared experience for listeners and dancers throughout the nation. As another writer remarked, 'sometimes when the music of the Savoy bands is coming "over the air" one pauses to think of the millions of feet that are moving in time with their saxophones and banjos'.[85] Bandleader Ramon Newton similarly described the influence of the radio on popular dance, writing that 'To-day, with the aid of this wonderful invention, a song that would probably never have been heard at either John O'Groats or Land's End, is known there as quickly as it is known and appreciated by those who dance to the Savoy Havana Band … while those thousands of others listen in, they are visualising the scene of happiness that the dancers create.'[86] Through these broadcasts, millions of Britons at the far reaches of the country were able participate in a simultaneous and communal experience of popular dance, and to share awareness of the most current trends whether or not they were enthusiastic dancers themselves.

As the motion picture industry transitioned from the silent to sound eras, film began to play a similar role to the radio in disseminating the dance hall experience to non-dancers. Approximately one sixth of the output of British filmmakers in the 1930s were musical films, and prominent dance bands commonly made appearances on cinema screens, playing music for dancers just as they did on the radio.[87] As one writer observed with respect to the number of famous bandleaders appearing in dancing films, 'only a few thousand people can hope to see such stars as Harry Roy, Henry Hall and Jack Hylton even when they go on tour, but with a film every little village gets a chance of seeing the men who entertain them on the air'.[88] The cinema, as Britain's most widespread leisure activity, was a critical means through which the experience of the dance hall was disseminated to the nation.

The experience of 'public' dancing was thus one that could be obtained in a wide variety of ways – even in the privacy of one's own home. The dancing public was constituted from a diverse group of Britons consuming popular dance to widely varying degrees in a multitude of different ways. There were those people who frequented public ballrooms and participated in the dancing. Yet even this group was not homogeneous, since people ventured out dancing with distinctive purposes and preferences. Beyond the walls of the palais, there were other Britons who listened to dance music on the radio, perhaps getting up to quickstep around the sitting room, but perhaps not. There were also those who merely read about or saw on film the latest occurrences and innovations in popular dance, without attempting to perform them or even learn more about them, but by which they were influenced. As time passed, and commercial leisure expanded in all realms and directions, popular dance became ever more ubiquitous and influential within British society. While not everyone could be found 'at the palais', the vast majority Britons were affected by popular dance, and the social issues and cultural meanings that were fostered by and forged through this leisure form.

Notes

1 MOA: TC 38/6/G, The Imperial Society of Teachers of Dancing (19 June 1939), p. 7.
2 'The Palais de Danse and the Profession: A Suggestion', *Dancing Times* (February 1926), p. 558.
3 James Nott, *Music for the People: Popular Music and Dance in Interwar Britain* (Oxford: Oxford University Press, 2002), p. 149.

4 'Public Dancing Halls', *Daily Mail* (20 January, 1919), p. 4.

5 'Super-Palace of Dancing', *Daily Express* (29 October, 1919), p. 7.

6 'Some Extracts from the Diary of Mr. Terpsichore-Pepys, 1919', *Dancing Times* (January 1920), p. 291.

7 Draycot M. Dell, 'Dance Halls of To-Day', *Popular Music and Dancing Weekly* (29 March 1924), p. 194.

8 Nott, *Music for the People*, pp. 153–4.

9 Robert Sandall, 'Light Fantastic', *London Daily News*, (2 June 1987), p. 23. Clipping from Hammersmith Borough Archives.

10 James McMillan, *The Way it Was, 1914–1934* (London: William Kimber & Company, 1979), p. 145.

11 'The Palais de Danse and the Profession: A Suggestion', p. 558.

12 See Nott, *Music for the People*, pp. 168–177.

13 Nott, *Music for the People*, p. 170.

14 Mona Vivian, 'Has the Dance "Craze" Come to Stay?' *Popular Music and Dancing Weekly* (10 January 1925), p. 229.

15 Draycot M. Dell, 'Dance Halls of To-day. No. 3 – Finsbury Park Palais de Danse', *Popular Music and Dancing Weekly* (22 March 1924), p. 177.

16 Nott, *Music for the People*, p. 170.

17 'Nottingham's Dancing Problem is … Too Many Girls!' *Popular Music and Dancing Weekly* (8 December 1934), p. 20.

18 Nott, *Music for the People*, p. 171.

19 Draycot M. Dell, 'Dance Halls of To-Day', *Popular Music and Dancing Weekly*, (15 March, 1924), p. 148.

20 'Modern Roman Palace', *Daily Express* (1 March 1920), p. 7.

21 'Diary of Mr. Terpsichore-Pepys, 1919', p. 291.

22 Draycot M. Dell, 'Dance Hall's of To-day. No. 1 – Wimbledon Palais de Danse', *Popular Music and Dancing Weekly*, (8 March 1924), p. 124; 'Nottingham's Dancing Problem is…Too Many Girls!', p. 20.

23 Horace Richards, 'Come Dancing Around Britain, No. 5 – Bright Bands at "Brum"!' *Popular Music and Dancing Weekly* (29 December 1934), p. 16.

24 'Tea Table Talk', *Daily Express* (24 February 1920), p. 3.

25 Nott, *Music for the People*, p. 171.

26 See Mica Nava, *Visceral Cosmopolitanism: Gender, Culture, and the Normalisation of Difference* (Oxford: Berg, 2007), pp. 19–40.

27 'The Wembley, Wibbly, Wobbly Dance', *Popular Music and Dancing Weekly* (14 June 1924), p. 150.

28 Margaret Black, 'On With the Dance – At Wembley', *Popular Music and Dancing Weekly* (5 July 1924), p. 208.

29 Nott, *Music for the People*, pp. 172–3.

30 Dell, 'Dance Hall's of To-day. No. 1', p. 124.

31 Nott, *Music for the People*, p. 157.

32 Tom Harrisson and Charles Madge, *Britain by Mass-Observation* (London: Harmondsworth, 1939), p. 141.

33 As quoted in Roma Fairley, *Come Dancing Miss World* (London: Newman Neame, 1966), p. 4.

34 Fairley, *Come Dancing Miss World*, pp. 20–2.

35 MOA: TC 38/3/A, C.L. Heimann (8 December 1938), p. 1.

36 For more on Heimann and the development of Mecca, see Nott, *Music for the People*, pp. 155–7. See also James Nott, *Going to the Palais: A Social and Cultural History of Dancing and Dance Halls in Britain, 1918–1960* (Oxford: Oxford University Press, 2015).

37 MOA: TC 38/3/A, C.L. Heimann, p. 2.

38 Irene Raines, 'London Ballroom News', *Dancing Times* (July 1939), p. 485.

39 MOA: TC 38/6/F, Danceland Questionnaire (April 1939).

40 Nott, *Music for the People*, p. 158.

41 Penny Summerfield, 'Mass-Observation: Social Research or Social Movement', *Journal of Contemporary History* 20:3 (July 1985): p. 440. See also Nick Hubble, *Mass Observation and Everyday Life: Culture, History, Theory* (London: Palgrave Macmillan, 2006); James Hinton, *The Mass Observers: A History, 1937-1949*, (Oxford: Oxford University Press, 2013).

42 MOA: TC 38/1/J, Hammersmith Palais (28 August 1939).

43 MOA: TC 38/1/A, Locarno (13 April 1939).

44 MOA: TC 38/6/F, Letter to the Mecca Agency (19 April 1939); MOA: TC 38/1/A, Easter Monday Morning (10 April 1939).

45 MOA: TC 38/1/A, Locarno (12 April 1939).

46 IWM: Documents.6498, Private Papers of Captain J S Gray (23 April 1944).

47 MOA: TC 38/1/A, Locarno (27 April 1939).

48 MOA: TC 38/1/B, Paramount (25 November 1939).

49 The Man Who Didn't Dance, 'The World's Greatest Dance-Hall', *Popular Music and Dancing Weekly* (2 February 1924), p. 32.

50 See the *Dancing Times*, October and/or November issues, between 1931 and 1939.

51 MOA: TC 38/1/A, Locarno (13 April 1939).

52 MOA: TC 38/1/A, Locarno (12 April 1939).

53 MOA: TC 38/1/A, Easter Monday Morning (10 April 1939).

54 Eric Hobsbawm, *Interesting Times: A Twentieth-Century Life* (London: Penguin Books, 2002), p. 81.

55 'The Coming Ballroom Season', *Dancing Times* (October 1933), p. 27.

56 Judith R. Walkowitz, *Nights Out: Life in Cosmopolitan London* (New Haven, CT: Yale University Press, 2012), pp. 183–94.

57 Richards, 'Come Dancing Around Britain, No. 5', p. 16.

58 MOA: TC 38/1/J, Forester's Hall (26 November 1938).

59 IWM: Documents.6498, Captain J S Gray (24 September 1941).

60 MOA: TC 38/2/A, Dance Promotion and Promoters.

61 On nightclubs, see Martin Pugh, *'We Danced All Night:' A Social History of Britain between the Wars* (London: The Bodley Head, 2008), pp. 216–20; Walkowitz, *Nights Out*, pp. 209–52.

62 MOA: TC 38/6/G, The Imperial Society of Teachers of Dancing (19 June 1939), p. 3.

63 Molly Carmichael, 'Watch Your Step', *Daily Mirror* (9 November 1935), p. 23.

64 Josephine Bradley, 'My "Cavalcade" of Dancing', *Popular Music and Dancing Weekly* (27 October 1934), p. 3.

65 Novice, Letter to the Editor, *Dancing Times*, December 1932, p. 298.

66 MOA: TC 38/1/A, Locarno (17 November 1938).

67 MOA: TC 38/1/A, Locarno (12 April 1939).

68 MOA: TC 38/6/F, Letter to the Mecca Agency (19 April 1939).

69 MOA: TC 38/1/A, Yam Night (23 February 1939).

70 MOA: TC 38/1/A, Yam Night (23 February 1939).

71 'The Coming Ballroom Season', *Dancing Times* (October 1934), pp. 43–4.

72 'A Word About Cabaret', *Dancing Times* (August 1924), p. 1060.

73 MOA: TC 38/3/F, Interview with Chaperlin (10 February 1939).

74 MOA: TC 38/1/A, Handsome Territorial Premiere (13 June 1939).

75 MOA: TC 38/1/A, Jitterbug Demonstration at Locarno (7 January 1939).

76 MOA: TC 38/1/A, Yam Night (23 February 1939).

77 MOA: TC 38/6/F, Danceland Questionnaire (April 1939).

78 See Nott, *Music for the People*.

79 Asa Briggs, *A History of Broadcasting in the United Kingdom, Volume II: The Golden Age of the Wireless* (London: Oxford University Press, 1965), p. 253.

80 Michael King, 'Playing to the World', *Popular Music and Dancing Weekly* (4 September 1926), p. 118.

81 Madge and Harrisson, *Britain*, p. 163.

82 'Savoy Bands to Keep on Broadcasting', *Daily Mail* (19 February 1926), p. 7.

83 IWM: Documents.94/370, Growing Pains: A Teenager's War, p. 51.

84 Ballroom Notes, *Dancing Times* (February 1926), p. 575.

85 King, 'Playing to the World', p. 118.

86 Ramon Newton, 'Hundreds of Miles of Music', *Popular Music and Dancing Weekly* (21 February 1925), p. 92.

87 Stephen Guy, 'Calling all stars: musical films in a musical decade', in Jeffrey Richards (ed.), *The Unknown 1930s: An Alternative History of the British Cinema, 1929–1939* (London: I.B. Tauris, 1998).

88 Howard Lawson, 'Band-leaders Are Becoming Film Stars', *Popular Music and Dancing Weekly* (20 July 1935), p. ii.

4

The dance evil: gender, sexuality and the representation of popular dance

In 1925, playwright J. Jefferson Farjeon wrote an article for the *Dancing Times* entitled 'The Dance Evil'. Despite its suggestive title, Farjeon's article was not an attack on dancing, but rather a lamentation over the way in which it was depicted on the stage. He argued that modern playwrights constantly vilified dancing in their work, although they themselves might not even be aware of it. The 'attacks are subtle', Farjeon wrote, 'the war is below the surface. Though we have yet to see the play entitled "Down with the Dance!" the war goes on, just the same.' Farjeon alleged that it was in the portrayal of characters who danced, or the settings in which dancing occurred on stage, which subtly maligned dancing. Pointing specifically to Noel Coward's latest play, *The Vortex*, Farjeon wrote that all the characters who danced were 'Vain people, silly people, dangerous flirts, and at least one drug-taker.' He further declared that while there was no direct condemnation of dancing in the play, 'in the author's attempt to portray a certain kind of atmosphere and a certain kind of company, dancing is brought in'. Significantly, Farjeon also acknowledged that Coward and other playwrights would undoubtedly protest against any accusation that they were denigrating dancing, because they were keen dancers themselves. In Farjeon's imagination, the other authors remonstrated: '"What is this? We don't condemn dancing! We dance ourselves!" or "What are you talking about? Dash it, sir! We *all* dance!"'[1]

In this article, Farjeon identified many of the negative cultural assumptions that circulated around popular dance, but also the strong tensions that existed between those assumptions and dancing's widespread popularity as a leisure form. He wrote his piece at the height of palais construction and just before the arrival of the Charleston – a moment of peak success for popular dance in Britain – but one during which the representation of this cultural form, its chief enthusiasts and professionals, and the public spaces where it took place, remained highly contested. In particular, dancing often sat at the centre of contemporary discourses of gender, class and sexuality, initiating reconsiderations of these categories of difference, while they in turn influenced how dancing was experienced and understood. This chapter will explore popular dance's central role in articulations of femininity and masculinity between the wars, as well as in the lived experiences of women and men. It will also show that public dance halls and paid dance partners were imbued with a taint of criminality and sexual immorality – underpinned by class – but that an active campaign was waged to ameliorate the reputations of both. An examination of the gendered discourses that surrounded dancing demonstrates that this leisure form was always prone to some degree of controversy, and was a site for the reification – but also the transgression – of lines of class, gender and sexuality. However, popular dance also became progressively more respectable and integrated into the national culture as the professionalisation and commercialisation processes described in the preceding chapters unfolded.

Butterflies and lounge lizards: popular dance and the redefinition of gender

In February 1920, the *Daily Express* published an opinion piece entitled 'The Dream Girl – And the Awakening', written by First World War veteran George E. Pearson. Describing the wartime experience, Pearson recalled, 'Out in France, or under the tropical sun, how often the temporary soldier saw in his cigarette smoke the face of a dear, affectionate, typical home-loving English girl … He would sigh and long for the day when again he could return to the "feminine" girl at home, and satisfy his heart's yearning.' Pearson claimed that this dream of finding such an ideal British woman to make his wife after the war was part of what helped him survive life in the trenches, yet he went on to describe feelings of shock and dismay upon his return to Britain, and his discovery that the 'dreamgirl' of his wartime fantasies no longer existed. Pearson suggested that while men had been sobered by their wartime experience, made more serious and learned the value of hard work, women had generally been changed for the worst. In dubbing this new embodiment of inferior femininity the 'dancing girl', Pearson also firmly articulated what he felt was her worst characteristic: a fanatical love of dancing. Under the heading 'Tired of Dancing', he reflected that prior to the war, dancing had been a pleasant diversion for both men and women, but that 'the girl of to-day lives only to dance. She is not happy unless the subject of conversation relates to the ballroom. Is this the type of wife that a man wants?' Pearson concluded his diatribe by noting that given the immense death-toll in the war, and the shortage of available husbands, the so-called dancing girl was 'doomed', and would be 'shelved'.[2]

These statements, and the article as a whole, created quite a stir, and over the next few weeks a national debate over the current state of British womanhood played out on the letters page of the *Daily Express*. Dozens of men and women weighed in on the discussion, and gradually two competing visions of British femininity were articulated and deconstructed. The so-called 'dreamgirl', the woman that Pearson suggested battle-weary men had been fantasising about throughout four long years of war and now favoured as a wife, was described as virtuous, modest, subdued, and fond of home and family. Her antithesis was the feminine figure alternately referred to as the 'modern woman', 'jazz-mad', the 'butterfly' or simply the 'dancing girl'. These women were said to be loud, flirtatious and lacking in good sense; they dressed provocatively, smoked and drank alcohol, and were above all obsessed with dancing.

Many of the initial letters received by the *Daily Express* in response to Pearson's article were written by men who whole-heartedly agreed with him, and who described their own disillusionment with the women they encountered upon returning to Britain after the war. Another veteran, who signed his letter 'Disappointed', wrote that while serving in Egypt he had also dreamed of 'the dear girls of home and the purity, brightness, and sweetness of the beautiful English home life'. Yet he had found upon his return that 'Instead of the girls of our fond imaginings we find them a madly given-over-to-dancing, theatre-going type. Not content with these as a mere diversion they have become in the present day an intoxicating passion.'[3] However, another large volume of mail came from women claiming to be the lost 'dreamgirl', and who lamented the advantages that their dance-mad sisters seemed to enjoy over them in attracting the opposite sex. As one woman wrote, 'it is not the quiet stay-at-home girl who gets the best time, however pretty she may be. It is the one who attends the dancing classes, smokes, and is out for a thorough go-ahead life, and the men seem to prefer her.'[4] This letter, and others like it, quickly inspired a whole new round of mail from men seeking to reassure these 'stay-at-home girls', and which condemned the dancing girl in even more vociferous terms. As one man asserted, 'The majority of men much prefer a girl of modest disposition – that is, one who does not smoke, flirt, or jazz.'[5] Another man similarly commented that 'no serious thinking man would ever ... look for his "dream girl" in a jazz-hall or night club'.[6] The position of many male correspondents is perhaps best summed up in a short statement by 'Lonely', who declared, 'The best women ... do not frequent the dance'.[7]

Despite the clear antipathy being directed towards dancing girls on the part of some veterans and frustrated dreamgirls, not all of the mail received by the *Daily Express* endorsed this castigation of women who danced. In fact, much of the significance of this debate resides in its illustration of how contested ideas about women – and dancing – actually were in the first years after the war. A letter written by 'A Girl of Nineteen' asked what was so wrong about young women having a little fun prior to marriage, when they would inevitably settle down and become 'serious'?[8] Other defenders of dancing women turned their wrath on the so-called dreamgirls, with one writer proclaiming that the reason these women could not find a husband was because they were desperate and narrow-minded, as demonstrated by their viewing 'harmless pastimes and pretty clothes as not quite "comme il faut"'.[9] Less contentiously, other correspondents argued that an enthusiasm for dancing did not necessarily imply excessive frivolity or immorality. Two self-described widows wrote the newspaper together to explain that, 'not all girls who frequent the dance hall go because they are of a frivolous turn of mind, but because they, too, are lonely and seek companionship'.[10] Another woman asserted that a desire to dance was not a sign of bad character, but rather that dancing simply provided a necessary outlet for women who were otherwise very serious and hard-working:

> Why do your correspondents persistently classify us into two groups – the dancing girl and the quiet, stay-at-home? Is there no combination of the two? Many a girl, after she leaves business, has to assist at home to relieve an overworked mother ... and yet we still find time to enjoy our youth, to go to dances and to fling dull care away. Are we to be counted heartless because of this?[11]

Nor were female dancing enthusiasts the only ones to argue that women could be industrious, devoted to family and fun-loving at the same time; to be 'dreamgirl' and 'butterfly' simultaneously. About a week after Pearson's original article appeared, the *Daily Express* printed another opinion piece on the question of British femininity by editor A. Beverley Baxter. Baxter was also a veteran who acknowledged Pearson's dreamgirl as a common fantasy during the war, but went on to argue that this was an emotional reaction to the front lines, and that 'this classifying of the elusive feminine into types is absurd'.[12]

This national dialogue continued in the pages of the *Daily Express* for over a month, and offered a vivid illustration of the dramatic challenges to the gender order that came during the war and its aftermath. Historians have well documented that, on the one hand, women's important contribution to the war effort as workers and sacrificing wives and mothers was acknowledged and rewarded with enfranchisement in 1918. On the other hand, the increased employment opportunities and greater personal independence that the war created for women was a subject of considerable social and political concern; the war had also reified traditional feminine roles – particularly associated with motherhood – as much as it had tested them, and the question of marriage, and what to do with the millions of 'surplus' women who were unlikely to marry given the numbers of men killed in the war, was a source of particular consternation. At the same time, the war's destructive impact on Victorian visions of martial masculinity, as well as on the lives, bodies and psyches of individual men, further destabilised gender relations.[13] The dreamgirl and butterfly debate was reflective of many aspects of this broader context, but also highlighted just how profoundly dancing was implicated in – and constitutive of – post-war gender anxieties.

In a moment of unsettled gender relations, dancing became a critical node around which ideas about both femininity and masculinity were expressed and contested. At the same time, gender shaped how popular dance – in a strongly transformative moment of its own – was represented and experienced. Social concerns of the 1920s centred on the so-called 'modern woman', also referred to as the flapper or – tellingly – the dancing girl, who was characterised by her short hair and more boyish fashions, lack of sexual inhibition and propensity for drinking, smoking, driving cars and general pursuit of pleasure. Yet significantly, these discourses exposed as much about contemporary views of dancing as they did about women – as did the fact that the dancing girl had a male counterpart. A close study of the shifting views of both the women and men who danced helps to unpack the efforts to redefine gender roles in the interwar years, and highlights the changing perception of dancing as a leisure form. While the representation and social position of dancing men and women was often negative, it was not exclusively so: dance enthusiasts of both sexes consistently defended their favoured pastime, and so did others on their behalf. In addition, as processes of standardisation and commercialisation helped to integrate popular dance into the national culture, it became a more respectable pursuit for women and men alike; it was also increasingly feminised as an experience and marketable commodity.

One of the principal sites where social concerns about popular dance and modern womanhood were closely intertwined was in the popular press. National daily newspapers in particular were a site which often (although not exclusively) reaffirmed traditional understandings of femininity and domesticity, and provided strong criticisms of modern women, who were largely represented as morally ambiguous, ill-equipped for women's conventional role as wife and mother, and excessively pleasure-seeking.[14] In this context, dancing was by far one of the most frequent examples deployed in order to document this immoderate pursuit of a good time. For instance, in the same month as the *Daily Express's* dreamgirl and butterfly controversy, another press debate illustrated the potential for even more harsh condemnations of dance-mad women. The fervour erupted in the wake of a lecture by Dr Murray Leslie at the Institute for Hygiene about the millions of 'surplus' women created by the war, which received widespread attention around the country. Within his comments Leslie suggested that the disproportion between the sexes was leading to an 'extraordinary diversity of type' among British women, and that more prevalent than ever was 'the frivolous, scantily clad, jazzing flapper … to whom a dance, a new hat, or a man with a car were of more importance than the fate of nations'.[15] He further commented that women's obsession with dancing meant that the men who were on offer as partners were in huge demand and inundated with invitations to dances. In this case, the resulting letters to the editor of the *Daily Mail* (at least the ones that were published), generally endorsed Leslie's criticisms of dancing girls. As one man expounded on the difficulty some women confronted in the marriage market, '"The frivolous, scantily clad, jazzing flappers, irresponsible and undisciplined" … are themselves a reason why so many men shrink from matrimony.'[16] Another correspondent's letter demonstrated that the controversies surrounding dancing girls had the potential to transform not only how people felt about modern womanhood – but about dancing. In direct response to Leslie's comments about the high demand for male dance partners, 'A Young Dancing Man' complained, 'As one of these unfortunates, I suggest that the worst thing any young man can do is to learn to dance. One he does so he becomes a slave to dancing, he spends all his money on it, and he never has a moment of his own from dancing.'[17]

The associations between dancing and frivolous, immoral behaviour by women also extended beyond discussions that were directly about the flapper/butterfly. In a divorce proceeding between a Mr and Mrs Everitt, which received extensive press coverage, Mrs Everitt was accused of adultery with a neighbourhood doctor. As the case progressed Mrs Everitt was painted as a repeat adulteress, bad mother and frequenter of nightclubs. Her husband's lawyer also pointed to Mrs Everitt's propensity for throwing weekend and evening parties that featured dancing to gramophone music, and the doctor's regular presence at these events, as further proof of her bad character and adultery. A wild picture of dancing, drinking, and debauchery was painted before the courts. However, in the judge's summation he cautioned the court not to assume that simply because Mrs Everitt enjoyed jazz and dancing she must be guilty of immorality. The very fact that the judge felt he had to make such a statement at all is revealing about contemporary notions that associated dancing with moral laxity and bad behaviour.[18] Nor was the Everitt case the only court case to reinforce the moral ambiguity that surrounded female dance enthusiasts. As Lucy Bland has shown, dancing – as a pastime or form of employment – was a prominent part of the ambiguous characterisations of women at the centre of several high profile slander, drug and murder trials in the early 1920s.[19]

Criticisms of dancing women also filtered into politics. While the Representation of the People Act 1918 granted the vote to British women for the first time, it did so only for those over thirty years of age, and social concerns about the flapper directly contributed to this continued disenfranchisement of younger women.[20] As efforts to extend the franchise more broadly persisted throughout the 1920s, the debate created yet another site where dancing was drawn upon to demarcate the difference between the productive and deleterious elements of British womanhood. In 1927, while presiding over the annual conference of the Women's Unionist Organisation, the group's chair, Lady Evelden, emphatically proclaimed that 'the great majority of women between 21 and 25 were not flappers who thought of nothing but dancing'.[21] While her comments were ostensibly designed to defend the reputation of young women and prove them deserving of the full rights of citizenship, she explicitly used dancing as an identifier for those women who merited exclusion from the national community.

In all of these examples, an enthusiasm for dancing was deployed as the chief characteristic of the modern woman who had emerged from the war, and about whom there was considerable social concern. Nor were these concerns confined to Britain: debates about the changing place of women in society should be understood in a wider international context, as many countries grappled with the alienation experienced by returning servicemen, and the belief that women had been significantly altered by the war and were excessive in their pursuit of amusement.[22] In the midst of a global dance craze, dancing became a useful demarcator through which these gender anxieties could be expressed. As dance scholar Julie Malnig has argued, protests against dancing 'always come back to fears of (and for) the feminine: that the dancing would wreak havoc on the morals and sexual development of women and girls, threaten their roles as the keepers of domestic sanctity of home and hearth, or tempt their susceptible sexual natures'.[23] Yet the inverse was also true, and post-war gender anxieties strongly influenced the representation of the popular dance culture that emerged in this period. Invariably appearing in any laundry list of modern feminine preoccupations alongside drinking, smoking and gambling, dancing became directly associated with bad behaviours. Social concerns about women thus became constitutive of social concerns about dancing and vice versa.

However, as the dreamgirl and butterfly controversy attested, the criticisms of women who danced were not universal or without rebuttal – particularly from the women themselves. In the same month as the *Daily Express* debate, the *Daily Mail* reported that it had been receiving a great deal of mail from members of the Young Women's Christian Association (YWCA) about the divisions arising within the organisation on the subject of women's dancing, theatre-going, smoking and card-playing. While the YWCA leadership apparently had concerns about the social activities of women living on their premises, the letters published largely defended dancing girls. One woman wrote, 'I feel that the working girl living in the YWCA has enough to put up with … without being deprived of any innocent enjoyment simply because some straight-laced folks say nay.'[24] A couple of days later a married woman who had lived at the YWCA while her husband was at war also decried the '"killjoy" element' that wished to prevent dancing on club grounds, and to limit women's ability to attend outside dances or the theatre. She argued that dancing could be an entirely innocent pursuit and to ban it would be 'catering solely for unduly solemn and serious young women'.[25] In both the debate within the YWCA, and through the press coverage of the controversy, women actively defended their right to the entertainment that dancing afforded, and disputed claims that this leisure form was frivolous or morally ambiguous.

Indeed, for all of the criticisms that a preoccupation with dancing had made women selfish, silly or immoral, there were equally those who celebrated the new opportunities for feminine self-expression and independence that this expanding leisure form enabled. In 1925, Barbara Miles, a world champion ballroom dancer, stressed that most women who danced did so for the mental and physical exhilaration this pastime provided, rather than to pursue romantic interests or engage in wild behaviour. As Miles expressed it, 'the motto of the modern dancing girl is "dancing for dancing's sake"'.[26] As was discussed in Chapter 1, because the movements of modern ballroom dances like the foxtrot and one-step were simple and less structured than their Victorian forerunners, they were seen to be symbolic and expressive of the breakdown of convention that accompanied the end of the war and the growing independence enjoyed by women. This autonomy played out not only in the dances, but in the space of the public ballroom, which was celebrated for having lost much of its Edwardian formality. As the *Daily Mail* remarked in 1919, 'The girl who has been working as a V.A.D. or in a Government office, travelling to and fro unattended, does not take kindly to the chaperon-controlled dance.' [27] Another writer likewise proclaimed that a 'spirit of feminine independence rules in the ball-room', and claimed that women no longer required an escort to a dance, could pay their own admission fee, and even locate their own dance partners by way of the professional 'pen'.[28] When it came to relations between the sexes at a dance, another writer asserted, 'Modernity has made us very sensible.'[29]

The 'spirit of feminine independence' was perhaps not quite as straightforward as these writers believed, since in reality many women continued to rely on 'treating' by male escorts to attend a dance, would never have dared hire a professional dance partner, or were barred from public ballrooms altogether by their parents. However, heightened levels of personal autonomy, as well as expanding employment opportunities and rising wages, did allow women to take control of their dancing experiences and leisure time more generally during the interwar years.[30] For many girls and women, dancing occupied a critical place in their social lives, comparable, as Ross McKibbin has memorably observed, to what 'sport was to boys'.[31] This was the case for women of all ages and backgrounds, although those most interested in dancing tended to be young and single, and how the interest was manifested was often class contingent. Working-class women frequented public dance halls with far greater frequency than middle-class women, whose interest in dancing – particularly in the early part of the interwar period – tended to be expressed through enrolment in dancing schools or attendance at dances sponsored by churches, tennis clubs or youth groups.

However or wherever women danced, it was, as Claire Langhamer has argued, 'a complex leisure experience which transcended the dance venue itself', and which provided them with new avenues for self-expression.[32] Women's fashions in this period were strongly influenced by the requirements of modern ballroom dancing or the Charleston. Many women read dance magazines and instruction manuals, knew the members of popular dance bands and their songs, and listened for new dance lessons given on the radio. They followed dance trends religiously, and experimented with new steps and figures at home.

For these reasons, women tended to be superior dancers to men, because they took it more seriously and devoted more time to practice. Some women also preferred to dance with each other at the dance hall, even when male partners were not at a premium; alternately taking the man's part, they believed they could obtain higher quality dance practise with each other than with a fumbling male partner more interested in romance. At the same time, as will be shown in the next section, visiting the palais could provide women, as well as men, with new degrees of social and sexual freedom.

That women were the primary consumers of popular dance was increasingly recognised, and dancing was feminised in a number of ways within British culture. Notably, advertising for products marketed to women, such as cosmetics, skin care products, female fashions and cleaning products, frequently used images or descriptions of dances to promote their wares. An advertisement for Camp coffee, for instance, played on women's traditional role as hostess by advising, 'When guests come into *your* dance or party on a cold winter night – warm them up with good coffee.'[33] Another ad promoted Odo-ro-no antiperspirant by showcasing an apparently odorous woman being observed by two men at a dance, one of whom commented, 'Pretty, yes – but *I'm* not dancing with her!'[34] Occasionally the use of dancing in marketing campaigns was even more overt. For several weeks in 1925, women's magazine *Home Notes* featured an advertisement for Twink clothing dye, which informed readers that if they mailed in the attached coupon along with a Twink carton front they would receive a free written dance lesson from famed professional Maxwell Stewart. In addition to advertising, women's magazines featured many articles related to dancing trends, and the ballroom was a frequent setting for the short stories contained within these publications. Daily newspapers also included information about new dances or the latest dance frock on their women's pages, and the dance press devoted special attention to women. For several years in the 1920s, for example, the *Dancing Times* featured a monthly column entitled 'Phillida goes dancing', which focused on issues of supposed feminine concern like fashion and romance, while relating Phillida's daily tours of the London dance scene.

Ballroom dancing also became an increasingly standard element of female education. It was understood within middle-class families that dancing was a social necessity for their daughters, who were typically enrolled in dancing schools as adolescents. In the physical education classes provided by schools or youth organisations, dancing was similarly emphasised for girls in a way it was not for boys. In a handbook on physical recreation for girls released by the Board of Education in 1937, dancing received an entire chapter and several additional mentions.[35] As the authors of the book remarked, 'it is thought that something in the way of a definite scheme of dancing will be welcome in a handbook dealing with recreative physical training for working girls and women, with whom dancing will probably be one of the more popular indoor activities'.[36] Conversely, the equivalent handbook for boys dedicated only a few pages to dancing.

This lack of attention to dancing in a book dedicated to male physical education is indicative of the different role that this cultural form played – or was believed to play – in the respective lives of men and women. However, dancing held a central position within post-war gender anxieties, and it was one that extended beyond deliberations over femininity to some of the equally fraught reconsiderations of masculinity. For instance, at virtually the same moment as the dreamgirl and butterfly debate, and the vociferous defence of the rights of YWCA women to dance, another press item expressed concerns about the so-called 'Lounge Lizards of London'. The piece asserted that the 'sleek, well-dressed dancing man, with his saponaceous, unctuous, suave manner, is an inevitable product of the dancing craze'. An ever-present feature of London's dance establishments, these suave dancing men were usually to be found preying on wealthy older women who could supply them with gifts and financial support. The newspaper further contended that it was commonplace for the 'dancing dandies' to seduce and then blackmail the women they courted, who were frequently married.[37] As this example suggests, the dancing man, like the dancing woman, was connected with deviant behaviour – seduction, or outright criminality, such as blackmail or robbery. For instance, another press report recounted a story about a paid dance partner, who after leaving his job as an instructor at a West End dance club, had begun accompanying a woman who was a former client to different dance venues around London – at a rate of about 20 to 25 shillings per evening. In the course of one of these nights out, at the newly opened Hammersmith Palais, the man in question, Cecil Ernest Oddy, had stolen two diamond rings from his patroness, and at the time of writing was standing trial for the crime.[38]

While anxieties about dance-mad women focused on all levels of the social hierarchy, views of the dancing man were shaped by class. As one commentator noted, a man who danced was 'ridiculed by his friends unless he belonged to the world of Society'.[39] The upper classes had more income and leisure time to devote to dance instruction and a greater number of social responsibilities that involved dancing. It was thus more acceptable for men of that station to dance than for their working- or middle-class counterparts. There were in fact a number of well-known dance enthusiasts among the elite and even within the Royal Family, including the Prince of Wales and his younger brother the Duke of Kent. However, prejudices directed against upper-class men, as well as those who performed gentility through fashion or manners – for being effete or decadent – were also part of the broader social context that shaped views of dancing men. The extensive press coverage of the so-called 'Bright Young Things', which centred on their wild parties (at which dancing was central) and their effeminate 'extreme fashions', also informed contemporary understandings of the man who danced.[40] The reference to 'dancing dandies' in the story above is particularly telling about the liminal gendered space within which enthusiastic male dancers operated. Dandyism was associated by some with 'sexual nonconformity' and queerness.[41] It was also characterised in this period, as Catherine Horwood has argued, by an 'un-British passion for clothes'.[42] Given the social requirement for men of all classes to dress up a little for an evening out dancing, in a lounge suit or even full evening dress, the pursuit of sartorial elegance became yet another point upon which to heap scorn on men who danced. As Melanie Tebbutt has shown, by the 1930s a 'dance-hall type' of man had emerged even among the working classes, who was derided for being over-sexed and 'flashily dressed'.[43]

The dancing man thus embodied a number of suspect masculine elements all at once – effeminacy and dandyism, dangerous sexuality, fervent pleasure-seeking and aristocratic excess. He was also often associated with foreignness, given the Continental tinge to the names and backgrounds of prominent male professionals like Santos Casani or Monsieur Pierre – and the alleged 'Latin' temperament required to perform dances like the tango. In all of these ways, the questionable manliness of dancing was interrogated, even among those who actively pursued it as a pastime or profession. In an interview with Mass Observation, for example, Major Cecil Taylor expressed dismay that after three hundred years of Taylor men working as dancing masters, his own son had refused to follow along, choosing instead to join the army because dancing 'wasn't a man's job'.[44] Men naturally did go dancing, but there was a notion that they did not – or should not – value it as a leisure pursuit as much as women did, and that skills on the dance floor were far less critical to their social success. As one writer observed, the dancing school was 'the last place in the world the average man will willingly visit'.[45] Despite this resistance to instruction, a *Daily Mail* column proclaimed that even the most inexpert male dancers seemed to have no compunction about asking a lady to take a turn about the floor, saying that 'Some unwritten law ordains that it doesn't matter how badly a man dances, although a girl, to get partners, must dance well.' The author, simply called 'A Dancing Woman', was good humoured about this state of affairs in the ballroom, however, concluding her article by stating that 'the man who cannot dance is usually such a jolly good sort that one suffers all his iniquities in silence.'[46] A female *Dancing Times* columnist made a similar observation, and suggested that men with dancing talent were often lacking in other virtues: 'If a man is a perfectly priceless dancer – then he's generally a bit of a bore. If he is the most intriguing thing ever, then he's generally a rotten dancer.'[47] Even for women who valued quality dancing, therefore, the man who was equally invested in the art was not always an appealing manly specimen.

Significantly, this one article from the *Dancing Times* aside, the dance press (usually serving as a voice for the dance profession) generally attempted to combat the notion that dancing was an unmanly pursuit, with the result that the man who danced – like the dancing girl – was a consistently contested figure. One article published by *Popular Music and Dancing Weekly* in 1924, for instance, was composed of a debate between two women over dancing's manliness, which began with one of them asking, 'Don't you think men who dance are rather effeminate?' However, despite this provocative beginning, the bulk of the discussion focused on drawing a distinction between the 'insipid … vapid and vain, floppy and foppish' dancing men of the past, and a more explicitly modern incarnation for whom dancing provided improved carriage, and mental and physical poise. As one of the authors put it, 'How different is the male dancer of to-day! He is alert and alive, brisk and bright, keen and so full of vigour and vim. To my mind, the average man of yesteryear is merely a travesty and a caricature of his successor of modern times.'[48] The notion that the dancing man of the interwar years was different from his historic predecessors was yet another manifestation of the belief that modern ballroom dancing, and the culture that surrounded it, were more in sync with the modern world. The image of a healthy male dancing body, 'alert and alive' and replete with 'vigour and vim', also stood in stark contrast to the masculine minds and bodies decimated in the trenches. In fact, as part of broader endorsements of its benefits to good health, dancing was often put forth as a way of 'winning war veterans back to health'.[49] In one case, professional Santos Casani employed an image of his own undressed body in an instruction manual in order to attest to the robust manliness dancing could instil (see Figure 4.1). In contrast

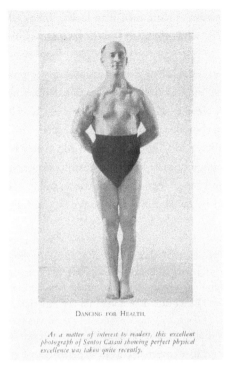

DANCING FOR HEALTH.

As a matter of interest to readers, this excellent photograph of Santos Casani showing perfect physical excellence was taken quite recently.

Dance professional Santos Casani shows off the benefits of dancing to the   **4.1**
masculine physique.

to the ballroom bore, seductive criminal and effete aristocratic dancing dandy, therefore, was a dancing man who embodied physicality, strength and recovery.

This modern dancing man was healthy and energetic, as well as poised, restrained and domesticated. As the *Dancing Times* remarked, 'Gone are the days when girls had to drag unwilling men to dances. To-day it is very nearly as natural for a man to go to a dance as it is for him to eat his dinner.'[50] Another dance press item reported,

> It is wonderful how big business men are turning towards dancing as a means of relaxation after the harassing labours of the day. Dance hall managers tell me that some of England's most prominent financiers can also claim the distinction of being first-rate dancers into the bargain.[51]

There was such an enthusiastic number of male dancers, another writer decreed, that they were starting to outnumber the women: 'parties [attending the dance halls] invariably consist of more men than ladies. The result is the ladies get a variety of partners, while the men – well the man wallflower is a modern innovation.'[52]

These descriptions established that it was perfectly appropriate for men to enjoy dancing – as long as that interest was balanced out by respectable employment and sociability. How a man behaved in the ballroom also helped to reveal something about his personality and character – he had certain duties to perform at a dance, and failure to do them adequately reflected poorly on him. A growing volume of press items and instruction manuals outlined how men should dress and deport themselves at a dance, and in one article providing guidance to would-be dance hosts and hostesses, the following advice was proffered:

> If you are fortunate enough to have a sufficiency of men, concentrate your attention on seeing that no girl is ever sitting out alone. Grab the nearest male, even if you have never seen him before, introduce him to the lone female, and leave them immediately. He will be a brute if he doesn't do his duty then.[53]

However, these requirements, and the representation of the ideal dancing man, existed in tension with many men's lived experiences of the dance hall. As Tebbutt has shown, there was considerable social anxiety for men, particularly among the working classes, associated with dancing correctly or being required to ask women to dance.[54]

Both the representation and the experience of dancing for men and women alike were thus complex and contradictory, and shaped by ongoing negotiations over gender and class. Popular dance provided a lens through which notions of femininity and masculinity were deliberated over and, in turn, gender anxieties strongly affected how dancing was perceived. However, negative representations of dancing girls and dancing dandies – while they never entirely disappeared – declined as Britain entered the 1930s. The use of dancing in marketing campaigns directed towards women, and its inclusion in female education, especially speak to its increasing societal integration as the interwar period progressed. This was in part owing to the broader re-stabilisation of the gender order with the passage of the 'flapper vote' in 1928 and the successful integration of new forms of British masculinity after the trauma of the war.[55] As the next section will show, the growing respectability of dancing was also tied to a broader campaign to ameliorate the reputation of the public ballrooms in which it took place.

Dance halls, nightclubs and the quest for respectability

In his autobiography, Claude Langdon, a one-time manager of the Hammersmith Palais, recalled of the early interwar years that 'some of the dance-halls which sprang up in our great provincial cities, as well as in London, did little to make dancing appear respectable as a pastime'.[56] As popular dance began to flourish in the 1920s, hundreds of spaces were built or transformed for that purpose, with dancing taking place in not only dance halls, but also restaurants, hotels, public houses, municipal and institutional halls and even churches. It was only certain public ballrooms that inspired negative comment, however, and the respectability of one dancing space over another was strongly influenced by the class of its chief clientele. As Robert Roberts recalled in his memoir of working-class life in Salford, near Manchester, the neighbourhood 'dancing rooms' had the reputation of being 'taboo' and 'low'.[57] Many middle-class girls were banned by their families from attending dance halls, even if they were permitted to attend classes in the attached dancing schools; while learning to dance was a social necessity for girls, the hall itself was perceived as morally ambiguous by many middle-class parents.[58] Responding to a survey by Mass Observation, one young woman said, 'I have never been in a dance hall ... I think of them has haunts of the less desirable sections of the lower classes.'[59]

However, the social dimensions of the dance hall were even more complex than a straightforward division between the working, middle and upper classes. Andrew Davies has shown that there was a hierarchy that distinguished one working-class hall from another, and marked certain halls as 'lower'; there were also a number of working-class girls who were banned from the dance hall by their parents for the very same reasons as their middle-class counterparts. As one woman interviewed by Davies recalled, 'I was never allowed to go dancing. My father used to say they were no good, [people] who went dancing.' Another woman recalled sneaking out to a Manchester dance hall against her parents' explicit wishes: 'My father would have killed me if he'd known. It was a right dive.'[60] Class prejudice influenced the reputation of public dancing spaces, but equally, individuals and families of the very social class a dance hall catered to might also reject patronising it in the quest to remain respectable.

Adding further layers of complexity to this picture is the fact that it was not solely working-class dance halls that were subject to social condemnation. Nightclubs, sometimes referred to as 'dancing clubs', attracted patrons from all classes, and could also be sites of interracial socialisation. Typically after-hours enterprises, these establishments commonly breached licensing laws related to the sale of alcohol and the regulation of music and dancing; they often possessed links to organised crime, and were subject to frequent raids by the police leading to criminal prosecutions, all of which received widespread press attention. Therefore, though nightclubs were largely a phenomenon of urban centres – especially the West End of London – Britons who never set foot in such establishments believed they understood what went on within them. The goings-on in nightclubs provided an extreme example of what also tainted social perceptions of all dancing spaces – overt sexual activity and criminal behaviour.

The possibility of romantic encounters was naturally a large part of the appeal of popular dancing as a leisure form. Sharing a dance or mingling in the tea room provided men and women with ample opportunity for forging romantic connections. As McKibbin has noted, dance spaces provided 'one of the few occasions where convention permitted [women] to take the sexual initiative', provided through such vehicles as 'Ladies' Choice' dances.[61] Many romances were thus initiated at the dance hall. As one man recounted to Mass Observation,

> I went with a friend of mine [to the Edinburgh Palais] one night to pass the evening; I met a girl who was very fond of dancing, and so the only way I could keep up the friendship was to learn dancing ... I go to the Edinburgh Palais every afternoon and evening I am off. Now I am married to the girl I met in this dance hall.[62]

Not only did the dance hall provide a place for the forging of romances, it was also a relatively acceptable destination for couples, particularly among the working classes, to go together throughout their courtship, and many romantic connections that began at a dance culminated in marriage.

Of course, public dancing spaces were also an important site for the initiation of more casual flirtations and sexual encounters. The degree to which sexual activity occurred *at* a dance depended to a great extent on the nature of the establishment. The reports filed by undercover police officers seeking to discover licencing violations revealed that nightclubs were a space wherein overt sexual behaviour tended to be readily condoned, often right on the dance floor.[63] As will be discussed at greater length below, prostitution was also prevalent in these establishments, infusing them with an even greater degree of sexual possibility. But though perhaps the most permissive, nightclubs were not the only venues in which sexual activity occurred. Some independent dance halls and private dances also tended to be more informal and tolerant of sexual behaviour. At the Spinners Hall in Bolton, which held dancing twice weekly, Mass Observation noted, '[Necking] much in prominence as evening wore on and especially after second interval.'[64] Other reports documented similar scenes, and even in the absence of overt sexual activity at dance halls, attraction was made evident through flirtation and the dancing itself. Upon his first visit to the Streatham Locarno, one observer for Mass Observation remarked, 'The aspect of the place was definitely lascivious and well designed for a place for sexual enjoyment. The sexual nature of dancing was obvious all the time. Why should the dancers dance in couples otherwise?'[65] Another observer said about the same hall, 'coming from middle class society, I was surprised at the amount of open intimacy, the numbers of arms round shoulders and the number of people holding hands quite openly'.[66]

For the most part, however, sexual conduct in the dance hall was circumspect. As another visitor to the Locarno remarked, 'There doesn't seem to be much sex about – dancing's the thing – not sex dancing specially [sic].'[67] Instead, sexual encounters arising in the dance hall generally took place outside the establishment. Typically if a man and woman had shared several dances over the course of the evening and were attracted to one another, the man would ask to 'see her home'. Since most young women still lived with their parents, any sexual activity tended to occur along the route home. Women had significant power in these interactions, basically directing whether or not they would occur. At the end of an evening's dancing at a hall in Deansgate, for example, Mass Observation noted, 'A few youths hung about outside the exit downstairs trying to "Click" with a girl – they were not very successful.'[68] Women's expanded incomes in the interwar period meant that many of them were willing to pay their own way into the palais rather than allowing men to cover costs with an expectation of sexual favours in return, although 'treating' did still occur.[69] While it is difficult to know the full extent and nature of sexual interactions originating in the dance hall, it is safe to say that they were a regular enough part of the experience of going to the palais for both men and women. Public knowledge of this fact was directly influenced the social perception of these venues.

Sexual competition was often a major catalyst to the second form of behaviour that diminished the public reputation of dance halls: violence and criminal activity. In 1920, the *Daily Mail* reported the story of a young women stabbed in the shoulder by her former fiancé after she arrived at a dance with another man.[70] On another occasion the *Mail* related a case wherein a man struck a woman in a hotel ballroom in Eastbourne after she refused to dance with him.[71] Not all dance hall violence originated in romantic entanglements, however. Alcohol was a leading cause of rough behaviour in dance spaces, leading to what dance promoters described as 'hooliganism' – characterised by physical fights and damage to property.[72] Davies has documented that considerable gang violence occurred in and around Manchester's dance halls.[73] Certain nights of the week were widely recognised as fighting nights in the city, and the Devonshire Street Ballroom was dubbed the 'blood bath' on Saturday evenings.[74]

However, it was nightclubs that were perhaps most responsible for inculcating the reputation for lawlessness and elicit activity that surrounded public dancing. Licensing violations, prostitution, drugs and organised crime were commonplace in these establishments. More importantly, these activities were widely reported in the press, which – just as with the butterfly and lounge lizard – played an important part in shaping the representation and social perception of dance venues. Kate Meyrick, operator of a series of different clubs at 43 Gerrard Street in Soho, and convicted multiple times throughout the 1920s for bribery and breaching licensing laws, became a veritable folk hero in endless press coverage of her indiscretions and arrests. One *Daily Express* article recounted a prosecutor's description of one of Meyrick's clubs: 'It is called a dancing club, but it would be no exaggeration to call it a dancing hell – an absolute sink of iniquity. It is a noxious fungus growth on our social life.'[75] In 1929 the *Sunday Sentinel* published an autobiographical series by Meyrick, outlining her experiences in London club life. Deliberately sensational and salacious, it revealed an environment replete with drugs, alcohol, violence and criminal activity; Meyrick also wrote a book, entitled *Secrets of the 43*, for additional public consumption.

In response to reports of this type, there were active attempts on multiple social fronts to 'clean up' and improve the reputation of public dancing establishments. Records indicate that abstract notions of character began to play a role in granting licenses for music and dancing to dance proprietors and promoters; according to the requirements of the Home Counties (Music and Dancing) Licensing Act 1926, county councils were to confer with local police as to the 'conduct and character of the applicant' prior to issuing a license.[76] Nightclubs were also of considerable interest to social purity organisations like the Public Morality Council and National Vigilance Association. They constituted a primary focus of the patrol work conducted by these groups, which also included patrolling for illegal gaming, excessive drinking and street solicitation; the organisations also frequently lobbied for increased police and legislative redress to curb the activities in these establishments. In 1930, the Metropolitan Police received a letter about 43 Gerrard Street from the London Public Morality Council that questioned, 'how it was possible for these proceedings to have continued in the samebuilding [sic] for so many years'.[77] Despite regular undercover operations, the police were limited as to what they could do to combat nightclub criminality until 1943, when they were granted additional powers to raid a venue without a warrant; in fact, until then, authorities were often complicit in allowing nightclubs to continue business as usual.[78] Finally, the dance profession also attempted to curb deviancy and improve the reputation of public ballrooms, particularly via their print media. In 1924 the *Dancing Times* featured a series of articles entitled 'Dance Clubs and the Law', wherein licensing laws were outlined for the benefit of proprietors and customers. That same year the magazine provided a written guide of dance venues in London, advising readers as to which were disreputable and should be avoided, and which were above approach and worthy of the business of respectable people.[79]

However, it was the dance hall industry itself that put in the strongest effort and made the greatest strides towards elevating the reputation of public ballrooms, as proprietors introduced numerous reforms in order to transform them into respectable, family oriented leisure venues. Of this effort, Langdon wrote, 'Not one in a million of the couples who dance today at the many palais throughout the country know that I had to fight to give them a wholesome, clean and cosy place where they could enjoy a dance.'[80] C. L. Heimann and Alan Fairley's biographer similarly extolled Mecca's efforts in this regard:

> Public dance halls had always been raw, rough, and dirty … [Heimann and Fairley] had to wipe out the old impression of dance halls; then they had to *prove* they could make them places for healthy recreation, where it was safe for ordinary boys and girls to meet and enjoy themselves.[81]

Particularly as dance halls consolidated into chains in the 1930s, there was a conscious effort on the part of proprietors to improve the reputation of their business and to expand their clientele.

Accordingly, at large chain dance halls a number of policies were put in place to regulate the behaviour of dancers. Alcohol was prohibited in the ballroom, and those who were visibly intoxicated were barred from entering. At certain halls, photographic records were kept of known trouble-makers, and those caught damaging property or engaged in physical violence were banned in the future.[82] There were also attempts to encourage patrons to bring their children to Mecca halls, particularly for the afternoon sessions, and to promote the idea that dancing was a 'family friendly' activity. For example, when Mecca introduced a series of novelty dances in the late 1930s, they were marketed towards children as much as adults; dance halls also became a common location for children's Christmas and fancy-dress parties. As Heimann and Fairley later told their biographer, 'Our whole policy is to bring families into all our pursuits.'[83]

Nor was it only the large chain dance halls that engaged in the effort to maintain good order at dances. In 1939, a group of private dance promoters formed the South London Dance Association (SLDA), with a mandate to conduct a joint effort to keep the 'rough element' out of dances. According to an interview with Mass Observation, the membership of the SLDA had been experiencing increasing problems of men forcing their way into dances at a greatly reduced entrance fee, often for nothing, and causing trouble. As a way of combating this problem, the names and descriptions of trouble-makers were taken and distributed around to other promoters in the group.[84] The SLDA was composed of working-class men who ran dance clubs as a side business, and the bulk of their patrons were of the same social level. Their efforts thus reflected an attempt on the part of working-class dance promoters to combat the classist attitudes that marked their dances and clientele as less respectable.

Accompanying the effort to give dance halls a more wholesome public image were deliberate attempts to monitor sexual behaviour. Some dance halls began to employ chaperones to patrol the ballroom and curtail overt sexual activity, a part that could also be played by the master of ceremonies (MC). Regarding a large dance hall in Douglas, *Popular Music and Dancing Weekly* noted, '[the MC] watches over the whole in such a way as at once to detect the slightest lapse from what ought to be, and, if this occurs, immediately puts it down'.[85] As one dance hall manager in Bolton told Mass Observation, 'There isn't any room for the funny business in the Modern Dance Hall as the people watch too keenly for that.'[86] At the Aspin Hall in the same town, a policy was put forward that women who left the hall at some point in the evening were not allowed to re-enter; this was to prevent couples from sneaking out for a brief sexual encounter and then returning to the dance. As the manager of the hall told Mass Observation, the restrictions 'keep the tone pretty decent'.[87] In this case, the onus for maintaining respectable relations with the opposite sex was clearly placed on women, but in certain contexts men's sexual freedom was equally curbed. At public dance halls, conduct was generally regulated in strongly heteronormative terms. Men dancing with other men was typically prohibited, and management made attempts to bar patrons who were known to be homosexual. Significantly, women dancing with women was not banned, and was indeed commonplace when male partners were scarce, or for the purposes of practice. While it seems more than likely that there were female same-sex couples in dancing spaces, the social acceptability of women dancing together shielded these women from the same discrimination.

It should also be noted that monitoring policies were often more fluid in practice. As was described above, sexual activity was a definite reality in and around some public ballrooms. Moreover, upon observing a same-sex male couple at a dance, Mass Observation discussed their presence with the event's promoter, who 'said there were several [same-sex couples who] tried to get in, but he kept them out, only allowing this one and his boy friend because they were quite harmless'.[88] Dancing spaces thus provided some space for the contestation and transgression of social mores, and the degree to which this occurred was largely dependent on the nature of the venue. Independent dances and dance halls were often the most flexible in terms of their supervisory policies, whereas chains such as Mecca, sitting atop the dance hall industry, was far and away the most stringent; the bigger the business, therefore, the tighter the restrictions on behaviour. A major element of the commercialisation of popular dance was the attempt to make dancing spaces respectable, and in that quest the dance hall industry instituted policies that reified conventional understandings of gender roles and sexual morality. These negotiations over class, gender, sexuality and respectability were also evident in debates about a particular form of dance hall employee: the paid dance partner.

The six-penny dance partner: prostitute or professional?

In Agatha Christie's classic 1942 novel *The Body in the Library*, Miss Marple is tasked with solving the murder of a young woman employed as a paid dance partner at a seaside hotel. In the course of her duties the woman had become close to a wealthy and elderly client who wished to adopt her, and there is a suggestion by other characters in the novel that she may have brought on her own death by reaching 'above herself' socially.[89] This fictional condemnation is revealing of a lingering stigma that surrounded the men and women who earned their living as paid dance partners in Britain's public ballrooms. Known by a variety of titles, including dance 'hostess', 'partner', 'teacher' and 'professional', these men and women usually occupied a particular area near the dance floor, often called the 'pen', where they could be hired by patrons who purchased tickets, usually at a rate of six pence per dance. However, the nature of dance partners' employment aroused considerable suspicion and scrutiny. For some, the notion of paying for a dance was viewed to be too close an approximation to paying for sex, and dance partners were frequently stigmatised as prostitutes and gigolos. The etymology of the word 'gigolo' is in itself revealing of the assumptions that surrounded this type of work; while modern readers would likely readily define the word as referring to a male prostitute, this was not always the case. The primary definition provided by the *Oxford English Dictionary* defines a gigolo as 'a professional male dancing partner or escort'. It is a testament to society's views of paid dance partners that the term linguistically evolved in the manner that it did, and relatively quickly. In 1939, a Mecca employee rejected the label entirely, emphatically declaring to Mass Observation 'I am a professional dance partner, <u>not</u> a gigolo'.[90] The discourses surrounding paid dance partners thus did much to cement an association between dancing and sexual immorality.

Yet like the social perception of dance enthusiasts of both sexes, views of dance partners were contested and contradictory. This was in part owing to the varied nature of these men and women's employment. In some cases, the cost of a dance typically went to the management, and dance partners earned only what they could procure from their clients in tips, refreshments and the occasional gift – whereas at other establishments staff were paid decent or even impressive wages. In particular, with the expansion of the dance hall industry, the desire to create a standard experience and elevate the respectability of the palais led to reforms to hours, pay and work conditions for dance partners. Those employed by the major commercial dance hall chains tended to be accredited teachers and competition dancers; in addition to selling dances, the inhabitants of the professional pen also provided the exhibition dances which were a standard feature of the dance hall programme, and considered themselves to be professionals. Indeed, in his autobiography, Victor Silvester recalled an occasion during his days as a dance partner, when he and a colleague were offered tips by a young woman who had spent considerable time dancing with each of them one evening; Silvester's colleague promptly returned the money, furiously demanding, 'What do you take me for – a waiter?'[91] Dance partners in his position were paid a standard salary by the venue that employed them and retained about half of what they brought in from clients. They might also make tips on top of their basic rate of pay – not all were so resistant to this additional financial benefit – yet still took pride in their professionalism.

But at other dancing establishments, particularly nightclubs, the reforms to work conditions that occurred at the large palais had little impact. Into the Second World War there were dance partners who continued to work only for tips and drinks, possibly with the management taking a percentage. From these earnings they would also have to provide themselves with the clothing, shoes and transportation needed to fulfil the requirements of their position. Frequently holding down another job as well, few of these men and women were trained teachers or professional dancers. In fact, in an interview with a dance partner at a Soho nightclub called the 'Blue Lagoon', Mass Observation discovered that dancing ability was not even a prerequisite for the women being put forward as dance partners at the club. Their role was largely to provide company to the patrons, and convince them to purchase more food and drink. In addition, unlike at the large palais, where the 'pen' was usually occupied by a roughly even number of the two sexes, nightclub hostesses were predominantly women. There is considerable evidence that under these circumstances the titles dance 'partner' or 'hostess' did often serve as euphemistic cover for prostitution.

In her interview with Mass Observation, the Blue Lagoon dance partner indicated that many of her fellow hostesses exchanged sexual favours for money, or at least held out the possibility of sex as a way of securing better tips from their male clients.[92] Records compiled by undercover police officers in the lead-up to raids on nightclubs offer additional insight into this type of sexual commerce. In Metropolitan Police reports the terms 'dance hostess' or 'dance partner' were often used interchangeably with 'prostitute'. Describing the scene at the El Morocco bottle party, for instance, one officer noted, 'Dance hostess[es] of the prostitute type are employed to entertain guests and coax them to buy drinks'.[93] A number of other reports written by police agents also revealed that they were propositioned by dance hostesses while working undercover. Recounting the details of a 1931 raid on an infamous club at 43 Gerrard Street, an officer wrote, 'The dancing instructresses have solicited me and on the night of the raid, the woman known as "Rosie" said to me: – "If you want a lady, I can arrange that with a friend, but I don't do that." '[94]

There was thus an active sex trade functioning within some dance establishments, and while it is clear that not all dance partners were engaged in prostitution, it is equally apparent that in these situations a woman's livelihood was in large part dependent on her ability to attract men and not the quality of her dancing. Police reports reflect rampant competition between dance partners to secure decent earnings, or at the very least to find someone to purchase their drinks and meals (usually breakfast, since peak operating time for nightclubs extended into the early morning hours). As one police report described, 'On 3 occasions, I saw quarrels between the dancing instructresses over men showing more favour to one than the other. On each occasion the women were on the point of fighting.'[95] These women were reliant on patrons not only for tips, but also for drinks, meals and cash. Such reliance had the potential to create a competitive and conflict-ridden work environment.

Even in the larger dance halls, where dance partners were not financially reliant on what they could procure from patrons, the relationship between partners and their clients was often not solely about dance instruction. Despite concerted efforts by management to hire professional dancers and keep paid partnering as respectable as possible, the line between dance and sexual partnering was often blurred. Many dance partners established a regular clientele, and gifts of varying degrees were common. Clients often attempted to move the relationship beyond the confines of the dance hall, something some partners were more willing to go along with than others. Charles Dilworth, the manager of Mecca's Royal dance hall in north London, told Mass Observation that the majority of the dance partners working for him were 'most moral', and kept their relationships with clients purely professional, because not to do so was likely to cost them the client in the end.[96] However, a female dance partner at the Royal told the social research organisation that she had to keep the fact that she was married a secret in order to maintain her clientele. She reported that some male customers were sexually aggressive with her, and that many of her regular clients made offers to walk her home or buy her dinner.[97]

Male dancer partners also forged relationships with patrons off the dance floor; they frequently escorted female clients to restaurants or other dance venues following their shift at the dance hall, and a number even travelled with their regulars. But as a male dance partner at the Royal informed Mass Observation, navigating the relationship with a client could be complex: 'This job has its amusing side and its sordid side ... This business is very intimate, unlike all others ... We get a lot of married women. They have more time and love dancing. Sometimes it goes farther and they take a passion for their particular teacher. Then come the complications. One must be shrewd.'[98] While the general state of affairs between dance partners and their regular clients was naturally extremely varied, there is little question that the relationships did occasionally become sexual. In Silvester's autobiography he details several romantic relationships with female clients, and one dance partner bragged openly to Mass Observation about the number of sexual conquests he had made.[99]

An undertone of sexual immorality was thus intrinsic to social perceptions of work as a dance partner. When Silvester informed his parents that he was leaving the army to accept a position as a dance partner at the Empress Rooms, his father was reported to have replied 'he never thought he'd live to see the day one of his sons turned gigolo'.[100] In the eyes of people like Silvester's vicar father, dancing simply did not represent respectable work, and dance partners were painted with the same brush that associated actresses and other performers with moral laxity. In the early 1920s, scandals, such as the slander trial that resulted from accusations of lesbianism against concert dancer Maud Allen – famous for her performances as Salome at the Palace Theatre prior to the war – had reinforced connections between professional dancing and sexual immorality.[101] These associations coloured the perception of paid dance partners and professional dancers more broadly.

The popular press was a chief vehicle through which a dubious view of the dance partner was disseminated. In an article describing the opening of the Locarno dance hall in Streatham in 1929, one newspaper observed that a guarantee the venue would be run along the 'correct lines' was the management's decision 'not to resort to the objectionable system of providing "six penny" dance partners'.[102] Dance partners also received negative attention in the extensive press coverage of police raids on nightclubs which violated licensing laws. In 1919 the *Daily Express* reported that club proprietor Kate Meyrick had been summoned to court for 'permitting the premises to be used as a resort of women of ill-repute'.[103] Meyrick herself, in a *Sunday Sentinel* series on her club at 43 Gerrard street, essentially acknowledged the sexual activities of the dance partners working for her, while accepting no complicity in their behaviour: 'When my dancing girls introduced their men friends to me as their brothers, I believed them, and I always warned them not to allow any men but these brothers to escort them home ... I am afraid dancing girls in those days were not as innocent as I thought them.'[104]

However, just as with the butterfly or lounge lizard, the representation of paid dance partners was ambiguous and contested. In April 1926 the *Daily Mail* featured a column in which the plethora of partners-for-hire at Britain's dancing establishments was discussed. Correspondent Patrick Chalmers noted that in the early 1920s a higher end hotel or restaurant that employed dance partners was viewed to have 'lost caste', but that 'gradually...a custom regarded as rather raffish ... became accepted as normal'.[105] Chalmers did caution, however, that it was far better practice to pay the partners a wage, rather than forcing them to work only for gratuities. The contradictory views of dance partners were also brought to light by a series of court cases involving women in this form of employment. In 1931, sixteen-year-old Marie Sibley, employed as a dance hostess at a London restaurant, sued her neighbour after she was bitten by his dog. A judgment was returned in her favour on the dog issue, but in delivering his verdict the presiding judge took the opportunity to decry the conditions under which Sibley was forced to work. Mr Justice McCardie pointed to Sibley's youth and working hours, and the fact that she had to provide the clothing and transport required for her job, as all being cause for significant concern. His greatest condemnation, however, was reserved for the fact that Sibley worked only for tips rather than paid wages. McCardie argued that this state of affairs provided 'a direct incitement to young girls to go beyond the bounds of propriety and sexual restraint'. He continued, 'It is quite plain that the more pleasing a girl was to a man the greater the fee that he was likely to give her.'[106] While there was no evidence presented that Sibley herself was engaged in prostitution, McCardie's comments once again directly linked professional dance partners with prostitution, and suggested that Sibley was in need of protection – a common undertone to representations of women who danced professionally or as a pastime.[107]

Two years later these connections were made even more explicit through another legal proceeding that drew widespread attention. Three men connected with the Kosmo Dance Club in Edinburgh were brought to trial in Edinburgh Sheriff Court for contravening the Immoral Traffic (Scotland) Act 1902 and the Criminal Law Amendment Act 1885. Asher Barnard, proprietor of the Kosmo Club, Edwin Jones, manager, and James Black, floor manager, were all charged with aiding and abetting prostitution, and living wholly or in part off the earnings of prostitution, through a system of 'booking out' the club's dance partners. The case was a source of intense public interest. The *Glasgow Herald* reported that on the first day of the trial 'a queue of men and women waited to gain admission to the courtroom'.[108] While the presiding judge, Sheriff Brown, opted to close the courtroom, the press was allowed to remain, and the details of the trial received extensive coverage in a large number of local and national newspapers. Later, when the jury returned their verdict, crowds of people assembled outside the courthouse, and a large police presence was also required.

Over the course of the nine-day trial, the inner-workings of the booking out system, the source of the criminal indictment against the Kosmo Club's management, was detailed through testimony provided by the accused, other club employees, taxi-drivers, clients and undercover police officers. A client could request a dance partner in person or over the phone at a cost of thirty shillings – ten of which went to the woman while the remainder was split by management – and then leave the club with her. While most of the dance partners and clients testified that they would then simply move on to another dance hall or party, a small number did admit that they were engaged in what was described throughout the trial as 'immoral purposes'. The jury clearly believed these witnesses rather than the majority and the accused, and found all three men guilty as charged; Barnard was sentenced to eighteen months in prison, while Jones and Black received three-month sentences.

Throughout the trial, the Kosmo Club's dance partners were represented in varied and contradictory ways. The prosecution attempted to portray the women as victims, under the control of the three accused men, while the defence's position shifted frequently. In cross-examining one of the dance partners, Barnard's attorney, Mr Blades, accused the witness of lying, suggested she lacked 'honour' and 'virtue', and at one point asked her, 'Is it possible to descend any lower?'[109] In his closing remarks, Blades also attempted to shift culpability for any illicit activity off the accused and onto the dance partners; he suggested that the ones who chose to engage in prostitution were not working under the direction of the club management but were merely smart businesswomen making the most of opportunities presented to them by the booking out system. However, he also argued that the dance partners *had* been victimised – not by his client – but by the trial itself:

> One of the cruellest of some very cruel things done in this case was the indiscriminate branding of these Kosmo dance partners as prostitutes ... These girls might be of lowly origin, but they were not entitled to be stigmatised and branded as the worst of womankind without positive proof. My heart was many times aflame ... at the treatment meted out to these defenceless girls.[110]

As the trial concluded, the presiding judge echoed McCardie's words in the Sibley case two years before; he lamented the work conditions of paid dance partners, and suggested that legislative reform might be required.

The Kosmo Club case represented the pinnacle of longstanding efforts to reform the working conditions of dance partners, from groups and individuals both within and outside the dance hall industry. Throughout the 1920s the Metropolitan Police received a number of letters from concerned citizens regarding what was taking place in after-hours dancing clubs, some specifically referencing the behaviour and plight of dance partners. Regarding one of Kate Meyrick's establishments, a correspondent wrote, 'there is reason to suppose that some of the rooms on the premises are used for worse purposes than drinking. A "Mrs. Stephenson" ... acts as a procuress and agent for the unfortunate girls employed as dancing partners, and will at any time obtain a girl to go home with a visitor on being paid a fee.'[111] Dance partners also drew the attention of numerous social purity organisations. The minutes of meetings of the National Vigilance Association (NVA) reveal that the organisation was concerned about working conditions of dance partners at the Portman Rooms as early as 1920.[112] The NVA raised the issue once again in response to Justice McCardie's comments in the Sibley case in 1931, as did the British National Committee, and both organisations had discussions based around the call for legislative reforms that followed the Kosmo Club case. The decision was made that local jurisdictions were to be encouraged to emulate the system in place in Glasgow, where a clause in the dance hall license issued by the city stipulated that paid dance partners must not be hired for any purpose outside the hall itself.[113]

Press attention and political pressure inspired the commercial producers of dancing to engage in greater degrees of self-regulation on the question of dance partners. The dance hall industry attempted to alter the taint that surrounded the job through reforms to working conditions and hiring practices. Increasing numbers of dance halls implemented a wage system, and steady pay meant that dance partners did not have to pattern their behaviour in order to maximise tips out of sheer financial desperation. Dance halls seeking greater respectability also sought out qualified dance instructors to fill their professional pens, highlighting dancing ability over personal charms in hiring their staff. Mecca in particular was strict about the behaviour and professionalism that was exhibited by partners when they were off the dance floor; upon observing dance partners in the professional pen at the Astoria dance hall engaged in pursuits like knitting or reading the newspaper, a writer for Mass Observation noted that they would never get away with doing so at a Mecca hall.[114] In the larger chains there was also increasing concern with issues of character – which effectively amounted to class – evident in hiring practices. As the *Weekly Telegraph* noted in 1939, in order to obtain a job as a partner at Mecca's Streatham Locarno dance hall, 'Applicants must be good dancers, speak in a cultured voice, have had a good education, and be able to provide faultless references.'[115]

The dance profession also made specific efforts to address the issue of paid dance partners, since the negative aspersions directed towards the latter had the potential to undermine the reputation of the former. In the report issued by the Official Board of Ballroom Dancing following the Great Conference in 1929, dance hall managers were encouraged not to allow dance partners to provide lessons unless they were qualified teachers.[116] While this was in part about the competition that untutored (and inexpensive) dance partners presented to the reputation and livelihoods of established teachers, this move by the profession also helped to inculcate the idea that dance partners should be trained professionals. Additionally, the profession used the dance press to ameliorate the reputation of dance partners. In a 1926 issue of *Popular Music and Dancing Weekly*, for instance, columnist 'Foxtrot' described the challenges of the job and wrote admiringly of the deftness with which they were often met:

> I spent an interesting time the other evening watching the professional partners at work. From what I saw, it is not enough to be a good dancer. You have got to possess plenty of patience and dance around as though you are enjoying yourself instead of working! I watched a certain lady partner dancing with various males, and it was truly wonderful to see the way in which she adapted her style to fit with her partner.[117]

This account contravened negative attitudes towards professional partners by emphasising their dancing talent and interpersonal skills.

Short stories in the dance press also painted dance partners in a sympathetic light. An illustrative example was *Popular Music and Dancing Weekly*'s serialised story entitled 'The Confessions of a Dancing Partner' – an account of life in the professional pen.[118] Rosie, the heroine of the tale, is a young, working-class woman from London who takes up a second job as a dance partner in order to support her sick mother – noble reasons which make her instantly sympathetic to the reader. The story also acknowledged public suspicions about this type of work, by portraying Rosie as conflicted over taking the job as a dance partner; on one level she is dazzled by the bright lights of the dance hall and the 'romance' of the work, but she also senses the derision of other people over what she does, particularly when the employer at her day job dismisses her for also working in the dance hall. However, eventually Rosie becomes reconciled to, and indeed a defender of work as a dance partner: 'Where once I had felt vaguely worried at being a dancing partner, where I had imagined that in some way I was lowering my dignity, I now realised that here was a position that was just as creditable as any other.'[119] The story concludes happily with Rosie marrying one of her clients, and the two of them opening their own chain of dance halls. A similarly favourable fictional rendering of professional dance partners appeared in *Modern Dance* in 1936. In this story, the heroine,

Isobel, takes up work as a dance partner in order to support her family after her upper-class husband finds himself out of work. Initially, Isobel's husband, Hugh, is strongly opposed to her employment, and imagines that she is having an affair with her exhibition partner. However, eventually Hugh comes to appreciate and respect his wife's work as a professional, full of admiration for 'the splendid and plucky way in which she had set out to do her bit towards raising them above water once more.'[120]

By the late 1930s, when the *Weekly Telegraph* examined the reforms to work conditions and more stringent hiring practices, the newspaper described working as a dance partner as a 'whole-time job as well recognised as that of a bank clerk'.[121] The comparison of a profession frequently equated with prostitution to work in a bank is telling about the strides towards respectability that dance partners had made by the outbreak of the Second World War – or at least of the strident efforts made by the dance hall industry to generate respectability for its staff. Rehabilitating the reputation of those who occupied the professional pen was part of the broader campaign to improve the social perception of public dance halls, described in the previous section. However, the controversies that surrounded paid dance partners never entirely went away. These men and women continued to exist in the same contested space between social condemnation and social acceptance that, as this chapter has shown, was characteristic of popular dance as a whole. The conflicting views of female and male dance enthusiasts, public dancing spaces and paid dance partners were all shaped by the range of cultural anxieties about gender, sex and class that plagued British society between the wars. Popular dance provided a vehicle through which these anxieties could be expressed and grappled with.

It should be noted that the controversies surrounding the people and places highlighted above were also about the nation. Social commentary about the flapper/butterfly was inflected with the sense that these women were behaving in a way that was fundamentally un-British, and that they were undeserving of the vote and the full rights of citizenship. Lothario dancing men, and 'gigolo' dance partners, possessed a foreignness that positioned them in stark contrast to stalwart and restrained British masculinity. The more controversial public dancing spaces – particularly nightclubs – 'prided themselves on their un-English atmosphere', bringing together under one roof Jewish managers, African-American jazz bands, Chinese gangsters and other inhabitants of cosmopolitan London.[122] Then there were the dances themselves – those that inspired the ardour of dance enthusiasts of both sexes, were performed in public ballrooms, and were theoretically taught by paid dance partners. Most of these dances

had arrived in Britain from elsewhere, and were infused with their own foreignness. As the next chapters will show, contestations over national identity were
also a prominent aspect of the evolution of Britain's popular dancing style.

Notes

1 J. Jefferson Farjeon, 'The Dance Evil', *Dancing Times* (January 1925), p. 439.

2 George E. Pearson, 'The Dream Girl – And the Awakening', *Daily Express* (16 February 1920), p. 6.

3 Disappointed, Letter to the Editor, *Daily Express* (19 February 1920), p. 4.

4 Elisabeth, Letter to the Editor, *Daily Express* (18 February 1920), p. 4.

5 Northcote, Letter to the Editor, *Daily Express* (23 February 1920), p. 6.

6 John Edwards, Letter to the Editor, *Daily Express* (26 February 1920).

7 Lonely, Letter to the Editor, *Daily Express* (25 February 1920), p. 4.

8 A Girl of Nineteen, Letter to the Editor, *Daily Express* (21 February 1920), p. 4.

9 Speedy Puss, Letter to the Editor, *Daily Express* (24 February 1920), p. 6.

10 Two Lonely Widows, Letter to the Editor, *Daily Express* (1 March 1920), p. 6.

11 Another Dream Girl, Letter to the Editor, *Daily Express* (24 February 1920), p. 4.

12 A. Beverley Baxter, 'The Charm of the Feminine', *Daily Express* (21 February 1920), p. 4.

13 On gender relations during and after the First World War see Billie Melman, *Women and the Popular Imagination in the Twenties: Flappers and Nymphs* (Basingstoke: MacMillan, 1988); Susan Kingsley Kent, *Making Peace: the Reconstruction of Gender in Interwar Britain* (Princeton, NJ: Princeton University Press, 1993); Joanna Bourke, *Dismembering the Male: Men's Bodies, Britain, and the Great War* (Chicago, IL: University of Chicago Press, 1993); Susan R. Grayzel, *Women's Identities at War: Gender, Motherhood and Politics in Britain and France during the First World War* (Chapel Hill, NC: University of North Carolina Press, 1999); Nicoletta Gullace, *'The Blood of our Sons:' Men, Women, and the Renegotiation of British Citizenship during the Great War* (New York: Palgrave MacMillan, 2002); Selina Todd, *Young Women, Work, and Family in England, 1918–1950* (Oxford: Oxford University Press, 2005); Lucy Bland, *Modern Women on Trial: Sexual Transgression in the Age of the Flapper* (Manchester: Manchester University Press, 2013).

14 See Adrian Bingham, *Gender, Modernity, and the Popular Press in Inter-war Britain,* (Oxford: Clarendon Press, 2004); Melman, *Women and the Popular Imagination*; Bland, *Modern Women on Trial.*

15 'The 1920s Girl', *The Times* (5 February 1920), p. 9.

16 Put off, Letter to the Editor, *Daily Mail* (6 February 1920), p. 6.

17 A Young Dancing Man, Letter to the Editor, *Daily Mail* (6 February 1920), p. 6.

18 'The Everitt Divorce Case', *The Times* (31 October 1919), p. 4.

19 Bland, *Modern Women on Trial.*

20 Judith R. Walkowitz, 'The "Vision of Salome:" cosmopolitanism and erotic dancing in Central London, 1908–1918', *American Historical Review* 108, No. 2 (April 2003): 25; Bland, *Modern Women on Trial*, pp. 4–6.

21 'Women Unionists and Franchise', *The Times* (27 May 1927), p. 13.

22 For a useful overview of these debates in different geographic contexts, see The Modern Girl Around the World Research Group, *The Modern Girl Around the World: Consumption, Modernity and Globalization* (Durham, NC: Duke University Press, 2008).

23 Julie Malnig, 'Women, dance, and New York nightlife', in Julie Malnig (ed.), *Ballroom Boogie, Shimmy Sham, Shake: A Social and Popular Dance Reader* (Urbana, IL: University of Illinois Press, 2009), p. 73.

24 'Y.W.C.A. Dancers', *Daily Mail* (5 February 1920), p. 5.

25 Padre's Wife, Letter to the Editor, *Daily Mail* (7 February 1920), p. 6.

26 Barbara Miles, 'Farewell Ball-room Romance!' *Popular Music and Dancing Weekly* (14 February 1925), p. ii.

27 'How We Dance', *Daily Mail* (15 January 1919), p. 4.

28 Nora Delany, 'Jazz Manners in the Ball-room', *Popular Music and Dancing Weekly* (27 February 1926), p. 112.

29 Teddie Gerard, 'May I Have the Pleasure?' *Popular Music and Dancing Weekly* (5 April 1924), p. 203.

30 Todd, *Young Women, Work, and Family in England, 1918–1950*, p. 220; Claire Langhamer, *Women's Leisure in England, 1920–1960* (Manchester: Manchester University Press, 2000), pp. 126–7; Judith R. Walkowitz, *Nights Out: Life in Cosmopolitan London* (New Haven, CT: Yale University Press, 2012), pp. 183–94.

31 Ross McKibbin, *Classes and cultures: England, 1918–1951* (Oxford: Oxford University Press, 1998), pp. 394–5.

32 Langhamer, *Women's Leisure in England*, p. 66.

33 *Daily Mail* (23 December 1926), p. 12.

34 *Daily Mirror* (26 November 1935).

35 *Recreation and Physical Fitness for Youths and Men* (London: HM Stationery Office, 1937, 1942); *Recreation and Physical Fitness for Girls and Women* (London: HM Stationery Office, 1937).

36 *Recreation and Physical Fitness for Girls and Women*, p. 10.

37 '"Lounge Lizards" of London', *Daily Express* (2 February 1920), p. 4.

38 'Girl's Paid Dance Partner', *Daily Express* (30 January 1920), p. 7.

39 Sophie Tucker, 'Let's Reverse', *Popular Music and Dancing Weekly* (14 November 1925), p. 69.

40 Catherine Horwood, *Keeping up Appearances: Fashion and Class between the Wars* (Stroud: Sutton Publishing, 2006), p. 146.

41 Paul R. Deslandes, 'Selling, consuming and becoming the beautiful man in Britain: The 1930s and 1940s', in Erika Rappaport, Sandra Trugden Dawson and Mark J. Crowley (eds), *Consuming Behaviours: Identity, Politics and Pleasure in Twentieth-Century Britain* (London: Bloomsbury Academic, 2015), p. 64.

42 Horwood, *Keeping up Appearances*, p. 149.

43 Melanie Tebbutt, *Being Boys: Youth, Leisure and Identity in the Inter-War Years* (Manchester: Manchester University Press, 2014), p. 215.

44 MOA: TC 38/6/G, The Imperial Society of Teachers of Dancing (19 June 1939), p. 6.

45 Tucker, 'Let's Reverse', p. 69.

46 A Dancing Woman, 'Men', *Daily Mail* (10 April 1926, p. 8).

47 Phillida Goes Dancing, *Dancing Times* (November 1920), p. 105.

48 Maggie Dickenson, 'Is Dancing a Manly Art?' *Popular Music and Dancing Weekly* (6 December 1924), p. 125.

49 E. J. Wass, 'Music that Heals', *Popular Music and Dancing Weekly* (8 May 1926), p. 56.

50 The Sitter Out, *Dancing Times* (October 1920), p. 2.

51 Around the Dance Halls, *Popular Music and Dancing Weekly* (12 April 1924), p. 232.

52 Around the Dance Halls, *Popular Music and Dancing Weekly* (8 March 1924), p. 124.

53 M. G. Hand, 'Arranging a Tennis Dance', *Popular Music and Dancing Weekly* (17 May 1924), p. 78.

54 Tebbutt, *Being Boys*, pp. 211–24.

55 See for instance, Paul Deslandes's recent work on male beauty and fashion in the 1930s: Deslandes, 'Selling, Consuming and Becoming the Beautiful Man in Britain'.

56 Claude Langdon, *Earls Court* (London: Stanley Paul, 1953), p. 51.

57 Robert Roberts, *The Classic Slum: Salford Life in the First Quarter of the Century* (Manchester: Manchester University Press, 1971), p. 16, p. 52, p. 216.

58 Horwood, *Keeping Up Appearances*, p. 99.

59 Quoted in Langhamer, *Women's Leisure in England*, pp. 68–9.

60 Andrew Davies, *Leisure, Gender, and Poverty: Working-Class Culture in Salford and Manchester, 1900–1939* (Buckingham: Open University Press, 1992), pp. 89–94.

61 McKibbin, *Classes and Cultures*, p. 395.

62 MOA: TC 38/6/F, Danceland Questionnaire (April 1939).

63 See, for instance: TNA: PRO, MEPO 2/4481: Mrs. Kate Evelyn Meyrick or Merrick: allegations of irregularities at The Cecil, The 43 and The Bunch of Keys Clubs, 1924–1934, Folder 1, 1922; Folder 3, 1924.

64 MOA: Worktown 48/D, Spinners Hall (30 December 1939), p. 6.

65 MOA: TC 38/1/A, Locarno (27 April 1939).

66 MOA: TC 38/1/A, Locarno (18 April 1939).

67 MOA: TC 38/1/A, Locarno (17 November 1938).

68 MOA: Worktown 48/C, Description and impressions of the Savoy Dance Hall, Deansgate, p. 2.

69 Todd, *Young Women, Work, and Family in England*, p. 220; Langhamer, *Women's Leisure in England*, pp. 126–7.

70 'Girl Stabbed at Dance', *Daily Mail* (14 January 1920), p. 5.

71 *Daily Mail* (10 April 1926), p. 7.

72 MOA: TC 38/2/A, SLDA General Meeting.

73 Davies, *Leisure, Gender, and Poverty*, pp. 92–4.

74 Langhamer, *Women's Leisure in England*, p. 68.

75 'Night Life in London Club', *Daily Express* (23 December 1919), p. 5.

76 TNA: PRO HO 45/20506: Entertainments: The Home Counties (Music and Dancing) Act, 1926: legal powers of County Councils to issue licences, delegate authority and institute proceedings, 1932–1943.

77 TNA: PRO MEPO 2/4481: Mrs. Kate Evelyn Meyrick or Merrick: allegations of irregularities at The Cecil, The 43 and The Bunch of Keys Clubs, 1924–1934, Folder 6, 1928–1930.

78 Walkowitz, *Nights Out*, pp. 209–52.

79 'London Dance Notes', *Dancing Times* (April 1924), pp. 737–41.

80 Langdon, *Earls Court*, p. 179.

81 Roma Fairley, forward to *Come Dancing Miss World* (London: Newman Neame, 1966), p. vii.

82 Langdon, *Earls Court*, p. 180.

83 Fairley, *Come Dancing Miss World*, p. vii.

84 MOA: TC 38/2/A, Lenny Haynes, p. 1.

85 George A. Wade, 'Running a Super Dance Hall', *Popular Music and Dancing Weekly* (8 August 1925), p. iii.

86 Quoted in James Nott, *Music for the People: Popular Music and Dance in Interwar Britain*, (Oxford: Oxford University Press, 2002), p. 187.

87 MOA, Worktown 48/D, Manager – Aspin Hall (8 January 1940), p. 16.

88 MOA: TC 38/1/I, Rye Lane (21 August 1939).

89 Agatha Christie, *The Body in the Library* (New York: Signet, 1941, 2000), p. 106.

90 Emphasis in original. See MOA: TC 38/3/G, Dance Professionals (12 March 1939).

91 Victor Silvester, *Dancing is My Life* (London: William Heinemann, Ltd., 1958), p. 41.

92 MOA: TC 38/4/H, The Blue Lagoon (14 April 1939), pp. 1–8.

93 TNA: PRO MEPO 2/4501: El Morocco Bottle Party, W.1: liquor irregularities, unlicensed music and dancing, complaints of rowydism and indecent literature, 1938–1940.

94 TNA: PRO MEPO 2/4481, Folder 7, 1931.

95 TNA: PRO MEPO 2/4481, Folder 7, 1931.

96 MOA: TC 38/3/F, Mecca Managers – Interview with Dilworth (18 March 1939), p. 2.

97 MOA: TC 38/3/G, Professionals at the Royal (25 May 1939).

98 MOA: TC 38/3/G, Professionals at the Royal (25 May 1939).

99 MOA: TC 38/3/G, Cyril (25 June 1939).

100 Silvester, *Dancing is My Life*, p. 40.

101 Walkowitz, 'Vision of Salome'; Bland, *Women on Trial*, pp. 15–54.

102 London Metropolitan Archives: GLC/AR/BR/07/4153, Untitled news clipping found in Locarno Dance Hall file.

103 'Night Life in London Club', *Daily Express* (23 December 1919), p. 5.

104 Kate Meyrick, 'My Ten Years behind the Scenes in London's Night-Life', *Sunday Sentinel* (13 February 1929), p. 13.

105 Patrick Chalmers, 'Dancing Partners', *Daily Mail* (23 April 1926), p. 8.

106 '15-Year-Old Dance Girl's Peril: Judge's Condemnation', *Daily Express* (20 November 1931), p. 3.

107 Bland, *Women on Trial*, pp. 55–101.

108 'Dance Club Charge', *Glasgow Herald* (30 November 1933).

109 'Night Life', *Edinburgh Evening News* (30 November 1933), p. 7.

110 'Guilty', *Edinburgh Evening News* (7 December 1933), p. 7.

111 TNA: PRO MEPO 2/4481, Folder 5, 1927.

112 Women's Library: FL195, 4NVA/1/1/07, Executive Committee Minutes, National Vigilance Association, Vol. 7, 29 October 1918 – 28 November, 1922.

113 'Dance Halls: Proposals to License Instructresses', *Edinburgh Evening News* (9 December 1933), p. 7.

114 MOA: TC 38/5/D, Astoria (5 December 1939), p. 3.

115 'Six Penny Partners', *Weekly Telegraph* (25 February 1939), p. 20.

116 Philip J. S. Richardson, *A History of English Ballroom Dancing* (London: Herbert Jenkins, 1946), p. 80.

117 Around the Dance Halls, *Popular Music and Dancing Weekly* (23 October 1926), p. iii.

118 See *Popular Music and Dancing Weekly*, 9 February 1924–8 March 1924.

119 'The Confessions of a Dancing Partner', *Popular Music and Dancing Weekly* (1 March 1924), p. 114.

120 A. H. Franks, 'Good Shoes', *Modern Dance* (August 1936), p. 24.

121 'Six Penny Partners', *Weekly Telegraph* (25 February 1939), p. 17.

122 Walkowitz, *Nights Out*, pp. 214–16.

5

English style: foreign culture, race and the Anglicisation of popular dance

In May 1920, Britain's leading dance professionals assembled in London and initiated the process that culminated in the creation of the English style of ballroom dance. As has been shown, the decision to standardise modern ballroom dancing was taken for several reasons, including a perceived need for consistency in what was being taught in dancing schools and a desire to insulate dancing from the attacks of critics. However, there was another critical dimension to the dance profession's efforts with respect to the English style, which was also exposed at the first informal conference. A dispute arose when some of those in attendance challenged various suggestions on standardisation offered by renowned dancer Maurice Mouvet (also known as 'Monsieur Maurice' or simply 'Maurice') on the grounds that he was not British. Of Belgian descent and born in New York City, Maurice had risen to fame prior to the First World War, alongside his partner Florence Walton, for their exhibitions of the tango and ragtime dances, and the pair had become international celebrities on a level that rivalled Irene and Vernon Castle.[1] Yet despite Maurice's lofty status and clear expertise, some of the teachers questioned, as Philip J. S. Richardson later recalled, 'what right had an American to attempt to teach English people how to dance'. Maurice's recommendations were eventually carried unanimously when other speakers pointed out that many of the dances under discussion were American in origin, and that as 'the greatest American dancer' Maurice was best positioned to offer an opinion on them.[2] However, the incident foreshadowed the ways in which the standardisation of the English style would be about considerably more than establishing a set form of steps and figures. As the interwar period progressed, popular dance became an important site of contestation over national identity and the growing influence in Britain of foreign – especially American – culture.

Anxieties about Americanisation were not exclusive to British dance professionals in this period. The entertainment industries that surrounded film, radio, popular music, music hall and theatrical dance, as well as dance halls, also expressed strong concerns about growing competition from American movies, music and stage acts. Various policies were thus enacted across Britain's entertainment economy to limit cultural imports from the United States, and, as this chapter will show, the dance profession found its own ways to combat foreign influence. Continually expressing that dancing was a manifestation of national character, temperament or race, the profession altered foreign dances through the standardisation process in a way that consciously 'Anglicised' them. In so doing, they reinforced and created a way to physically embody a vision of national identity defined in terms of social and regional unity; nationalist idioms such as reserve, civility and refinement; an emphasis on discipline and technique; and sexual restraint and whiteness. They saw the English style as entirely distinctive from – and superior to – the foxtrots and tangos of the Americas or Europe, and dancing technique and prowess became a way of differentiating the British from foreign and racial others. Additionally, the English style soon became more than a bulwark against Americanisation at home – it became a product that could be exported abroad, as the British dance profession's syllabus of modern ballroom dances was marketed to and adopted by teachers and dancers around the world.

The evolution of the national style of popular dancing, and the interactions between its producers and consumers, reveal a complicated picture of foreign influence and 'Americanisation' in Britain during the interwar years. While anxieties about American influence were seemingly real for some dance professionals, they also continued to rely heavily on the United States as a source of new dances to perform and teach. Like the dancers they instructed, professionals were generally fascinated by the latest developments in that country. Consequently, as they Anglicised foreign dances and crafted home-grown dances such as the five-step, trebla and six-eight, the profession's statements about, and responses to, Americanisation are often better understood as a marketing strategy than genuine expressions of concern. At the same time, with the export of the English style, Britain's professional dancers became important participants in shaping popular dance not only domestically, but globally. In these ways, the dance profession operated as much in concert with foreign culture as against it, disseminating the British national style abroad, and continuing to seek out new imports from the United States and Latin America. Importantly, as Britain entered the 1930s, this quest for new foreign dances was partly in response to a growing awareness among professionals – but also within the dancing public – that the English style was too reserved and regimented, and perhaps even too English. Dancers who grew impatient with the 'civility', 'refinement' and technical precision of the English style embraced dances such as the Cuban rumba and American truckin' as a means of restoring creativity and vitality to the dance floor, and in so doing constructed and performed alternative national imaginaries with their dancing bodies.

The English style and the nation

In the preface to his 1946 book *A History of English Ballroom Dancing*, Philip Richardson reflected on his subject, observing that over the past three decades Britain had 'undoubtedly taken the lead in the development of modern ballroom dancing'. He continued by acknowledging that very few of the ballroom dances that had attained prominence during that period had actually originated in Britain, but proclaimed that the standardisation of the English style had been the critical intervention to the evolution of superior technique around the world. As Richardson put it,

> Other countries may have supplied the raw material and the dancers of New York, being nearer the source of that material, may have been the first to experiment with it, but it was the teachers of England who first analysed the crude steps, reduced order out of chaos and evolved that modern technique which has made the English style paramount over three-fifths of the globe.[3]

Of the dances that formed the original standard four of the English style – the foxtrot, the one-step, the tango and the modern waltz – none had originated in Britain. Yet through the process of standardisation the dance profession made deliberate efforts to transform these dances – and the many other foreign dances that were subsequently imported to Britain – into something identifiably British. Consistently asserting that dancing was an expression of national character, temperament, or racial characteristics, professionals sought to create a style that was unifying across social and geographic divisions, and entirely distinctive from that of other countries. Critically, the movements they emphasised were those they believed best expressed British reserve, refinement, moderation, restraint and other related descriptors, while the ones they eliminated were those they deemed overtly sexual or associated with blackness. The end result was a dancing style that emphasised and physically embodied dominant and racialised visions of national identity, which British dance professionals were then able to market at home and abroad.

There were a variety of ways in which Britain's ballroom dancing style was constructed as a 'national' one. The accessibility of dancing as a leisure form – given the alleged simplicity of modern ballroom dances, the incessantly stated desire among professionals that its evolution should be directed by the tastes and preferences of the dancing public, and the low cost of an evening's dancing that came with the rise of the palais – connected popular dance with ideals of social inclusion and national unity. Dancing was a leisure practice open to all Britons, regardless of age, class, gender or region. This idea that dancing was 'democratic' only grew stronger as the interwar period progressed and dancing was envisioned as something that distinguished the British from the more autocratic political systems emerging on the Continent. In addition, since a major objective of standardisation was to deflect criticisms away from the new dances, the development of the English style was about making modern ballroom dancing not only accessible – but acceptable – to the whole of the national body. As has been shown, modern ballroom dances, their chief enthusiasts, and the public spaces where they were performed, often reinforced or fostered divisions of class, gender, sexuality and generation. Yet importantly, popular dance – and the emergence of a national style – was simultaneously constructed as an inculcator of social and national cohesion.

The unifying and collective impulse within the development and representation of the English style extended to geography as well. Despite the exclusionary character of the very name 'English' style within a country constituted by four nations, it was meant to represent the way that Britons danced from London to Edinburgh to Cardiff to Belfast. While 'English style' was predominately used to describe the standardised dances, 'British style' was occasionally employed, and many people argued that the national ballroom dancing style should be called 'British' rather than 'English'. This was not simply rhetoric, but rather a reflection of one of the primary goals of the standardisation of dance steps: to create a style that was legitimately nationwide with respect to how it was taught and performed. Therefore, since London teachers and London ballrooms were inevitably at the centre of the popular dancing world – both in terms of the quality of the dancing and the establishment of new trends – there was a consistent effort within the profession to bridge the gap between town and country.

As the standardisation process progressed, there was significant concern among professionals about the quality of dancing outside the capital. As one competitive dancer wrote in the *Dancing Times* in 1922, 'Despite the fact that … in the Provinces the modern dance has been in vogue for some considerable time, the standard of dancing prevailing there is still exceedingly poor.' Critics like this one pointed to the poor facilities for dancing beyond large urban areas, and the inferior quality of instruction, and were determined to remedy these problems. As the same author noted, he was 'exceedingly anxious ... to lay seeds which will blossom forth into a healthy desire among Provincial dancers to emulate the high standard of proficiency now shown by many of their London friends'.[4] The profession addressed provincial deficiencies in a variety of ways. London-based teachers communicated with their provincial counterparts through the mail and the press, trying to elevate their training and by extension the training of their students. Leading professionals like Richardson and Victor Silvester also travelled a great deal, offering their services as judges in competitions and facilitating exhibitions. The profession's concern with improving the dancing abilities of all Britons grew out of many of the same factors that had played into the decision to standardise the steps of the English style in the first place: to insulate dancing from criticism and to secure their own financial interests by drawing more people towards formal instruction. But these professional efforts also inaugurated a quest for national uniformity in the style, content and quality of popular dance.

By 1927, Richardson suggested that real headway had been made, writing in the *Dancing Times*, 'The improvement in dancing in the provinces is steadily maintained. At some places ... the standard is well up to the average London standard.'[5] However, in contrast to Richardson, there were also those – both within and outside the profession – who disputed that London was so far ahead of the rest of the country in popular dance. One London professional who attended a dance in a small village in 1925 had significant praise for both the quality and energy of the dancing she observed there, especially in comparison to what went on at many elite dances in the capital: 'The keenness and enthusiasm of the dancers, apart from the standard of their dancing, which was very high – was pleasantly refreshing after the languorous, what-a-beastly-bore attitude of dancers who sway and swirl, toddle and crawl in the somewhat artificial atmosphere of some of London's most exclusive ballrooms.'[6] Others argued that a town and country divide perhaps existed among professional dancers, but not within the dancing public. As one writer for *Popular Music and Dancing Weekly* noted, 'I would say that for individual exhibition dancing London takes the lead, but if I were asked to find Britain's best amateur dancer I would first search the provinces and try London as a last resource.'[7] Similarly, when asked about where the best dancing was to be found by Mass Observation, a dance hall manager in Bolton responded, 'For the general public I should say Liverpool and Manchester. Of course there are no experts outside London comparable with London experts ... Our good amateurs will look like novices against those in London.'[8]

Other observers beyond the capital disputed not only that Londoners were superior dancers, but also the idea that London was or should be the place that established trends for the rest of the country. In an interview with *Popular Music and Dancing Weekly*, the manager of the Palace dance hall in Douglas, on the Isle of Man, declared, 'We here in the North do not *follow* London; we frequently set the fashion ourselves.'[9] The *Liverpool Echo* likewise observed in 1926,

> Twice this week I have seen, in print, slighting references to 'the provincial style.' It is time Londoners learnt better than this. There may have been a provincial style in the derogatory sense a few years ago, but since then there has been no difference in favour of London ... [It] is in big provincial centres like Manchester and Liverpool that the fate of dancers is decided.[10]

Even if they did not claim to be setting the 'fashion', many dancers outside the capital made efforts to stay current and keep up with what the rest of the nation was dancing, and to what music. As the manager of a Bolton dance hall told Mass Observation, 'The people are very up-to-date. They expect to hear all the tunes that are being played on the wireless.'[11] Members of the dancing public could be as invested as the dance profession in shaping the national style, no matter where they lived in the country. Given the diversity within the dancing public, nationwide stylistic uniformity was an unrealistic aspiration that was never fulfilled – but the existence of this effort firmly embedded dancing within discourses about national unity and the creation of a distinctively British culture.

Nothing demonstrated this agenda more clearly than what proved to be a central issue in the development of the English style, which was to distinguish British dancing from the way in which the same dances were performed in other countries – especially the United States. The successful standardisation of steps and figures was itself something that differentiated British dancing, since American professionals were never able to attain the same level of national uniformity among teachers and the dancers they instructed. While American dance teachers, like their British counterparts, spent considerable time in the 1910s and 1920s experimenting with and giving order to the steps of ragtime and jazz dances, national standardisation efforts largely failed owing, as Juliet McMains has argued, to the immense geographic breadth of the United States.[12] For British teachers, in contrast, the development of the English style was not only about creating a standard technique for dancers throughout the British Isles: it was about altering foreign dances in way that made them more identifiably British.

As the English style evolved throughout the 1920s, those who oversaw the process consistently argued that wherever the dances being standardised had come from, British ballroom dancing was now something entirely transformed and distinctive. As Richardson observed in the *Dancing Times* in 1923, 'though we still get our ingredients abroad, we always mix them together to suit our own tastes'. Using as an example the nation's favourite dance, he continued, 'The ingredients of the foxtrot came from America, but the foxtrot as danced to-day in London is essentially an English dance, with considerable difference from its prototype in New York.'[13] Major Cecil Taylor, president of the Imperial Society of Teachers of Dancing, echoed this belief that American dances were significantly made over in Britain, proclaiming in an interview with Mass Observation: 'modern ballroom dancing is due to American influence without question but on every occasion it has arrived in England it has been pulled to pieces by the experts and has had cuttings and trimmings – cuttings taken off and trimmings added to – which have made it worthy of acceptance'.[14] The process was described even more explicitly by champion competition dancer, Nancy Bramall, who explained in *Popular Music and Dancing Weekly* that 'new dances … imported from other countries are strictly censored by the experts before being presented to the British dancer, and ugly or ungainly movements are eliminated'.[15]

At the root of this transformative process was the conviction that dancing style was expressive of national identities, which were alternately described in terms of character, temperament or race. As part of a survey of the state of popular dance across continental Europe, for instance, Maxwell Stewart observed, 'Every nation has its own individual form of dancing, and a nation's character is shown in its dancing.'[16] Another writer, in an article describing American dancing, similarly commented that 'dancing is an expression of life which is influenced by the national character. Therefore, little differences will always remain between the different continents.'[17] In these and the many other references to national distinctions in dancing, 'character', 'temperament' and 'race' were generally used interchangeably, referencing aspects of a people's personality and inner qualities, alongside their bodily capabilities. In keeping with longstanding definitions, 'racial' differences were simultaneously understood as the distinctions between those of different countries and skin tones.

Significantly, this interest in national and racial differentiation was not confined to dance professionals, but built upon and interacted with a more widespread concern with the nature of Englishness/Britishness in this period. As Peter Mandler has argued, 'the years between the world wars were the heyday of the idea of the English national character'.[18] The experience of the war fostered a sense of unity among those who had survived it, as well as an acute awareness of the differences among nations that had come from identifying enemies and interacting with allies. Everywhere from politics, to the hard and social sciences, to popular culture and the arts, there were strong efforts to unpack the essence of the national character and the common characteristics that united the people of all classes and regions, even as these characteristics tended to be defined as English rather than British. In creating the English style, British dance professionals also entered into this fray, crafting a national ballroom dancing style that was constructed in direct reference to prominent ideas about the national character – such as reserve, moderation, temperateness and civility. While many of these characteristics had been seen to define the English/British since the Enlightenment, they took on new importance after 1918 when an emphasis on peacefulness and moderation emerged as a means of combating fears of brutalisation that resulted from the war.[19] However, the national dancing style that was crafted through the process of altering and standardising foreign dances did more than simply reinforce or express ideas about national identity: it embodied and physically performed them. British dance professionals of the interwar period were cognisant of the connections between dancing and cultural identity formation. They believed that the national and racial characteristics of the British – as well as of other nations – were something that was bodily expressed through their movements in the ballroom.

In this context, professionals contended that foreign dances required British dancers to act in ways that ran contrary to their very nature as Britons. In their original form, what they termed 'Latin' dances such as the tango were too overtly sensual and too uninhibited for the reserved British temperament. In 1914, shortly after the tango's arrival in Britain, one writer remarked derisively that 'as danced in England by English people, [it] is petulant rather than passionate, as mild and mellifluous as a spray of hawthorn swaying to and fro in a breeze from the West. It is not in the least like the erotic prowl *a deux* of which travelers in Spanish America … speak with bated breath.'[20] The notion that British reserve made an effective performance of the tango a near impossibility was also frequently used to account for the dancing public's reticence in embracing the dance. As Santos Casani mused, 'It was said, rightly or wrongly, that English dancers had not the temperament for this most graceful Southern dance: in any case, the tango was not a success.'[21] In the case of American dances, they were said to be too stunt-filled, boisterous and unrefined for British tastes and abilities. This same critique was levelled against dances from the animal dances, through the Charleston, to the jitterbug, which also required – in in their unmodified forms – a degree of energy and abandon that was purportedly unnatural in the British. For instance, when a new dance called the 'College Swing' achieved considerable success in the United States after being introduced in a Betty Grable film, one dance magazine speculated that it was unlikely to succeed in British ballrooms, since it required 'for its complete enjoyment the ability to abandon oneself entirely to its quick rhythm. In fact, one should let oneself go to an extent of which but few English folk are capable.'[22]

The standardisation of the English style, and the subsequent modification of the multitude of other foreign imports that followed on the heels of the standard four, was thus also about Anglicising them. As the *Dancing Times* commented in 1924, 'The foxtrot, as danced in London to-day, is an English dance, in spite of its American beginning, and we much prefer to dance it in our own way.'[23] That 'own way' signalled a variety of changes that were made through the standardisation process to the foxtrot and other dances. First, British technique firmly stressed correct hold and balance. Dance scholar Theresa Buckland has described the requirements as follows: 'The torso was to move as an unbroken block: that meant no rotation of the pelvis, or moving it from side to side or sent back and forth; the shoulders were to be held straight and down, with no hunching and no movement back and forth.'[24] A careful distance was maintained between dancing partners, and all manner of jerking, shaking, or grinding was eliminated. This eased both the un-British demand for – and the social anxieties about – the close bodily contact between partners and overt sexuality that dances such as the tango, foxtrot, one-step and modern waltz had inspired in their rudimentary forms. Instead the English style was designed to conform to ideals of respectable femininity and masculine restraint.

Second, the dances were recreated to be fluid and graceful, with more of an emphasis on gliding rather than trotting. The kicks, dips, lifts, 'freak steps' and general 'stunting' that professionals believed characterised American and Continental dancing were all eliminated. Rather, as Maxwell Stewart expressed it, the English style was 'stately, graceful, and quiet, consisting of long, gliding steps and sweeping turns'.[25] In British ballroom dancing, strong emphasis was placed on precise technique, rather than on creativity, improvisation or dynamism. As the standardisation process was later described in a commemorative book about the Grafton Rooms dance hall in Liverpool, 'With that wonderful facility which we seem to have in Britain for toning down the eccentricities in imported dances the first wild movements of jazz became more and more subdued and the modern ballroom dancing with a definite technique was really on the way.'[26]

The elimination of 'eccentricities', wildness and particular movements from American dancing also had a marked racial dimension. Dance scholars have established that most dance forms native to the United States – from the eighteenth century Virginia jig to the dances of the Jazz Age like the foxtrot, Charleston and jitterbug – were in fact blended amalgams of African, African-American and European-American traditions. From black America came elements such as improvisation, close holds, torso undulation, call-and-response and strutting, while the European influence included partner dancing, and aspects of Celtic jigs and German reels.[27] Dances of Latin American origin like the tango or rumba were likewise hybrid creations that emerged from the multi-racial societies of South America and the Caribbean, but their blackness was not a prominent element of their reception in Britain; rather, 'Latin' dances were associated with exoticism and sensuality, or more pejoratively with effeminacy or laziness.[28] In contrast, despite their equally creolised geneses, most American dances of the Jazz Age were understood as African American in origin on both sides of the Atlantic.[29] Indeed, in Britain, the actual provenance of American dances was even less clear, since they were received second hand and often after they had already been appropriated and altered by white American dancers like the Castles or Maurice. In this muddled context, the simplest instinctive reflex was often to equate 'American' with 'African American'.

A language of race was thus central to the efforts by British professionals to grapple with the growing number of American dance imports and the process of standardising the English style. Commentary ranged from sanguine acknowledgments of the African-American origins of many of the dances to overt racial prejudice. In 1919, in an impassioned plea for a restoration of the waltz to common practice, dancing teacher Edward Scott wrote in the *Dancing Times*,

> Depend upon it, when the wheel of fashion takes another turn, as the nigger minstrels depart, with all their baggage of banjoes, drums, motor-horns, tin-plates, and frying-pans, the ever youthful waltz will again be welcomed with open arms,

and the discomfited jazzers, fox-trotters and one-steppers will, nolens volens, succumb to her irresistible sway.[30]

Even proponents of American dances employed racist invective in describing them. Another columnist who wrote monthly about her eager forays into London's terpsichorean nightlife observed that modern ballroom dancing 'originated from the niggers ... and that it requires neither brains nor ordinary intelligence'.[31]

The racial origins of American dances were an ever-present feature of the commentaries surrounding them, and the same racist tropes appeared time and again as new imports from the United States were introduced throughout the interwar period. When the blues arrived in Britain in 1923, for instance, the *Dancing Times* noted that it 'originated with the Darkies in the Southern States of America'.[32] Racialised language was even more in evidence with the introduction of the Charleston in 1925. As was shown in Chapter 2, upon its initial appearance in Britain, the dance engendered a great deal of controversy. Like all of the American dances that had preceded it, the Charleston was viewed to be too wild and boisterous for the refined British ballroom, something which was articulated in profoundly racist terms. One *Daily Mail* correspondent, for example, declared the dance to be 'a series of contortions without a vestige of charm or grace, reminiscent only of the Negro orgies from which it derives its creation'.[33] Reacting to the controversy, the dance profession stepped in just as it had with the foxtrot and one-step, and adapted the American version of the dance into the 'flat progressive Charleston' by eliminating its energetic kicks and more unruly movements. The goal was to circumvent public criticism and bring the Charleston in line with the other dances of the English style and, accordingly, the British character.

Yet significantly, as the furore over the Charleston dissipated, the *Dancing Times* published an article that was revealing about what was really at the root of efforts to tone down the Charleston and to standardise the steps of the English style more broadly. Entitled the 'Negro Influence in Dancing', the article charted the long-term influence of African-American culture on British music and dance. Starting with the minstrel performances of the mid-nineteenth century, the author's analysis moved steadily forward in time, acknowledging that often the 'white man has ... learnt something from the negro'. But arriving at the moment that ragtime and jazz dances emerged from African-American communities, the author wrote,

Of course, [these dances] had to be refined and adapted to civilised life before [they] could be countenanced in European ballrooms. The sawing movements of the arms, shaking shoulders, and close embraces, the incessant tom-tom beating and clatter had to be modified. The Charleston has been so adapted, and in its reformed character seems to be a welcome addition to the ballroom répertoire.[34]

A few months later, Silvester offered a similar assessment of the way that British professionals would 'crib' movements from African Americans, but then had to give them 'style, polish and finish' in order to make them worthy of 'the best ballroom dancers in the world [in this country]'.[35]

These statements in what was ostensibly the dance profession's 'paper of record' made explicit the racial undertone to the standardisation of the English style and the ongoing Anglicisation of American dances. Frequent references to 'freakish' and 'eccentric' steps, as well as 'stunting' or 'wildness' in professional descriptions of American imports were racially encoded, and their elimination – through 'polish and finish' – altered black dances in a way that brought them in line with dominant understandings of national identity which equated English/Britishness with whiteness. Britain's status as a colonial power had long established a racialised nationalism, but, during the interwar years national cohesion was in part re-stabilised by othering Britain's small population of people of colour, which encompassed people of African, South Asian, West Indian and Chinese descent.[36] The whiteness of Englishness/Britishness was asserted as a bulwark against national challenges ranging from the trauma of the war, to the Depression, to the weakening of the Empire. Efforts to whiten black dances were thus consonant with this dominant racialised articulation of national identity.

British professionals were not alone in this undertaking to whiten black dances. As Danielle Robinson has shown, the process of modifying the untamed, intimate, and inventive dances of ragtime into the formalised modern ballroom dancing had commenced with American professionals – most notably the Castles, as well as Maurice and Walton – who sought to elevate the dances' respectability and market them to a middle-class audience by 'defusing [their] racial threat'. Even the characteristics that would come to embody the very Englishness of the English style, such as 'restraint' and 'refinement', had American antecedents, as they were bestowed upon the process of removing 'ragtime's references to blackness by containing its exuberant physicality and sexuality'.[37] The influence of American professionals on the early stages of the British standardisation process also extended to their physical presence: as has been shown, Maurice was in attendance at the first informal conference, and in the autumn of 1918 Irene Castle had visited Britain and provided comments on jazz music and dances which were reported on as authoritative in the *Dancing*

Times.[38] The transformation and commodification of what were perceived to be black dances into the mainstream and respectable modern ballroom dancing was thus accomplished through processes of modification and whitening that extended across and were moulded by professionals on both sides of the Atlantic.

Although they collaborated with their American counterparts on a process that actually began in the United States, British professionals believed that the end result was entirely in keeping with the character, temperament and racial composition of their own country. The English style was regularly compared to the dancing of foreign and racial others, and proclaimed to be superior. In describing its movements and technique, specific descriptors such as grace, steadiness, sedateness, moderation, restraint, refinement, reserve and civility, were all invoked and attached nationalistic meanings to British dancing. As early as 1921 an official for what would become the Imperial Society of Teachers of Dancing declared to the *Daily Mail* that 'the Englishman has become the best dancer in the world. His dancing is very much steadier and infinitely more graceful than that of the American, the Frenchman, or the German'.[39] The *Dancing Times* similarly observed a year later:

> There is none of the roughness or harshness of the American execution seen in a British ballroom, nor is there anything of the svelt movement of the Latin. The Britisher's execution lies somewhere between these two, and in its highest expression becomes a thing of grace and rhythm such as is the admiration of the dancing world. This is founded upon the Englishman's unfailing instinct for moderation.[40]

Beyond the profession, the same national idioms were affirmed by other figures in the dancing world as well. For example, Savoy hotel bandleader Ramon Newton described British dancing as 'sedate' and 'restrained', observing it was far more graceful than what he had witnessed during his time as a musician in North America.[41] Teachers and others who inhabited the professional realm believed that compared to the way in which the same dances were performed abroad, the British execution was more graceful, refined and ultimately superior. As Nancy Bramall summed it up, 'you have only to ask anyone who has travelled abroad to learn that British dancing is better conducted and healthier in every way than the dances to be found in any other country'.[42]

Indeed, British dance professionals did travel frequently, and were able to base their assessments of British dancing versus that of other nations on the observations they made while touring and teaching abroad. In the wake of a stint on the Continent in 1932, Silvester proclaimed in the *Dancing Times* that 'the Anglo-Saxon nations make better ballroom dancers than those of the Latin or southern group'. He attributed this superiority to the fact that those of 'Anglo-Saxon' descent were 'more controlled' and possessed a 'steadier temperament', further claiming that after the British the Germans had the best technique in Europe because their 'national characteristics' made them more 'hard-working, thorough and methodical'.[43] A few years later, following his own tour of Europe, Maxwell Stewart agreed with Silvester that northern Europeans like Germans and Danes – who had by this time adopted the English style technique in their classes and ballrooms – were the strongest dancers on the Continent. He also offered comments on the French, writing that they 'take their dancing with a lively spirit and atmosphere', and he found much to admire in the 'gay, *joie de vivre*' on display in French ballrooms. However, Stewart still concluded that 'compared with our English style, their dancing is apt to appear jerky and rather of an erratic nature'.[44] A similarly dissonant critique was levelled against American dancing by professional Thomas Bus following a tour of public ballrooms in the United States. Bus was extremely impressed with the 'utter abandonment and freedom with which these people dance', but affirmed that the 'execution [of technique] would not stand a comparison with the English style'.[45]

Professionals thus acknowledged that British dancing could be deficient to that of other nations in terms of energy and passion – or even natural ability – but believed that what British national characteristics enabled was discipline, concentration and a commitment to technique. For instance, in a *Dancing Times* article entitled the 'Supremacy of the English Style', married professionals Josephine Bradley and Douglas Wellesley-Smith decreed that the British were without a doubt the 'best dancers in the world'. But in attempting to account for that superiority the authors joked that it was not owing to 'our innate sense of rhythm – we haven't one'. In a way that affirmed the connections between nation, race and dancing ability, Bradley and Wellesley-Smith acknowledged that Americans and the European 'Latin' races in particular had natural advantages the British lacked, but remained inferior dancers because 'they know nothing of the English style and technique'.[46] Silvester likewise believed that the strength of technique evident among British dancers easily trumped temperamental or racial affinity. In an effort to counteract public reluctance to engage with the tango, for example, Silvester vehemently disputed what he believed to be a widely proliferated notion that 'unless you have Latin blood in your veins, it is impossible to dance it. Never was there such a ridiculous fallacy in the history of ballroom dancing.'[47]

British dance professionals had a vested interest in arguing for the superiority of the technique that they had devised: it was the basis of their business as teachers of dancing and provided a marketable commodity which was sold via classes, public performances and instruction manuals at home – but also abroad. As much as the English style was articulated as an expression and physical embodiment of the British national character, it was equally seen as a technique that could be emulated by and marketed to foreigners. Despite the many statements in the very same article linking national temperament to the execution of dancing, in the 'Supremacy of the English Style', the authors also had this to say about the national technique: 'We refer to it as "English," not because there is anything particularly English about it, but merely because our first-class dancers have been the first to discover and exploit it.'[48] That discovery and exploitation was what had made Britain, in the minds of many both within and beyond the dance profession, the centre of the ballroom dancing world.

The English style and the world

In 1922, within only two years of the beginning of the standardisation process, Richardson observed: 'One must have some criterion by which one can judge the attempts of dancers in any particular dance … In the foxtrot and one-step one first looked to America, whence they came; now one looks to the best exponents in London.'[49] A decade later, Richardson's *Dancing Times* believed the reach of British technique had extended even farther. As the opening pages of an issue from 1935 put it, 'With the possible exception of the United States of America all the world looks to-day to Britain in matters appertaining to ballroom dancing, and what she does to-day Europe, Asia, Africa and Australasia will hope to do to-morrow.'[50]

What this meant in specific terms was that as the technique of the English style of ballroom dancing was formalised, it was exported abroad. While none of the dances that formed the English style had originated in Britain, what British professionals provided – to a degree that the countries of origin for many of these dances had not – was a syllabus of standard steps and figures that could be used in instruction. As Silvester observed, 'It is now an accepted and undisputed fact that the majority of the nations in Europe have adopted what has come to be known as the English style … and are doing their best to emulate us.'[51] Taylor put it even more succinctly, bragging to Mass Observation that, 'Everyone wants to dance the London style no matter where they live. Without question London leads the world in social dancing.'[52]

International dance competitions – amateur and professional alike – were another important way in which the British asserted their technical supremacy and motivated foreigners to adopt the English style. As Silvester told Mass Observation, 'All the continental countries copy English styles, mainly because English couples win all the competitions'.[53] Professionals like Silvester expressed great pride at the degree to which British teams dominated international dance competitions throughout the interwar period. One *Dancing Times* article, for instance, described recent British defeats at the hands of the United States in golf, France in tennis, Germany in football and Australia in bowls, but concluded by asserting, 'there is still one kind of championship that *cannot* be taken from us by all the rest of Europe put together – and that that is a *Dancing Championship*'.[54]

Another result of British supremacy in competitive ballroom dancing was that the annual Blackpool championship gradually attained international rather than solely national importance. By 1935, the *Dancing Times* argued that it was at Blackpool that innovations in the foxtrot, quickstep or waltz were 'crystallised' in the performances of competitors, and non-British dancers seeking to perfect the English style followed these developments with rapt attention. As the magazine put it, 'It is therefore no exaggeration to say that hundreds of thousands of people all over the world are interested in and indirectly affected by the decisions of the Adjudicators in the "Empress Ballroom".'[55] In fact, the student became the master when a Danish team actually defeated the British at the two countries' annual competition in 1938, much to the great perturbation of the British dance press. But even as their home-grown dancers were challenged, the British profession's annual championship was increasingly acknowledged as the marquee ballroom dancing event around the world. An editorial in *Modern Dance* affirmed this predominance, by comparing Blackpool to another national event that had achieved global import: 'The All-British Championship has become the world's championship, as is the case of the tennis at Wimbledon, which is really only an "All-England" title, but again justly regarded as the "blue riband" of the tennis contests throughout the globe.'[56]

Importantly, it was not only British professionals who affirmed the supremacy of their technique and its growing influence abroad. In 1933 the *Dancing Times* published a reflection entitled 'European and American Dancing Compared', written by Japanese contributor James Hyojiro Kato. Describing his first introduction to modern ballroom dancing during his travels to Europe and the United States immediately following the First World War, Kato recalled that at that time, the United States – as the country of origin for jazz music and dances such as the foxtrot – enjoyed 'world-leadership' in ballroom dancing, and Europe and Asia alike took their cues from America. However, on a subsequent world tour in 1931, Kato suggested that the tables had turned; his expectations for American dancing were 'miserably crushed', and he found that the country had 'gone astray' and 'completely off the right path of progress'. European ballroom dancing, in contrast, was in a state of 'new splendour'. Particularly impressive to this Japanese traveller was Britain, where he found the ballroom dancing to be 'artistically refined' and 'technically studied and developed'. In so doing, Kato echoed the descriptions of the English style supplied by its own creators, and also made a case for Britain's growing global supremacy in ballroom dancing technique. As he observed, 'It now goes without saying that England has taken the position once held by America, and will continue to lead the ballroom dancing of the world for many years to come.' Although at his time of writing some American and French influence was still evident in the ballroom dancing technique of his own country, Kato believed in 'a few years time the English style will completely dominate the whole dancing population in Japan'.[57]

That the comments provided by this Japanese aficionado – as well as similar testimonials contributed to the *Dancing Times* by Germans, Americans and several other foreign dancers – appeared in the dance profession's premier magazine suggests that they were not unmediated by British teachers seeking to further reinforce the superiority of their technique. However, they do still speak to the global dissemination and impact of the English style as the interwar period progressed. As it was perfected and formalised, the British national ballroom dancing style was adopted as the preferred technique in dance classes, competitions and public ballrooms across Europe, throughout much of the British Empire, and in many other countries around the world. This expanding interest in British technique created new professional opportunities for British teachers. The instruction manuals of figures such as Silvester and Santos Casani were marketed internationally, and British dance professionals were in high demand abroad as teachers and exhibition dancers – bringing their technique along with them. In particular British teachers spent a great deal of time on the European continent, performing in Paris and maintaining schools in the resort towns of the south of France; by the late 1920s, commentators observed that the influence of the English style was clearly discernible in Parisian dancing. British professionals also commonly visited other European countries such as Germany and Denmark, while in return, teachers from as far away as Eastern

Europe and Scandinavia visited London to 'brush up on their dancing' and 'acquire the style about which they have heard so much'.[58]

The influence of the British dance profession and the English style extended beyond Europe as well. Accreditation of teachers in places such as South Africa, Australia and India drew upon the standards approved by the Official Board of Ballroom Dancing. In 1933, the *Dancing Times* published a list of just a few of the many countries where dance professionals trained in British schools were then teaching, which included Australia, Canada, China, India, Rhodesia, South Africa, Spain, Switzerland and the United States.[59] It should be noted that despite the presence in that year of British teachers in cities like Miami, Los Angeles and Winnipeg, for the most part American-style ballroom steps continued to hold sway in North America until the 1960s, when the English style became the 'International Style' and was adopted in the United States, Canada and ballroom dancing classes and competitions throughout the world.[60] However, in the interim, British technique still had a considerable impact on North American dancing. British teachers took up extended residencies in New York and other cities, to see what was new in dancing across the pond, but also to provide reciprocal instruction in the English style. In one such case, married dance team Alec and Maud Mackenzie reported that they had found 'the dancers over there are much intrigued with the quickstep'.[61] British teachers were also encouraged to advertise in American dance periodicals, so that the growing number of American tourists to London would know where to locate instruction in the local style. Among them were many professional dancers, who – although the English style was not consistently adopted in the United States – were still eager to participate in 'teacher's weeks' alongside their European counterparts and to learn the latest in British dancing. Indeed, the global impact of the English style technique was such that on the occasion of the fifth anniversary of the Great Conference and the formal establishment of the standard four, Silvester observed, 'It must be very gratifying to Mr. Philip Richardson to know that the syllabus recommended by the Official Board has been adopted and copied throughout the world.'[62]

The creation of the English style and the international dissemination of British ballroom technique thus challenges a straightforward picture of encroaching Americanisation around the world during the interwar period. The dances of the Jazz Age – which, while often identified as American and exported globally by way of New York, were generally hybrid creations of American, Latin American, African and European traditions already – were recreated on the ground in Britain, and then exported abroad as something distinctive and identifiably British. This had important cultural ramifications, providing a means for producers and consumers of popular dance alike to grapple with and physically perform British national identity. But the creation of the English style was also financially driven, and provided the dance profession with a marketable commodity, which was sold domestically and internationally. Framing the dissemination of British technique in explicitly economic terms, the *Dancing Times* observed in 1935:

> In these islands some millions of pounds are invested in what may be called the 'dancing industry' and, at present, in this industry our 'trade balance' with the rest of the world is in our favour. We not only set the example but we send our dances, our dancers and our teachers to the four corners of the globe.[63]

However, even as the British profession grew to be ascendant in ballroom dancing technique, the national style it had created faced new challenges from at home and abroad.

Foreign culture, commercial nationalism and popular dance

The British dance profession firmly believed in – and advertised their technique on the basis of – the conviction that foreign dances were transformed, and even made superior, through the processes of standardisation and Anglicisation. Nonetheless, concerns about the strength of foreign influence on British popular dance persisted. Professionals had what might best be described as ambivalent relationship with the United States in particular. They continued to make strong use of the United States as a source for new dances that they could introduce to the dancing public, but they framed aspects of their marketing – particularly for a series of home-grown, 'British' ballroom dances that were launched starting in the mid-1920s – in explicitly anti-American terms. The ultimate failure of this marketing campaign, however, revealed that the specific Britishness of the English style, or the British-made dances the profession had created, was of far less concern to the dancing public. Indeed, the more technically precise the English style became, the more everyday dancers, musicians, dance hall proprietors and even some members of the dance profession expressed concern that it was too difficult and growing stale. By the 1930s, all of these parties began to seek out new ways to reinvigorate popular dance, turning even more regularly towards foreign imports, and exploiting alternative avenues such as motion pictures, in the quest for novelty. The result was that the vision of the nation expressed on the country's dance floors gradually began to challenge the reserve, refinement and whiteness emphasised by the English style.

Even as professional dancers carried out the process of altering and Anglicising foreign dances through the standardisation of the English style, there were those who saw the need for a dance that was British in *creation* rather than merely in evolution. As exhibition dancers Marjorie and Georges Fontana mused in the *Dancing Times*, 'England is rapidly taking her place as the foremost dancing nation of the world ... Does it not seem a pity that we have to go abroad for all our new dances? Are we not clever enough in this country to evolve something ourselves?'[64] In the wake of such comments, there were several notable attempts to answer the call for a ballroom dance that was completely British-made. The first of these was the 'five-step', which was developed by composer Harry Davson and dancer George Cunningham, and was a ballroom dance set in 5/4 time, distinguishing it from the foxtrot's 4/4 or the waltz's 3/4.

The five-step received a substantial amount of publicity in the dance and popular press, and was endorsed by celebrities such as bandleader Jack Hylton. The promotional campaign also explicitly touted the home-grown Britishness of the dance. As *Popular Music and Dancing Weekly*'s columnist 'Fox Trot' reported in June 1924, 'We can congratulate ourselves at last a new dance has been invented which can bear the trade stamp of "Made in England".'[65] But despite the best efforts of the media and the dance profession to promote this British-made dance, the five-step failed to catch on with the dancing public in any meaningful way. The bottom line was that the British origins of the five-step could not compensate for its weaknesses as a dance. It was overly complicated, and the distinctive time signature meant that there was a shortage of songs to which it could actually be performed. The intense promotional campaign may also have worked against the dance in the end. Richardson speculated that part of the problem with the five-step was that in their eagerness to embrace a new – and British – dance, teachers and the press gave it such a flurry of attention that its limitations were very quickly exposed.[66]

However, the failure of the five-step did not preclude several other attempts to develop home-grown ballroom dances. Only two years later, the 'trebla' appeared, and was even more explicitly trumpeted for its British creation and sensibilities. Named for one of its creators Albert ('trebla' when the letters were reversed) Barnett, the dance was heavily promoted – especially as a bulwark against Americanisation. Barnett and his partner, Nora Chilo, staged daily demonstrations of the dance at their studio, and it received widespread coverage in the dance press and a number of instruction manuals. The *Dancing Times* alone featured full-page advertisements for the trebla for over a year. An illustrative example contained the image of a lion – traditional heraldic symbol of Great Britain – bookended by the phrase 'British & Best' (see Figure 5.1). Building upon the global reputation of the English style, the advertisement suggested (contrary to any real evidence) that the trebla was already 'the dance sensation of the British Empire and the Capitals of Western Europe'. The text further advised readers: 'Don't be dominated entirely by American Invasions!!! Learn the TREBLA the All-British Non-Sequence Dance.'[67] Another advertisement even more overtly presented the trebla as a stem against the tide of American influence, by employing testimonials for the dance from the popular press. As the *Referee* affirmed: 'It is an entirely British dance, not a hybrid product of American origin, like most of our dances.' The *West London News* similarly averred: 'It is hoped that [the Charleston] will soon be superseded by "The Trebla", which is a simple and graceful dance and is entirely British.'[68]

5.1   Advertisement for the trebla, an original 'British' ballroom dance.

However, despite the widespread and intensely nationalistic promotional campaign, the trebla had as little impact on British popular dance as its predecessor the five-step. The same failure awaited the 'six-eight', another new dance which the profession as a whole agreed to throw its collective weight behind and 'push' following the Great Conference in 1929. Again the creation of British dance professionals, the six-eight was designed to accompany 'old English dance measures' written in 6/8 time (and perhaps avoid the problem of the five-step's lack of accompanying tunes). But according to the *Dancing Times*, the six-eight did more than resurrect old national songs: it fulfilled a public clamour for national dances. As the magazine put it, 'For years the Press have been crying out "Why cannot we have British dances for British ballrooms?" The Six-Eight is a big step in that direction.'[69]

The dance profession thus framed the creation – and especially the promotion – of home-grown ballroom dances in direct opposition to the expanding influence of American culture in Britain. From the very first conference of dancing teachers in 1920, some professionals were clearly wary of American influence, as their criticisms of Monsieur Maurice's contributions had demonstrated. Their subsequent efforts to distinguish the standard four of the English style from their equivalent American dances, and to develop home-grown British ballroom dances, also had strong nationalistic undertones and were influenced by broader concerns about Americanisation within British society. But while dance professionals may have possessed legitimate anxieties about Americanisation, those fears were belied by their own consistent interaction with and co-optation of American cultural products. Leading professionals travelled frequently to the United States, and those who could not looked eagerly to others for the latest news and innovations. For instance, when ex-pats Alec and Maud Mackenzie returned to London from New York for a brief stay, they advertised in the *Dancing Times* on the basis that they could provide 'a limited number of lessons and hold Teachers' Classes in all the latest developments in American Ballroom Dancing'.[70] Another British teacher described the influence of the United States on professionals in Britain in slightly exasperated terms, noting that whenever New York City in particular introduced anything new in dancing, 'the [British] dance profession stops in its tracks to hear the news and alters its course accordingly'.[71] Ultimately, the profession's general readiness to import any new dance sensation that took hold in the United States operated in constant tension with its efforts to construct an intrinsically British dancing style.

A similar incongruity was evident in efforts by other entertainment industries to subvert American influence in the interwar years. Throughout the 1920s and 1930s, American music, films and performers became increasingly common on British cinema screens, bandstands and stages. This inspired a protectionist reaction from the home-grown industries surrounding these cultural forms. As Peter Bailey has argued, in the 1920s the Variety Artists Federation became 'fiercely protectionist and racist' in the face of the growing number of American performers on the music hall stage, and attempted to curb the number of foreign acts.[72] The Musicians Union (supported by the Ministry of Labour) followed suit in 1935, and imposed a ban on 'aliens', which was clearly directed primarily towards the large number of American bands (many of them featuring black musicians) operating in Britain.[73] At the same time, the British film industry, fearing the predominant popularity of Hollywood movies, also worked with the government to pass the 1927 Cinematograph Films Act, which introduced the notorious quota system, in which a certain percentage of films shown in Britain had to be British-made.

However, the outcomes of these initiatives were largely ambiguous. As Bailey has shown, by the 1930s music hall was being celebrated for its 'exemplary Englishness', while showcasing a distinct Anglo-American hybridity in its actual acts.[74] In the case of cinema, the quota system did help to stimulate production within the British film industry, but also led to the creation of the so-called 'quota quickies' – poor quality, low cost films designed to meet the requirements of the quota – which ultimately tarnished the reputation of British film.[75] With respect to musicians, many British dance bands did achieve success and renown, while the number of American bands working in Britain dropped. However, government documents suggest that the British ban was motivated by more than concerns about foreign competition, but was also a reaction to a parallel ban on foreign acts in the United States. In the mid-1930s this prohibition left famed British bandleader Jack Payne unable to land in New York to take up a planned American tour, a slight which received much publicity in Britain.[76]

In this context, the nationalistic rhetoric present in the advertising for British-made dances, and the whole process of 'Anglicising' foreign dances, should at least in part be understood as a marketing strategy rather than as a legitimate attempt to curb Americanisation. Professionals commodified the nation and used American cultural encroachment as a way of promoting and selling their home-grown dances, in an example of commercial nationalism. Indeed, contradicting their alleged fears of Americanisation, is the fact that

– even as they marketed the five-step, trebla and six-eight on the basis of their Britishness – professionals continued to import new American dances as well, as part of ongoing efforts to locate 'standard five', boost dance class enrolments and sell instruction manuals. Also significant is what the reception of the five-step, trebla and six-eight all revealed about the preferences of the dancing public: notably, a dance's Britishness was not enough to guarantee it would be a success. These dances clearly lacked other qualities that the dancing public valued more than national origin, a fact made further apparent by a growing sense of impatience with the English style that began to be manifested in various quarters as Britain moved into the 1930s.

Importantly, the more the English style was formalised, the more contested it – and by extension the ways that it articulated the national character – became within the dance profession and dancing public alike. Even as the English style was embraced abroad and British expertise was celebrated, there were growing concerns that the technique was too precise and excessively regimented. The standardisation of steps and figures meant that there was a 'correct' and 'incorrect' way to dance, which some feared stifled creativity and innovation, and would ultimately make dancing stagnant and dull. As early as 1923, a *Dancing Times* article suggestively entitled 'The Dullness of English Dancing', provided a disheartening description of the average British ballroom:

> the real joy of dancing is conspicuous by its absence. Steps have become rather too conventional with the best dancers owing to the influence of competitions which have led to standardisation, which … is all to the good as long as individuality is not killed.[77]

While there were those who described British ballroom dancing as refined and graceful, there were equally others who saw it as uninspired, phlegmatic and boring. And while the precision, refinement and reserve of the English style was said to be an expression of the national character, some argued that both dancing style *and* national temperament would benefit equally from a little shaking up. In the early stages of the dance craze, the *Daily Mail* asked, 'is it not to the credit of the Jazz band that it has caused the Englishman to lay aside some of his traditional reserve for once to let himself "go," and to show that he really is enjoying himself?'[78] An anonymous teacher likewise claimed in 1926 that one of the great virtues of the Charleston was that it was 'fun' enough to have knocked some of the severity out of the 'solemn-faced British dancer'.[79] As this revealed, even some professionals, despite their belief in the superiority of British technique, admitted that British ballrooms lacked the energy and vitality of their foreign equivalents. As Maxwell Stewart observed in 1930, 'Surely it is not incompatible for "good style" in dancing as we know it in England to be joined with that "joie de vivre" which is such a feature of Continental ballrooms?'[80] Thomas Bus likewise concluded following his tour of the United States that the British could learn something from American dancers, and 'let slip our reserve a little and to give a larger place to the natural element and the element of joy'.[81]

Among the strongest critics of British dancing technique were musicians, who found it to be incompatible with the way they wanted to play music. In the late 1930s, in a lecture before the Coventry branch of the National Association of Amateur Dancers, musician Sonny Rose offered some comments about British ballroom dancing that caused a considerable stir and were reprinted in a dance magazine. Rose began his remarks with the provocative assertion: 'Dancing lacks vitality to-day. The present dances halls are temples of boredom. How could I possibly express to you in words how completely boring playing in a palais can be to musicians.' He continued by bemoaning that in being forced to play music at the tempos needed to properly execute the English style, good musicians were 'muzzled' and 'confined', and that 'Dancing has choked the music that created it.' He concluded by telling the assembled amateur dancers, 'In your efforts to promote good dancing you are strangling and killing the dance halls.'[82]

This speech was only one salvo in what had been years of debate between musicians and dance professionals over the speed of music for dancing. Many within the profession, as well as enthusiasts of technique within the dancing public, complained that dance bands played at too fast and erratic a tempo to comply with the standard steps of the English style. 'Hot' jazz and swing were especially criticised in this respect, with the contention being that dance bands were more invested in musical innovation than in the needs of dancers. Therefore, starting in the late 1920s professionals, such as Bradley and especially Silvester, were at the forefront of devising a solution to this problem, which was to modify and regulate the tempo of dance music to be more suitable accompaniment for the standard four. The result was what became known as 'strict tempo' dance music, and both Bradley and Silvester assembled orchestras which became synonymous with this new musical style.

Strict tempo was touted as the ideal style of music *for* dancing, something that was distinctive from 'dance music'. Both styles continued to co-exist, however, and each had its own proponents. Jazz fans and musical aficionados were highly derisive and dismissive of strict tempo, since they felt it stifled originality and creativity. However, professionals and dance enthusiasts saw the value in the smoother, unvarying rhythm of strict tempo, because it made the standard dances easier to perform correctly. As Taylor explained to Mass Observation,

> too often [the bands] play to please themselves and not the public … Different bands have their own ideas. Some make you want to dance. Some make you feel you want to have a drink. Victor Silvester's orchestra will always make you feel you want to move. With it you have perfect time, perfect rhythm, and beautiful melody.[83]

The two musical camps often squared off in print, and while it was anathema to musical purists and jazz fans, strict tempo had many adherents. Notably, by the time of Silvester's death in 1978, his orchestra's strict tempo dance records had sold more than 75 million copies.[84]

The clear support for strict tempo among professionals, as well as many within the dancing public, demonstrates that there was a strong commitment to the English style among both the producers and consumers of popular dance. However, they also gradually became aware that some novelty and flexibility in British dancing was necessary. By the 1930s, the dancing public began to 'vote with their feet', and sought out new dances that enabled improvisation and creativity, and required less training. For its part, the profession generally demonstrated a willingness to accept innovations that might rejuvenate popular dance, but would occasionally balk when these innovations challenged the technique – along with all of its attendant meanings about the national character – of the English style.

One of the dances to emerge in this context was the Cuban rumba, which arrived in Britain around 1931. Like the tango before it, the rumba was a dance of Latin American origin, but which came to Britain by an indirect route – some professionals seem to have first learned of it in New York, and others in Paris. Despite their recent efforts to craft home-grown dances, British professionals were interested in the rumba for all of the same reasons they latched on to any new dance: novelty, evolution of their art, but especially financial exigency. As Britain descended into the Depression, dance teachers were concerned about maintaining their businesses, and as the *Dancing Times* laconically put it after advising its professional readership to push the rumba, 'we believe there is money in it'.[85] As with the tango, there were some within the profession who felt that the dancing public would not embrace an 'exotic' Latin dance. Alex Moore contended that as 'attractive as this dance is, it is entirely opposed to English temperament'.[86] The rumba did in fact take a few years to catch on. Looking back on the recent dancing season during the summer of 1932, Richardson observed that there had been, 'what I may describe as a half-hearted invasion of our ballrooms by Cuban music which has drifted over from the States'.[87] This lukewarm start notwithstanding, within a year or two there was enough public interest in the rumba that dancing schools were advertising on the basis of their ability to provide instruction in the dance. In 1933, Silvester noted that 'to the surprise of most of us' the rumba was gaining in popularity.[88] Subsequent reports from dance hall proprietors reveal that in the latter half of 1930s the rumba was a regular feature on dance programmes throughout the country; it did not receive as many plays as the quickstep or foxtrot, but was at least as common as the tango.

Part of the reason for this success was that the profession adopted a novel 'wait and see' attitude when it came to the rumba: teachers promoted it, and offered lessons in the dance, but the Official Board made the decision not to standardise its steps right away. As Richardson advised his readership, 'Our Quick-steps, Fox-trots and Valses are so standardised to-day that I am sure it will give an added interest to dancing if this Cuban music be left as a *Danse libre* to which we can all step as the fancy moves us.'[89] A standard version of the dance was eventually formalised (in fact, several 'standard' versions briefly emerged when some teachers ignored Richardson's advice and set out to do it themselves, creating much consternation within the profession), and the rumba would go on to become a staple dance of the Latin branch of ballroom competition. But in delaying this process for a few years, the profession uncharacteristically did more than pay more than lip service to the idea that they wanted the dancing public to take the lead in shaping the national style. Professionals also appear to have been responding to concerns that ballroom dancing had become too rigid and technical, since in counselling his readers not to standardise the rumba right away, Richardson tellingly suggested they leave it to the nation's best dancers to 'play with' for a while.[90]

The other effect of the rumba's success was to inaugurate a more general enthusiasm for 'Latin' dances, which after the mid-1930s became a more prominent element of British popular dance. Professionals carried out an umpteenth attempt to create a new tango variation that would ensnare the public, but several other new Latin dances came from a different source: motion pictures. With the advent of the sound era, Hollywood entered into what has often been called a 'golden age' of movie musicals, a trend that was mimicked in British domestic film production. Approximately one-sixth of the output of British filmmakers in the 1930s was musical films, often so-called 'backstage' stories, in which a nebulous plot provided context to a series of variety acts.[91] But in addition to cinematic entertainment, what musical films offered was a stable of new dances, which commercial producers saw as potential additions to popular dance. As one magazine mused in 1935, 'Will the screen give us a new ballroom dance craze?'[92]

In Britain, the trend of transferring a dance from cinema to ballroom began with the 'carioca', a dance first introduced in *Flying Down to Rio*, the 1933 film that launched the legendary partnership of Fred Astaire and Ginger Rogers. Prior to the release of that film, Astaire was already a major celebrity in Britain. Born in Omaha, Nebraska in 1899, he had achieved child stardom alongside his older sister Adele as a popular vaudeville act. However, starting in the 1920s, the pair's career and international fame skyrocketed as much from their performances on the London stage as from those on Broadway, as the twosome moved back and forth across the Atlantic with revues like *Stop Flirting* (1923) and *Funny Face* (1928).[93] When his sister married and retired in the early 1930s, Astaire turned to Hollywood to launch the next phase of his career. Cast alongside Rogers as the supporting players in *Flying Down to Rio*, the duo's performance of the carioca became the stand-out scene in the film. Now a bona fide film star in addition to a dance celebrity, Astaire eventually made nine more films with Rogers – including a biographical film about Vernon and Irene Castle – most of which were tremendously successful on both sides of the Atlantic.

As performed on screen by the virtuoso Astaire and Rogers, dances like the carioca required too much floor space and too high a degree of difficulty for the average British dancer. But to remedy these issues, enterprising members of the dance profession and dance hall industry capitalised on the interest in musical films by adapting certain screen dances for the ballroom. The manager of the Plaza dance hall in Glasgow, for example, introduced a simplified, more accessible version of the carioca, which garnered significant attention in the dance press and was featured on dance programmes in Scotland and throughout the country for several years.[94] Mass Observation reports from 1939 reveal that at that point the carioca still enjoyed approximately as many plays and drew about as many dancers to the floor as other 'Latin' dances such as the rumba and tango.[95] Dances from other Astaire and Rogers films, including the 'continental' and the 'piccolino', were also later adapted for the public ballroom, as were a several dances developed for British films. For instance, the 'caranga', created for the 1935 film *Brewster's Millions*, was given substantial publicity and step-by-step instructions in *Popular Music and Dancing Weekly*.[96] While none of these dances had the impact of the carioca – which was itself only a moderate success – most shared what one observer called a 'definitely Latin stamp about them'.[97] It was a Latin stamp defused by way of the United States and reimagined in Britain, but collectively this series of Latin American or Latin American-inspired dances provided a vital alternative to the unyielding steps and nationalistic meanings associated with the English style. An amorphous 'Latin' flavour was injected into British dance culture, similar to that which Christina D. Abreu has identified in commodified Cuban culture of the mid-twentieth century United States, and characterised by 'nonblackness, tropical escape, and sanitised exoticism'.[98]

Meanwhile, Hollywood films were an important vehicle for introducing the British dancing public to new American dances as well. In an interview with Mass Observation, Mecca's leading teacher, Adele England, pointed to the influence of the movies as a way of accounting for the growing public interest in a dance step known as 'truckin''. As she told the observer, 'They see the films, see Fred Astaire and so on doing these steps so they think they will have a go.'[99] This interest in Astaire and Rogers, their films and the dances they introduced speaks to the expanding fascination with American culture as Britain progressed through the 1930s. As Eric Hobsbawm has argued – having reflected upon the allure of America from his vantage point as both a historian and as one who grew up in this period as a young man enamoured with jazz – American cultural imports were often of interest merely because they were American.[100] Many Britons saw America as inherently exciting, exotic and modern, and despite the inherent racism in commentaries about American cultural imports, their perceived blackness was also a large part of what made them intriguing.[101] Moreover, with respect to dancing, the conduits for cultural transmission of American products – motion pictures, radio, recorded music and print culture, and professional and personal travel – only continued to expand. This meant that the dancing public was less reliant on established intermediaries like the dance profession to obtain knowledge of new trends, although commercial producers did continue to play an instrumental role.

Truckin', the dance referenced by Adele England in her interview with Mass Observation, provides a revealing glimpse into the British reception of American popular dance imports – particularly those associated with blackness – and of the negotiations that occurred over them between producers and consumers. In the 1930s, various dance steps and figures that accompanied a new jazz variation known as 'swing' began to make their way across the Atlantic. Once again dance professionals were at the forefront of disseminating knowledge of swing and its attendant dances. In the spring of 1932, Bradley published an account in the *Dancing Times* about a recent trip to New York where she visited Harlem and first 'discovered' the Lindy hop.[102] Named in honour of Charles Lindbergh's successful transatlantic flight, the Lindy had developed in the African-American dance halls of New York's Harlem, particularly the Savoy Ballroom, starting in the late 1920s. The dance was characterised by improvisational and occasionally independent movements when partners broke apart. Holding on to their partner with one hand during these 'defining swing-outs', dancers improvised rhythmic movements, while continually separating and coming back together.[103] Following Bradley's American visit, there was no immediate push to bring the Lindy to Britain, but over the next few years some of its elements and other movements associated with black dancing gradually filtered across the pond. Some were present in a group dance known as the 'Big Apple', while others were collectively referred to as 'truckin''.

In the United States, truckin' generally referred to one particular movement in the Lindy hop – a strutting walk with shoulder swagger, and one wagging finger raised in the air – by which partners came back together following a breakaway. In Britain, however, truckin' appears to have included the Lindy's truckin' step, with other elements of the dance incorporated under this different name. Mass Observation descriptions indicate that dancing couples maintained a loose hold – sometimes with only one arm – as they bent forward, wiggled their hips and swung their legs; breakaways and swing-outs were also common. But truckin' looked a little different each time it was performed, and there are frequent references in the reports to dancers 'making it up as they go along'. Importantly, the dance encouraged the creative improvisation that had been resolutely stamped out of British ballroom dance through the standardisation process. Truckin' was also clearly associated with black culture in the minds of British producers and consumers, for which it was decried by a professional who witnessed an exhibition of the dance put on by American champion dancers in Manchester in no uncertain terms:

> The champions were coloured people; they performed the most un-English movements you could imagine – negroid in the extreme ... How much better would it be if the management gave us demonstrations by British dancers of repute, and thereby created the incentive to raise the standard of ballroom dancing.[104]

Much about the reception of truckin' by the dance profession is revealed in these comments. On the one hand, items in the dance press from throughout the 1930s show clear interest in swing and its associated dances among professionals, since they were always on the lookout for a new dance sensation, and many of them shared the broader public fascination with American culture. On the other hand, as the Mancunian correspondent bluntly articulated, truckin' reintroduced to the British ballroom many of the elements the profession had attempted to quash in standardising the English style and in toning down the Charleston. The dance had no standard form, it called for movements that were perceived to be at odds with the British national character, and it was decisively associated with blackness. For some professionals, truckin' represented a clear threat to ballroom dancing, and undid all of their hard work to create a national style that was reserved and refined, committed to standard technique, and white.

Yet despite professional ambivalence, there is evidence that truckin' remained of considerable interest to a significant number of people within the dancing public. This interest was stoked by Britain's other commercial producer – the dance hall industry – which saw truckin' as a potential novelty that they could use to draw patrons to the palais. A number of public ballrooms, especially in London, began providing exhibitions and special sessions for the dance, and Mass Observation reports from the late 1930s reveal that it enjoyed substantial popularity and prevalence.[105] Indeed, some enthusiasts trucked above and beyond the parameters established by the special sessions provided by management. Truckin' was engaged in during foxtrots and quicksteps, and as one observer noted, 'One couple even managed to concoct truckin to waltz time.'[106] It appears that much of the enthusiasm for the dance was based in its general American-ness; as Mass Observation noted with respect to the origins and public knowledge of the dance, 'Rogers and Astaire are at the base of it.'[107] However, racial difference was also a visible aspect of the production and consumption of truckin'. Most of the exhibition dancers hired by the dance hall industry were black, and many of the truckin' couples described by Mass Observation were interracial, usually a black man and a white woman.

The choice made by some within the dancing public to adopt truckin', and their physical performances of the dance, retained significant cultural power for shaping the vision of national identity that was expressed on the dance floor. As foreign dances like the rumba and truckin' arrived in Britain via the cinema and dance hall industry – with increasingly less mediation by the dance profession – the dancing public was able to either reify or challenge the understanding of national identity that had been constructed and commodified through the standardisation of the English style. In adhering to the instruction of professionals in ballroom dancing, dancers performed the vision of the nation established by the English style – in which Britishness was refined, restrained and white. However, in choosing to adopt, and in performing a dance like truckin', the dancing public created and embodied alternative meanings and national imaginaries. Truckin' was not as rigidly defined in its movements, and was livelier than the English style; it embodied a vision of the nation that was less associated with reserve and refinement, and connected with American-style expressions of freedom and democracy. This was even more the case with the successor to truckin', the jitterbug, which was introduced to thousands of Britons by actual Americans during the war years. The image of the nation associated with a dance like truckin' was also more fluid with respect race, as the claims of white superiority that upheld Britain's colonial system and national self-understanding, existed in tension with many Britons observations of, and desire to experiment with, African-American dance forms. At the same time, as will be discussed in Chapter 8 in relation to the jitterbug, performing what were perceived to be black dances could also provide white dancers with new ways to assert racial hegemony.

Ultimately what a dance such as truckin' made manifest was that the vision of national identity embodied through popular dance was fluid rather than fixed, and in a constant state of evolution on the nation's dance floors. While for the most part the English style and all of its attendant associations remained the dominant popular dance form and national imaginary, foreign dances increasingly provided opportunities for a reconsideration and performance of different meanings, in which embodied Britishness was less reserved and more racially fluid. These alternative visions of the nation were then experienced and expressed by individual dancers, and observable to their fellow Britons in the ballroom. The growing influence of American popular dances also pointed to the declining influence of the dance profession in determining what would be essayed in the public ballroom. While the profession was ascendant in ballroom dancing technique – at home and abroad – by the late 1930s, ballroom dancing faced new competition from other styles as to what would form the basis of *popular* dance. Truckin' was one aspect of this, while the other was a boom in so-called novelty dances. The latter was directed by Britain's other commercial producer – the dance hall industry – which proved to have a similarly ambivalent relationship to American cultural products. Even as it promoted truckin' and later the jitterbug, the industry launched the Lambeth Walk – the greatest British dance success the world had ever seen – which was marketed in explicitly anti-American terms.

Notes

1 Mark Knowles, *The Wicked Waltz and Other Scandalous Dances: Outrage at Couple Dancing in the 19th and Early 20th Centuries* (Jefferson, NC: McFarland, 2009), p. 74.

2 Philip J. S. Richardson, *A History of English Ballroom Dancing* (London: Herbert Jenkins, 1946), pp. 43–4.

3 Richardson, *A History of English Ballroom Dancing*, p. 9.

4 Morry M. Blake, 'Get the London Style', *Dancing Times* (February 1922), p. 424.

5 The Sitter Out, 'Ballroom Notes', *Dancing Times* (April 1927), p. 21.

6 Mona Vivian, 'Has the Dance "Craze" Come to Stay?' *Popular Music and Dancing Weekly* (10 January 1925), p. 229.

7 Zetta Mor, 'Can London Produce the Best Dancers?' *Popular Music and Dancing Weekly* (28 March 1925), p. 182.

8 MOA: Worktown 48/C, Astoria Palais de Danse (18 December 1939).

9 George A. Wade, 'Running a Super Dance Hall', *Popular Music and Dancing Weekly* (8 August 1925), p. iii.

10 'Dancing Time on Merseyside', *Liverpool Echo* (24 March 1926), p. 10.

11 MOA: Worktown, 48/D, Manager – Aspin Hall (8 January 1940).

12 See Juliet McMains, *Glamour Addiction: Inside the American Ballroom Dance Industry* (Middletown, CT: Wesleyan University Press, 2006), pp. 71–86.

13 'Ballroom News', *Dancing Times* (October 1923), pp. 17–19.

14 MOA: TC 38/6/G, Imperial Society of Teachers of Dancing (19 June 1939), p. 7.

15 Nancy Bramall, 'The Truth about British Dancing', *Popular Music and Dancing Weekly* (24 October 1925), p. 16.

16 Maxwell Stewart, 'Continental Style', *Dancing Times* (October 1939), p. 17.

17 Thomas W. Bus, 'My Impressions of America's Dancing', *Modern Dance and the Dancer* (January 1939), p. 15.

18 Peter Mandler, *The English National Character: The History of an Idea from Edmund Burke to Tony Blair* (New Haven, CT: Yale University Press, 2006), p. 143. See also pp. 143–95.

19 Jon Lawrence, 'Forging a peaceable kingdom: war, violence, and fear of brutalisation in post-First World War Britain', *Journal of Modern History* 75 (September 2003): 557–89.

20 Quoted in Jo Baim, *Tango: Creation of a Cultural Icon* (Bloomington, IN: Indiana University Press, 2007), p. 56.

21 Santos Casani, 'The Dances of To-morrow', *Popular Music and Dancing Weekly* (31 May 1924), p. 112.

22 'America's Latest Craze', *Modern Dance and the Dancer* (4 August 1939), p. 16.

23 Dancer, 'To the Dance Bands of London', *Dancing Times* (March 1924), p. 615.

24 Theresa Jill Buckland, *Society Dancing: Fashionable Bodies in England, 1870–1920* (Basingstoke: Palgrave Macmillan, 2011), p. 192.

25 Stewart, 'Continental Style', p. 17.

26 Liverpool Record Office, Liverpool Libraries, Hq79333GRA, *Grafton Rooms: Souvenir Brochure on the Occasion of our Silver Jubilee, 1924–1949* (1949), p. 30.
27 Jurretta Jordan Heckscher, 'Our national poetry: the Afro-Chesapeake inventions of American dance', in Julie Malnig (ed.), *Ballroom Boogie, Shimmy Sham, Shake: A Social and Popular Dance Reader* (Urbana, IL: University of Illinois Press, 2009); Julie Malnig, 'Women, dance, and New York nightlife', in Julie Malnig (ed.) *Ballroom Boogie, Shimmy Sham, Shake: A Social and Popular Dance Reader* (Urbana, IL: University of Illinois Press, 2009); Danielle Robinson, *Modern Moves: Dancing Race During the Ragtime and Jazz Eras* (New York: Oxford University Press, 2015).
28 Christina D. Abreu has identified a similar tendency towards understanding Cuban culture in terms of its 'nonblackness' in the mid-twentieth century United States. See Christina D. Abreu, *Rhythms of Race: Cuban Musicians and the Making of Latino New York City and Miami, 1940–1960* (Chapel Hill, NC: University of North Carolina Press, 2015).
29 Robinson, *Modern Moves*, pp. 64–9.
30 Edward Scott, 'About Waltzing', *Dancing Times* (March 1919), p. 201.
31 'Phillida Run Away – From Dancing', *Dancing Times* (July 1921), p. 789.
32 'Ballroom Chat', *Dancing Times* (October 1923), p. 19.
33 'The Charleston Dance – A Protest', *Daily Mail* (26 April 1926), p. 7.
34 F.A. Hadland, 'Negro Influence in Dancing', *Dancing Times* (April 1927), p. 73.
35 Victor Silvester, 'The Blues', *Dancing Times* (September 1927), p. 649.
36 Lucy Bland, *Modern Women on Trial: Sexual Transgression in the Age of the Flapper* (Manchester: Manchester University Press, 2013), p. 72.
37 Robinson, *Modern Moves*, p. 92.
38 See *Dancing Times*, November 1918-February 1919. See also, Richardson, *A History of English Ballroom Dancing*, pp. 37–9.
39 'Best Men Dancers', *Daily Mail*, (9 August 1921), p. 3.
40 G. E. Fussell, 'Racial Temperament and the Dance', *Dancing Times* (January 1922), p. 405.
41 Cyril Ramon Newton, 'A Few Notes by a Band Conductor', *Popular Music and Dancing Weekly* (9 August 1924), p. 53.
42 Bramall, 'The Truth about British Dancing', p.16.
43 Victor Silvester, 'Continental Dancing', *Dancing Times* (June 1932), pp. 245–7.
44 Stewart, 'Continental Style', p. 17.
45 Bus, 'My Impressions of America's Dancing', pp. 14–15.
46 Josephine Bradley and Wellesley-Smith, 'The Supremacy of the English Style', *Dancing Times* (July 1930), p. 368.
47 Victor Silvester, 'This Season's Tango', *Dancing Times* (January 1932), p. 460.
48 Bradley and Wellesley-Smith, 'The Supremacy of the English Style', p. 368.
49 'Ballroom Gossip', *Dancing Times* (March 1922), p. 521.
50 'The Championships', *Dancing Times* (July 1935), p. 354.
51 Silvester, 'Continental Dancing', p. 245.
52 MOA: TC 38/6/G, Imperial Society of Teachers of Dancing (19 June 1939), p. 7.
53 MOA: TC 38/5/G, Victor Silvester (30 May 1939), p. 3.

54 Bradley and Wellesley-Smith, 'The Supremacy of the English Style', p. 368.

55 'The Championships', *Dancing Times* (July 1935), p. 354.

56 Editorial, *Modern Dance* (June 1936), p. 1.

57 James Hyojiro Kato, 'European and American Dancing Compared', *Dancing Times* (October 1933), pp. 21–2.

58 Silvester, 'Continental Dancing', p. 247.

59 'Teaching Overseas,' *Dancing Times* (December 1933), pp. 328–9.

60 McMains, *Glamour Addiction*, p. 88.

61 *Dancing Times* (February 1929), p. 650.

62 Victor Silvester, 'Steps that every ballroom teacher should know', *Dancing Times* (February 1935), p. 572.

63 'The Championships,' *Dancing Times*, p. 354.

64 Marjorie and Georges Fontana, 'Ballroom and Exhibition Dancing', *Dancing Times* (December 1920), p. 176.

65 Around the Dance Halls, *Popular Music and Dancing Weekly* (7 June 1924), p. 138.

66 The Sitter Out, *Dancing Times* (September 1924), p. 1129.

67 'Can you dance the Trebla?' *Dancing Times* (September 1927), p. 632.

68 'Trebla Season', *Dancing Times* (December 1926), p. 350.

69 'Sidelines on the Six-Eight', *Dancing Times* (October 1929), p. 20.

70 Advertisement, *Dancing Times* (June 1930), p. 158.

71 Margaret Einhert, 'Some New York Dance Impressions', *Dancing Times* (September 1929), p. 524.

72 Peter Bailey, 'Fats Waller meets Harry Champion: Americanisation, national identity, and sexual politics in inter-war British music hall', *Cultural and Social History* 4:4 (2007), 497.

73 Marc Matera, *Black London: The Imperial Metropolis and Decolonization in the Twentieth Century* (Oakland, CA: University of California Press, 2015), p. 150.

74 Bailey, 'Fats Waller Meets Harry Champion', p. 505.

75 Ross McKibbin, *Classes and Cultures: England 1918–1951* (Oxford: Oxford University Press, 1998), pp. 427–8.

76 TNA: LAB 8/1926: Minutes of a deputation from the Agents Association, Entertainment Protection Association, Paramount Theatres Ltd and the Association of Ball Rooms and Dance Halls regarding admission of foreign bands to this country: decision to refuse permits to American bands and press communique, 1934–1961.

77 K.M.B., 'The Dullness of English Dancing', *Dancing Times* (October 1923), p. 16.

78 'Irresistible Jazz', *Daily Mail* (January 29, 1919), p. 4.

79 A Teacher of Dancing, 'The Truth About the Charleston', *Popular Music and Dancing Weekly* (7 August 1926), p. 38.

80 Maxwell Stewart, 'Tango on the Continent', *Dancing Times* (November 1930), p. 159.

81 Bus, 'My Impressions of America's Dancing', pp. 14–15.

82 Sonny Rose, 'Has Dancing Progressed', *Modern Dance and the Dancer* (January 1939), p. 19.

83 MOA: TC 38/6/G, The Imperial Society of Teachers of Dancing (19 June 1939), pp. 3–4.

84 Ian Driver, *A Century of Dance: A Hundred Years of Musical Movement, from Waltz to Hip Hop* (London: Hamlyn, 2000), p. 144.

85 'Encourage the Rumba', *Dancing Times* (July 1934), p. 350.

86 Alex Moore, 'Ballroom Dancing Made Easy', *Modern Dance and the Dancer* (November 1936), p. 5

87 The Sitter Out, 'Ballroom Notes', *Dancing Times* (July 1932), p. 353.

88 Victor Silvester, 'The Ballroom Rumba', *Dancing Times* (January 1933), p. 445.

89 The Sitter Out, 'Ballroom Notes', *Dancing Times* (October 1931), p. 39.

90 The Sitter Out, 'The Ballroom in 1934', *Dancing Times* (December 1934), p. 287.

91 Stephen Guy, 'Calling all stars: musical films in a musical decade', in Jeffrey Richard (ed.) *The Unknown 1930s: An Alternative History of the British Cinema, 1929–1939* (London: I.B. Tauris, 1998).

92 Leonore Manning, 'Will the Screen Give Us A New Ballroom Dance Craze?' *Popular Music and Dancing Weekly* (13 July 1935), p. 20.

93 For more on Astaire's career, see his autobiography: Fred Astaire, *Steps in Time: An Autobiography* (New York: Cooper Square Press, 1959, 2000). See also Kathleen Riley, *The Astaires: Fred and Adele*, (Oxford: Oxford University Press, 2012).

94 Horace Richards, 'Come Dancing Around Britain – No. 1: Glasgow Greets the Carioca', *Popular Music and Dancing Weekly* (24 November 1934), p. 12.

95 MOA: TC 38/1/A, Locarno (8 November 1939).

96 'Here's the Caranga!' *Popular Music and Dancing Weekly* (5 January 1935), p. 7.

97 Manning, 'Will the Screen Give Us a New Ballroom Dance Craze?' p. 20.

98 Abreu, *Rhythms of Race*, p. 1.

99 MOA: TC 38/5/G, Dancing Teachers (5 June 1939), p. 4.

100 See Eric Hobsbawm, 'Jazz Comes to Europe', *Uncommon People: Resistance, Rebellion, and Jazz* (New York: Norton, 1998); Eric Hobsbawm, *Interesting Times: A Twentieth-Century Life* (London: Penguin Books, 2002).

101 Mica Nava, *Visceral Cosmopolitanism: Gender, Culture, and the Normalisation of Difference* (Oxford: Berg, 2007), p. 80; Bailey, 'Fats Waller Meets Harry Champion', p. 498; Matera, *Black London*, pp. 145–77.

102 Josephine Bradley, 'A Trip to New York', *Dancing Times* (March 1932), p. 684.

103 Karen Hubbard and Terry Monaghan, 'Social dancing at the Savoy', in Julie Malnig (ed.), *Ballroom Boogie, Shimmy Sham, Shake: A Social and Popular Dance Reader* (Urbana, IL: University of Illinois Press, 2009), p. 133.

104 Mancunian, 'Manchester Murmurs', *Modern Dance and the Dancer* (December 1935), p. 5.

105 MOA: TC 38/1/A, Observations in Dance Halls – Locarno; M-O A: TC 38/1/B, Observations in Dance Halls – Paramount.

106 MOA: TC 38/1/B, Paramount (20 March 1939).

107 MOA: TC 38/1/A, Locarno (17 November 1938).

6

Doing the Lambeth Walk: novelty dances and the commodification of the nation

In the late 1930s, the British nation was gripped by a dance craze unlike any it had witnessed since the start of the modern dance era. As Mass Observation famously observed, 'you could find them doing the Lambeth Walk in Mayfair ball-rooms, suburban dance-halls, cockney parties and village hops'.[1] But even this statement went only some distance towards conveying the profound impact of this simple, silly, 'novelty' or 'party' dance. Like many dances for the public ballroom, the Lambeth Walk began life as a theatrical number, performed by comedian Lupino Lane in the comedy-musical *Me and My Girl*. The show centred on the character of Bill Snibson, a cockney from Lambeth in south London, who inherits an earldom but finds it difficult to adapt to life among the elite.[2] The high point in the musical came when Bill, as played by Lane, led a grand dinner party in a dance number called the Lambeth Walk, in which the company swaggered and strutted about the stage, rolling their shoulders and swinging their arms in what was purported to represent the 'typical Cockney walk'.[3] The dance's name thus referenced the walking movements of working-class Londoners, but also a short road called Lambeth Walk just south of the river Thames.

Lane's stage dance was soon adapted by C. L. Heimann and the Mecca chain of dance halls as a novelty for their patrons, and it was this ballroom version of the Lambeth Walk that became a phenomenon which transcended both theatre and palais. The king and queen were widely reported to have performed the dance, and many of Britain's leading stars of stage and screen participated in a celebrity performance at the Coliseum. The Lambeth Walk became a staple number during the pantomime season of 1938–39, to the point that Lane's production company had to threaten lawsuits for copyright infringement.[4] At the same time, Lane himself was able to capitalise on the success of the ballroom version of his dance, as he produced both television and film adaptations of *Me and My Girl* within two years.[5] Providing additional evidence of the Lambeth Walk's popularity, it soon inspired a flurry of copycats. In the months after its release, dozens of new party dances were created by dance professionals and ballroom proprietors, such as the 'boomps-a-daisy', the 'gazook', the 'trek', the 'cherry hop', the 'all change walk' and the 'palais stroll', to name only a few. Regarding the veritable explosion of novelty dances, the *Daily Mail* observed that 'the Lambeth Walk has a lot to answer for'.[6]

Meanwhile, the Lambeth Walk song and dance became so well known that they developed a cultural currency that could be drawn upon in many different contexts, ranging from the ridiculous to the poignant. The Labour Party composed a campaign song to the melody, while other companies and organisations exploited its commercial possibilities, producing parodies such as 'The Printers' Walk' for a meeting of printers in Brighton.[7] As international tensions mounted, and the Second World War erupted, Britons used the dance to express their camaraderie, fortitude and good humour. In the post-war period, children sang the song and performed the dance at parties, while a pub in south London long bore the name 'Lambeth Walk'. In these ways, the Lambeth Walk retained a lingering resonance long after it had disappeared from Britain's dance floors and airwaves, raising the question as to what it was about this dance that caused it to have such a tremendous and long-lived impact.

The fervour for the Lambeth Walk represented a different kind of dance craze than those that had surrounded the foxtrot or the Charleston in the 1920s. This chapter will show that while there were a variety of reasons for the dance's remarkable success, a major element of the craze that surrounded the Lambeth Walk was its commercial promotion and public acceptance as a quintessentially *national* dance. Unlike the vast majority of the dances being performed in Britain, the Lambeth Walk was created by a British dance professional. It was based on a musical number from a British theatrical production, and was performed to a song written by a British composer. It was produced and promoted by a British company, and first introduced in British ballrooms. The dance was also viewed by many – largely erroneously – to be a genuine working-class dance with a long and established history within British culture. Meanwhile, so big a success did this British-made and British-themed dance prove to be that Mecca tried to replicate its triumph with a series of follow-up dances. During the final years of the 1930s Mecca introduced the Chestnut Tree, the Park Parade, the Handsome Territorial and Knees Up, Mother Brown, all of which were modelled on the Lambeth Walk's formula for simplicity and British thematic content. The dances summoned and circulated prominent idioms about national identity during the 1930s: they glorified the nation's heritage and natural beauty, endorsed conservative institutions like the monarchy and the army, and generally emphasised Englishness rather than Britishness.[8] Yet given that they were created in the last months before the outbreak of the Second World War, the dances also anticipated the transition to wartime understandings of the British nation, by celebrating the 'ordinary' Briton and the country's democratic spirit.[9]

However, for all of the Mecca novelty dances' patriotic undertones, the company's primary motivation in creating the Lambeth Walk and its successors was to make money: through record and sheet music sales, and most of all by attracting more patrons to the company's dance halls. To do so, Mecca specifically marketed the dances on the basis of their British origins and character. Beneath a veneer of merriment, Mecca's promotional efforts on behalf of the novelty dances also clearly demarcated what was *not* British, in strongly anti-American and racialised terms. In this way, the Mecca novelty dances represented an apogee of the commodification of national identity that began with the English style of ballroom dance. Mecca explicitly sought to sell its dances on the basis of their Britishness, while also heralding them as a bulwark against Americanisation – but in keeping with the mechanisms of commercial nationalism, the reception of Mecca's 'British' dances was more complicated than the company likely anticipated. Significantly, with the exception of the Lambeth Walk, the dancing public largely rejected the alleged Britishness of the Mecca dances, and it was not their nationalist themes but their merit as dances – as well as the level of enjoyment which they bestowed – that determined whether or not they were successful. Once again the nation's popular dance culture, and the national imaginaries that it expressed and embodied, were negotiated between the producers and consumers of dance.

The birth of a dance

From the outset, the production of the Lambeth Walk and other Mecca novelty dances was driven by the company's continuing desire to attract greater numbers of patrons to its dance halls. The origin of the dances can be traced back to an evening in March 1938, when Heimann, Mecca's managing director, attended a performance of *Me and My Girl* at the Victoria Palace Theatre in London. As Heimann would later tell the story, for months he had been seeking out a new dance – one that could be performed by dancers of all ages and classes, regardless of whether they had training in ballroom dancing – and sitting in the audience watching Lane strut about the stage cockney-style, he believed he had found just the dance.[10] Heimann quickly secured Lane's permission to adapt the Lambeth Walk for the dance hall, and to develop the ballroom version he turned to Adele England, the principal of the dancing school attached to Mecca's Streatham Locarno dance hall. What England went on to create was a very simple group dance, in which dancers circled the floor in partners, singing the Lambeth Walk song and sauntering with the supposed cockney swagger; at requisite intervals in the song they would slap their knees and hoist their thumbs in the air, yelling 'Oi!'

At the most basic level, the Lambeth Walk was a sequence dance, a style that required dancers to perform the same arrangement of steps in repetition. Sequence dancing was nothing new in the 1930s, since prior to the advent of the waltz, most Georgian dances were of this style; sequence dances like the lancers and the quadrille had also been common in the Victorian period. However, sequence dancing had largely fallen out of vogue with the ascent of modern ballroom dance, and in creating the Lambeth Walk, Heimann and England also likely drew inspiration from several other 'party' dances that were circulating around the dance halls at the same time. Mass Observation, which undertook a thorough study of the Lambeth Walk in 1939, further speculated that the dance was really a derivation of the American cakewalk. If accurate, this suggestion – which has been supported by some modern scholars – is replete with irony, given that, as will be shown, the Lambeth Walk's un-American-ness became a major feature of both its production and consumption.[11]

Once England had created the ballroom version of Lambeth Walk, Mecca turned to the task of promotion. Heimann and England quickly staged an exhibition of the dance at the Locarno, and the company launched an active publicity campaign, working with music publishers and the BBC to promote both the song and dance. England then travelled throughout the country providing demonstrations of the Lambeth Walk at different Mecca dance halls, where, as she reported to the *Dancing Times* in May 1938, 'without exception the public received it with enthusiasm, crowding on to the floor and requesting it several times during one session'.[12] It did not take long for the Lambeth Walk to catch on. Not only Mecca halls, but dance venues throughout the country were soon complying with the public demand for the fun and infectious new dance. The Lambeth Walk's impact on British culture also quickly transcended the ballroom, and in fact transcended the nation itself: the dance was successfully exported beyond the British Isles, to the European continent, throughout the Empire and to the United States. One New York correspondent for the *Dancing Times* wrote to the magazine in October to announce that the Lambeth Walk was being demonstrated in department stores, taught in dancing schools such as Arthur Murray's, and performed 'everywhere from Fifth Avenue to Harlem'.[13] The dance was also embraced by Hollywood, appearing in several American movies throughout 1939. On the Continent, the Lambeth Walk was a major success, even as diplomatic tensions increased and rumours of war rumbled. As a poet memorably remarked at the height of the Munich Crisis, 'while dictators rage and statesmen talk, all Europe dances – to The Lambeth Walk'.[14]

It is not hard to imagine why the Lambeth Walk appealed to dancers – in Britain and abroad. In the first place, the dance was simply good fun, and helped restore what contemporaries often referred to as the 'party spirit' to the ballroom. The song that accompanied the dance was also admired, described as 'catchy' or 'ear haunting'.[15] The Lambeth Walk was easy to learn, and it helped to counteract the perception that popular dance had grown stale and excessively technical. More than two decades had passed since the emergence of modern ballroom dancing at the end of the First World War, and the English style – once considered to be innovative and provocative – had become for many Britons overly complicated and too rigidly standardised. Lessons were a virtual necessity for anyone wishing to dance 'correctly', the opportunity for which was limited to those who had the time, inclination, and money for instruction. Even for those adequately trained in them, the standard four ballroom dances had grown a bit tiresome. No new dance had caught on in a significant way since the Charleston, and for years observers of dancing had speculated that something was needed to shake things up in the ballroom.

Into this void entered the Lambeth Walk, which was fun, fresh and distinctive. In the words of the *Dancing Times*'s Philip J. S. Richardson, the Lambeth Walk – and the numerous novelty dances that followed in its wake – was comprised of 'ridiculously simple steps – so simple that they can be picked up by a roomful of people in five minutes'.[16] England also framed the appeal of her party dance in relation to the perceived challenges of ballroom dancing: 'In the four standard dances, concentration is needed to execute them correctly, so it is as well to have on the programme certain numbers in which everyone may relax and forget the serious side of dancing: and the "not so advanced" dancers may feel happy and at ease.'[17]

Additionally, as Richardson observed, although sequence dancing was 'old as the hills', it was new to the 'present generation' of dancers.[18] This style of dance provided a novel experience for dancers who had grown weary of foxtrot and tango variations. According to one magazine, the Lambeth Walk freed the British dancing public from,

> every law of 'rise and fall,' 'contrabody movement,' 'sway,' etc., and up rise these non-dancers, these wallflowers, these nobodies, and take the floor, the band puts on paper hats and lets itself go, and the party spirit is amongst us.[19]

However, the dearth of successful new dances over the preceding decade had not been for lack of trying: as has been shown, hundreds of dances of varying quality – both home-grown and imported – had been introduced by the dance profession in an effort to locate 'standard five', and spark interest in instruction. Nor was the Lambeth Walk even the first group dance to appear in this period. Once again, America had led the way. In early 1938, the Big Apple was imported from the United States by British teachers in search of a new dance to introduce to their students. The dance was purportedly named for the African-American nightclub in Columbia, South Carolina, where it originated, and it required participants to form a circle and to perform certain steps derived from the earliest forms of swing dancing – such as truckin', Suzy-Q and the Charleston swing – in response to the calls from a leader. While the *Dancing Times* claimed that the Big Apple generated a great 'party spirit' among dancers – the same description that would later be applied to the effect produced by the Lambeth Walk – it failed to catch on in any substantive way.[20] Richardson speculated that the steps set to 'hot' jazz were too difficult for the average British dancer, and that they felt self-conscious during the portion of the dance that required them to 'shine' – meaning to dance solo in the centre of the circle.[21] Meanwhile, a British party dance, the palais glide, which possessed a hazy history but had purportedly been created almost a decade earlier in Yorkshire or the Midlands, also re-emerged in London around the same time as the Big Apple. In this simple dance, participants stood side by side in a line, linked arms and proceeded to 'glide' across the floor. The palais glide was more of a success than the Big Apple, but only after the Lambeth Walk had taken off and spurred greater enthusiasm for these types of dances.

The novelty, simplicity and enjoyment provided by the Lambeth Walk therefore do not wholly account for its 'phenomenal success'.[22] Rather, it was Mecca's promotional campaign that set the Lambeth Walk apart from the Big Apple, palais glide, or the dozens of other new dances that appeared in the 1930s. The substance of Mecca's marketing of the dance is best encapsulated in a comment Heimann made to the *Star* newspaper during the summer of 1938: 'there has never been anything quite like "The Lambeth Walk" in English dancing. Practically everything popular here came from America. "The Lambeth Walk" has changed all that. It has the happy spirit of the old English round dances.'[23] Heimann's statements reflected the two main features of how Mecca promoted the Lambeth Walk: it was British-made, in a time when so much British popular culture originated in the United States, and it was English/British in its style and content, perhaps even harkening back to older national dance forms.

Yet critically, Mecca was not the only source to perpetuate these ideas: the nationalist themes at the centre of the company's marketing campaign resonated strongly throughout British society. The dance profession, the dance bands, the popular media, the social research organisation Mass Observation, and even some residents of Lambeth itself, embraced and further perpetuated the manufactured vision of national tradition represented in Mecca's Lambeth Walk, as well as its significance for slowing the encroachment of American culture. The Lambeth Walk phenomenon thus strongly displayed Mecca's power to shape popular dance (and the national culture more broadly), but was also more complicated than a manifestation of cultural manipulation by a commercial producer. In the production and consumption of the dance, Mecca and the public negotiated the meanings surrounding – and the performance of – the Lambeth Walk in ways that made the dance, whatever its real origins, a recognised part of the national culture and a physical enactment of national identity.

First, Mecca personnel, but also many contemporary observers outside the company, believed that the success of the Lambeth Walk marked an important reassertion of British cultural autonomy. England told Mass Observation that it was the greatest 'English' dance success the world had ever seen.[24] In turn, Mass Observation's Tom Harrisson wrote in the *Picture Post* that British music and dancing were at last making a stand against the sea of American imports, referring to the Lambeth Walk as 'the biggest blow to American influence'.[25] Harrisson argued that the dance's success represented a real challenge to American cultural supremacy, not just at home but abroad, an idea that was even more widely espoused once the Lambeth Walk was exported to the United States. For instance, in late 1938, Jack Payne, one of Britain's leading bandleaders, commented in the *Evening News*: 'ever since Irving Berlin tickled our feet with his little masterpiece "Alexander's Ragtime Band," American composers ... have been giving us foxtrots and quicksteps lauding the panoramic delights of every State within the Union ... it is pleasing to find at long last that the compliment can be whole-heartedly reciprocated'.[26] After years of attempts to quell the influence of foreign culture on popular dance, now at long last the British dance community had a bona fide hit to call its own. Not only was this dance British-made, it represented British culture to the outside world through its very steps and themes.

Indeed, the Lambeth Walk's creators marketed the dance not solely as a bulwark against American cultural dominance, but for being genuinely British in its history and style. While the modern genesis of Mecca's Lambeth Walk was not concealed, strong efforts were made by those involved in its creation to establish a longer tradition for the dance. For instance, Lane helped to confirm the authenticity of the Lambeth Walk when he told Mass Observation: 'I got the idea from my personal experience and from having worked among cockneys. I'm a cockney born and bred myself. The Lambeth Walk is just an exaggerated idea of how the cockney struts.'[27] The composer of the song, Douglas Furber, likewise claimed to have drawn inspiration from working-class people in his Yorkshire childhood.[28] The architect of the ballroom version of the Lambeth Walk, England, also frequently reinforced Lane and Furber's contention that the song and dance captured the genuine movements and culture of the cockney. As she told the *Dancing Times* shortly after the dance's creation,

> It was characteristic of the Costers that they walked with a slight side-to-side movement, with a swing of the arms, and, as each hand came forward, an upward jerking of the thumbs for a few inches … It set the foundation stone … for the "Lambeth Walk" making a truly English dance.[29]

In the same article, and later on in a short instructional book that she wrote about the Lambeth Walk and the other Mecca novelty dances, England reminded readers that there had been a music hall song called the 'Lambeth Walk' back around the turn of the century, popularised by comedian Alec Hurley.[30] There was seemingly no direct connection between Hurley and England's Lambeth Walks, but England and her Mecca employers latched on to this longer history as a key element of the publicity surrounding the dance.

England told a rather different story about the origins of the Lambeth Walk to Mass Observation, however, and one that presented strong evidence that she and her employer's primary interest in creating the dance had been pecuniary. In an interview with the social research organisation, England said that she had not drawn inspiration from, nor even investigated cockney culture before developing the steps of the dance. Instead, England said that she had designed the Lambeth Walk solely based on her knowledge and experience of what proved popular in the dance halls.[31] In mimicking Lane, a self-professed cockney, England may well have believed there was a trace of realism to the dance's movements, but authenticity was not her priority. Her comments to Mass Observation confirmed that Mecca's principal motive in developing the Lambeth Walk was not to celebrate or restore a national cultural tradition, but rather to create a popular dance that would bring people into the company's dance halls. But in order to so, the dance's creators were happy to perpetuate the notion that it had a long and established history.

Notably, the precise details of this history were often confused and contradictory. Cockneys were traditionally associated with the East End of London – those born within 'the sound of Bow bells', referencing the ringing bells of St Mary-le-Bow church – rather than a south London neighbourhood like Lambeth. Yet by the time that Lane and subsequently England were creating the Lambeth Walk, the appellation had become associated with working-class Londoners more broadly, making the dance plausible as a cockney tradition.[32] In addition, the Lambeth Walk was not always specifically associated with cockneys: its creators, and the many others who would ultimately engage with the dance's origins, also frequently called it a 'coster' dance. This shortened version of 'costermonger' referred to any person who sold fruit or vegetables from an outdoor stand, regardless of geographic location. Among the Lambeth Walk's creators and other analysts of the dance, its regional origins were in fact traced back to everywhere from Hampstead Heath to Yorkshire.

The contradictions in the Lambeth Walk's history clearly arose from the fact that it was the creation of a dance teacher in 1938 rather than a longstanding feature of working-class culture. However, the Lambeth Walk's muddled backstory seems not to have mattered to the millions of Britons who loved it: whether it was because of Lane's cockney background or the existence of the old Alec Hurley music hall song, there was just enough about the dance and its movements that rang true for Britons. More than likely, they could see the flaws in Mecca's hazy history of the dance but chose to disregard them, and, as will be shown, they soon found ways to make the dance their own regardless of its contemporary origins, class focus or regional specificity. Importantly, numerous individuals and social groups were soon backing Mecca's claims that the Lambeth Walk represented an intrinsically British cultural tradition.

The dance profession, in conjunction with the popular media, was one of the most effective forces for validating the Lambeth Walk's legitimacy. Seeking a history for the dance, the *Manchester Guardian* turned to Major Cecil Taylor, president of the Imperial Society for Teachers of Dancing, who duly reported that 'costers on Hampstead Heath danced like this sixty years ago'.[33] Editors at the *Modern Dance and the Dancer* also wrote that they had conducted their own study of the dance's evolution, confirming that it 'originated at the fairgrounds of London, when the costers took their concertinas, combs and paper, and danced with their donahs'.[34] A newsreel that featured footage of both the palais glide and Lambeth Walk being performed at the Streatham Locarno referred to the latter as 'an honest to goodness cockney number'.[35] Richardson and the *Dancing Times* also regularly confirmed the cockney or coster origins of the Lambeth Walk, though in a more tentative way that hinted at an awareness of how tenuous the connections between Mecca's dance and real cockney tradition truly were. As the magazine remarked in December 1938, 'The fact that to some extent the "Lambeth Walk" does conventionally represent the reputed movements of the London Cockney ... may account for its success and the comparative failure of imitations which have not the same slight historical background.'[36] In this statement, the most important periodical about dancing in Britain suggested that the dance was 'to some extent' authentic and that the historical background of the dance was 'slight', but confirmed it nonetheless.

Beyond the dance community, real-life Lambethians were also eager to lay claim to the dance. In interviews conducted by Mass Observation in the actual Lambeth Walk – a short road in south London – many local people willingly confirmed that the song and dance had a long history, dating back perhaps as far as half a century, and that the latest incarnation was merely a revival. However, most Lambethians suggested that the earlier version of the dance that they knew went by a different name. One woman recalled that she performed the Lambeth Walk, 'oh years ago when we were little shirt buttons. Fifty years ago. We called it the jig.' Another man remembered that prior to Lane's version, 'We had our own show. It hadn't any name. But we always used to say "Oi!"'[37] In these comments, local Lambethians established a direct connection between Mecca's Lambeth Walk and the history and customs of their class and neighbourhood, helping to further cement the dance within British culture.

The idea that the Lambeth Walk was a longstanding feature of Lambeth cultural life was perpetuated by many participants and spectators of the dance outside the borough as well. In a list establishing the origins of Mecca's Lambeth Walk, Mass Observation's Charles Madge and Tom Harrisson put in the number one position, 'the cockneys of Lambeth and elsewhere whose walk [Lupino] Lane imitated'.[38] Research conducted by the social research organisation also showed that approximately a quarter of British people surveyed believed that the dance had originated with 'Lambeth, costers or Cockneys'. One observer told Mass Observation, 'I understand the Lambeth Walk is a coster dance, and I imagine it originated with the costers and girls promenading.'[39] Many within the British public thus identified something historically British in Mecca's Lambeth Walk, regardless of its contemporary origins, and reinforced the dance's legitimacy as much as its creators did. Another observer of the dance remarked, '[the] thing that struck me was the way the dancers seemed to throw themselves into the part, as though they were play-acting, especially the men, who seemed to fancy they were costers, imitating their mannerisms.'[40] These comments additionally conveyed how much of the meaning in the Lambeth Walk was constructed in its physical performance. As Richardson observed in a radio interview, novelty dances required participants to engage in a 'bit of acting'.[41] Indeed, who performed the Lambeth Walk, and where and how they did so, shifted the meanings that the dance expressed in accordance with individual preferences and regional customs.

Importantly, there was great variety to how the dance was performed throughout the country. England told Mass Observation that 'people will do [the Lambeth Walk] in their own way'.[42] Another observer of the dance remarked that 'nobody seems to do it the same', while the *Dancing Times* noted that 'not one couple in a thousand is doing it as taught'.[43] The ways in which the dancing public altered the Lambeth Walk were particularly significant for the vision of the nation that it expressed and embodied. With its London focus and Mecca's many references to the remarkable local and international success of an 'English' dance, the Lambeth Walk fell short of comprehensively representing the whole of the nation. So by changing the steps or adapting the dance in ways that reflected their specific locality, the British people effectively extended its geographic range and made the dance more legitimately national in scope. In Scotland, dancers changed the customary 'Oi!' at the end of the Lambeth Walk to an 'Och aye', in a playful bid to inject local flavour.[44] Among the flurry of copycat dances that emerged in the Lambeth Walk's wake were a significant number of regional variations, including the Margate walk, the Southend walk, and the Blackpool walk. Other localities eschewed the 'walk' designation but retained the spirit of the Lambeth original when creating the Highland swing, the Scottswood shuffle, the Clapham prom and the Deptford dip. In their physical performance of the Lambeth Walk (or its regionally specific imitations), therefore, the dancing public transformed the meanings associated with the dance well beyond those espoused by Lane or the Mecca organisation. In this way, it was not merely rhetoric – produced by Mecca or elsewhere – that connected the Lambeth Walk to British national identity; rather, the dancers' bodies constructed and instantiated British national identity during their performances of the dance.

While Britons extended the geographic scope of the Lambeth Walk beyond one short London road to encompass more of the country, they tended to confirm its working-class themes. One woman remarked that the dance was 'common, particularly the "Oi" bit at the end, and I think it is lovely to be common and let yourself go in these days of refinement'.[45] Scholars have noted that the source material for the Lambeth Walk presented a benign and idealistic vision of the British class system. As Raphael Samuel and Alison Light observe, in *Me and My Girl*, 'The working class, however rough their ways, are basically harmless; the aristocracy, however stuck-up, benevolent; the English a race of lovable eccentrics.'[46] Stephen Guy similarly argues with respect to the film version of the show that it was in the Lambeth Walk that 'The meeting of the classes is symbolised.'[47]

The dance retained these associations in its transition to the public ballroom. While a hint of mockery or even class prejudice was occasionally a feature of comments concerning the Lambeth Walk, many Britons clearly believed that in their performance of the dance they were paying tribute to the working classes, and nurturing social harmony. Only weeks after the dance was created, a newsreel that introduced it to filmgoers asserted that this was a dance for all Britons, regardless of social background. The narrator encouraged viewers: 'whatever walk of life you may be in, try the Lambeth Walk'.[48] As another fan of the dance noted, 'I always feel that it draws all classes of society together … The whole thing gives out friendliness and makes me like the costers better.'[49] Lane himself remarked, 'rich and poor alike – there is no class distinction about dancing. Anyone can do the "Lambeth Walk" and nearly everyone does'.[50] The simplicity of the dance enabled all Britons to participate, whether or not they could afford instruction in ballroom dancing. The communal performance of the Lambeth Walk also inspired feelings of camaraderie and allowed Britons to imagine that they were one happy dancing unit. As the *Dancing Times* observed, 'it is the community spirit, the idea of many folk doing the same movement in unison that grips them'.[51] While the classes would rarely have mingled in the performance of the Lambeth Walk, its phenomenal success and ubiquity further reinforced the idea that it was a shared national experience.

The feelings of social unity evoked by the Lambeth Walk, as well as the celebration of the 'ordinary' Briton represented in the cockney or coster, anticipated ideals about national identity that became dominant once the country entered the Second World War. During the so-called 'people's war', the nation's self-understanding was inextricably tied to ideas about national unity, social levelling and the vital role played by the average person in winning the war. Gareth Stedman Jones has argued in fact that the ordinary Briton was often personified in the cockney.[52] Thus, as the threat of war grew in the final years of the 1930s, the Lambeth Walk helped to cultivate the vision of the nation that would eventually fight. At the same time, the incongruity of a very silly dance rising to global prominence in the same moment as the international situation drastically deteriorated was not lost on contemporaries. Following the resolution of the Munich Crisis, *The Times* observed that had war not been averted, both Britain and Germany would have been marching off to the fight to the same popular dance tune.[53]

As international tensions mounted, the Lambeth Walk's creators also sought to associate the dance with the battle lines being drawn across Europe, using this as yet another point upon which to promote the dance. In January 1939, Mass Observation's Harrisson wrote an article for the *Picture Post* which charted the creation and distribution of Mecca's first follow-up to the Lambeth Walk, the Chestnut Tree. The article featured an interview with Heimann, who said this about the appeal and importance of the Mecca novelty dances:

> I claim, rightly or wrongly, that the Lambeth Walk and Chestnut Tree are typically English. The difference between the English people and those who follow Hitler and Mussolini as I see it, is between the arms of Hitler and Musso, and the arms of the King. Musso puts his hand over his head and everyone else does and that means the rule of iron. The King puts his hand above his head and everyone else does when they sing The Chestnut Tree, and that means democracy.[54]

Heimann suggested that it was their very ability to follow a leader in dance rather than in marching that distinguished the British from their future military enemies in Nazi Germany and Fascist Italy. When the Lambeth Walk was later banned in these countries, Heimann further declared to Mass Observation that the dances were simply 'too peace making' for the likes of Hitler and Mussolini.[55]

The rejection of the Lambeth Walk by fascist leaders, as well as its ease and accessibility, and the physical enactment of social harmony represented in its movements, cultivated another important idea about the dance: that it reflected Britain's long history of democracy. Once again, this was a notion that the producers of the Lambeth Walk were pleased to endorse, and Heimann often proclaimed that his novelty dances showcased the nation's democratic spirit.

Lane was another proponent of this idea, stating in in an interview that 'ours is a truly great democratic nation, and such institutions as the "Lambeth Walk" make it more so'.[56] However, it was not only Heimann and Lane who perceived there to be a democratic impulse in the Lambeth Walk. Mass Observation's Harrisson and Madge justified the inclusion of an entire chapter about the dance in a book about the national reaction to the Munich Crisis by noting, 'we may learn something about the future of democracy if we take a closer look at the Lambeth Walk'.[57] In the spring of 1939, in reference to the Lambeth Walk and party dances in general, one writer for the *Dancing Times* proclaimed: 'No longer can we treat these dances as frivolities. They have become important, they are international, and truly democratic.'[58]

The idea that the Lambeth Walk expressed democracy and the national spirit clearly had resonance for the dancing public as well. When war finally erupted in September of 1939, the people's favourite dance was deployed in a multitude of ways to help them make sense of the conflict. Within a few weeks of the declaration of war, a parody entitled 'Hitler's Lambeth Walk' began to circulate in penny pamphlet form, with the lyrics changed to mock Nazi leaders and describe an easy Allied victory.[59] A propaganda film entitled 'Lambeth Walk – Nazi Style' was later produced, in which scenes of a Nazi rally from Leni Riefenstahl's *Triumph of the Will* were re-edited to show German soldiers goose-stepping in time to the song. The road in south London actually called Lambeth Walk also became a site through which Britons were able to measure the impacts of the war and to express the nation's endurance. The *Evening Standard* followed a group of children from Lambeth Walk to Surrey as a means of examining the effects of the evacuation. In the first days of the Blitz, the *Daily Sketch* photographed a group of Londoners performing the Lambeth Walk amidst the ruins resulting from a recent German air raid (see Figure 6.1). The caption beneath the image read: 'The gallant Cockneys of Lambeth Walk refuse to be downhearted. They still keep up their famous dance, and they can smile'.[60] Britons used the Lambeth Walk to express their resilience and good cheer in the face of the German bombing campaign, physically embodying the Blitz spirit through dance. As will be shown in Chapter 7, this was to become a dominant characteristic of popular dance during the war years, as it came to represent the nation's spirit, endurance, and democracy.

The Lambeth Walk thus came to retain a host of cultural meanings that extended well beyond Heimann's original goal of creating a simple party dance that would bring the masses into Mecca dance halls. While the marketing of the dance was calculated from the beginning, the promotional campaign also

DANCING AMID RUINS
DOWN LAMBETH WAY

In spite of the damage caused in the Lambeth Walk area during the latest Nazi raids, the gallant Cockneys of Lambeth Walk refuse to be downhearted. They still keep up their famous dance, and they can smile. See also Page 2

6.1   Londoners dance the Lambeth Walk to express their fortitude and good spirits after an air raid.

expanded and mutated in accordance with the popular response to the dance. Mecca, the ballroom dance profession, and the dancing public all jointly affirmed the Lambeth Walk as a reassertion of British cultural autonomy, and as a celebration of working-class culture, social harmony and democratic ideals. Through these negotiations, the Lambeth Walk became a part of the national culture and a way to physically embody national identity. However, the commercial interests that had motivated Mecca's creation of the Lambeth Walk were made once again apparent in the production of the company's subsequent novelty dances, and resulted in a very different response from the dancing public.

'The Lambeth Walk has a lot to answer for'

The craze for the Lambeth Walk had in no way abated when Mecca premiered its second novelty dance, the Chestnut Tree, in November 1938. With this dance, and the three that followed it, Mecca maintained the formula that had been so successful with the Lambeth Walk: all of the dances were designed to be relatively simple to learn, and were based around national themes. In the case of the Chestnut Tree, the dance was inspired by a newsreel image of King George VI joining in a camp sing-along of the old folk song 'The Village Blacksmith' taken sometime in the summer of 1938. The widely seen image of the king tapping his head in the tradition of the folk song provided inspiration to composer Jimmy Kennedy, who was charged with coming up with Mecca's next novelty dance tune.[61] Kennedy, along with his brother, Hamilton, and Tommy Connor, recreated the 'The Village Blacksmith' as 'The Chestnut Tree', and once again England developed the dance. In the same simple style as the Lambeth Walk, dancers circled the floor mimicking the growth of a tree, before boisterously exclaiming 'CHESTNUTS!'

Mecca's promotional campaign for the Chestnut Tree was more systematic, and on an even grander scale, than the one it had instigated for the Lambeth Walk. Heimann and his public relations manager, Byron Davies, gave the Chestnut Tree a national launch, debuting the dance simultaneously at every Mecca dance hall in the country on 15 November 1938. In this way, Mecca proposed, the different parts of the nation could learn and share in the newest dance at the exact same moment. At each hall, on-staff professional dancers first demonstrated the dance, and then invited patrons to join in, with the words to Kennedy's song prominently displayed on large banners around the halls so that people could sing along. England herself introduced the dance at the Streatham Locarno, and later went on tour to promote the Chestnut Tree around the country. The company also sent advance publicity about the dance – including instructions on steps, images, music and lyrics banners – to the press and non-Mecca dance halls free of charge, in the hope that they would further spread word about its newest novelty dance. Finally, Mecca joined forces with Peter Maurice Music Company to promote and distribute the Chestnut Tree song. On the same day that the dance debuted in Mecca halls, Jack Payne's band launched the song on the BBC, and sheet music and gramophone records went up for sale, each with written or recorded instructions on how to perform the dance.

Less than four months later, a similar and even more costly promotional campaign was undertaken for Mecca's third novelty dance, the Park Parade, which received its national premiere on 8 March 1939. Thematically the Park Parade was based around a couple taking a romantic stroll in the park on a summer's day; the dance's big finish, along the lines of 'Oi' or 'Chestnuts!'

required dancers to shout 'Yippee, ain't love grand!' The Park Parade was also said to be more of a 'real' dance than its predecessors, with a change from foxtrot (4/4) to waltz (3/4) time halfway through. The steps were once again designed by England, to go along with a song composed by Arthur Young, Tommy Duggan and Anthony Page. Like the Chestnut Tree, the Park Parade had a simultaneous debut at all the Mecca halls throughout the country, and the dance was made the grand finale of a variety show at the London Hippodrome, premiering there on the same evening. It also received even more advertising than the Chestnut Tree, with posters on the sides of buses and in the London Underground, and as an additional promotional tool Mecca introduced a free gift at the Park Parade launch. During the dance's demonstration at Mecca halls nationwide, real straw hats were distributed to patrons to sport during the dance – not paper 'carnival novelties', Mecca was quick to note, but real hats that would cost four to six shillings in a shop – which were meant to complement the outdoor theme.[62] Indeed, Mecca's commitment to promoting its novelty dances is perhaps best displayed by the escalating costs involved. According to Heimann's interview with Mass Observation, Mecca spent £500 promoting the Lambeth Walk, £1,000 on the Chestnut Tree and £3,000 on the Park Parade.[63]

Both the Chestnut Tree and the Park Parade enjoyed credible, if short-lived, success. Fans of novelty dances deemed the Chestnut Tree simple and enjoyable, while more serious dancers tended to prefer the Park Parade's added complexity. Though neither dance attained anything like the status of the Lambeth Walk, they were generally well received. Mecca was far less successful, however, with its fourth novelty dance, the Handsome Territorial. With a song composed by Kennedy and Michael Carr, and dance movements by England, the Handsome Territorial was described by many as more of a march than a dance. Comprised of the same type of simple movements as its predecessors, the climax required the dancers to shout 'BOOM!' while performing a military salute. The dance was introduced during the summer of 1939, on the eve of the outbreak of the Second World War, and with its military theme, Mecca promoted the dance as being particularly topical, and 'astoundingly appropriate to current events'.[64] With these claims, the company began to ease into a business strategy that would characterise its activities during the war, wherein the war crisis itself was used to market dancing.

The Handsome Territorial debuted at the Locarno on 13 June 1939, but with far less fanfare than the Chestnut Tree and Park Parade. England told Mass Observation's Alec Hughes that Mecca wanted to see if another dance could be successful without a large promotional campaign.[65] No doubt the reduced publicity accounts to some extent for the Handsome Territorial's lack of impact, yet it must also be attributed to the inferiority of the dance. Hughes's report suggested that even some of its creators seemed dubious about the quality of the dance. England believed that Heimann's determination to release a new novelty every few months diminished the quality of what was being produced. As she told Mass Observation, 'it is mad to bring out so many dances, though I am the last who should say it … These things just come to you. You might just think of a good idea, like Lambeth Walk, and make a success of it. But you can't do that when you have to turn them out on a certain date.'[66] England later admitted to being nervous about touring the country with the Handsome Territorial, and apparently with good reason. At the dance's Locarno premiere, once the professionals had completed the exhibition, no dancers joined in at all. When the dance was introduced at the Paramount several days later, the reception was little better. Patrons at both premieres described the dance as 'daft', 'crazy' and 'awful'. Hughes overheard one woman remark to her friend about England and her new dance, 'I think I could write better than that myself.'[67] Another woman stated, 'of course I'm not going to dance a thing like that. They'd have to drag me on the floor first.'[68] Hughes himself concluded that the dance was 'still born'.[69]

Yet the Handsome Territorial's chilly reception did not stop Mecca from proceeding with the launch of its next dance, nor did the outbreak of war in September 1939. On 12 December of that year, Heimann and England premiered Knees Up, Mother Brown at the Paramount dance hall in London. Like the Lambeth Walk, the dance had its roots in an old music hall song, and promotional materials were once again provided free of charge to the press and non-Mecca halls. Despite Britain's changed reality, Mecca's primary concern was clearly still profit, as the company informed other dance hall proprietors that it was 'at your service to make dancing prosperous in war time'.[70] In fact, the outbreak of the war goes some distance towards explaining why Knees Up, Mother Brown made little real impact; it was in competition with another, perhaps more timely novelty dance, the black-out stroll, produced by one of Mecca's competitors that same autumn. But there was also less eagerness among some members of the dance hall industry and dancing public to embrace Heimann's latest novelty; they had lost patience with the Mecca dances and their fly-by-night popularity. As the manager of the Aspin Hall in Bolton told Mass Observation, 'I've not bothered with the last one – Knees Up, Mother Brown. [Mecca has] written to me about it … but I reckon it isn't worth bothering about. Why take all the trouble to get the stuff to learn it and then put it across for it to die out in about a week? It's not worth it.'[71]

The waning interest in Mecca's novelty dances was in spite of the company's persistent claims that, like the Lambeth Walk, all of the dances were easy to master and 'typically English'. As she was in the planning stages for the Lambeth Walk follow-ups, England told Mass Observation, 'we want to keep them all English now'.[72] Accordingly, the dances were all designed by British musicians and dancers, and contained what were purported to be national themes. The Chestnut Tree was based on an old folk song, celebrated rural village life, and through the image of the king that inspired the dance, had connections to that most British of institutions, the monarchy. The Park Parade also celebrated an aspect of Britain's natural beauty – the urban park – and pushed nostalgia through the addition of the straw hat, which was supposed to harken back to an old fashion trend, the 'strawyard', and to a past era in general. Byron Davies, Mecca's head of publicity, said about the Park Parade, that 'the spectacle of a ballroom filled with couples with the men all wearing straw hats, creates an atmosphere reminiscent of the good old days when the only Sunday amusement was to listen to the band in the park'.[73] The Handsome Territorial, though less about nostalgia than about the 'topical' threat of a looming war, paid tribute to another traditional and conservative national institution, the army. Like the Lambeth Walk, the Handsome Territorial also glorified the average, everyday Briton by focusing on a low-ranked foot solider rather than an officer, as the lyrics to the song demonstrated:

> He wasn't a Gen'ral
> He wasn't a Colonel
> He wasn't a Major
> He wasn't a Captain
> He wasn't a Sergeant
> He wasn't a Corp'ral
> Just a member of the rank and file[74]

Finally, Knees Up, Mother Brown was based on an old music hall song, and like the Lambeth Walk, was marketed as a song and dance with genuine cockney origins.

With these themes, the Mecca novelty dances reproduced and commodified a vision of the nation that was prominent in popular culture of the 1930s: nostalgic references to Britain's past, and espousals of the nation's natural beauty. The Mecca dances were also more concerned with glorifying England, rather than Britain, part of the common interwar tendency towards an inward-focus on 'Little England'. At the same time, the Handsome Territorial's celebration of the foot soldier, just like the Lambeth Walk's evocation of the everyday working man, anticipated important aspects of wartime national identity, with its emphasis on the critical role played by the average person in winning the war. Heimann's frequent espousal of the novelty dances' 'democratic spirit' also hinted at the ways in which dancing would come to distinguish the democratic British from their authoritarian enemies during the war years. The Mecca novelty dances thus helped to construct and circulate dominant ideals about interwar and wartime national identity, while also converting those ideals into products to be sold.

The effort to reproduce national idioms through the Lambeth Walk follow-ups was not the only way in which their Britishness was affirmed. As with the Lambeth Walk, Mecca and the creative teams in its employ attempted to distinguish the dances from American cultural imports, often in strongly racialised terms. In articulating what he believed to be the appeal of the Chestnut Tree, one of the song's composers, Connor, told Mass Observation, 'English dances should be for the English – [people are] getting tired of what I call Harlemesque.'[75] Meanwhile, Mecca's press release for the Chestnut Tree strongly echoed the language employed by the dance profession during its own efforts to Anglicise African-American dances and create the English style: 'the dance itself is severely ENGLISH. So many of the new and short-lived dances that have been introduced in recent years have been American, and based on negro rhythms not suited to the English temperament'.[76] The Mecca novelty dances, like the English style of ballroom dance, thus firmly established national identity as white, and against an American other.

However, despite the fact that with the Chestnut Tree, the Park Parade, the Handsome Territorial, and Knees Up Mother Brown, Mecca strived to replicate exactly the combination of factors that had produced the phenomenal success of the Lambeth Walk – simplicity and national themes – each was less successful than the last. No doubt part of the reason for this was that some of the 'novelty' in novelty dances had simply worn off. The dancing public was overwhelmed with five of these dances in less than two years, not to mention the dozens of non-Mecca novelty dances that came and went in the same time period, and had grown weary of the repetition. Yet mere boredom on the part of the public does not wholly account for waning support for the Mecca creations, especially since the outbreak of the war saw a resurgence of interest in party dances. Rather, the reception of the Mecca dances presents a more complex picture about the consumption of popular dance, and the part played by dancers in determining what cultural meanings would be associated with and performed through a dance. Significantly, in articulating their feelings about the four dances, the dancing public and the dance profession called upon the first element of Mecca's rhetoric about its dances – simplicity and accessibility – but rarely the second – Britishness. If a person liked novelty dances, they tended to like the new ones produced by Mecca; if they did not like novelty dances, they disliked Mecca's dances as much as any others. As with the five-step and trebla a decade earlier, the dances' Britishness seemed to play little part in determining how Britons reacted to them. In sharp contrast to how they had received the Lambeth Walk, proponents and critics alike focused on the other four novelties' value merely as dances, not 'British' dances.

As has been shown, all of the Mecca novelty dances were designed with a view towards universal appeal. With the Lambeth Walk the focus had been on its simplicity, and the idea that it was a truly democratic dance that anyone could take part in. Mecca pushed this idea with its other four novelty dances as well, even to the point of suggesting that they were appropriate for children. Special morning sessions were held at some Mecca halls to teach children the new dances free of charge. Images of young children were also common in advertisements for the dances. For instance, the promotional materials for the Handsome Territorial noted that like its predecessors, 'it is entirely free from any taint of "sex" and therefore appropriate for Parties and for Children'.[77] In this way, the novelty dances also played a part in Mecca's continuing efforts to 'clean up' the dance halls and to market dancing as a family friendly leisure activity. However, the company's formula for cultivating broad-based interest in its dances was even more involved than simply making them easy to learn and respectable. Mecca wanted its dances to have widespread appeal, and the subtle differences between them were targeted at separate consumers. Since dancing was often perceived to be a leisure pursuit dominated by the young, England deliberately inserted elements of the polka, an old-time dance, into the Chestnut Tree, thinking that this would make it more appealing to older dancers.[78] With the Park Parade, Mecca attempted to appease the critics of novelty dances who argued that they were not really dances at all, by introducing more complexity, and a mid-dance switch from foxtrot to waltz time. With its various novelty dances Mecca tried to ensure that there was something for everyone, an idea that was also reflected in how the novelties were performed in the dance halls. Mecca halls often played the novelty dances together in a sequence known as the 'Heimann Medley'. Patrons therefore knew that if they liked the Park Parade more than the Chestnut Tree, they did not have to wait long for their favourite dance to be played, and, Mecca likely hoped, would not leave the dance floor.

The distinctions between the various Mecca novelty dances did figure into their reception to a considerable degree. Some dancers liked the Chestnut Tree or the Park Parade for the very reasons that Mecca had predicted. In a survey conducted jointly by Mass Observation and Mecca's dance magazine, *Danceland*, many respondents noted that they preferred the Park Parade to the Chestnut Tree because there was 'more to it', and it was more of a 'real' dance.[79] As one man wrote, 'the Park Parade has more charm and style than the Chestnut Tree, it has variety and more opportunity for real dancing as compared with the rather miming actions of the Chestnut Tree'.[80] Most patrons therefore had their personal favourite among the novelty dances; there was also some variation from hall to hall, town to town, in terms of whether it was the Chestnut Tree, the Park Parade or even the Handsome Territorial that was most popular. How a dance would 'go over' also often depended on the location or simply the night in question. Novelty dances tended to be very successful at private dances, where everyone generally knew one another and were less inhibited and concerned about looking foolish. Mass Observation also noted that all of the Mecca dances were enthusiastically performed at a New Year's Eve dance in Bolton; something about the festive atmosphere of the holiday was conducive to the communal merriment of novelty dances. The observer noted, 'the effect produced [by the dances] was one of terrific excitement. The band was playing full blast, everyone was singing the words … and the floor was vibrating [and] sinking a good 4–6 inches in the centre of the room.'[81] But though there was considerable diversity as to when, where, and why people enjoyed novelty dances, there were some common sentiments put forth by enthusiasts of the dances, often directly corresponding to Mecca's intentions. Proponents suggested that novelty dances had restored fun to the ballroom; that they were simple and enabled even the most inexperienced dancers to participate; that they were a welcome change from twenty years of foxtrot variations. Many of those responding to the *Danceland* questionnaire also simply expressed that the dances were 'happy'.[82]

Among members of the dance profession, the response to the Mecca novelty dances was decidedly mixed. The majority of professionals acknowledged that the dances were fun, and had restored 'sociability' to the ballroom. Some further affirmed that novelty dances had renewed public interest in dancing, and expressed the hope that once the novelties got people to enter the palais they would be inspired to take up ballroom dance in a more serious manner. James Quinn, a professional dancer who along with his partner Florence Mills was Mecca's chief demonstrator of the novelty dances, told Mass Observation, '[these dances get] people to dance who otherwise would not. They learn simple dances like this and, finding they like them, it encourages them to learn the more complicated ballroom dances.'[83] Teacher Alex Moore similarly wrote in the *Dancing Times* that novelty dances '[have made] ballrooms much brighter, and [have] also had the effect of inducing thousands of non-dancers literally to "walk" on the ballroom floor for the first time.'[84] Taylor went so far as to proclaim that 'the Lambeth Walk came as a godsend. The ballroom had become so melancholy for want of something of a joyous nature that the Lambeth Walk brought back to the ballroom what had been lacking for 20 years.'[85] However Taylor, and other prominent members of the dance profession such as Silvester, also categorically asserted that the novelties were not 'real' dances.

This was the mantra most often take up by professional critics of novelty dances, who further lamented that because of their similarity to sequence dancing the novelties were old-fashioned and halted the progressive development of modern ballroom dance. As Monsieur Pierre wrote in the *Modern Dance and the Dancer*, 'I am disappointed because I consider we should go *ahead* not *backwards*.'[86] Other professionals were concerned about more than technique, suggesting that the silly novelty dances presented a threat to the integrity of the British ballroom. Scottish dancing teacher and ballroom manager John Gillespie wrote a very critical letter to the *Modern Dance and the Dancer* suggesting that dancers were being 'tortured' by the rush of party dances, and that it was paramount that the profession 'make an effort to stop this hectic rush of stupid novelties'.[87] Most dance professionals, whether they approved of novelty dances or not, dismissed them as passing craze that would not have the same enduring appeal as the four standard ballroom dances. In his 1944 book, *The Ballroom Dancer's Handbook*, A. H. Franks explained that the guide would contain no discussion of party dances at all, since:

> most of them are too ephemeral for serious contemplation; they have no foundation in technique and are produced chiefly for the diversion of the unhappily vast army which remains ignorant of the joy to be won from mastery of the four standard dances.[88]

Even England acknowledged that most of her dances were likely to fade out quickly.[89]

It should be noted that many dance teachers' distaste for the novelties resided in the effect that these dances had on their financial interests. As one professional complained to Mass Observation, because novelty dances were simple to learn the craze for them had caused a real slump in dancing school attendance.[90] In a radio interview, Richardson similarly recalled that upon the introduction of these dances, 'A few [teachers] grumbled that their business was slipping away from them.'[91] However, more enterprising professionals seized upon the economic opportunity afforded by public enthusiasm for party dances. For instance, despite the aforementioned Monsieur Pierre's misgivings about them, he and his partner Doris Lavelle soon created their own novelty dance – the 'boomps-a-daisy' – which was accompanied by a song written and performed by singer Annette Mills. Just like Mecca's dances, the boomps-a-daisy was said to be inspired by British history and culture, specifically the 'naughty nineties'. In advertising and exhibitions of the dance, demonstrators sported late-Victorian fashions, particularly gowns with a pronounced bustle, which related to the dance's primary movement – a naughty 'boomps', wherein partners bumped hips. As Monsieur Pierre's about-face indicates, many within the dance profession – despite initial avowals that the craze for novelty dances simply could not last – soon jumped on the bandwagon. The most visible sign of this capitulation came in 1939, when a new sequence dancing category was introduced at the profession's premier competition at Blackpool, in which competitors created and exhibited new group dances.

Meanwhile, the criticisms of novelty dances did not arise solely from within the dance profession. Despite attempts by Heimann and the popular press to disseminate the idea that all of the Mecca novelty dances equalled the success of the Lambeth Walk, there is no question that they were not universally beloved. In particular, some dancers worried about looking ridiculous performing the silly movements. A dance hall manager in Bolton noted, '[though] the crowd are quite prepared to laugh at the staff doing them they do not take them up well themselves. They feel conspicuous doing them'.[92] Another hall manager suggested that rather than being worried about looking silly, the patrons at his establishment simply took ballroom dancing too seriously to engage in novelties: 'It wouldn't go here ... I don't think that sort of dance catches on. The public dancers are dancers here.'[93] The feelings of many novelty dance critics were perhaps best summed up in one man's response to the Chestnut Tree, which was recorded by Mass Observation: 'Silliest damn thing I've ever seen.'[94]

Public and professional reaction to the Mecca novelties was thus significantly divided, but what is most striking about the diversity of feeling is that, in contrast to the response to the Lambeth Walk, there was little discussion of their thematic content. The British dancing public embraced the nationalist nostalgia and anti-American themes in the Lambeth Walk, and upon the first introduction of the Chestnut Tree, there was some continuation of these narratives. In his article for the *Picture Post*, for example, Harrisson expressed enthusiasm for the fact that the new dance 'talks English, not American'.[95] But for the most part Britons remained resistant or indifferent to the idea that the other Mecca novelty dances were 'typically English'. In fact, when they did acknowledge any national elements to the dances, it was often in derisive terms. An American visitor to the Streatham Locarno, for instance, upon observing an exhibition of the Handsome Territorial, remarked to Mass Observation, 'it's screwy. That's what you call an English dance, isn't it?'[96] A sixteen-year-old girl said about the Park Parade, 'Oh it's like the Lambeth Walk – daft. That's the trouble with this country. When they have a thing they keep imitating it, till you get fed up with it.'[97] Some dancers also expressed concerns, shared by professionals, that novelty dances constituted a threat to the true British dancing represented by the English style. One letter to the editor of the *Modern Dance and the Dancer* observed, 'it is conceivable that in 1938, when the whole world is looking to the British style of dancing as the best in the world ... that we should lower the dignity of the ballroom by introducing such dances'.[98] Another letter expressed similar concerns: 'For years style and grace have been the main features of British dancing. Now, with [novelty dances] all has been forgotten.'[99]

Therefore, although the other Mecca novelty dances had as much claim to being genuine national cultural traditions as the Lambeth Walk, the British public proved reluctant to identify anything authentic in them. In attempting to account for this, it must be recalled that almost two years passed between the creation of the Lambeth Walk and the launch of Knees Up, Mother Brown. This was a crucial time period, in which Britain moved closer to war, and ideas about national identity transitioned accordingly. As notions of national and imperial unity became increasingly prevalent, celebrations of Little England such as those evoked by the Mecca novelty dances were bound to lose some of their appeal. While popular cultural celebrations of landscape, history and heritage would remain prevalent throughout the war years as well, in this transitional moment, the new ideals of the wartime nation may well have been more potent. In this context, it seems likely that if any of the Mecca novelty dances was to have been embraced for its national themes, it would have been the Handsome Territorial. Not only was it 'topical', but like the Lambeth Walk it celebrated the ordinary Briton, which was commensurate with wartime understandings of national identity. However, unlike the Lambeth Walk, it was not admired as a dance, and quality clearly played as much, if not more of a part than thematic content in determining whether a dance would be admitted into the national culture.

The abject failure of the Handsome Territorial suggests that there was also another important factor at work in the dancing public's failure to accept the Mecca novelty dances as British. Some people clearly saw through the commodification of the nation represented in the dance, and viewed the content as exploitative. Hughes speculated in his report for Mass Observation that the timing of the dance was designed to coincide with the introduction of conscription in the summer of 1939, and he was not the only one to express this belief or that it might be inappropriate or insensitive. A Locarno band member told Mass Observation, '[the Handsome Territorial] is a fuckin' marching tune. I think [Mecca is] trying to cash in on the conscription business. They may get away with it.'[100] These comments reflected a level of awareness about Mecca's efforts to commodify the nation in the production and marketing of popular dance. The dancing public was conscious – probably even with the Lambeth Walk – of the commercial processes at work in Mecca's production of its novelty dances, even while receiving and performing them. While the case of the Lambeth Walk demonstrated a clear willingness on the part of the public to accept the vision of national culture that the dance hall industry produced, a closer look at the reception of all five Mecca novelty dances shows that consumers equally had agency in determining what vision of the nation they would accept, transform or simply reject.

Finally, while British popular dance had long espoused a racialised vision of national identity, by the late 1930s Mecca's insistence that their dances were not American and not black perhaps proved to be more of a hindrance than a selling point. Many Britons were increasingly enthusiastic about American cultural imports in any form. Moreover, Mecca's establishment of its novelty dances as explicitly English and explicitly white occurred at the very moment that a new dance originating in black America was first making its way across the Atlantic. In the same year that Britain was introduced to the Chestnut Tree, the Park Parade and the Handsome Territorial, it was also introduced to the jitterbug, which was to redefine British popular dance during the war years. Thus, while the dancing public eagerly accepted the authenticity of the Lambeth Walk, it did not infer anything truly national about Mecca's follow-up dances. Part of the reason seems to have been a cognizance that Mecca was using these supposedly British dances as a self-interested means of bringing people into their halls. Another contributing factor may well have been that Mecca's

anti-American, expressly white vision of the nation held little appeal for a
dancing public about to be swept away by swing music and the jitterbug. But
while the response to Mecca's nationalistic marketing of its novelty dances was
ambiguous, throughout this campaign the company developed and refined
the business strategies that would carry it through the war years.

Notes

1 Charles Madge and Tom Harrisson, *Britain by Mass-Observation* (London: Harmondsworth, 1939), p. 139.
2 For more on the stage production of *Me and My Girl*, see Raphael Samuel and
   Alison Light, 'Doing the Lambeth Walk', in Raphael Samuel (ed.), *Patriotism:
   The Making and Unmaking of British National Identity, Vol. III* (New York: Routledge,
   1989).
3 Madge and Harrisson, *Britain*, p. 141.
4 Jonah Barrington, 'Oi! No Doin' the Lambeth Walk in the Pantos', *Daily Express*
   (11 November 1938), p. 3.
5 *Me and My Girl* was one of the first musicals to be shown on the new medium
   of television. With respect to the film, Lane took advantage of the popularity of
   the ballroom dance by re-titling the adaptation *The Lambeth Walk*. For more on
   the film, see Stephen Guy, 'Calling All Stars: Musical Films in a Musical Decade',
   in Jeffrey Richards (ed.), *The Unknown 1930s: An Alternative History of the British
   Cinema, 1929–1939* (London: I.B. Tauris, 1998).
6 'I See Life by Charles Graves', *Daily Mail* (2 March 1939), p. 8.
7 It should be noted that Mass Observation believed this song was never actually
   used by the Labour Party, although a copy of the lyrics remain in the Mass
   Observation Archive. See MOA: TC 38/2/D, Lambeth Walk cont'd (1939); *Sussex
   Daily News* (6 February 1939). Clipping from MOA: TC 38/1, Additional Material
   (6 February 1939).
8 On interwar national identity, see Alison Light, *Forever England: Femininity,
   Literature and Conservatism Between the Wars* (London: Routledge, 1991); Alex
   Potts, 'Constable Country between the wars', in Raphael Samuel (ed.), *Patriotism:
   The Making and Unmaking of British National Identity, Vol. III* (New York: Routledge,
   1989); Jeffrey Richards, *Films and British National Identity: From Dickens to Dad's
   Army* (Manchester: Manchester University Press, 1997); Krishan Kumar, *The
   Making of English National Identity* (Cambridge: Cambridge University Press,
   2003); Peter Mandler, *The English National Character: The History of an Idea from
   Edmund Burke to Tony Blair* (New Haven, CT: Yale University Press, 2006);
   Matthew Grimley, 'The religion of Englishness: puritanism, providentialism, and
   "national character", 1918–1940', *Journal of British Studies* 46 (October 2007),
   884–906.
9 See Angus Calder, *The Myth of the Blitz* (London: Jonathan Cape, 1991); Sonya
   Rose, *Which People's War? National Identity and Citizenship in Britain, 1939–1945*

(Oxford: Oxford University Press, 2003); Wendy Webster, *Englishness and Empire, 1939–1965* (Oxford: Oxford University Press, 2007); Susan R. Grayzel, *At Home and Under Fire: Air Raids and Culture in Britain from the Great War to the Blitz* (Cambridge: Cambridge University Press, 2012).

10 Roma Fairley, *Come Dancing Miss World* (London: Newman Neame, 1966), p. 60.

11 Ross McKibbin, *Classes and Cultures: England, 1918–1951* (Oxford: Oxford University Press, 1998), p. 409.

12 Adele England, 'The Lambeth Walk', *Dancing Times* (May 1938), p. 170.

13 The Sitter Out, 'What will follow the Lambeth Walk?' *Dancing Times* (October 1938), p. 33.

14 Editorial, 'Peace and the "Lambeth Walk" ', *The Times* (18 October 1938).

15 See, for example, The Sitter Out, 'What will follow the Lambeth Walk?', p. 32.

16 'All About the Party Dance', *Dancing Times* (October 1939), p. 14.

17 England, 'The Lambeth Walk', p. 170.

18 'All About the Party Dance', p. 14.

19 Eric Y. Tilley, 'Slow Foxtrot or Lambeth Walk', *Modern Dance and the Dancer* (May 1939), p. 18.

20 'The Big Apple', *Dancing Times* (February 1938), p. 681.

21 'All About the Party Dance', p. 15.

22 The Sitter Out, 'What will follow the Lambeth Walk?', p. 33.

23 'This Man Made the World Shout "Oi!" ', *The Star* (16 August 1938). Clipping from MOA: TC 38/2/G.

24 Madge and Harrisson, *Britain*, p. 161.

25 Tom Harrisson, 'The Birth of a Dance', *Picture Post* (7 January 1939), p. 46.

26 Jack Payne, 'About this Lambeth Frolic', *Evening News* (15 December 1938), p. 11. Clipping from MOA: TC 38/2/E.

27 Madge and Harrisson, *Britain*, p. 159.

28 See Samuel and Light, 'Doing the Lambeth Walk', p. 267.

29 England, 'The Lambeth Walk', p. 170.

30 Adele England, *How to Dance C.L. Heimann's Novelty Dances* (London: Danceland Publications, 1942), p. 16.

31 Madge and Harrisson, *Britain*, p. 159.

32 See Gareth Stedman Jones, 'The "Cockney" and the nation, 1780–1988', in David Feldman and Gareth Stedman Jones (eds), *Metropolis-London: Histories and Representations Since 1800* (London: Routledge, 1989).

33 'The Birth of a Dance', *Manchester Guardian* (26 July 1938), p. 10. Clipping from MOA: TC 38/2/G.

34 'Oi!,' *Modern Dance and the Dancer* (July 1938), pp. 11–12.

35 'New dances for everybody', British Pathé newsreel (25 April 1938). Located at www.britishpathe.com/video/new-dances-for-everybody/query/lambeth+walk. Accessed 27 October 2014.

36 The Sitter Out, 'Ballroom Notes', *Dancing Times* (December 1938).

37 Madge and Harrisson, *Britain*, pp. 144–7.

38 Madge and Harrisson, *Britain*, p. 141.

39 Madge and Harrisson, *Britain*, p. 166.

40 MOA: TC 38/2/C, Material used for Lambeth Walk Chapter in Britain.

41 'All About the Party Dance', p.14.

42 Madge and Harrisson, *Britain*, p. 161.

43 Madge and Harrisson, *Britain*, 167; The Sitter Out, 'What will follow the Lambeth Walk', p. 33.

44 Madge and Harrisson, *Britain*, p. 163.

45 Madge and Harrisson, *Britain*, p. 173.

46 Samuel and Light, 'Doing the Lambeth Walk', p. 267.

47 Guy, 'Calling All Stars', p. 112.

48 'New dances for everybody', British Pathé newsreel.

49 Madge and Harrisson, *Britain*, p. 171.

50 Lupino Lane, 'About This (You know) Walk', *Answers* (10 December 1938), p. 9. Clipping from MOA: TC 38/2/E.

51 The Sitter Out, 'What will follow the Lambeth Walk?' p. 33.

52 Stedman Jones, 'The "Cockney" and the nation', pp. 272–324.

53 Editorial, 'Peace and the "Lambeth Walk"', *The Times* (18 October 1938).

54 Harrisson, 'The Birth of a Dance', pp. 48–9.

55 MOA: TC 38/3/A, C.L. Heimann, (12 March 1938).

56 Lane, 'About This (You know) Walk', p. 9.

57 Madge and Harrisson, *Britain*, p. 140.

58 Irene Raines, 'London Ballroom News', *Dancing Times* (April 1939).

59 MOA: TC 38/6/A, Jazz Literature (12 April 1939).

60 'Dancing Amid the Ruins Down Lambeth Way', *Daily Sketch* (19 September 1940).

61 Tom Harrisson, 'Birth of a Dance', p. 45.

62 MOA: TC 38/3/D, Press Bulletin – Park Parade.

63 MOA: TC 38/3/C, Park Parade (8 February 1939).

64 MOA: TC 38/3/E, Press Bulletin – Handsome Territorial.

65 MOA: TC 38/1/A, Handsome Territorial (13 June 1939).

66 MOA: TC 38/5/G, Interview with Adele England (5 June 1939).

67 MOA: TC 38/1/B, Handsome Territorial (14 June 1939).

68 MOA: TC 38/1/A, Handsome Territorial (13 June 1939).

69 MOA: TC 38/1/A, Handsome Territorial (13 June 1939).

70 MOA: TC 38/7/B, Flyer for Knees Up Mother Brown (December 1939).

71 MOA: Worktown 48/D, Aspin Hall (8 January 1940).

72 Madge and Harrisson, *Britain*, p. 161.

73 Byron Davies, 'Dance that Revives a Fashion', *The Entertainment Organiser and Club Secretary* 10 (March 1939), p. 63. From MOA: TC 38/3/D, Park Parade Literature.

74 Sheet music for Handsome Territorial. From MOA: TC 38/3/E.

75 MOA: TC 38/3/A, Chestnut Tree (15 November 1938).

76 MOA: TC 38/3/A, Press Bulletin – Chestnut Tree.

77 MOA: TC 38/3/E, Press Bulletin – Handsome Territorial.

78 MOA: TC 38/3/A, Chestnut Tree (7 December 1938).

79 MOA: TC 38/6/F, Danceland Questionnaire (April 1939).

80 MOA: TC 38/6/F, Danceland Questionnaire (April 1939).

81 MOA: Worktown 48/D, Bolton Palais (1 January 1940).

82 MOA: TC 38/6/F, Danceland Questionnaire (April 1939).

83 MOA: TC 38/3/A, Chestnut Tree (7 December 1938).

84 Alex Moore, 'Will the War Change the English Style?' *Dancing Times* (March 1940), p. 357.

85 MOA: TC 38/6/G, Imperial Society of Teachers of Dancing (19 June 1939), p. 2.

86 Monsieur Pierre, 'Those Sequence Dances!' *Modern Dance and the Dancer* (May 1938), p. 14.

87 John R. Gillespie, Letter to the Editor, *Modern Dance and the Dancer* (January 1938).

88 A. H. Franks, *The Ballroom Dancer's Handbook*, 2nd ed. (London: Isaac Pitman and Sons, 1944), p. vi.

89 MOA: TC 38/5/G, Interview with Adele England.

90 MOA: TC 38/5/G, Interview with John Rowe (16 February 1939).

91 'All about the party dance', p. 16.

92 MOA: Worktown 48/D, Aspin Hall (8 January 1940).

93 MOA: Worktown 48/C, Astoria Palais de Danse (18 December 1939).

94 MOA: TC 38/3/A, Chestnut Tree (15 November 1938).

95 Harrisson, 'The Birth of a Dance', p. 49.

96 MOA: TC 38/1/A, Handsome Territorial (13 June 1939).

97 MOA: TC 38/1/A, Locarno (29 April 1939).

98 Robert Gledhill, Letter to the Editor, *Modern Dance and the Dancer* (December 1938), p. 21.

99 A. Calloway and C. Smith, Letter to the Editor, *Modern Dance and the Dancer* (January 1938), p. 20.

100 MOA: TC 38/4/A, Mecca Bands (27 May 1939).

7

Dancing democracy in wartime Britain

In November 1945, only a few months after the Second World War had drawn to a close, a writer for the magazine *Britannia and Eve* remarked, 'Future historians may say that Global War gave dancing and dance music a new lease of life ... Wherever the fighting men of air, sea or land camped down, and girls were to be got, they organised a weekly dance. There was more dancing in the war than in normal peace time years.'[1] A few years later, Victor Silvester echoed these words about the profusion of dancing in wartime, writing in his book *Dancing for the Millions*, 'It is perhaps not insignificant that the great dancing boom in Britain began when this country was threatened with invasion and when bombs were dropping. It stood our people in good stead then, and it has done so ever since, for the boom has never abated.'[2] Then decades later, a twenty-first century newspaper retrospective about the Liverpool Blitz, entitled 'We Danced As They Bombed', featured the following memory from a serviceman who was a regular visitor to the Grafton Rooms dance hall: 'One Saturday night a bomb dropped in the alley between the Grafton and the Olympia. The ceiling was peppered by shrapnel coming through the roof... The dancing continued to the strains of Mrs Wilf Hamer on the piano. She played until the all-clear sounded.'[3]

These comments all attest to how deeply popular dance was embedded within the experience and memory of the Second World War in Britain, particularly as a representation and expression of fortitude, good cheer and social unity in the face of the war's difficulties and dangers. From the first days of the war, through the threat of German invasion and the Blitz, to the arrival of American military forces in 1942, the notion was widely proliferated that the British people continued to dance merrily and in even greater numbers than before the war. Espousals of a dance 'craze' or 'boom' resembled discourses that surrounded dancing in the wake of the First World War, but there were some noticeable differences. By 1939, popular dance was a markedly more respectable pastime than it had been in 1919, acknowledged and even promoted as an important means of boosting morale, and for fostering a sense of community among Britons, as well as between Britons and their military allies. While criticisms of excessive pleasure-seeking – especially by young women – arose once again, they were less explicitly connected with or channelled through discourses about popular dance. Finally, the dance craze of 1919–20 was often described as a manic, escapist lark in which Britons reacted to and sought to forget the traumas of war. In contrast, the dancing boom of 1939–45 was said to be occurring during the Second World War itself, constructing and physically embodying many of the ideals about how and why Britain was fighting.

The cornerstones of British national identity in wartime were a collective belief in national unity and the levelling of the class system, duty and service, equality of sacrifice, and good cheer and grace under fire. It has long been established by historians that this vision of the British nation at war was deliberately crafted by popular culture, the media, the government and the people themselves, and often falters under critical examination.[4] However, a consideration of popular dance during the war clarifies some of the tensions and contradictions that existed within the social experience of the conflict, and have shaped its historical representation. During the war, dance became a powerful and important expression of the nation's high spirits, resolve and togetherness in the face of hardships like bombing – in ways that were exploited as propaganda, and used as a form of marketing for commercial producers of dancing – but also possessed real meaning for millions of Britons. While social conflicts of class, gender, sexuality and race were in no way eliminated and were in some cases exacerbated during the war – sometimes even through events that transpired in public dancing spaces – a belief in social unity, and the strength of Britain's democracy, was deeply felt. This chapter will show that the dance floor was an important site where these ideals were constructed, expressed and experienced, and that the 'people's war' could exist, even if it was only in the ephemeral moment of dance.

'We danced while they bombed'

When war erupted on 3 September 1939, all places of public amusement in Britain, including dance venues, were immediately closed owing to the fear of imminent aerial bombardment by the enemy. For a number of years government officials had been debating the best policy to enforce regarding cinemas, theatres and dance halls, concerned not only about the potential casualties should a large entertainment venue take a direct bomb hit, but the effect on morale that the deaths of mass numbers of theatre-goers, movie-watchers or dancers might have. However, officialdom was equally cognisant of the important role that entertainment could play in maintaining morale, particularly if the war was a long one.[5] Thus, by mid-September, when the expected air raids failed to materialise, dance halls and other public ballrooms were permitted to reopen.

Almost immediately the idea began to proliferate that Britain was embroiled in a dance craze, the likes of which had not been seen since the end of the First World War, or perhaps ever in history. The *Evening Standard* remarked in November that 'you have only to go to Quaglino's, the Dorchester, Grosvenor House, the Café de Paris, or the May Fair to see that dancing is the most popular wartime amusement'.[6] Citing the comments of famed bandleader Joe Loss, the *Bristol Evening World* went even further, declaring in December that 'Dancing is enjoying the biggest boom in its history – not forgetting the heady days of the Charleston.'[7] The *Dancing Times* also proclaimed the existence of a wartime dance craze, observing a few weeks into the conflict, 'It takes more than a war to empty Hammersmith; [the Palais] is, in fact, doing better business than ever, with Miss Betty Lyons still presiding and seeing to it that there is some competition or novelty every night in the week.'[8] The same article additionally reported that in West End hotels and restaurants, dancing was in 'full swing'. As dance band drummer Anthony Crombie later recalled in an interview with the Imperial War Museum, 'it was tremendous [in the dance halls.] Everybody was ... going for it hell for leather. No tomorrow ... nobody knew whether they were going to see the next day so it was a now or never type philosophy.'[9]

As Crombie speculated, the uncertain future undoubtedly fuelled a desire to dance and have fun during these early stages in the war, but to do so was not without its challenges. In particular, the black-out made navigating the dark streets difficult and even dangerous, and much of the coverage of the dance craze stressed the British people's determination to confront these obstacles for the sake of an evening's dancing. The provincial reporter for the *Dancing Times* noted in late 1939, 'The Ritz Dance Hall [in Manchester] is apparently the most popular place in town. People are still flocking in every evening, without regard for either black-outs or bad weather.'[10] For many people, the dance hall represented a space of light in the darkness, where good spirits and feelings of camaraderie reigned. As the manager of Bolton's Aspin Hall told Mass Observation, 'The blackout makes the need for a central place of brightness, and … noise [which] are perhaps more essential than they were before the war … [In the hall] there is increased light to make up a brilliant contrast with the blackout, which is oppressing everywhere else in town.'[11] Another Mancunian correspondent for the magazine *Modern Dance* wrote in October 1939 that Manchester had been a gloomy place since war had broken out, but described the excitement with which people greeted the reopening of the city's dance halls:

> Despite the black-out and the black look-out, I, in common with many others I should imagine, donned dancing shoes and made for the nearest hall, dived in, through darkened doorways, and stood blinking in the light and thought how heavenly it is to dance again – and this after only a fortnight without … Before a few dances were over, I found quite happily that all the dancers were singing as well as dancing – in fact, it almost became community singing – and it really did help us all to feel more cheerful.[12]

Reports like this one produced a vivid picture of Britons' willingness to brave the black-out and overcome anxieties about the war not only to have a little fun, but to participate in the sense of community being forged in the public ballroom. From the first weeks of the war, popular dance became an important representation and expression of the resilience, cheerfulness and social unity that characterised the dominant vision of the British people at war.

Among the most strident disseminators of this image of stalwart Britons choosing to dance rather than succumb to fear or distress were American war correspondents. Eager to stimulate sympathy and regard for the British people in the United States, these foreign journalists helped reinforce images of togetherness and resilience arguably even more than their local counterparts. In one of his famed broadcasts to the United States during the early months of the war, Edward R. Murrow declared that he had been investigating London nightlife, describing it like this:

> Business is good; has in fact improved since war came. There are more dance bands playing in London's West End now than in the months before peace went underground. Many establishments where one could eat without musical distraction in the old days have now engaged small orchestras. Customers want to dance. [Ballrooms and night-clubs] are jammed nearly every night. People come early and stay late. I left one place at 3:30 the other morning. No one else showed any disposition to leave and so far as I know they may be there still, singing *The Beer Barrel Polka* and trying to dance on an overcrowded floor.[13]

Nor was Murrow the only one to use the persistence of dancing as evidence of the high morale in Britain. In late August 1940, just days before the start of the Blitz, Murrow's colleague, Eric Sevareid, recorded a broadcast from the 'great big dance floor' at the Hammersmith Palais, surrounded by what he described as 'the biggest crowd I ever saw trying to dance in one place at one time'. When an air raid siren had gone off moments before the broadcast, the bandleader had announced they would keep playing should people want to stay; only a few dancers cleared the floor, while the rest 'put up a big cheer and went on with their song'. Sevareid concluded his comments by describing the hall's location and the people in the crowd: 'We're a long way from Berkeley Square. We're a six penny bus ride from the heart of London … This is not Mayfair. Nobody comes here to be seen or to see. They come to dance, for the pure pleasure of dancing … and these shopgirls, these workers, these grocers clerks, these people who make up the stuff of England, they dance wonderfully well.'[14] Like Murrow, Sevareid's report emphasised the determination and good spirits of the British people, displayed through their eagerness to dance, even in the face of a potential air raid. But he additionally called attention to the predominantly working-class clientele of the hall, reinforcing predominant idioms that the 'ordinary Briton' was the truest embodiment of the nation at war.

As Sevareid's transitional broadcast suggests, Britain's desire to 'keep dancing through' became an even more critical image as the situation on the battle front changed and the so-called 'Phoney War' progressed into a long series of military setbacks, and the start of the Blitz. During the German bombing campaign, dance was employed as an illustration of the British people's courage and grace under fire, particularly by the press. Frequent reports showed stalwart Britons literally dancing in the streets, even after a raid. For instance, one *Daily Mirror* headline proclaimed, 'LET THE PEOPLE SING? YOU CAN'T STOP 'EM!' and printed beneath this declaration was a photograph of Londoners dancing in the bomb-ravaged streets of the East End, jovial and defiant in the face of enemy attempts to crush morale through terror bombing.[15] Another report in *Dance News* described the tenacity of dancing in Plymouth, which sustained periods of heavy bombing: 'The people of that much-bombed city of Plymouth are still keeping up their spirits by various pastimes – the most popular is dancing on the famous Plymouth Hoe.'[16] Dance venues also inevitably sustained bomb damage, often while patrons were in attendance, and these incidents provided another way to vividly exemplify the Blitz spirit. In one case, the crowd reaction after an attack on a London dance hall was described as follows in *The Times*: 'When the bombs fell the lights in the dance hall went out, dancers were flung to the floor and debris cascaded down. A sailor shouted as the hall was plunged into darkness, "Keep steady, stand against the walls." The dancers obeyed and there was no panic.'[17] On another occasion, according to *Dance News*, a destructive raid did not even halt the dancing: 'When an enemy plane dropped heavy bombs on a South Coast town on October 7, the band in a large dance hall played on, and the dancers continued as though nothing had happened, although many of the windows had been blown out.'[18]

Particular attention was given to the persistence of dancing in Dover, which suffered under both heavy bombing and enemy shelling across the English Channel from occupied France. In a short book about the siege entitled *Britain under Shellfire*, one journalist marvelled that under such conditions as the town was facing, Dover still staged weekly dances at the town hall:

> *Every* Monday. The enemy is but 21 miles away, but dances will be held *every* Monday! On the average, Dover sees three dances per week, and seldom are they postponed through war causes. One occasion saw the orchestra vie with German gunners as to which could make the most noise: dancers remained swaying to the rhythm of war and a 'hot' band!

Stories like this, the writer further commented, showed the 'carry on' spirit of a town living under the shadow of German long-range artillery.[19] A similar account came from *Dance News*, which reported that on one occasion, 'While the shells were bursting overhead, some 200 dancers in the Dover hall were applauding a demonstration of ballroom dancing.'[20] In another front-page article, the newspaper called Dover 'Britain's No. 1 front-line town', noting that 'Dancing has often continued while bombs were falling and when the crash of anti-aircraft guns has almost drowned the music.'[21] Dancing thus offered journalists a vivid and frequently dramatic symbol of the British people's defiance, bravery and good spirits, and it was widely deployed by both the dance and popular press to cement the general perception that the nation would 'carry on' whatever trials might emerge.

Significantly, although the notion that Britons continued to dance merrily in the face of wartime dangers and deprivation was a potent idea, the reality of the situation was more complex. Interviews with various dance hall managers conducted by Mass Observation revealed that when leisure spaces first reopened in September 1939, the return of patrons was in many cases accomplished at a slow trickle rather than at a mad dash.[22] The assistant manager of the Astoria ballroom in Charing Cross Road attributed the gradual build to the fact that at first the dance hall was only permitted to open in the afternoons. However, once evening hours were extended to eleven o'clock, business at the Astoria did resemble something like the dance craze being described in the popular press. In fact, the Astoria's manager reported that the hall was doing better than it had been before the war, and that at other venues in the same franchise, in Brighton, Liverpool and Birmingham, as well as at his competitors' halls, business was 'outstandingly good'.[23]

Further evidence of a dancing boom is provided by the fact that during the war the Association of Ballrooms petitioned the Home Office to remove the ban against dancing on Sundays in order to meet public demand for the pastime.[24] A number of spaces not previously used as ballrooms were also turned over for the purpose in order to accommodate eager dancers. As the editor of the popular music periodical *Melody Maker* told Mass Observation, 'In some cases, from information I receive in letters from all over the country, enterprising band leaders have taken over derelict halls and are running their own dances – places like church halls and the like which have been left empty due to the war.'[25] Perhaps the most significant example of this expansion came when the Royal Opera House in Covent Garden was converted into a Mecca dance hall in December 1939, remaining one of the country's premier leisure venues for the duration.[26] In addition, as the next section will detail, military and civilian authorities became important new hosts of dances, as they sought to provide entertainment to service personnel and war workers. By the autumn of 1944, cinema managers reported that dancing had surpassed going to the pictures as the 'Forces delight' and favourite form of entertainment.[27]

For many people, the appeal of dancing in wartime resided in the very reasons being cited in the press and by the dance hall industry, particularly the brightness and merriment contained within the dance hall. As one woman recalled regarding the Grafton Rooms in Liverpool, 'Outside we had the black-out, so it was great to walk into a bright, warm, and pleasant atmosphere.'[28] Such was the allure of dancing spaces that many Britons were willing to go to considerable trouble and effort in order to spend an evening at one. In an interview with Mass Observation, the manager of the Streatham Locarno mentioned a couple who used to drive in from Croydon to dance at the hall at least three nights a week; once the war began and fuel was rationed, he assumed he would no longer see them, but then the couple began appearing regularly on bicycles.[29] Similarly, in his wartime diary, Captain J. S. Gray described being part of group of soldiers and civilians who journeyed over twenty miles one evening just to reach a dance.[30] Another diary, kept by land girl Muriel Merritt, revealed that she cycled, bussed and walked all over Sussex to attend village dances at least once a week throughout her posting, while Leeds factory worker Louise White, recorded that she and other women war workers regularly spent afternoons out dancing prior to commencing work on the night shift, a practice that no doubt made for a long and exhausting day.[31] In fact, White frequently attended dances twice daily, going to one dance hall for the afternoon programme and another in the evening, illustrating how often the most determined dancers engaged in their favourite pastime even in wartime.[32]

Personal accounts also support the idea that dancing helped to sustain morale, and in spite of the danger from bombing. Drummer Crombie recalled that in the West End clubs where he performed during the Blitz, 'Morale was very high and a good time was being had by all, notwithstanding the fact that outside all hell was breaking loose.'[33] In another case, a wartime teenager recalled in a memoir, 'Entertainment was discovered to be a great morale booster and people were willing to take a chance on the bombs.'[34] Of the bleak period that followed the defeat of the British Expeditionary Force in Western Europe and the evacuation of Dunkirk, a Dover woman similarly recalled, 'there were many lighter moments. Cocktail parties and dances were held … They did much to boost up our morale.'[35] Even when the war intruded directly into the experience of the dancing, many Britons retained good spirits and humour. A few weeks into the Blitz, journalist Phyllis Warner described the scene in the ballroom at the Savoy hotel, as those present kept dancing throughout an air raid: 'As we danced … the guns added unrehearsed effects, so that we heard "A nightingale – bang – sang in – thud – Berkeley Square – crash" and "Franklin D. – woof – Roosevelt Jones – smash." Nobody appeared to mind.'[36] Several months later, in March 1941, two bombs landed right in the middle of the dance floor of the Café de Paris near Piccadilly Circus. It was an immense tragedy, in which dozens of people were killed, including members of the band. However, one witness to the event recalled that her husband later said of the evening, 'At least we didn't have to pay for our dinner.'[37] While many of these examples were retrospective accounts, the fact that they lingered on as important memories only further validates the importance of dancing as a creator and symbol of cheerfulness and resilience in wartime.

Dancing was also attractive as a wartime leisure activity for more practical reasons. The Astoria's manager attributed an increase in his business to ongoing wartime restrictions, such as the black-out. As he told Mass Observation, 'The Blackout helps us inasmuch as the boys and girls who go dancing before the war used to go dancing some nights, to the pictures on others, and on other nights would parade around and look at the shops. But now every night they have to go inside somewhere.'[38] Another dance hall manager in Bolton similarly reported that war conditions sent more pleasure-seeking Britons to the dance halls, 'owing to the fact that at the weekend people are not able to travel out of town'.[39] He also noted that while public attendance was up above pre-war levels, the hall was still losing out on the reduced number of private dances. The wartime dancing boom was therefore as much about limited alternative entertainment options as it was about boosting morale or defying the enemy. It was also an inconsistent boom. Talk of a dance craze was prominent during the fall and winter of 1939–40, the period known as the 'Phoney War', when war had been declared between Britain and Germany but very little was happening on the battle front. Anticipation of darker days to come likely did contribute to a desire to live in the moment, as drummer Crombie suggested, but dancing also simply provided Britons with something to do throughout this waiting game. For example, bandleader Loss attributed the crowded dance halls to the number of men in uniform who were killing time while awaiting their deployment.[40] Yet when the military situation changed, so too did the nation's desire to dance.

Importantly, despite contemporary celebrations of an ongoing dance craze, data compiled by the Home Office reveals that attendance at leisure venues dropped considerably during periods of heightened crisis in the war, such as the launch of the German offensive in the spring of 1940, or the start of the Blitz later that year.[41] In May 1940, as the German blitzkrieg tore across Western Europe, the press secretary of Grosvenor House wrote to Tom Harrisson at Mass Observation concerning a survey about dancing that the social research organisation had planned to undertake at the hotel, but had decided to abandon: 'I was half a mind to suggest putting it off myself as, with the latest War developments … the mood of the people is not to go out nearly so much at night to make whoopee in the West End.'[42] Some reports in the press also confirmed that not everyone was in the mood to dance. In the same issue of *Modern Dance* that described the zeal for dancing in Manchester, another correspondent wrote about the situation in Scotland: 'At the moment of writing most of the Scottish halls have reopened, but under circumstances that could not be more unhappy. Many people have at present not the time nor the inclination for the gay atmosphere of the ballroom, and black-out regulations and the restricted travelling facilities have seriously curtailed the activity of the others.'[43] Contemporary diaries and personal accounts also make clear that for all the times that Britons continued to dance merrily to the accompaniment of bombs and shells, there were just as many occasions where an attack or even just a warning would clear the floor or prematurely shut down a dance. Thus, the dance craze was a powerful symbol and propaganda tool, but not always a social reality. Not all Britons greeted the outbreak of war in a frenzy of dancing, and the realities and restrictions of wartime could make attending a dance more of a challenge than they were willing to confront.

In this context, commercial producers of dancing faced new challenges of their own: namely, how to stay in business for the duration. Resourceful hall managers and dance professionals therefore cultivated ways to keep people dancing, most notably by transforming dancing into a patriotic act. From the first days of the war the dance profession and dance hall industry enlisted in the war effort with gusto. Dance celebrities joined the military or took up war work to much fanfare, and prominent members of the professional community launched the 'Dancers' Victory Fund' to support various wartime causes. Established connections between the dance hall and radio industries were also put to good work: the BBC broadcasted a show live from the Hammersmith Palais called 'Services Spotlight', which featured celebrity entertainment for those in the armed forces. In this way, the industry sought to celebrate Britons directly engaged in the war effort: dance halls provided reduced rates to patrons in uniform, and covered their walls with pleas to women to take up war work. In 1941, the Mecca-Locarno in Leeds sponsored a special event to encourage women to take up work in the factories, even commissioning a new dance tune that reassured them, 'You look just as sweet in your overalls.'[44]

Like this one, special events at dance halls were pervaded with war themes. Many public ballrooms hosted 'Gas Mask Balls' to encourage Britons to carry this vital piece of protection from chemical warfare. Mecca in fact devoted an entire week to this cause, while another enterprising manager in Burnley constructed special hooks around his ballroom's dance floor, so that patrons could store their masks to better facilitate dancing, but in the event of an attack they would be much more readily accessible than in the cloakroom.[45] In response to a request from the Ministry of Supply, dance halls throughout the country began coordinating paper salvage drives, hoping to collect a hundred tons of paper per month.[46] Various halls also drew upon dancing's reputation as a morale-booster, inaugurating 'Let's Be Cheerful' weeks at different points throughout the war. In other cases, dance band competitions required participants to play wartime songs, such as 'Tipperary' or 'Roses of Picardy', and many amateur dance competitions instituted policies whereby at least one member of competing teams had to be in uniform. In 1941, Mecca halls throughout the country hosted a series of competitions where participation was limited to civil defence workers. The series concluded with a grand finale at the Streatham Locarno, where participants received prizes and representatives from the Home Guard and the ARP staged a parade around the hall before 2,000 spectators.

The financial proceeds from these special events were generally donated to war causes, which was another prominent feature of wartime dances: throughout Britain, everywhere from the village hall to the large corporate palais, dances small and large were used to raise money for the war effort. Special collections were taken, or entrance fees were donated, to a range of causes: hospitals, the Red Cross, St John's Ambulance, the Home Guard, and to special funds which supported the building of warships, airplanes and tanks. In one notable example, the Manchester Ritz hosted a 'Tank Week' in 1941, during the course of which a large inflatable tank was pushed around the ballroom; as they danced across the floor patrons could drop a few coins upon its surface, and by week's end the hall had raised 56 pounds.[47] In a multitude of ways, therefore, Britons were encouraged to think of dancing not just as a form of entertainment, but as yet another way to do their 'bit' for the war effort.

Undoubtedly many dance promoters and hall managers were motivated by their own sense of duty and patriotism in undertaking the initiatives described above. However, they also clearly sought ways to keep people dancing, and commercialised dominant national idioms as a way to protect their business interests. Notably, the dance hall industry was not above self-promotion for its wartime good works. In the fall of 1940, Mecca sent a letter to a number of media outlets and business acquaintances, including Mass Observation, which read:

> This is not, in any sense, a business communication, but you may be interested to know that despite many difficulties we have kept business going, continuing the employment of nearly a thousand people; helping financially any that have been 'called up'; collecting large sums for various deserving causes. We also organised the 'Don't Talk League' which has been very successful, and we are handing over the whole money, without any deductions whatever, to the British Sailors' Society. Moreover, – an achievement of which we are rather proud – we have opened no less than 12,000 War Savings Accounts for our patrons. We merely mention this to show that we have done our 'Bit', – don't you think it rather good?[48]

The letter demonstrated that Mecca did much to support the war effort in real terms, but its leaders also clearly wanted to ensure that the public knew it was doing so. On another occasion, the company spoke directly to its patrons via *Dance News*: '[Have] you noticed that, unlike everything else you purchase [since the war began], your Dancing in a Mecca Hall costs you exactly the same as it did in pre-war days – that is, unless you are in uniform, and then, in many instances, it costs you less.'[49] By drawing attention to Mecca's support for the war effort and those fighting it, the company's leaders undoubtedly hoped to cement good will for its brand, and entice more people into its dance halls.

In this and a number of other ways, producers of popular dance capitalised upon the war, and dominant ideologies about the fighting nation, in order to enhance, or at least preserve their businesses for the duration. In dozens of advertisements, which generally featured the cartoon image of a uniformed man and his female date, Mecca suggested to patrons that they meet their 'friends in the Forces' at the company's dance halls. Wartime marketing campaigns also emphasised the relative safety from bombing of dancing schools and public ballrooms; this was certainly in part about protecting dancers, but also about ensuring that they continued to patronise the venue or studio. Many dance teachers changed their hours to comply with the black-out, or advertised on the basis of their studio's proximity to air raid shelters. The Savoy hotel converted one of its basement ballrooms into a shelter where it continued to provide dining and dancing, and later mattresses and pillows so that its patrons did not need to brave the dangerous streets at the end of the evening.[50] In the same way, Mecca's Paramount dance hall was promoted as 'London's most comfortable air-raid shelter'.[51] The Café de Paris, a night-club located below street level, was also specifically advertised as one of the safest places in London to dance – a marketing strategy that proved tragically ironic when the club was destroyed during a raid in March 1941.

Some of the larger dance hall chains also created new songs and dances that reflected war themes, and exposed the ongoing commercial competition between them. In the fall of 1939, the Astoria dance hall, in conjunction with its chief bandleader, Loss, created the 'black-out stroll', another so-called novelty or party dance. The start of the war saw a renewal of enthusiasm for these group dances, which helped forge and express the feelings of merriment and camaraderie that characterised the wartime dance hall. As the *Liverpool Evening News* suggested in October 1939, novelty dances helped to 'enliven the atmosphere', and served as a physical embodiment of social unity in action.[52] Established pre-war favourites like the Lambeth Walk continued to appear regularly on dance programmes, but war themes began to be incorporated into a new crop of dances. The first was the black-out stroll, which was set to a song by Tommy Connor of Chestnut Tree fame, and was performed with the same simple sequential movements as previous novelty dances. However, the black-out stroll also contained a new twist: halfway through the dance the lights in the ballroom were shut off, and everyone switched partners. For this reason, the *Daily Mirror* rather meanly declared that the dance was ideal for 'wallflowers' – the women usually deemed too unattractive or untalented to secure partners under the lights.[53]

The references to the black-out in the dance's title and execution were not the only ways in which the war was put to work in the creation and marketing of the black-out stroll. In an interview with Mass Observation, Connor said that he wanted to do his 'duty' as a songwriter and produce a dance that would showcase and promote the gaiety of the wartime ballroom, while also acknowledging its changed demographics and helping to forge acquaintances among dancing strangers:

> My main reason for getting the dance out was to get one which would allow a change of partner, and also to bring an atmosphere of jollity to the dance floors. There [has] been a 75% change of face in the ballroom since the war began. Evacuees are going into ballrooms they have never been in before. This [dance] gives them the party spirit ... It gives everyone a reason to meet everyone else. I am dancing with you. At the end of 32 bars I am dancing with someone else. If only a few words pass between you there is a communal atmosphere and you can always renew the acquaintance next week.[54]

As Connor observed, the evacuation and military service meant that many Britons were migrating throughout the country, and entering dance venues where they might not know many people: the black-out stroll was designed to remedy that situation, providing a way for people to mingle. According to Connor, the dance was a physical enactment of the national unity that the war was allegedly producing. Of course, drawing upon ideals of social cohesion as a marketing strategy was one thing: getting the people to buy into them was yet another. Upon first observing a performance of the dance at the Astoria, Mass Observation's Alec Hughes reported that only about half the participants actually switched partners during the 'black-out' as they were meant to.[55] Clearly wartime dancers continued to assert considerable control over their dancing experience, just as they had in peace-time.

Meanwhile, not to be outdone, Mecca replicated the efforts of its competitor, the Astoria, and delivered its own war-themed novelty dance. The 'tuscana' was designed to mock the military setbacks of the Italian Army following its invasion of Greece. To the beats of a song that advised dancers to 'just retreat', dancers walked in a circle taking one step forward, and then three steps back.[56] Developed by Adele England, the tuscana (like the Lambeth Walk and its successors) was given a national launch at Mecca halls throughout the country. The company also released a special souvenir issue of *Dance News* to commemorate its new dance, so that '[after the war] it will be a happy reminder of all of the glad times you spent with us'.[57] The tuscana and black-out stroll undoubtedly provided some of the same moments of communal merriment bestowed by all novelty dances, though neither appears to have been more than a brief success. However, the creation of the two dances underscores the ways in which competing dance hall chains utilised the war, and dominant ideologies about national unity, in a bid to protect their financial interests in a trying time.

Indeed, the longer the war went on, the more challenges there were for the dance hall industry. Increasing numbers of dance establishments were either bombed out or commandeered for war purposes. For instance, the Winter Gardens in Blackpool, which contained the famed Empress Ballroom, was re-purposed to train military personnel in Morse code, and to equip servicemen for overseas service. At the same time, more and more dance hall staff and musicians were drafted into war work and military service, making it difficult to keep public ballrooms running. Like many industries, one strategy dance establishments adopted was to hire more women, who began working as hall managers, masters of ceremony, musicians and bandleaders to an unprecedented degree. Still, staffing issues posed enough of a problem that the dance press also began to argue that commercial dancing should be considered a vital service. *Dance News* proclaimed in an editorial in December 1941 that 'Entertainment including dancing should be considered as one of the national services, almost as important as war work in the factories.'[58] The newspaper further contended that dancing was vital to morale, and made those who frequented dance halls all the more productive in their own service to the war effort. As the editors advised their readers, 'Dance and be happy, so that you may work harder for victory.'[59]

These claims by the dance hall industry and dance press that dancing was critically important to morale and productivity had another backdrop as well: ongoing national debates about whether recreation was appropriate in time of war. At various moments in the conflict, particularly when things looked dire on the battlefront (such as in the spring of 1940 or after the fall of Singapore in 1942), individuals ranging from newspaper editors, to factory owners, to parliamentarians questioned whether entertainments should be discontinued given the crisis. While dancing was not a major focus of these discussions – which tended to be most critical of sports and gambling – the pressure was felt keenly enough that in 1941 *Dance News* offered an editorial that argued the suggested bans on entertainment were 'absurd'. As the editors further proclaimed, 'This paper has no false ideas about the problems, the trials, and the difficulties which beset us in the present conflict for freedom and peace … We do know that no man, or woman can work continuously and give of his best, without relaxation or pleasure. Where better to relax than in the comfort and cheerfulness of the modern dance-hall.'[60] Two years later, *Danceland* featured a similar editorial, which pointed out that even the government believed that recreation was a critical aspect of the war effort, adding that 'A few hours spent dancing renews and refreshes war-jangled nerves.' This opinion piece even more explicitly linked dancing to the reasons Britain was fighting a war at all, by proclaiming, 'Dancing epitomises the freedom for which we are fighting and is the negation of all that dictators hold dear … So treasure the liberty that allows you to dance as you please.'[61]

These editorials – in media published by Mecca's publishing arm, Danceland Publications – are illustrative of another important aspect of wartime marketing by the dance hall industry, which directly connected dancing with the goals of the war effort, the tyranny of the enemy, and Britain's freedom and democracy. Producers continually contrasted the strength and character of British dancing to growing restrictions in Germany and occupied Europe. This was a strategy that had been developed even before the war, when Mecca claimed the Lambeth Walk and its other novelty dances reflected Britain's democratic spirit, and were 'too peace-making' for Hitler and Mussolini. Once war had been declared, the dance press paid close attention to efforts by the Nazis to stamp out dances the regime deemed degenerate, or to shutter dancing spaces as a form of social control over Germans and those Europeans they had conquered. News reports described the closure of dance halls in Berlin, and the outlawing of dancing in places under occupation such as Paris and the Channel Islands. One story detailed the violent attack on a group of local men by German soldiers outside a dance in Norway, after Norwegian women had refused to dance with their occupiers, whose presence eventually cleared the hall.

The links between dancing, freedom, and anti-fascism were also cemented by lighter press items that implied the persistence of British dancing was a major source of aggravation to the enemy. For instance, a cartoon featured in *Dance News* portrayed an exasperated Hitler showing a British newspaper

(*Dance News*, no less) to his ally, Mussolini, and exclaiming in frustration, 'Ach, Musso! See this, they're still dancing!' (see Figure 7.1). In response, Mussolini could only scratch his head in confusion. Presumably the two cartoon dictators saw the fact that Britons continued to dance as a sign of their enemy's enduring morale, reinforcing the idea that Britain's dance craze was synonymous with its defiant stance against German aggression. There may even have been some truth to the idea that the Germans were monitoring British dancing. The infamous Lord Haw-Haw, an Irish fascist who fled to Germany at the outbreak of war and transmitted demoralising radio programmes back to Britain, referenced famous dance halls on multiple occasions; both the Barrowlands ballroom in Glasgow and London's Hammersmith Palais were threatened with targeting by German bombers. But the cartoon light-heartedly proclaimed that British dancing could not be stopped, whatever challenges might emerge. Additionally, a second cartoon that appeared in *Dance News* a few weeks after the first suggested that the same could not be said of the Germans in the face of the British air offensive. This sketch depicted a lone radio broadcaster (who

Dance News imagines Hitler and Mussolini lamenting the endurance of dancing in wartime Britain.   **7.1**

bore a striking resemblance to Hitler) standing before a completely empty German dance floor, and being forced to lie about his fellow citizens' morale and eagerness to dance: 'Friendts abroad, Berlin is not vorried by R.A.F. bombs, no. Now listen to gay music from der crowded Wilhelmstrasse dance halle.'[62]

Eventually the reports and images that connected dancing with freedom and anti-fascism coalesced into a short book entitled *Stepping Out*, published by Danceland Publications. Within its pages, author James Mackenzie prompted his readers to imagine venturing out dancing one evening and finding every dance establishment closed. 'Yet this is very largely the position in dictator and dictator-occupied countries', Mackenzie opined, 'when force rules and freedom goes and with it dancing which so truly expresses a freedom of spirit and action that is distasteful to rulers and conquerors.'[63] If this message was not clear enough, the cover of *Stepping Out* was emblazoned with the declaration, 'Where Freedom Reigns, There's Dancing', and the opening pages proclaimed:

> Dancing and freedom are words that go hand in hand. You can't have one without the other ... You are free, within broad limits, to do as you please and go where you please – to the sixpenny 'hop' round the corner, or to the comfortable magnificence of the West End hotel. No one questions your right. You exercise it in the normal course of things as a free citizen in a free country.[64]

Through print media, therefore, producers argued that the opportunity to dance was directly related to freedom and democracy, and something that distinguished the British from their enemies and those living under occupation. In a wartime society where dancing was frequently employed as a symbol of resistance and defiance before the enemy, the dance hall industry reinforced these ideals, while undoubtedly hoping to capitalise upon them financially.

The notion that dancing was an expression of freedom, democracy and resistance against the enemy was not solely a dance hall industry marketing ploy, however. These ideas should also be understood within broader contemporary discourses that saw British popular culture as something democratic, which best defined the nation, and distinguished Britain from its enemies. As Peter Bailey has argued, in the late 1930s a parallel discourse existed around music hall, in which humour and the 'pleasures of the people' became symbolic of democracy and national solidarity, and stood in contrast to the militant and coercive uses of leisure by the less fun-loving and convivial Nazis.[65] Democratic attributes were thought to be displayed through a range of popular cultural forms in this period, ranging from the circus to horse racing.[66] In addition, the wartime enthusiasm for dancing was exaggerated and even exploited by commercial producers and the press, but it was not entirely fabricated. As has been shown, many Britons did continue to dance for a wide variety of reasons, and they often understood their consumption of dancing in terms of freedom, democracy and resistance to the enemy. For instance, journalist Phyllis Warner effectively echoed the sentiments put forth by the *Dance News* cartoon described above, when she recorded in her wartime diary following a rollicking dance on New Year's Eve 1940, at the height of the Blitz: 'Would that Hitler could have seen us. I think he'd have found it darned disheartening.'[67] While producers commodified patriotism and national identity, consumers also connected popular dance with the ideals that surrounded the war, and used the ballroom as a space to grapple with divisions of class, gender and race, and to express social unity.

Democracy on the dance floor

In his survey of London nightlife during the early days of the war, Murrow remarked on the understated nature of the clothing being worn at dances, even in places 'where a few months ago evening dress was as important as the ability to pay the check'.[68] In the face of clothes rationing, and in a show of solidarity with those who possessed more limited pre-war wardrobes, Britons who would normally have dressed formally for a dance often abandoned this practice for the duration, and evening dress was eliminated as a requirement in most dance competitions. In general, as another writer observed after the conflict had ended, the 'formality and the trimmings' were removed from wartime ballrooms.[69] The tendency towards dressing down, combined with the plethora of uniforms in the mix, meant that in certain respects the ballroom appeared more homogeneous than ever before, with visual markers of class and affluence significantly reduced. At the same time, the wartime ballroom was a space of unprecedented diversity. Colonial troops and other allies, often representing different races, mixed and mingled on the dance floor. Ideals of social levelling and imperial unity were strikingly on display as Britons moved about the floor.

Despite pervasive ideals about the 'people's war' and 'people's empire', it has been well established by historians that class, gender and racial conflicts were in no way eliminated during the war, and were in some cases exacerbated by wartime conditions. Social interactions prompted by the evacuation and military service were permeated with class prejudice, and the divergent experiences of rationing and bombing contravened notions of 'equality of sacrifice'. Persistent hierarchies of class and gender also shaped conceptions about who was adequately doing their bit for the war effort, and imperial unity was belied by the experiences of many black colonial subjects who suffered racist treatment in the Britain. As this section will show, events at dances sometimes reflected or perpetuated these lingering social divisions. However, the ballroom was also a place where social unity was performed and experienced, and dancing enabled Britons to practice and express the ideals that surrounded their war effort – even if only temporarily in the moment of dance – and in spite of the darker undercurrents of social conflict that characterised wartime society.

First, the conditions of wartime prompted significant degrees of social mingling on the dance floor, of Britons of different ages, regions and even classes. Most public ballrooms retained their pre-war clienteles, but there were also opportunities for the transgression of class lines in wartime. In reference to the traditionally elite Café de Paris, for example, the *Evening Standard* noted near the beginning of the war that a 'democratic change has come over London nightlife. The dancers ... bore the stamp of districts as far afield as Wimbledon.'[70] An important factor in promoting greater mingling of Britons of different backgrounds was the geographic movement of large numbers of people associated with the evacuation, war work or military service. These realities meant that many people were likely to visit dancing spaces well beyond their neighbourhood dance hall, perhaps for the first time, a phenomenon the novelty dance the black-out stroll had attempted to capitalise upon. The wartime experiences of army captain Gray provide a good illustration of these migrations. Gray, who was an avid amateur dancer before the war, travelled around Britain a great deal due to frequently changing military postings. He attended dances in every sort of venue from small churches to large chain dance halls, in locations ranging from Dover, Llandudno, Newcastle and London. His diary also reflects that he made friends and acquaintances in all of these places largely by attending dances, typically finding a local woman who he would regularly partner with.[71]

Within the military itself, wartime circumstances also permitted less formality and greater degrees of socialising across ranks than would have been permitted in peace time. In 1944 a committee of the Air Council of the Royal Air Force officially approved a practice that had become increasingly prevalent at bases around the country – that of 'all-ranks' dances. The committee cited the distance of bases from towns or cities; a more economical use of bands, time and labour; scarcity of partners for multiple dances; and the fact 'that "all-ranks" dances bridge the gap between officers and airmen' as valid reasons for allowing such dances at the discretion of station commanders.[72] Official protocol was often disregarded at dances outside the control of military authorities as well. One woman serving in the Wrens, the women's branch of the Royal Navy, recalled, 'As I was only a non-commissioned person … we were not meant to mix with officers, and often red tape was across the dance hall. But often we broke the rule.'[73] Murrow also noted that ballrooms were a strange mélange of ranks, even with respect to partnering; it was not uncommon to see a 'sergeant of the Women's Auxiliary Fire Service being pushed about the dance floor by a private'.[74] Of course, like so many temporary wartime measures, this mixing of servicemen and women of varying ranks and social backgrounds lasted only for the duration. By 1948 the Air Council had decreed that 'the considerations which gave rise to the war-time decisions to allow "all-ranks" dances are … [no longer] desirable or necessary in peace-time'.[75]

Beyond the British armed forces, dancing provided a way of celebrating and cementing relations with Britain's military allies. Dances were held to commemorate occasions such as Red Army Day, as a way of honouring the Soviet Union. Polish pilots and Free French soldiers were a common presence at dances wherever they were serving, while colonial troops, particularly from Canada and the Caribbean, also passed time at dances. In 1943, the documentary film *West Indies Calling*, which focused on the subjects from the Caribbean who were in Britain contributing to the war effort, concluded with some of their representatives merrily participating in a dance, and imperial unity being visibly displayed on the dance floor. When the United States entered the war in late 1941 and American military personnel began to arrive in Britain, dancing soon became an important means of solidifying the Anglo-American alliance. The British government saw dances as a way of welcoming American forces and making them feel more at home, while US military bases and American Red Cross clubs reciprocated by hosting dances in return. American dances were popular not only as a way to forge good relations, but because the food, drink and other luxuries on offer at these events were viewed as positively miraculous to Britons who had suffered under three years of rationing. Commercial dance providers also embraced the Americans: led by Mecca, most dance halls provided free entry to American troops for the first few weeks after their arrival.

However, the American 'invasion' also introduced a number of new social tensions to Britain. Some of the greatest anxieties related to young women, and the enthusiasm that many of them expressed for the 'Yanks'.[76] As historian

David Reynolds has observed, 'next to the caricature of the "oversexed" GI, the image of the "ever-ready" British female is probably the most durable myth of the American occupation', and women who were perceived to be in active pursuit of GIs faced considerable social condemnation.[77] Sonya Rose has shown that public commentary primarily circulated around young, working-class women, or so-called 'good-time girls', who were accused of promiscuous behaviour and of prioritising their own amusement above the needs of the war effort and general social good.[78] Yet significantly, despite the fact that, like the flapper of the 1920s, the good-time girl of the 1940s was condemned for excessive pleasure-seeking, dancing was only occasionally referenced in descriptions of her behaviour. Instead, public criticism tended to focus on young women's interactions with GIs and their conduct in the streets and parks, and outside military encampments.

This lack of scrutiny was in spite of the fact that dancing played a prominent role in relationships between British women and GIs. Dance halls were a principal site for 'yank-hunting', and dancing ability was a considerable part of the appeal of GIs, who were considered to be superior dancers to British men – at least when it came to American dances, such as the wartime favourite, the jitterbug.[79] There were also fringe benefits to socialising with GIs – everything from cosmetics and nylons to food and drink. One memoirist recalled that she and her friends viewed the food provided at American dances with incredulity and excitement, noting that they 'were prepared to be polite and even try to Jive or Jitterbug in order to partake in such a feast'.[80] However, a clear distinction emerged between dancing with and actually dating GIs. As another woman described it, 'the Yanks were all over. You danced with them but you knew what kind of reputation you would get if you went out with Americans.'[81] Wartime women saw dancing as a socially acceptable route to meeting GIs, but knew that to extend the relationship beyond the dance floor was to risk social condemnation. One war worker remembered: 'The GIs would send yellow cabs to the factory to pick us up when we finished work ... We'd have a dance and a laugh and then they'd send us back again, there was nothing more to it.'[82] Undeniably sexual relationships between British women and American GIs did begin at dances, but it was clearly the sex and not the dance that provoked outrage.

When dancing did enter into contemporary discourses about moral laxity and pleasure-seeking women, it was more often drawn upon in the women's defence. Like the so-called good-time girls, another target of scrutiny during the war years was the Auxiliary Territorial Service (ATS), the women's branch of the British Army. Falling victim to lingering concerns about women's military service in general, the ATS were subjected to a 'whispering campaign' that accused them of immoral behaviour. Attempts to defend these women, and argue for their strong character and innocent pursuit of amusement, often invoked dancing. In a 1941 *Daily Telegraph* article, the newspaper's correspondent in York declared: 'Many of these girls come to this town for a time. They work hard and they like an evening's dancing now and then ... It would be hard to find much wrong with a life like theirs.'[83] That same year, Lord Trenchard stated in a speech to the House of Lords, 'There are too many people ... who think because they see places like big hotels crowded with young girls dancing in mufti that they are not doing their bit. I gather that most of them, if not all, are working hard and are only enjoying an hour or two of relaxation in the evening.'[84] Lord Trenchard's comments revealed that there were those who continued to condemn women who danced. Likewise, land girl Emily Weaver, who had trained as a dance professional before the war, observed in her memoir that the farm family she lived and worked with were suspicious of her past, and she learned 'to keep quiet about the dancing'.[85] Yet condemnation of women who danced was increasingly a minority opinion. In addition, attacks against those 'dancing in mufti' were sometimes directed against men as well, as part of a more general concern about 'shirking'; what anxieties there were about dancing during the war years were less gendered than those in the 1920s. The predominant view was that dancing provided hard-working Britons of both sexes with well-deserved entertainment, rather than perpetuating immorality.

The growing respectability of dancing, even in the face of wartime anxieties about pleasure-seeking and promiscuity, was further reinforced by the endorsements given to this leisure practice by conservative institutions ranging from the military to the church. Despite the whispering campaign directed against its servicewomen, the ATS included dancing as part of the curriculum for its physical education courses. In 1942, a Bloomsbury hotel was converted into a hostel for women officers and other ranks who visited London for training or as part of their duties, and during the reconstruction the hotel's ballroom was maintained to provide 'excellent dancing facilities' for the women in residence.[86] Dancing was in fact viewed to be an ideal activity for young women who the needs of the war effort had sent far from home. The Women's Voluntary Service frequently organised dances at the social centres created for the female factory workers who had relocated to take up war work, as a way of alleviating homesickness.

Dancing received a stamp of approval from many religious leaders as well – even though this group tended to be among the most vocal critics of pleasure-seeking women and moral laxity. In 1943 the Archbishop of Canterbury gave a well-publicised address at a meeting of the Church of England Men's Society, in which he decried the 'really alarming collapse of honesty and sex morality'.[87] Similar concerns were raised at different points by figures at every level of church hierarchy, from bishops to parish preachers, representing all Christian denominations, but dancing was not a significant feature of the diatribes on issues ranging from out-of-control youth, sexual activity and alcoholism. At a Methodist Church conference in Birmingham in July 1943, many of these issues were again under discussion, but significantly, the assembly also sanctioned dancing as a morally safe form of amusement by voting to permit dancing on church premises.

The conference's endorsement of dancing was not without its detractors. Most notably, Lord Rochester cautioned his colleagues that 'Dancing has been known to lead to impurity of thought, desire, and practice. The most difficult fight that we men have is the fight for purity of thought, character, and life, and there are few forms of pleasure in modern society which make that battle more difficult than dancing.'[88] However, the remarks of eighty-nine year old Dr Scott Lidgett in defence of dancing were those most widely reported in the press:

> It seems to be assumed in some quarters ... that directly you say that dancing may be an incidental and subordinate feature of an evening meeting, our young people will at once break out into Saturnalia ... This is a travesty. There has been no excess as far as I know... Trust [young people] under the adequate oversight and control of ministers and trustees to have some liberty, and you may be sure that that liberty will not be abused.[89]

Lidgett's comments were met with loud applause, and when the issue came to a vote, the conference voted to permit church dancing by a large majority. Letters to the editor in the days that followed indicate that the Church's decision was also greeted with enthusiasm by the public. One man wrote to the *Leicester Evening Mail* that Lidgett had shown 'wisdom' in his remarks, further commenting, 'Surely there is no case to made out for condemning ordinary dances, a form of relaxation and entertainment that has given pleasure throughout the ages? ... This killjoy attitude simply won't do in 1943.'[90]

As the war progressed, dancing in church halls grew increasingly common. While some church leaders faced resistance when they began to provide dances, it was usually only from a minority within their communities. Taken together, the endorsement of dancing by government, military and religious leaders, and the absence of dancing from debates about good-time girls and service-women, attests to its growing respectability by the Second World War. Modern dances and public dancing spaces would always have their detractors, but the different positions that this leisure form occupied in discourses about excessive pleasure-seeking and moral laxity in 1920 and 1940 are striking, and serve as strong evidence of its incorporation into the national culture. However, although many of the gendered tensions surrounding popular dance had been reduced by the war years, there was one way in which they continued to provoke social conflict: when they intersected with race.

The British nation had long experience with racial difference by the 1940s, and not simply via exposure to imperial culture or African American popular culture. African-American performers had been touring the country since the 1840s, and black communities sprang up, particularly in port towns, in increasing numbers from the eighteenth century onwards. However, during the Second World War, the presence of large numbers of colonial war workers and service-men, particularly from the West Indies, as well as African-American GIs, rendered racial difference far more visible within Britain's borders, and prompted a renegotiation of internal race relations.[91] In particular, though most Britons were grateful for the military and economic support of these colonial and American allies, and wished to make them welcome, there was strong anxiety about sexual relationships between black men and white British women.[92]

Given that romantic entanglements frequently began at dances, anxieties about interracial sex occasionally played out on the dance floor, and produced violent results. In 1943, the *Sunday Pictorial* newspaper recounted the story of Arthur Walrond, a Jamaican journalist who was now serving as a sergeant in the Royal Air Force, and who described being assaulted by a British Army officer after he had danced with a woman at a dance in Lancashire.[93] On another occasion, two British sisters, upon observing that a group of black GIs were largely being ignored at a dance in Somerset, invited them to the floor during a 'ladies choice' number. The father of the two women was later approached by another man at the event, who demanded to know 'what his daughters were doing dancing with coloured troops'.[94] A third incident provides further insight into the complex space dancing occupied in wartime race relations. In 1943, the case of Learie Constantine, a government welfare officer and cricket star of Caribbean birth, grabbed national attention when he and his wife were barred from staying at a London hotel due to a colour bar. In general, the government, press, and public expressed outrage over this occurrence, and demanded redress for the humiliation of a British subject. However, when a local church synod met to pass a resolution against racist policies of the sort encountered by Constantine, one clergyman encouraged caution, asking whether those present would 'care to see their people dancing with these men'.[95] Whether it was because of the close physical proximity created by dancing, or ongoing associations between dancing and sex, once race entered into the mix, anxieties about dancing clearly persisted.

Yet the feelings of outrage sparked by the Constantine hotel ban are more consonant with the predominant reaction to incidents of discrimination and racist violence experienced by black men in Britain during the war – even at dances. Significantly, most incidents of dance floor racism originated not with British attendees, but with their white American allies. Particularly GIs who came to Britain from the segregated South frequently voiced objections and responded with violence when they witnessed British women dancing with black men, regardless of whether the men in question were American citizens or British subjects. The same Walrond, who suffered one attack by a British man at a dance, was violently accosted a second time by an American soldier who objected to him asking a woman to dance on another occasion in Bury St Edmonds. Government documents also reveal a clear escalation in dance floor violence following the arrival of the US Army. One report pertaining to the Grafton Rooms in Liverpool noted that West Indian war workers had been frequenting the hall since they began to arrive in Britain in 1941, but once Americans also began patronising the venue, the dance hall had 'degenerated on occasion into a racial fighting ground between coloured British subjects and white Americans'.[96] In another incident, four Americans, two white and two black, were arrested in the town of Huyton, near Liverpool, in August 1942 as a result of a street fight outside a pub. The Home Office report describing the episode noted: 'The cause of the trouble appears to have been due, to the U.S. white troops resenting Coloured troops associating with local females at local dance halls.'[97] Official documents show that many within the British government were under the impression that some Southern white men visited dance halls with the express intention of using physical force to stop black men from dancing with white women.

Black men were not the only targets of racist protests in the ballroom; the women who danced with them were also the subject of considerable scrutiny. Avice Wilson, a young British woman who later married a GI, recalled being 'chided' by a different American for dancing with a Jamaican RAF corporal at a dance near Chippenham in 1943.[98] Another woman believed that, 'If you danced with coloured Americans, you were blacklisted by the white ones. They kept a list at the camp of these girls and passed it to the new troops coming in.'[99] Women who partnered black men therefore also suffered abuse and condemnation, both on and off the dance floor, since anxieties about miscegenation were at the centre of debates about women's promiscuity and pleasure-seeking during the war years. However, the links between dancing and romantic possibilities were more often presumed by the Americans rather than the Britons in attendance at dances.

Incidents of racist violence presented another major challenge to the dance hall industry, particularly as many within its ranks attempted to promote their ballrooms as spaces of safety, patriotic action and social harmony. A common response was thus to subvert potential conflicts by banning those who were perceived to be the root of the problem: namely, black men. A number of dance halls implemented full or partial colour bars, and in some cases justified this action by placing the responsibility for violent incidents on the men of colour – even though it is clear from the evidence that they were far more frequently the victims rather than the instigators of racial clashes. For example, one Liverpool dance hall manager who banned black servicemen and war workers from his establishment, told the *Warrington Examiner*: 'At first I was proud of my "United Nations" ballroom, but the United Nations personnel were anything but united. They quarrelled, flashed knives, and made white girls fear to refuse to dance with them.'[100] However, unlike this man, most dance hall proprietors were motivated by financial concerns rather than racial prejudice in their implementation of colour bars. When the Home Office protested against the extension of colour bars in dance halls throughout northern England, hall managers argued back that the number of white patrons was so much larger than the number of black patrons that to ban the former rather than the latter would be very bad for business.[101]

As this Home Office protest demonstrates, the government strenuously objected to the establishment of colour bars, and other dance halls sought out alternative ways to curb racial violence without incurring protests from the government. Of Mecca's many dance halls, the Paramount on Tottenham Court Road consistently attracted the largest black clientele, even before the outbreak of war. It was in fact known as the circuit's 'jitter hall', a place where one could both witness and freely perform African-American dances such as the jitterbug. But here too racial conflict increased exponentially once large numbers of US troops began patronising the venue in 1942. In response, Mecca did not institute a full colour bar, but introduced a policy whereby black patrons could only enter the hall if they brought their own dance partner, since, the management believed, most violent incidents seemed to occur after a black man asked a white woman to dance. However, as the widow of one of C.L. Heimann's partners, Alan Fairley, recalled in her memoir, Mecca soon received an official protest about this requirement from the Colonial Office.[102]

Dance hall colour bars clearly flew in the face of government policy. Something that is apparent in both official documents and public statements is that the British government was committed to ensuring that American-style segregation practices not be imported to Britain. The British prided themselves, and had built their Empire on, what they perceived to be their more liberal racial thinking, promulgated through benevolent rule and the proliferation of democracy. As Sonya Rose has argued, the racial conflicts that were manifested during the war years threatened to undermine the whole imperial system and one of the fundamental bases of British national identity.[103] With this in mind, British officials knew they could not be in the business of supporting colour bars, which were imposed not only in dance halls but other public spaces ranging from pubs to hotels. As the Minister of Information, Brendan Bracken, wrote in the *Sunday Express* in September 1942, 'the British government is in favour of putting an end to this prejudice as quickly as possible'.[104] However, despite such statements, the government was also very concerned with not alienating Britain's vital military ally. From officialdom, there was often a lot of talk and very little action when it came to protecting black GIs or their own colonial subjects from dance floor violence.

In fact, another incident demonstrated that British officials were not just apathetic but occasionally obstructionist when it came to supporting the rights and personal safety of black men in British dance halls. In 1943, the manager of the Casino dance hall in Warrington refused to eject a Jamaican war worker after a group of white Americans objected to his presence in the ballroom. Soon after, the dance hall was placed out of bounds by US Army authorities, for reasons that were likely both to avoid potential conflicts and punitive towards the venue. Importantly, the ban against the Casino did not remain confined to US troops; shortly thereafter, British and Canadian military personnel were also directed to boycott the Casino. This policy seemed to affirm the fears expressed by many dance hall managers about what might happen if they demonstrated support for their black rather than white patrons, but it also generated a great deal of controversy. The situation at the Casino received significant coverage in the press, and even merited the attention of Parliament, when the Member for Warrington posed a question in the House of Commons about what had motivated the military ban. The government would not concede that the boycott was motivated by racial tensions, but rather attributed it to overcrowding.

This explanation seems not to have convinced many within the public, however, who expressed outrage that the Casino manager was not being supported in his refusal to implement a colour bar, and they did so in terms that reflected democratic ideals and wartime national identity. One letter to the editor of the *Warrington Examiner* asserted:

> With the right of the American authorities to decide what is best for their own I am not prepared to argue; but when the British powers-that-be take a similar step, I think a great deal should be said … [The Casino manager] is entitled to stand up for the rights of coloured people without having to be persecuted … He will be assured the hearty support of every true Briton and anti-Fascist.[105]

For this writer, colour bars represented a threat to a vision of the nation defined in terms of freedom, racial tolerance and democracy, and to the very ideals upon which Britain was fighting the war. The letter differentiated Britain from its fascist enemies, but also from its most important military ally, suggesting that American segregationist practices were something Britain must not emulate.

A similar response was elicited by the experiences of Walrond, the Jamaican airman who was twice violently accosted for dancing with a white woman – once by a British man and once by an American. Following the second incident, Walrond wrote a letter to the Colonial Office demanding protection from such dangers and indignities, and suggesting that the racism they displayed might mean that Britain was not that different than the fascist regimes it was fighting. 'Is it fair, is it just,' Walrond questioned, 'to ask me to risk my life nightly over enemy territory when, behind me, I have left something as treacherous to humanity as any "ism?" The very same day that Walrond wrote his letter, he was killed while taking part in a bombing raid over Germany, a tragic end that drew even more attention to his story. The *Sunday Pictorial* wrote a whole article about Walrond's experiences, under a headline that demanded: 'What are we going to do about this?' Calling Walrond 'a devoted son of the Empire', the newspaper argued that it was time for the British public to acknowledge the immense contribution being made by black colonial subjects in the war against Nazi Germany, and to protect them from violence and persecution in dance halls and elsewhere.[106]

The public reaction to racial conflicts in dance halls was often on the side of the black men, particularly with colonial workers and soldiers who were perceived to be 'doing their bit' for the war effort with as much diligence and patriotism as white Britons. When told by an American not to dance with a Jamaican airman, memoirist Wilson recalled replying, 'But why, [when] they voluntarily came over before you did to fight for us.'[107] There were also instances when Britons came to an even more active defence of black men who suffered persecution or racist attacks. On some occasions, when black men were physically assaulted for dancing with white women, British men were known to jump into the fray. American civil rights activist Walter White recorded just such an incident in *A Rising Wind*, an account of his wartime travels through Britain, during which time he interviewed many black GIs:

> One [man] had told of the distinguished British family inviting a group of American soldiers to their home for dinner and dancing. Everything moved smoothly during the meal, but when one of the Negro soldiers danced with one of the English women, he had been assaulted by a Southern white soldier. A free-for-all followed in which the British took the side of the Negroes.[108]

Coming to the aid of those victimised by racist attacks enabled Britons to physically enact the ideals for which they were fighting the war. On occasion, the dance floor became a space to perform not only social levelling and national cohesion, but also imperial and racial unity.

Efforts to instil racial harmony on the dance floor should naturally not be overstated. As the evidence above demonstrates, Britons from the clergy to government officials to dance hall managers and patrons were just as capable of racist feeling and action as white American GIs, and broader anxieties about miscegenation did reintroduce apprehensions about dancing and sexual immorality that had been reduced in other contexts. Moreover, after 1945, when growing numbers of black colonial subjects began making their way to Britain, the number of colour bars and other manifestations of racism in public dancing spaces grew exponentially. But during the war itself, when Britons used the space of the dance hall to perform their democratic ideals, this often extended to racial inclusiveness. As the next chapter will show, in this more fluid racial environment, they also revised their opinion of black dances, and latched on to a new American import that further enabled them to dance democracy.

Notes

1 C. Patrick Thompson, 'And Now…to Dance', *Britannia and Eve* (November 1945), p. 56.
2 Victor Silvester, *Dancing For the Millions* (London: Odhams Press, 1949), p. 38.

3 'We Danced As They Bombed', *Liverpool At War*, Special Publication of *Liverpool Echo* (2003), p. 14. Clipping from Liverpool Record Office, Liverpool Libraries, Hf942.753LIV.

4 See Angus Calder, *The Myth of the Blitz* (London: Jonathan Cape, 1991); Sonya Rose, *Which People's War? National Identity and Citizenship in Britain, 1939–1945* (Oxford: Oxford University Press, 2003); Juliet Gardiner, *Wartime: Britain, 1939–1945* (London: Headline Publishing, 2004); Wendy Webster, *Englishness and Empire, 1939–1965* (Oxford: Oxford University Press, 2007); Susan R. Grayzel, *At Home and under Fire: Air Raids and Culture in Britain from the Great War to the Blitz* (Cambridge: Cambridge University Press, 2014).

5 TNA: PRO HO 45/18141: Places of Public Entertainment in Time of War, Report for the Home Office, 1938–1939.

6 'Corisande's News for Women', *Evening Standard* (22 November 1939), p. 11.

7 'Dancing is Biggest Boom in History', *Bristol Evening World* (2 December 1939). Clipping from MOA: TC 38/1/A, Miscellaneous.

8 Irene Raines, 'London Ballroom Notes', *Dancing Times* (November 1939), p. 74.

9 IWM: Sound Archive.11844, Transcript of interview with Anthony Crombie (1986), p. 2.

10 'Provincial Notes', *Dancing Times* (November 1939), p. 85.

11 MOA: Worktown 48/D, Manager – Aspin Hall (8 January 1940).

12 'Manchester Notes', *Modern Dance* (October 1939).

13 Edward R. Murrow, *This is London* (New York: Simon and Schuster, 1941), p. 41.

14 IWM, Sound Archive.20240, French civilian comments on Hammersmith Palais during Second World War (24 August 1940).

15 Quoted in Jean R. Freedman, *Whistling in the Dark: Memory and Culture in Wartime London* (Lexington, KT: University of Kentucky Press, 1999), p. 127.

16 'Dancing on Plymouth Hoe', *Dance News* (30 August 1941), p. 1.

17 'Bomb casualties killed in dance hall', *The Times* (17 March 1941), p. 4.

18 'Bombed, But Danced On', *Dance News* (18 October 1941), p. 1.

19 Frank Illingworth, *Britain Under Shellfire* (London: Hutchison & Company, 1942), p. 42.

20 'Dover Still Dances', *Dance News* (13 September 1941).

21 'Dover Dances to Shell-Fire', *Dance News* (4 April 1942), p. 1.

22 MOA: TC 38/5/D, Astoria (5 December 1939), p. 2; MOA: Worktown 48/D, Dance and Dance Halls; MOA: TC 38/6/A, Jazz Since the War Began.

23 MOA: TC 38/5/D, Astoria (5 December 1939), p. 2.

24 TNA: PRO HO 45/24083: Entertainments: Sunday dancing: proposals to extend facilities, 1926–1950.

25 MOA: TC 38/5/A, Editor – Melody Maker (27 October 1939).

26 For more on the Royal Opera House as a dance hall, see Francesca Franchi, 'Mecca Comes to Covent Garden', *About the House: The Magazine of the Friends of Covent Garden* (Spring 1991), 12–20.

27 'Dancing Beats Films', *Danceland* (September 1944), p. 8.

28 'We Danced As They Bombed', p. 14.

29 MOA: TC 38/1/A, Chaperlin (1 November 1939), p. 4.

30 IWM: Documents.6498, Private Papers of Captain J S Gray (20 April 1940).

31 IWM: Documents.2860, Private Papers of Miss M E Merritt.

32 IWM: Documents.3347, Private Papers of Mrs L White.

33 IWM: Sound Archive.11844, Crombie, p. 13.

34 IWM: Documents.94/370, Growing Pains: A Teenager's War, pp. 18–19.

35 IWM: Documents.127, Private Papers of Mrs V Rayner, p. 15.

36 IWM, Documents.3208, Private Papers of Miss P Warner, (4 October 1940), p. 2.

37 IWM: Sound Archive.10345, Interview with Ruth Wittmann (4 September 1988).

38 MOA: TC 38/5/D, Astoria (5 December 1939), p. 1.

39 MOA: Worktown 48/C, Astoria (18 December 1939).

40 'Dancing is Biggest Boom in History'.

41 TNA: PRO HO 186/229: Entertainment, Restriction on public amusements, Public Entertainments; Decision Regarding Entertainments Emergency Period, May 10, 1940.

42 MOA: TC 38/8/D, Correspondence, Letter from H.E. Smith to Tom Harrisson (21 May 1940).

43 'Scottish Notes', *Modern Dance* (October 1939).

44 'Girls Are Just As Sweet in Overalls', *Dance News* (8 November 1941), p. 1.

45 See *Dancing Times*, October 1939.

46 'Paper Chase! Our Great Drive for Salvage in Every Dance Hall', *Dance News* (6 December 1941).

47 'Tank in Dancehall', *Dance News* (11 October 1941).

48 MOA: TC 38/7/B, Letter from C.L. Heimann to Mass-Observation (October 1940).

49 'Twixt You and the Editor', *Danceland* (February 1941), p. 3.

50 IWM, Documents.3208, Miss P Warner.

51 MOA: TC 38/1/B, Paramount (21 October 1939), p. 1.

52 'Dancing Notes', *Liverpool Evening News* (13 October 1939). Clipping from MOA: TC 38/4/A.

53 'Wallflowers, Here's Your Dance', *Daily Mirror* (18 November 1939), p. 10.

54 MOA: TC 38/5/D, Tommy Connor (5 December 1939), p. 2.

55 MOA: TC 38/5/D, Astoria (5 December 1939), p. 5.

56 MOA: TC 38/2/B, Publicity Materials for The Tuscana (1941).

57 *Dance News* (February 1941).

58 Editorial, *Dance News* (6 December 1941).

59 Editorial, *Dance News* (20 December 1941).

60 Opinion, *Dance News* (19 July 1941), p. 2.

61 'War Time Tonic', *Danceland* (September 1943), p. 2.

62 *Dance News* (30 August 1941).

63 James Mackenzie, *Stepping Out* (London: Danceland Publications, 1944), p. 6.

64 Mackenzie, *Stepping Out*, p. 5.

65 Peter Bailey, 'Fats Waller meets Harry Champion: Americanisation, national identity, and sexual politics in inter-war British music hall', *Cultural and Social History* 4 (2007), 495–509.

66 On circuses see Sandra Trudgen Dawson, 'Selling the circus: Englishness, circus fans and democracy in Britain, 1920–1945', in Brett Bebber (ed.), *Leisure and Cultural Conflict in Twentieth-Century Britain* (Manchester: Manchester University Press, 2012).

67 IWM, Documents.3208, Miss P Warner, (31 December 1940), p. 4.

68 Murrow, *This is London*, p. 41.

69 Thompson, 'And Now…to Dance', p. 8.

70 Quoted in Philip Ziegler, *London at War, 1939–1945* (London: Pimlico, 2002), p. 52.

71 IWM: Documents.6498, Captain J S Gray.

72 TNA: PRO AIR 2/8865: R.A.F. dances for all ranks – policy, 1944.

73 IWM: Documents.3029, Private Papers of Mrs A Parkhurst, p. 2.

74 Murrow, *This is London*, p. 41.

75 TNA: PRO AIR 2/8865.

76 See Rose, *Which People's War?*; David Reynolds, *Rich Relations: The American Occupation of Britain, 1942–1945* (New York: Random House, 1995); Juliet Gardiner, *'Over Here:' The GIs in Wartime Britain* (London: Collins & Brown, 1992); Graham A. Smith, *When Jim Crow Met John Bull: Black American Soldiers in World War II Britain* (London: I.B. Tauris, 1987).

77 Reynolds, *Rich Relations*, p. 262.

78 Rose, *Which People's War?*, pp. 71–92.

79 Ross McKibbin, *Classes and Cultures: England, 1918–1951* (Oxford: Oxford University Press, 1998), p. 396.

80 IWM: Documents.94/370, Growing Pains, p. 98.

81 As quoted in Philomena Goodman, *Women, Sexuality and War* (Basingstoke: Palgrave, 2002), p. 135.

82 As quoted in Goodman, *Women, Sexuality and War*, p. 132.

83 Stewart Sale, 'A.T.S. Morals Defended', *Daily Telegraph* (23 December 1941), p. 5.

84 'Let Women Run the A.T.S.', *Daily Telegraph* (26 November 1941), p. 3.

85 IWM: Documents.1238, Private Papers of Miss E E Weaver.

86 'Ballroom for Service Girls', *Dance News* (4 April 1942).

87 'Moral Laxity: Primate's Appeal to Men', *Leicester Evening Mail* (10 July 1943), p. 5.

88 'Dr. Scott Lidgett Defends Church Dances', *Leicester Evening Mail* (14 July1943), p. 4.

89 'Dancing and Cards', *Liverpool Daily Post* (15 July 1943), p. 2.

90 Anti-gloom, Letter to the Editor, *Leicester Evening Mail* (15 July 1943), p. 3.

91 Laura Tabili, *We Ask for British Justice: Workers and Racial Difference in Late Imperial Britain* (Ithaca, NY: Cornell University Press, 1994); Rose, *Which People's War?*; Bill Schwarz, 'Black metropolis, white England', in Mica Nava and Alan O'Shea

(eds), *Modern Times: Reflections on a Century of English Modernity* (London: Routledge, 1996), pp. 176–207.

92 See Smith, *From Jim Crow to John Bull*; Rose, *Which People's War?*

93 Geoffrey Carr, 'What are we going to do about this?' *Sunday Pictorial* (19 September 1943), p. 6.

94 Quoted in Gardiner, *Wartime*, p. 486.

95 'Synod and Insults to Coloured Folks', *Western Mail & South Wales News* (16 September 1943), p. 3.

96 TNA: PRO, LAB 26/55: Colour Bar – Manchester and Others.

97 TNA: PRO, HO 45/25604: War: US Forces personnel stationed in the UK: possibility of friction between white and coloured troops, 1942–1944.

98 IWM: Documents.3403, Private Papers of Mrs A R Wilson (1946).

99 Quoted in Gardiner, *'Over Here'*, p. 156.

100 'Two Dance Halls Ban Coloured Men', *Warrington Examiner* (8 December 1943).

101 TNA: PRO: LAB 26/55: Colour Bar – Manchester and Others.

102 Roma Fairley, *Come Dancing Miss World* (London: Newman Neame, 1966), pp. 71–2.

103 Rose, *Which People's War?*, p. 239.

104 Brendan Bracken, 'Colour Bar Must Go', *Sunday Express* (20 September 1942), p. 2.

105 Letters to the Editor, *Warrington Examiner* (11 December 1943), p. 4.

106 Carr, 'What are we going to do about this?', p. 6.

107 IWM: Documents.3403, Mrs A R Wilson.

108 Quoted in Les Back, 'Nazism and the call of the jitterbug', in Helen Thomas (ed.) *Dance in the City* (New York: St. Martin's Press, 1997), p. 190.

8

The 'infernal jitterbug' and the transformation of popular dance

In April 1940, just as the 'phoney war' was about to become a lot less phoney, C. L. Heimann and the Mecca organisation announced their latest novelty – an adaptation of an imported American dance called the jitterbug. In promotional materials for the new dance, the dance hall circuit proclaimed: 'The interest and enthusiasm for Jitterbug Dancing is now well-established, having withstood the condemnation it at first received – it is characteristic of the present epoch; it is demanded by youth; it has progressed without any sponsoring. It has, in fact, asserted itself despite the efforts of many sections of the Dancing profession to eliminate it!'[1] In this statement, much about the history of the jitterbug's cultural trajectory in Britain was revealed. The jitterbug was a dance primarily favoured by the young, and came to be seen as the ideal dance to best reflect and express the wartime moment. It also had many detractors – within the dancing public, dance profession and dance hall industry – but endured owing to the efforts of its enthusiasts. Indeed, the production and consumption of the jitterbug was particularly emblematic of the patterns of cultural negotiation – now well established – that had determined the style and progression of popular dance since the 1920s.

The popular dance culture that 'boomed' during the war was more explicitly Americanised than what had preceded it, owing to the presence of large numbers of American servicemen in Britain, and the craze for the jitterbug. Commercial producers made the same efforts to Anglicise the dance that had occurred in response to foreign imports throughout the interwar years, but importantly, the dancing public – increasingly enthralled with cultural products from across the pond and surrounded by actual people from the United States – demonstrated a strong interest in the 'authentic', American jitterbug. Through their acceptance or resistance to the jitterbug, Britons grappled in microcosm with the broader social changes, racial transformations and ideas about national identity that characterised wartime society. Moreover, the jitterbug represented a critical shift in dancing styles for the British, in that it had no standard steps and figures, and encouraged improvisation and independent movements. Like truckin' or the Lambeth Walk, the jitterbug offered welcome relief to dancers weary of foxtrot variations, and heralded the changes that were coming to popular dance as Britain entered the post-war world.

The jitterbug comes to Britain

The jitterbug was the American dance most closely associated with swing, an evolution in jazz that occurred in the 1930s, and which was characterised by written arrangements which were performed by big bands.[2] In fact, the term 'jitterbug' originally referred to the fans of the musical style rather than any particular dance movements, and swing and the jitterbug were inextricably connected on both sides of the Atlantic. There was a tendency among jitterbugs to intersperse their dancing with pauses simply to listen to the music, which was one of the primary reasons it inspired the wrath of serious ballroom dancers. The movements of the jitterbug were presaged by dances like the Big Apple, and especially the Lindy hop, elements of which had made their way to Britain in the late 1930s as truckin'. Indeed, historian Sherrie Tucker describes the jitterbug as the 'mainstreamed doppelgänger' of the Lindy, as the dance transitioned out the ballrooms of Harlem to be appropriated by and captivate the younger generation across the United States.[3] Likewise in Britain, the jitterbug possessed many similarities to truckin'; it was characterised by energetic, inventive movements – kicks, lifts, spins, finger wags and especially the 'breakaway', in which partners separated and then rhythmically came back together. It too was an exuberant dance that encouraged creativity and improvisation, and occupied considerable space on the dance floor. However, for reasons that will become clear the jitterbug would go on to have a much wider reach than its predecessor.

While perhaps irrevocably associated in popular memory with the American presence in wartime Britain, the jitterbug actually crossed the pond even before the war had started. According to one (possibly apocryphal) story in a contemporary history of the dance, the jitterbug's British life began in January 1939, when a 'coloured couple', probably American, began jitterbugging in the corner of the dance floor at Mecca's Paramount dance hall in London.[4] Having attracted a fair amount of attention from other patrons, they were asked to give an impromptu exhibition of the dance on the bandstand by the hall's manager, R. T. Davis. Although there may be some truth to this tale, it should be acknowledged that the jitterbug would not have seemed as dramatically novel to the British dancing public as it implies. The name 'jitterbug' may have been new to Britain, but swing movements had been growing in influence for several years.

Throughout 1939 the jitterbug became an increasing fixture at the large dance halls in urban centres, but remained to some degree specialised knowledge. Mass Observation reports indicate that the dance was demonstrated at a number of London halls, but was practised on the dance floor by only select members of the dancing public.[5] On 20 November of that year, Britain's first jitterbug competition was staged at the Paramount, which had become known and was promoted by Mecca as the nation's primary 'jitter hall'. The competition largely consisted of a dance marathon, the endurance form of dance contest that was widespread in the United States throughout the Depression but had enjoyed less success in Britain.[6] While the principal goal in a marathon was just to keep on dancing, competitors were also required to stay in rhythm with the music or be disqualified. This event, which received considerable attention in the popular and dance press, did much to further widespread knowledge of the jitterbug throughout the country.

Over the next months and years, the jitterbug expanded its influence throughout Britain in a variety of ways. Additional dance competitions took place, transitioning away from the marathon-style towards more traditional British formats, and then in January 1940 the first All-England Jitterbug Championship was held at the Paramount. Through these competitions, as well as exhibitions and the sale of magazines and swing sheet music, the dance hall industry did much to promote the jitterbug – in spite of a distinct ambivalence to the dance felt by some proprietors. The jitterbug also received considerable attention in the press, and was a prevalent feature in Hollywood movies; films such as the Ginger Rogers vehicle *Bachelor Mother*, or the Marx Brothers' production *The Big Store*, introduced the jitterbug to scores of British cinema-goers.[7] Finally, with the arrival of foreign servicemen from across the Atlantic – first Canadians and especially Americans starting in 1942 – the British jitterbug era entered a new, more pronounced phase. The thousands of American servicemen stationed around the country, often in rural areas that lacked a large palais through which urbanites had previously encountered the jitterbug, now introduced the dance to the masses.

Upon its initial appearance in the nation's ballrooms, attempts at the jitterbug by British dancers were seen to be simplistic compared to how the dance was performed in the United States. As a jitterbug demonstrator who toured the country for Mecca told Mass Observation, 'You don't see the real jitterbug dancing over here. In America they throw the girl over their back. They have her leg under their arm and give her a twist and then throw her over their back. They dance till they drop exhausted – that's proper jitterbug. They go on and on and on till they drop. They will last 25 minutes.'[8] Outside of London, attempts at the dance were even more amateurish, at least to the eyes of Mass Observation's Alec Hughes, who wrote of the jitterbug dancing in Bolton, 'Their jitter had none of the London ease, nor any of its intricacy and skill. They just jigged about, having a good time ... None tried any really complicated steps.'[9] The presence of the Americans was therefore important for spreading the influence of the jitterbug, but also for altering and ameliorating the way in which the dance was performed in Britain. Prior to the arrival of the American forces, one teacher even advised British dancers to take a look at some of the Hollywood films featuring the jitterbug in order to learn how to better perform it, since according to him, 'the English version is very, very crude'.[10]

Like so many dances that had come to Britain from America, opinions about the jitterbug within the dance profession, dance hall industry and dancing public were markedly divided. Some contemporaries were enthusiastic about a new and innovative dance, while others were suspicious or dismissive; bandleader Joe Loss, for instance, stated in 1939 that he saw no future for the jitterbug.[11] Much of the debate over the dance echoed the one that had surrounded the Charleston almost two decades earlier. There was bemusement, amusement and in some cases vehement objections to the wild, untamed nature of the jitterbug. As one witness to the dance recalled, 'it seemed a bit strange ... it seemed like they were circus acrobats'.[12] In particular, the jitterbug's wild steps, kicks and breakaways could be disruptive to patrons engaged in more conventional ballroom pursuits. Regarding one visit to a wartime dance hall, keen amateur J. S. Gray recorded in his diary that the floor was 'simply packed out with Yanks [and] Canadians, with jitter-buggers everywhere, so it was almost an impossibility to get in any serious dancing'.[13]

Just as they had with the Charleston, many dance halls took measures to curb the disruptive effects of the dance. As the Mecca jitterbug demonstrator told Mass Observation, 'They have had to ask the people at the Paramount if they would mind not doing the jitterbug to ordinary quicksteps. I do it. You see you kick peoples [sic] ankles and they don't like it and complain.'[14] On another occasion Mass Observation recorded that people 'dancing in the ordinary fashion seem to find it rather annoying as the evening wears on and the jitterbug fans become worked up'. The report went on to explain that, responding to the complaints of other patrons, the dance hall's master of ceremonies requested that dancers not engage in jitterbugging during the general dancing, but promised that there would be a special session later in the evening. The three or four eager jitterbugs who participated in this special session then apparently drew considerable interest from the other dancers as an exhibition, but the observer speculated that non-jitterbugs were equally keen not to have to continue sharing dance floor space with them afterwards.[15] Other halls also created special jitterbug sessions during an evening's dancing, in order to better control the dance and keep jitterbugs from disrupting other patrons. On a visit to the Royal dance hall in north London, for example, a writer for Mass Observation recorded the presence of a sign that asked jitterbugs 'to confine their activities to dances specially played for them at 4.30, 5.30, 8.30, 9.30, and 10.30'.[16]

Some halls went further than demarcating special sessions for the jitterbug, but instead attempted to ban the dance altogether, and placed signs announcing the prohibition around the dance floor. In addition to the annoyances the jitterbug caused for other patrons, the dance wreaked havoc on diligently maintained dance floors, leading to costly repairs for ballroom proprietors. The industry also feared public criticism over the jitterbug's imagined improprieties, since it was a dance that caused women to be lifted high in the air and flung about the dance floor, with their skirts often raised over their heads. A commonly expressed view was that the jitterbug was 'not nice'.[17] Clinging to the tenuous grip on respectability that they had developed for their establishments throughout the interwar years, dance hall managers feared social purity advocates who might use the jitterbug to renew their castigations. Consequently, if they did not ban the dance entirely, the dance hall industry attempted to establish limits on *how* it was performed. A report for Mass Observation described the efforts of the manager of the Paramount in this respect:

> He said that on the American nights they had jam sessions, but only short ones as the dancers went wild, eyes rolling, skirts flying and in general working themselves up into a frenzy. Mr. Davis explained that the management wanted them to enjoy themselves but when the dancing started turning into immoral display they called the jam session off and played waltzes [etc.][18]

Similarly, during a jitterbug marathon in Leeds, one dance step in which the female partner fastened her legs around the male partner's body to be spun around was banned from competition for its alleged impropriety.[19]

If they could control when and how it was performed, however, many within the dance hall industry perceived that there were advantages to embracing the jitterbug. Once again Heimann and Mecca were at the forefront of these efforts; confronted with strong public enthusiasm for the latest American import, Mecca quickly jumped on the jitterbug bandwagon. Throughout 1939, even while extolling the home-grown virtues of the Lambeth Walk and its successors, Mecca began making moves to capitalise upon the growing jitterbug phenomenon. The circuit hired dancers, often American, to stage exhibitions of the dance at Mecca halls around the country, and began to advertise the Paramount as a place where patrons could 'see our famous jitterbugs'.[20] Mecca halls became a primary location for many special jitterbug-themed events, and marathons and competitions were held at the Paramount, Locarno, and Royal Opera House. Considerable attention was also paid to the jitterbug in Mecca's various periodicals, and in 1942 the company's print arm published a short book dedicated to the new dance, entitled *Swing Fever Jitterbug*.

Meanwhile, the dance profession greeted the jitterbug with the same degree of bemusement and ambivalence that it had greeted novelty dances only a short time earlier. In responses to a survey of dancing teachers conducted for the book *Swing Fever Jitterbug*, the dance was described as everything from a 'nuisance dance' to 'undignified' to 'very fascinating'. Of those queried, Major Cecil Taylor was the most disapproving, making the comment that 'Jitterbug is a horrible thing and most detrimental to dancing in general. I advise its total banishment.'[21] Even the professionals who were less opposed to the jitterbug expressed concerns that it might undermine or diminish the English style. Yet despite these misgivings, most professionals believed that any new dance that sparked the interest of the dancing public was a thing to be welcomed. In 1938, when swing dancing first began to take hold in Britain, a writer for *Modern Dance* observed that its success was 'inevitable', because for too many years the 'ballroom routine remained unchanged; the average dancer had become lethargic and consequently in the mood to accept a new form of dancing'.[22] Like novelty dances, the jitterbug entered into and revived a popular dancing scene that had grown stale, and this was seen as a positive development by most professionals. As Monsieur Pierre told the writers of *Swing Fever Jitterbug*, the dance was 'a welcome change from the standard dances and is likely to increase in popularity … it should benefit dancing'.[23] Alex Moore described what he witnessed at a jitterbug competition as 'the most disgusting and degrading sight I have ever seen in a ballroom', and something which could not possibly make a discernible contribution to the future of ballroom dance, and yet still went on to assert that the dance was a useful novelty for wartime dance floors.[24]

In terms of how the dancing public responded to the jitterbug, negative feelings were inspired against the dance for the havoc it often created on the dance floor. As Gray recorded in his diary regarding a visit to a dance hall in Brighton, 'Went to Sherrys [sic] again in afternoon. Swamped out today by U.S.A. soldiers indulging in the infernal "jitterbug".'[25] Ballroom dance enthusiasts like Gray, who took their favoured pastime seriously, shared the concerns of professional dancers that the jitterbug constituted a threat to the 'real' or 'true' dancing of the English style. As one concerned dancer wrote in a letter to the editor of *Modern Dance*, 'While I agree that at a dance all types have to be catered for, I am aggrieved by the fact that Swing is growing into a pernicious canker and spoiling dancing altogether. I have visited various places and find the tendency to make all Foxtrots and Quicksteps into Swing.' The correspondent went on to warn that unless the dance profession took action, they might be witnessing 'the deterioration of modern ballroom dancing as we know it now'.[26]

Other dancers, especially younger men and women, were far more enthusiastic about the jitterbug, however. Introduced to the dance by American GIs, a memoirist described it as 'infectious and energetic'.[27] The jitterbug was fun and lively, and provided a respite from the standard four ballroom dances. As another woman who partnered visiting Americans recalled, 'We English girls took to it like ducks to water. No more slow, slow, quick, quick slow for us. This was living.'[28] The strong appeal of the jitterbug was also conveyed in a 1942 letter from pilot Philip Mortimore to his girlfriend; listening to the wireless in the mess as he wrote to Doreen, Mortimore remarked, 'It wouldn't be dignified and sergeant-like to get up and start jitterbugging in the mess although I feel like it. It's funny how it gets you.'[29] Even Gray, though frequently exasperated by the 'infernal' jitterbug, was forced to acknowledge in his diary on one occasion that the dance produced a good time: 'Went to the Regent Dance Hall in the evening and as might have been imagined it was full to overflowing with the Canadians taking full charge and "jitterbugging" all over the place!! As a dance it was hopeless but everyone was enjoying themselves and the bar was full!!'[30] So although the jitterbug was not universally beloved, and even at the height of its wartime popularity Britons were more likely to be foxtrotting than jitterbugging, the dance maintained a devoted following.

Indeed, it is important to note that the jitterbug was understood as another dance craze that was largely initiated by the dancing public. Victor Silvester believed that the dance had developed 'at random in its own turbulent way', quite removed from the intervention of the profession or industry.[31] The strength of the public's enthusiasm for the dance was also a main theme of the Mecca-produced *Swing Fever Jitterbug*. In the opening pages of the book, the author observed: 'Crazy? Maybe. Acrobatic contortions not fit for the ballroom? Perhaps. But the public liked it and asked for more.' The booklet further contended that jitterbugs would not be dissuaded by efforts to curb the spread of their favourite dance: 'Large notices "No Jitterbugging Allowed" did not stop all the enthusiasts, many of whom got into a corner to whisk and twirl away.'[32] About the dance, Heimann himself remarked: 'If people want a thing they will have it.'[33] This conviction appears to have been at the root of Mecca's pragmatic and profit-minded decision to embrace the jitterbug.

Anglicisation, authenticity and the jitterbug

Although Mecca had spent most of the preceding two years marketing its novelty dances on the basis of their Britishness and un-American-ness, officials at the company clearly sensed that the latest dance sensation from the United States presented an opportunity. The dance hall chain soon went further than providing exhibitions of jitterbug– it directly appropriated and Anglicised the dance, releasing 'C.L. Heimann's Refined Jitterbug' in 1940. Adapted by Adele England of Lambeth Walk fame, this toned-down version eliminated the suggestive movements and wild lifts and kicks that created havoc on dance floors and prompted concerns about impropriety. Describing the Mecca version of the jitterbug as 'refined' also associated it with longstanding descriptions of both the English style of ballroom dance, and the national character. Further connecting it with processes of Anglicisation, the refined jitterbug was explicitly promoted as a follow-up to Heimann's 'British' novelty dances, and publicised using many of the same marketing strategies. In addition to a special launch of the dance at the 1940 All-Britain Jitterbug Championship at the Locarno, Mecca coordinated with the Peter Maurice Music Company to release relevant sheet music, for which the two companies chose the very popular Glenn Miller swing tune 'In the Mood'. Credit was given where credit was due, and the cover of the sheet music was emblazoned with a large image of Miller; however, in one corner a small photograph of Heimann was also present, and consumers were advised that they were buying the music that went along with *his* 'jitterbug novelty'. The pamphlet contained the music to 'In the Mood', as well as diagrams and instructions on how to perform the jitterbug.[34] The company thus recreated and repackaged the dance in a way that reinforced and commodified many of the same nationalist idioms contained within the marketing of the English style and British novelty dances.

Nor was Heimann the only one to advocate the creation and marketing of a 'refined' jitterbug more appropriate for British ballrooms: the idea simultaneously gained traction within the dance profession. Despite his personal distaste for the dance and belief that it could have no permanent impact, Moore suggested that there was room within British dancing for a 'mild' jitterbug. Another proponent of a mild or refined jitterbug was Silvester, who remarked in the survey for *Swing Fever Jitterbug*: '[The jitterbug] is a vital force providing it is modified. All lifts, throws and other exaggerated movements should be entirely eliminated. These movements are acrobatics, which is not dancing, and quite unsuitable for the ballroom. If ever this form of dancing is to develop, the standardisation of a few simple basic steps is essential.'[35] Silvester's idea was to standardise and Anglicise the jitterbug much in the same way as he and other professionals had formalised the English style and modified the Charleston. By 1944, Silvester had taken action, working in association with Heimann to produce the 'jive', a modified, subdued form of the jitterbug that expanded upon efforts that began with Heimann's refined version. Already a renowned bandleader with his strict tempo orchestra, Silvester now formed a new Jive Band in order to record and sell music to accompany the new dance, and, along with Mecca's Danceland Publications, released a book on the subject, entitled *This is Jive*. According to Silvester, the jive was designed to appease enthusiasts and critics of the jitterbug alike. As he described it, 'The Jive is as clever as the Jitterbug was crude. Danced slowly it can be graceful. Danced quickly, it can be just as bright and snappy without being boisterous.'[36]

Just like the creation of the English style and the flat progressive Charleston, the movement to create a 'refined', 'mild' and more British version of the jitterbug was encoded with the language of race. Although the jitterbug had already been appropriated and mainstreamed out of the black Lindy hop by white America, it retained associations with blackness when it arrived in Britain. Renewed references to 'freak steps' and primitivism began to reappear in the dance press, while critics of the dance castigated it in racist terms, and asserted that it was antithetical to Britishness. As one provincial correspondent for the *Dancing Times* proclaimed, 'Jitterbugs, Truckin', and those ungraceful, un-English, and sometimes vulgar gyrations are not acceptable in Blackpool's ballrooms.'[37] Beyond the profession, a London magistrate condemned the dance as a 'sex exciter for negroes'.[38] The process of 'refining' the jitterbug, and eliminating its more boisterous, wild and suggestive movements, was therefore once again about whitening a black dance, and making it more respectable. In the promotional materials for the refined jitterbug and later the jive, the American dance's perceived racial origins were also significantly downplayed.

At the same time, in racial discourses that surrounded this latest American import, the tone had changed in slight, but meaningful ways, since the days of the foxtrot or Charleston, and which had been hinted at through the reception of the jitterbug's precursor, truckin'. The enthusiasm for the jitterbug was amplified by the physical presence of so many Americans – black and white – in public ballrooms, and during the war, as has been shown, the dance floor was a space wherein social and racial unity were actively performed. Indeed, the unresolved tension between anxieties over interracial dancing and miscegenation, and the desire to eliminate colour bars and preserve Britain's self-understanding as the centre of a liberal, racially harmonious empire, was mirrored in attitudes towards the blackness of the jitterbug. There were a growing number of people in the popular music and dance hall industries, dance profession and dancing public, who acknowledged the perceived blackness of the dance in a manner that sought not to suppress, but rather to highlight or endorse. The racial origins of the dance, and the expertise of black jitterbugs in performing it, were acknowledged and even celebrated – yet often still in language that perpetuated racial stereotypes and made claims for white supremacy.

In a chapter of *Swing Fever Jitterbug* on the origins of the jitterbug, author James Mackenzie challenged critics of the dance who had 'dismissed [it] as "negro stuff"'. 'True dancing', Mackenzie argued, was 'based on rhythm, and nowhere is true rhythm more naturally performed than by the negro. The white man may not have the same facility but he can learn much of the art of true dancing by watching the negro.'[39] Other commentators also reinforced the talents of black dancers in performing the jitterbug, particularly in comparison to white dancers. As the Mecca demonstrator interviewed by Mass Observation put it, 'You watch a coloured man dance and a white. There is an entire difference. The coloured man is born to dance like that.'[40] This recognition of black expertise was also affirmed by the increasing interest expressed by some white Britons in knowing how black dancers perceived their performances of the dance. *Swing Fever Jitterbug* asked an African-American dancer about the British jitterbug, purportedly being told 'It's O.K., but they don't let themselves go.'[41] Mass Observation also interviewed two truckin' demonstrators at the

Streatham Locarno in order to get their opinion about British attempts at black dances, one of whom remarked, 'there's just something missing in the English'. This dancer's partner elaborated further, telling the social research organisation, 'I guess it is born in us. The rhythm is there. It originated in the negro. It comes easy to us. There is a natural rhythm in our bodies. The English are much better at ballroom dancing than at this sort of dancing. They are inclined to be too stiff. They make it look too much like work.'[42] Meanwhile, rather than moving to instantly stamp out the movements that were perceived to be 'black' in the jitterbug, some Britons sought to preserve and copy them. In another interview with Mass Observation, two white women who performed exhibitions of the jitterbug at Mecca halls said that they had learned the dance from black dancers: 'We practice with the coloured people. They are marvellous. They were never taught nothing. They just dance. They learned it from birth. We picked it up from them.' It was also with a degree of satisfaction that the women revealed that they had been deemed superior jitterbugs by the dancers who had trained them, better even than black women: 'We've been told [by] coloured people [that] we swing better than dark girls.'[43]

Importantly, the declining interest in Anglicised dances and the growing appreciation for the aesthetics of black performance did not necessarily translate into new levels of racial toleration within British society. The notion of black 'expertise' or natural affinity for the jitterbug provided black dancers with a degree of cultural authority in the eyes of white Britons, but it also perpetuated longstanding and problematic biological assumptions about racial difference. For instance, *Swing Fever Jitterbug* asserted that the talents displayed by black dancers in performing the jitterbug, as well as the steps of the dance, could be traced back to their ancestors' 'far-off jungle days'.[44] Within the shifting racial discourses that surrounded the dance, there were also new ways for white dancers to make claims for superiority. The two women jitterbugs mentioned above laid claim to the African-American dance and made it their own by proclaiming that they had improved upon its performance in comparison to black dancers. As they told Mass Observation: 'We were at the Paramount and one evening they put us on the centre stand. We can do anything that any of the coloured people can do as far as swing is concerned.'[45] Much in the same way, in *Swing Fever Jitterbug*, immediately after author Mackenzie suggested that Britons could learn something from African Americans about dancing, he remarked: 'It is interesting to recall that one of the first jitterbug marathons ever held in this country was won by a young English couple in spite of the fact that an experienced coloured couple were competing.'[46]

In this statement was an implicit suggestion of white superiority, even in the performance of what was understood to be a black dance. British jitterbug enthusiasts reified racial differences and claims for white supremacy, even while being attracted to and embracing the blackness of the dance. As Danielle Robinson has argued with respect to ragtime dancing in the United States, in performing movements perceived as black, white dancers could assume a 'temporary' blackness, which ultimately underscored their ability to 'take blackness on and off' – in a way black dancers could not – and affirmed their whiteness.[47] The allure of the jitterbug in its un-Anglicised, unrefined, un-whitened form was thus less about racial tolerance, and more about the accelerating attraction to American cultural imports. Heightened by the fact that so many were introduced to the jitterbug by actual Americans rather than one of Britain's commercial producers of dancing, Britons wanted to experience the dance in its authentic form, of which blackness was considered to be an important part. Especially for the younger generation, the American-style jitterbug was a respite from the staid, refined, increasingly old-fashioned foxtrot; the dance was fun, exotic, and intrinsically modern.

Indeed, the jitterbug's modernity was borne out in a number of ways. First, the dance was decisively associated with young Britons, and it was their interest in it which spurred the phenomenon on. This was in part owing to the belief that the jitterbug required too much energy and abandon for older dancers. One dance teacher told the *Star* newspaper that it was only because of the young that the jitterbug was able to attain any sort of foothold in Britain, since the dance called 'for far more energy, abandon, rhythm, and lack of self-consciousness than anyone beyond the teens possesses'.[48] *Swing Fever Jitterbug* even quoted a doctor who suggested that it might be dangerous for anyone over the age of thirty to attempt the jitterbug.[49] Whether it was to defend or criticise it, many observers acknowledged that this was a dance for the next generation. As one elderly woman who had been introduced to the jitterbug by her granddaughter remarked, 'It looks a bit modern to my idea, but I remember years ago how annoyed my parents were when I told them I had danced the Boston Two Step at a dance. No doubt if I were a young girl to-day I should be jitterbugging with the best of them.'[50] The rise of a new generation – the children of those who had been at the forefront of the modern ballroom dancing craze in the 1920s – brought with it another moment of transformation for British popular dance. The jitterbug represented the start of a critical transition, wherein inventive, individualised and occasionally independent steps began to supplant the standardised and technically precise ballroom dances. As one dance journalist noted, after the war 'It hardly seems likely that [the young] will be content with the old, accepted order of dancing.'[51]

As this comment implied, another way in which the jitterbug's modernity was reinforced was through its direct association with the time period during which it was created. Just as the foxtrot and one-step were said to be ideal expressions of the post-Armistice dance craze and 'roaring', ultra-modern 1920s, the jitterbug was strongly connected with the wartime moment where it came to prominence. As *Swing Fever Jitterbug* put it, there was just 'something in the air that helped [the jitterbugs] along'.[52] The jitterbug provided 'vigour and spontaneous good feeling', as well as 'an outburst of gladness in the face of the depressions and war scares'.[53] Alex Moore similarly told readers of the *Dancing Times*, 'Remember ... that there is a war on, and that ... many people turn to the ballroom for mental relaxation. For such people I feel that ... a mild form of the "Jitterbug" dancing is a welcome innovation.'[54] Elsewhere in the profession's premier magazine, the editors advised teachers that whatever their concerns, the public interest in the dance made sense in wartime.[55] It has also been argued that the jitterbug had particular appeal for young women, who felt it physically expressed the greater freedom and independence they enjoyed as a result of their participation in the war effort.[56] More generally, the untamed energy and fun of the jitterbug made it an ideal dance through which people could dispense with war-related fears and concerns, and it embodied the informality and exuberant spirit of the wartime ballroom. As drummer Anthony Crombie recalled,

> Prior to the war ... [dance] music was keyed down very low, rather sedate kind of offering, more wallpaper than music, and suddenly with the oncoming of the war people had all this frustration and pent up energy that needed to release and I think the American style music provided the opportunity to get rid of those energetic impulses via dancing.[57]

Significantly, in a moment when dancing was deployed to express the nation's resolve and good cheer, the lively and carefree jitterbug had a natural valence and impact. The improvisational nature of the dance released dancers from the rigid standardisation of the English style, and all of the latter's attendant associations about national identity. Rather, with its spirit, spontaneity and individualism, the jitterbug produced alternative national imaginaries that were consonant with dominant wartime ideologies, and indicative of the growing influence of American culture and dogma. As historians of the Depression-era and wartime United States have shown, swing and the jitterbug were intrinsically associated with American national identity; the vibrant and uninhibited sounds and movements, experienced and performed on dance floors that had allegedly been racially integrated, seemed to embody and express 'freedom, individualism, ethnic inclusiveness, democratic participation'.[58] While these associations have been subject to scholarly critique, they loomed large within American society during the war and in the decades since.[59] They also had considerable allure for wartime Britons, who were attracted to American culture and equated dancing with democracy. In addition, the jitterbug provided a vital connection to Britain's American ally, and represented another point of differentiation between the nation and its German enemy. Both the British and the Americans used Nazi prohibitions against jazz in propaganda as a way of highlighting the differences between democracy and fascism, and underlining the justness of the Allied cause.[60] Lending even further weight to these associations was the fact that swing music and the jitterbug were employed as a form of cultural resistance by non-conformist youth – the so-called 'swing kids' – within Nazi Germany. In the jitterbug, therefore, many of the impulses that directed wartime popular dance more broadly coalesced: the desire to have fun and live in the moment, as well as the belief in democracy, inclusivity and social unity.

In sum, in subtle but critical ways, the jitterbug craze demonstrated that popular dance in Britain was on the cusp of another major upheaval. It was a dance primarily enjoyed by younger Britons, who were a generation removed from the men and women who had embraced the foxtrot, and who were now seeking to foment their own dancing revolution. While the ballroom dance profession still wielded significant authority throughout the jitterbug years, there were further signs that its influence might be on the wane in favour of the dance hall industry, since it was Mecca, and teachers like Silvester who now worked alongside the company, that were at the forefront of developments with respect to the jitterbug. The racial discourses that surrounded the jitterbug also represented both continuity and change with how dances of African-American origin had been greeted in the past: some Britons attempted to preserve the blackness of the dance, while others were engaged in the now well-established processes of Anglicisation and whitening that resulted in the 'refined jitterbug' and the jive. Finally, the dance's improvisational nature, and the solo rather than partnered steps that would follow the breakaway, provided a stark contrast to the standardised movements of modern ballroom dancing. It had not happened yet, nor would it for some time, but ballroom dancing was gradually being replaced as the nation's primary popular dance style.

Notes

1 MOA: TC 38/1/A, Press announcement for All-Britain Jitterbug Championship (1940).
2 David Stowe, *Swing Changes: Big-Band Jazz in New Deal America* (Cambridge, MA: Harvard University Press, 1994), p. 5. See also Lewis Erenberg, 'Things to come: swing bands, bebop, and the rise of a postwar jazz scene', in Larry May (ed.), *Recasting America* (Chicago, IL: University of Chicago Press, 1989), pp. 221–45; Sherrie Tucker, *Dance Floor Democracy: The Social Geography of Memory at the Hollywood Canteen* (Durham, NC: Duke University Press, 2014).
3 Tucker, *Dance Floor Democracy*, p. 3.
4 James Mackenzie, *Swing Fever Jitterbug* (London: Danceland Publications, 1942), p. 28.
5 See MOA: TC 38/1/A, Locarno; MOA: TC 38/1/B, Paramount; MOA: TC/38/1/C, Royal Tottenham.
6 Carol Martin, *Dance Marathons: Performing American Culture in the 1920s and 1930s*, (Jackson, MS: University of Mississippi Press, 1994).
7 Mackenzie, *Swing Fever Jitterbug*, pp. 57–60. See also Karen Hubbard and Terry Monaghan, 'Social dancing at the Savoy', in Julie Malnig (ed.), *Ballroom Boogie, Shimmy Sham, Shake: A Social and Popular Dance Reader* (Urbana, IL: University of Illinois Press, 2009), p. 141.
8 MOA: TC 38/4/H, Frivolity (4 June 1939), pp. 1–2.
9 MOA: Worktown 48/C, Astoria Palais de Danse (18 December 1939).
10 Mackenzie, *Swing Fever Jitterbug*, p. 76.
11 'Dancing is Biggest Boom in History', *Bristol Evening World* (2 December 1939). Clipping found in MOA: TC 38/1/A, Miscellaneous.
12 IWM: Sound Archive.11830, Transcript of Interview with William Amstell (1986), p. 16.
13 IWM: Documents.6498, Private Papers of Captain J S Gray (5 May 1943).
14 MOA: TC 38/4/H, Frivolity (4 June 1939), p. 2.
15 MOA: TC 38/2/B, Jitterbugs (10 August 1940).
16 MOA: TC 38/1/C, Royal (1 December 1939).
17 Mackenzie, *Swing Fever Jitterbug*, p. 81.
18 MOA: TC 38/1/B, Mr. Davis on Swing (8 March 1939).
19 Mackenzie, *Swing Fever Jitterbug*, p. 30.
20 MOA: TC 38/7/B, Pamphlet for Paramount Dance Hall (1940).
21 Mackenzie, *Swing Fever Jitterbug*, pp. 68–78.
22 Harry Kahn, 'Swing', *Modern Dance* (February 1938), p. 13.
23 Mackenzie, *Swing Fever Jitterbug*, p. 69.
24 Alex Moore, 'Will the War Change the English Style: The Jitterbug Menace', *Dancing Times* (March 1940).
25 IWM: Documents.6498, Captain J S Gray (25 January 1944).
26 M. S. Hale, Letter to the Editor, *Modern Dance* (March 1938), p. 23.
27 IWM: Documents.94/370, Growing Pains: A Teenager's War, pp. 98–9.

28 Quoted in Juliet Gardiner, *'Over Here:' The GIs in Wartime Britain* (London: Collins & Brown, 1992), p. 114.

29 IWM: Documents.12777, Private Papers of P P Mortimore (22 October 1942).

30 IWM: Documents.6498, Captain J S Gray (27 December 1941).

31 Victor Silvester, *This is Jive* (London: Danceland Publications, 1944), p. 18.

32 Mackenzie, *Swing Fever Jitterbug*, p. 10.

33 Mackenzie, *Swing Fever Jitterbug*, p. 31.

34 A copy of the sheet music for 'In the Mood' described is found in MOA: TC 38/7/A, Songs (1940).

35 Mackenzie, *Swing Fever Jitterbug*, p. 76.

36 Silvester, *This is Jive*, p. 21.

37 'Provincial Notes', *Dancing Times* (October 1939), p. 37.

38 Quoted in James Nott, *Going to the Palais: A Social and Cultural History of Dancing and Dance Halls in Britain, 1918–1960* (Oxford: Oxford University Press, 2015), p. 224.

39 Mackenzie, *Swing Fever Jitterbug*, p. 12.

40 MOA: TC 38/4/H, Frivolity, (4 June 1939), pp. 2–3.

41 Mackenzie, *Swing Fever Jitterbug*, p. 44.

42 MOA: TC 38/1/C, Truckin' – Lagey and Heyward (1 June 1939), pp. 1–2.

43 MOA: TC 38/1/A, Jitterbug Demonstration at the Locarno (1 July 1939).

44 Mackenzie, *Swing Fever Jitterbug*, p. 12.

45 MOA: TC 38/1/A, Jitterbug Demonstration at the Locarno (1 July 1939).

46 Mackenzie, *Swing Fever Jitterbug*, p. 13.

47 *Modern Moves: Dancing Race during the Ragtime and Jazz Eras* (New York: Oxford University Press, 2015), pp. 73–9.

48 'Young Sheffield Goes "Crazy" Dancing', *The Star* (31 July 1941). Clipping found in MOA: TC 38/4/A.

49 Mackenzie, *Swing Fever Jitterbug*, pp. 34–5.

50 Mackenzie, *Swing Fever Jitterbug*, p. 83.

51 Mackenzie, *Swing Fever Jitterbug*, p. 10.

52 Mackenzie, *Swing Fever Jitterbug*, p. 10.

53 Mackenzie, *Swing Fever Jitterbug*, p. 83, p. 30.

54 Moore, 'Will the War Change the English Style: The Jitterbug Menace'.

55 'Ballroom Notes', *Dancing Times* (December 1939), pp. 141–2.

56 Les Back, 'Nazism and the call of the jitterbug', in Helen Thomas (ed.) *Dance in the City* (New York: St. Martin's Press, 1997), p. 195.

57 IWM: Sound Archive.11844, Transcript of interview with Anthony Crombie (1986), pp. 5–6.

58 Stowe, *Swing Changes*, p. 99.

59 Tucker, *Dance Floor Democracy*, pp. 9–10.

60 Back, 'Nazism and the Call of the Jitterbug'.

Epilogue
Come dancing – popular dance in post-war Britain

In 1946, a story in *Dance News* described how two teenaged girls, upon discovering that their local dance hall had banned the jitterbug, were so distraught that they tried to stow away aboard a ship bound for the United States.[1] Their attempted exodus to the country they deemed to be more aligned with their cultural tastes is indicative of the ongoing tensions that surrounded popular dance and American culture as Britain entered the post-war period. The jitterbug – now more widely established as the jive – did not depart the British Isles along with the American military at war's end, and dance hall proprietors, dance professionals and the dancing public remained significantly divided over the dance. The controversies over the jive often echoed those that had circulated around dancing since the ragtime era, in that this latest sensation was decried for being un-British, ugly and a promoter of immorality. The same year the two keen jitterbugs attempted their escape to America, a local priest in Lancashire decried the jive as the 'work of the devil', and as a 'debased form of art which stimulates the lowest passions'. However, in the same town the elderly councillor responsible for local entertainments defended his jivers by remarking, 'If this is the work of the devil then let us have more of it, for a happier, healthier, well-conducted crowd of young folk I have rarely seen.'[2] The criticisms and defences of the jive were thus strikingly similar to those that had surrounded the animal dances, tango, Charleston and jitterbug during the preceding three decades. Yet importantly, other aspects of the jive debate signalled that the late 1940s was a critical moment of transition for British popular dance. Among producers and consumers alike there was dissension over whether to embrace the improvisational, Americanised dancing styles that the jive represented, or to resolutely re-establish the English style of modern ballroom dancing.

As Britain once again transitioned from war to peace, popular dance was at a crossroads. In some respects, it seemed that the dance culture that had developed over the course of the previous three decades, and which had played such a vital social and cultural role during the war, would simply carry on and even blossom according to established patterns. Public ballrooms that had been commandeered during the war were steadily restored to their original purpose, and dance hall construction was an active part of re-building efforts in the wake of damage from bombing.[3] Dance instruction thrived into the 1950s, and also expanded, when American dance school chain Arthur Murray entered the British market. In keeping with pre-war trends, popular dance continued to be disseminated throughout society in a variety of other ways beyond the walls of the palais and dance studio. Holiday camps in the burgeoning Butlin's chain began opening ballrooms on their premises, and popular dance was widely circulated via the radio, records, film, as well as the new medium of television. In January 1948, Victor Silvester transferred his popular *BBC Dancing Club* from the radio to the television. A year later, Mecca (which was also a sponsor of Silvester's programme) launched its own dance-themed television show, *Come Dancing*. Both programmes emphasised professional demonstrations and instruction in ballroom dance, as well as competitions and general dancing.

The advent of ballroom dancing on television also showed that the dance profession and the English style still enjoyed considerable influence in the immediate post-war period. What one newspaper called in 1946 the 'smooth flowing unhurried style that is typically English, and with a little practice is easy to learn', still had many advocates, dominated the programme at most dance halls, and was for many people the style that continue to best embody the nation.[4] The English style's international reputation was also quickly re-established and continued to grow after the war. Ballroom dance aficionados around the world looked to British professionals for guidance and leadership in technique. As one South African visitor put it in 1947, 'My impressions of the ballroom dancing world in London have been extremely favourable during my short stay in the home country. After all London is the centre of all art and the standard of dancing here certainly upholds the tradition.'[5] Around the same time, Silvester's strict tempo records were exported to America, providing further evidence of the global impact of the English style and its accompanying music, and foreign teams began to seek out British dance competitions in greater numbers. In 1948, for instance, Australia's champion ballroom dance team came to London to compete in the *Star* Championship, relying on their home-grown training in the mother country's technique. The British dance profession's presence and influence in Europe was also gradually reasserted with the defeat of Nazi Germany and the end of the German occupation of much of the Continent. In 1947, the first dance competition to be held in Germany since the Nazi regime placed restrictions on dancing took place in Hanover, within the British occupation zone. A year later, the annual Anglo-Danish dance contest of the pre-war years was held for the first time in a decade, with the Danes narrowly defeating the British team in a repeat of the shocking loss of 1938.

Incidents like this provoked some angst and served as a bellwether that with the growing internationalisation of the English style, the British might not remain dominant in their native ballroom dancing style forever. A number of professionals were quite chagrined by a letter to the *Dancing Times* from one of their Dutch colleagues in 1946, which suggested British technique had become too fast, gymnastic and theatrical, and had gotten on the 'wrong track' since he last visited Britain before the war.[6] British dance professionals were also aware that in the battle for dancing 'hearts and minds', their ballroom dance technique was doing battle with American styles abroad as well as at home. In 1949, professionals Alex Moore and Pat Kilpatrick visited Germany to lecture about and provide demonstrations of English style ballroom dances at the first conference of that country's new Official Board. About this visit, *Danceland* observed that in the wake of the war, German dancing was at a 'crossroads', and the English style needed to be bolstered in order to keep the Germans from adopting the 'rhythmic loose' style of the Americans.[7]

By the final years of the 1940s, the dance profession took several steps to introduce new regulation and to ensure its ongoing supremacy in modern ballroom dancing: efforts were made to formalise a 'revised technique' for the English style, and to solidify the distinctions between the amateur and professional categories in dance competitions. In April 1948, the Official Board of Ballroom Dancing also convened the 'World's Ballroom Dancing Congress', to which they invited foreign teachers from around the world to Blackpool to learn – or to catch up on – the latest in the English style technique following the long disruption of the war years. Of the three hundred people present at the conference, there were representatives from across Europe, and from as far away as India, Ceylon and Australia. Participants attended classes and demonstrations in the standard four dances, and listened to lectures on topics such as the history of the English style.[8] Then in 1950, Philip J. S. Richardson spearheaded the creation of the International Council of Ballroom Dancing, in order to formalise the procedures for international competitions – an organisation that endures to this day as the World Dance Council.

Significantly, these measures helped to protect the integrity of the English style and the British profession's international supremacy, but they also created even further distance between professionals – with their technical precision – and the average members of the dancing public. This growing divide was acknowledged by an article in *Lancashire Dance News*, published shortly after the war, which proclaimed, 'A continual contention of the palais patron has been that the majority of professional dancers and demonstrators are content to bask in the comfort of their success without attempting to bring about a liaison between themselves and their public – the people from whom they derive their income'. This author argued that more than ever before demonstrations at the palais operated at too high a level to provide any real tutelage to the average dancer; he accused professionals of resting on their laurels, without realising that it was now usually the bands rather than the exhibition teams that drew the largest crowds to a dance hall.[9] A letter to the editor of the *Dancing Times* similarly complained that the performances he witnessed at dance championships – while beautiful and impressive – were 'entirely unsuited to the congested floors of ballrooms to-day'. This writer wanted to see competitors exhibit 'how the dances should be danced IN A BALLROOM, and so raise the standard of dancing, which has a modern tendency to degenerate to "jigging" and "jiving"'.[10] Another criticism of the competition system in the late 1940s was that it always rewarded the same teams; one observer argued that adjudicators needed to 'encourage the plodders' by allowing less established competitors to make it past preliminary heats.[11]

As has been shown, there had always been a disjuncture between the ballroom dancing of exhibitions and competitions, and what transpired in public ballrooms, but this gap clearly widened in the years after the war. Professionals and the more serious dancers within the dancing public were increasingly concerned about the declining technique in public dance halls. One letter to the editor of *Danceland*, for example, argued that only a few palais patrons really knew how to dance, and that 'even those few are obstructed by the majority, who just "mug around" with their arms and feet anywhere but in the correct steps and rhythm, with the great idea they are dancing'.[12] Continuing efforts were made to encourage instruction and raise the standard of dancing among casual dancers – and perhaps build bridges between them and the profession. For instance, Silvester, arguably Britain's most famous professional dancer, worked particularly hard to diminish growing perceptions that the English style was difficult or overly technical. Through the *BBC Dancing Club*, and his ongoing career as an author of instruction manuals, he advertised a 'Magic Way' method towards ballroom dancing prowess, guaranteeing that 'non-dancers will be able to take the ballroom floor in public with confidence after the first lesson'.[13]

However, despite efforts like these, an idea that had arisen even before the war – that the English style was too niche and technically precise – plagued ballroom dancing and professional dancers more and more in the late 1940s. The observations of an Indian observer, visiting Britain in 1947 for the first time in twelve years, provided additional insight into why ballroom dancing was increasingly marginalised as a popular style. Dancer Delicia Husna Jehan was dismayed to find a significant decline in the 'social aspect' of ballroom dancing since her last visit, and suggested it was 'becoming too professional and ... drifting from the original idea'. She concluded her observations of the British dancing scene by asserting that 'we need to win back the original social pleasure of the ballroom'.[14]

In reality, the 'social pleasure' of the ballroom had endured and even increased in the years after 1945, although what Britons danced was diversifying beyond the English style more than ever before. The post-war years witnessed a growing interest in American square dancing, while a significant segment of the dancing public favoured 'old-time' dances – such as the Victorian waltz, lancers, and polka – which had been a rising trend in some public ballrooms since before the war. Party dances also continued to be an important attraction and marketing strategy for the dance hall industry. Mecca in particular attempted to once again replicate the successful formula it had devised with the Lambeth Walk, by introducing new novelties that were British-themed, fun and simple enough to draw untutored dancers to the palais. For example, in 1946 the company launched the ''Ampstead way' in conjunction with the film *London Town*, which, although referencing a different part of London – Hampstead rather than Lambeth – seems not to have diverged significantly from its successful predecessor's 'cockney swagger'.[15] The following year, Mecca followed up 'Ampstead way with the 'royal minuet', a new dance devised by Adele England to commemorate Princess Elizabeth's coming of age. Like so many novelty dances before it, the royal minuet represented a flagrant example of the commodification of a traditionally English symbol by the company, however, ironically, there was no specific mention of the princess, since by law no member of the Royal Family could be named in anything which might be 'commercially exploited'.[16]

Unquestionably the jive served as the most visible and dramatic challenge to ballroom dancing after the war, however. While they had shown some willingness to accept it as a wartime novelty, many professionals and keen amateurs now raised strong objections to the dance, arguing that it was a threat to the correct execution of the English style, which they claimed the majority of people still preferred. A letter to the editor of *Danceland* from a dance enthusiast in Dorset expounded in frustration, 'Just when we thought we were beginning to see the last of the jive, it rears its ugly head again! Will the jivers never realise that they are hopelessly outnumbered?'[17] Not only were the jive's boisterous movements disruptive to those attempting a foxtrot or waltz, jivers had a tendency to halt mid-dance to enjoy the music of the band. In fact some swing fans chose not to dance at all, but simply stood on the dance floor near the bandstand to listen to the music concert-style, blocking any hope of progressive dancing. A related issue was that in many cases the irregular musical arrangements played by the 'swing inspired' dance bands were unconducive to a correct performance of the English style, leading one commentator to argue that bandleaders needed to 'Silvesterise' their orchestrations (a reference to Silvester's strict tempo dance music); improvised 'hot' swing, he argued, was appropriate for concerts, but not for ballrooms.[18] Proponents of the English style claimed that if a renewed push for strict tempo and ballroom dancing was not made, the country risked all of its dance halls becoming 'jive palaces'.[19]

Another correspondent to *Danceland* also expressed his distaste for the jive, but suggested a possible course of action that implied he understood that it was not likely to disappear from the nation's ballrooms: 'I for one appreciate orthodox dancing, and [jivers] infuriate me with their blank stares as they wiggle a foot there, and a twist there. Why don't the powers that be organise a dance-hall in each town or city to cope with these would-be killers of a noble art and thus eliminate a large cause of the discomfort and annoyance felt in present-day ballrooms.'[20] This writer's proposal that there should be designated spaces or even designated dance halls for swing music and the jive was in fact a solution that was devised in some the larger cities where public ballrooms were plentiful. Various dance hall proprietors responded to objections to the jive by banning the dance and emphasising ballroom dancing, while others deliberately catered to the 'jive-minded'.[21] As this state of affairs was succinctly described in *Danceland* in October 1947, 'managers in many halls were (a) inviting jitterbugs, (b) banning them, (c) roping them off – or (d) chucking them out'.[22] Meanwhile, other halls took to focusing on ballroom dancing one night and then the jive on the next, in an effort to determine what drew the greatest crowds and would ultimately be the most profitable for them. As this suggests, contemporaries were cognizant that the battle being waged between ballroom dancing and the jive represented a larger deliberation over the content of the country's dancing style, and the vision of the nation that it embodied. As Mecca professional James Quinn mused, 'It is fascinating to consider whether, remaining foreign to our true natures, jive will prove to have been nothing but a temporary superimposition and will die a natural death ... or whether the widespread enthusiasm with which it was accepted did indeed indicate a need for some new form of expression.'[23]

The jive did not 'die a natural death', nor did the English style – at least not immediately. Both continued to be danced in the nation's public ballrooms throughout the 1950s. However, the fundamental stylistic distinctions between them represented a broader choice that was gradually being made about the future of popular dance in Britain. Unlike the specific and formalised movements of ballroom dancing, the jive had no required steps and encouraged improvisation. Though the jive was still generally a partner dance, dancers frequently broke apart and engaged in independent movements. The jive was thus a herald of the twist, and the many other solo dances that would come to characterise the rock 'n' roll and disco eras. The expanding interest in the jive, and the dances that followed in its wake, also continued to undermine the cultural influence of the dance profession. As early as 1947, a letter to the editor of *Danceland* hinted at the waning authority of dance professionals, when its author rather derisively speculated as to why they were so resistant to the jive: 'Personally, I think it is because they can't do it. It may be due to the fact that it is beyond most of the teachers. I only know two schools where it is on the syllabus.'[24]

In the face of competition from new Americanised styles, as well as the declining public interest in the directives and instruction of dancing teachers, by the 1960s, the English style had been effectively divorced from popular dance. With the end of its heyday, many dance studios were forced to fold, and even the fate of the palais de danse seemed tied to the decline of the 'old-fashioned' ballroom dancing with which it was so strongly associated. In the later decades of the twentieth century, more and more dances halls closed their doors owing to competition from nightclubs and discotheques, or were converted for other purposes.[25] Importantly, the English style did live on as the competition standard, not only in Britain, but around the world – even conquering America at long last. As Juliet McMains has observed, it is ironic that Britain's national style, as well as the competition and accreditation systems its professionals had devised, reached this pinnacle of success and global influence 'at the exact moment ballroom dancing was at its nadir as a social activity'.[26] Ballroom dancing would also have a strong second act in British and global popular culture, with the remarkable success of celebrity dance competition television shows such as *Strictly Come Dancing* (the twenty-first century successor to Mecca's *Come Dancing*) and its many copycat programmes around the world, such as America's *Dancing with the Stars*.

For much of the first half of the twentieth century, however, the English style of ballroom dancing was the fulcrum around which British popular dance revolved. It was at the centre of multiple entertainment industries, and drew millions of people to dance classes and dance halls, as well as to their wireless sets or local cinemas. Ballroom dancing was the basis for a mass market of instruction manuals, newspapers and magazines, gramophones and sheet music, new fashion trends, and a range of other products. While the English style was not the only element of popular dancing in this period, other dances – from the Charleston to the Lambeth Walk – often represented a reaction to it, or were eventually tamed by its standards. The English style also highlighted Britain's position within expanding global systems of popular cultural exchange. Faced with an onslaught of foreign music and dances during the Jazz Age – which in some cases they embraced, and in other cases they resisted – the British people took up these dances, and from them were able to create something intrinsically their own, before sending it back out into the world to re-shape the culture of dozens of other countries. Most importantly, the popular dances of this period provided a way for Britons to engage with the critical issues of the day, such as the status of women in society, the changing racial make-up of the country, and international relations and global warfare. With their dancing bodies, Britons affirmed and challenged social barriers, and imagined who they were as a people and what their place was in a changing world.

Notes

1 Peter Probe, 'Dancers' Diary', *Northern Dance News Weekly* (7 September 1946), p. 2

2 'Work of the Devil', *Lancashire Dance News* (27 April 1946).

3 James Nott, *Going to the Palais: A Social and Cultural History of Dancing and Dance Halls in Britain, 1918–1960* (Oxford: Oxford University Press, 2015), pp. 72–98.

4 'Do Dancers' Tastes Change?' *Northern Dance News Weekly* (13 July 1946), p. 4.

5 Sylvia E. Clark, 'A South African Looks at Britain', *Danceland* (May 1947), p. 11.

6 Eddy L. Kuypers, 'As Others See Us', *Dancing Times* (March 1946), p. 295.

7 'Alex Moore Takes English Style to Germany Again', *Danceland* (July 1949), p. 13.

8 'World's Ballroom Congress', *Dancing Times* (June 1948), pp. 478–81.

 9 James Burleigh, 'The Palais-Goer and the Pro', *Lancashire Dance News* (11 May 1946), p. 1.
10 Jack Aitken, Letter to the Editor, *Dancing Times* (June 1948), p. 499.
11 'Encourage the Plodders', *Lancashire Dance News* (4 May 1946).
12 J. R. Whitehead, Letter to the Editor, *Danceland* (November 1947), p. 2.
13 'Silvester Teaches "Magic Way" by Television', *Danceland* (February 1948), p. 5.
14 Delicia Husna Jehan, 'Why We Dance', *Dancing Times* (February 1947), p. 261.
15 'Another Kissing Dance', *Northern Dance News Weekly* (20 July 1946), p. 1.
16 See *Danceland* (May 1947).
17 Letter to the Editor, *Danceland* (September 1947), p. 2.
18 Melvin Dunn, 'Stop Swinging It', *Lancashire Dance News* (27 April 1946).
19 'Do Dancers' Tastes Change?', *Northern Dance News Weekly* (13 July 1946), p. 4.
20 B. W. Eadon, Letter to the Editor, *Danceland* (April 1947).
21 'Jivers & Old Timers Battle on Merseyside', *Danceland* (January 1948), p. 16.
22 John Martin, 'It's our Tenth Birthday', *Danceland* (October 1947), p. 2.
23 James Quinn, 'The British Style', *Danceland* (May 1947), p. 4.
24 Letter to the Editor, *Danceland* (September 1947), p. 2.
25 Nott, *Going to the Palais*, pp. 92–8.
26 Juliet McMains, *Glamour Addiction: Inside the American Ballroom Dance Industry* (Middletown, CT: Wesleyan University Press, 2006), p. 89.

Select bibliography

Archival collections

BBC Written Archives Centre
Hammersmith Borough Archives
Imperial War Museum
  Department of Documents
  Sound Archive
Liverpool Record Office
London Metropolitan Archives
Mass Observation Archive
Museum of Liverpool Life
National Archives, Kew
  Records of the Air Ministry and Royal Air Force (AIR)
  Records of the Colonial Office (CO)
  Records of the Home Office (HO)
  Records of Departments responsible for Labour and Employment matters (LAB)
  Records of the Metropolitan Police Office (MEPO)
National Archives of Scotland
Royal Opera House, Covent Garden
Theatre Museum
Women's Library

Newspapers and periodicals

Britannia and Eve
Cheltenham Chronicle and Gloucestershire Graphic
Daily Dispatch
Daily Express
Daily Mail
Daily Mirror
Daily Telegraph

Dance News
Danceland
The Dancing Times
Eastern Mercury
Edinburgh Evening News
Evening News
Evening Standard
Hereford Times
Home Chat
Home Notes
Huddersfield Daily Examiner
Ladies Field
Lancashire Dance News
Leeds Mercury
Leicester Evening Mail
The Leytonstone Express and Independent
Liverpool Echo
London Daily News
Melody Maker
Modern Dance
Modern Dance and the Dancer
Northern Dance News Weekly
Popular Music and Dancing Weekly
The Star
Top Spin
Sunday Chronicle
Sunday Sentinel
Walthamstow, Leyton, and Chingford Guardian
Warrington Guardian
Warrington Examiner
Weekly Telegraph
Western Mail and New South Wales

Printed primary sources

Astaire, Fred, *Steps in Time: An Autobiography* (New York: Cooper Square Press, 1959, 2000).

Atherton, J. and W. Atherton, *Empress Ballroom and Palais de Danse, Wigan* (Liverpool: Ports and Cities Publishing Co., 1926).

Casani, Santos, *Casani's Self-Tutor of Ballroom Dancing* (London: Cassell and Company, 1927).

Casani, Santos, *Casani's Home Teacher: Ballroom Dancing Made Easy* (London: Heath Cranton, 1936).

Castle, Victor and Irene Castle, *Modern Dancing* (London: Harper & Bros., 1914).

Christie, Agatha, *The Body in the Library* (New York: Signet, 1941, 2000).

Collier, John and Iain Lang, *Just the Other Day: An Informal History of Britain Since the War* (London: Hamish Hamilton, 1932).

Cook, Raymond, *Shell-Fire Corner Carries On: A graphic description of the War's Events at England's Gateway* (London: Headley Brothers, 1942).

England, Adele, *How to Dance C.L. Heimann's Novelty Dances* (London: Danceland Publications, 1942).

England, Adele, *The ABC of Dancing* (London: Danceland Publications, 1942).

Fairley, Roma, *Come Dancing Miss World* (London: Newman Neame, 1966).

Franks, A. H., *The Ballroom Dancer's Handbook*, 2nd ed. (London: Sir Isaac Pitman & Sons, 1944).

Graves, Robert and Alan Hodge, *The Long Week-End: A Social History of Great Britain, 1918–1939* (New York: W.W. Norton & Company, 1940, 1994).

Harrisson, Tom, 'Whistle While You Work,' *New Writing* I (Autumn 1938): 47–67.

Harrisson, Tom and Charles Madge, *Britain by Mass-Observation* (London: Harmondsworth, 1939).

Hay, Ian, *Peaceful Invasion* (London: Hodder and Stoughton, 1946).

Illingworth, Frank, *Britain Under Shellfire* (London: Hutchison & Company, 1942).

Jephcott, A. P., *Girls Growing Up* (London: Faber and Faber, 1942).

Joseph, Shirley, *If Their Mothers only Knew: An Unofficial Account of Life in the Women's Land Army* (London: Faber and Faber, 1946).

Langdon, Claude, *Earls Court* (London: Stanley Paul, 1953).

Mackenzie, James, *Swing Fever Jitterbug* (London: Danceland Publications, 1942).

Mackenzie, James, *Stepping Out* (London: Danceland Publications, 1944).

Meyrick, Kate, *Secrets of the 43: Reminiscences by Mrs. Meyrick*, (London: J. Long, 1933).

Mitchell, A. Cosmo, *Allan's Ballroom Guide: An Authentic Description of All Dances in General Use* (Glasgow: Mozart Allan, 1926).

Moore, Alex, *Ballroom Dancing* (London: Isaac Pitman & Sons, 1942).

Murrow, Edward R., *This is London*, Elmer Davis (ed.) (New York: Simon and Schuster, 1941).

Richardson, Philip J. S., *A History of English Ballroom Dancing* (London: Herbert Jenkins, 1946).

Roberts, Robert, *The Classic Slum: Salford Life in the First Quarter of the Century*, (Manchester: Manchester University Press, 1971).

Silvester, Victor, *Modern Ballroom Dancing* (London: Herbert Jenkins, 1927, multiple editions).

Silvester, Victor, *This is Jive* (London: Danceland Publications, 1944).

Silvester, Victor, *Victor Silvester's Magic Way to Ballroom Dancing* (London: Danceland Publications, 1947).

Silvester, Victor, *Dancing For the Millions: A Concise Guide to Modern Ballroom Dancing* (London: Odhams Press, 1949).

Silvester, Victor, *Dancing is My Life* (London: William Heinemann, 1958).

Silvester, Victor and Philip J. S. Richardson, *The Art of the Ballroom* (London: Herbert Jenkins, 1936).

Spain, Molly, Fred Haylor, Phyllis Haylor and Charles Scrimshaw, *As We Dance* (London: The Dancing Times, 1938).

Spowart, Ella, *Ballroom and Services Dance Instructor: War Edition* (London: The Homeland Association, 1942).

Taylor, Cecil H., *Old Time and Novelty Dances* (London: The Dancing Times, 1944).

Tearle, Robert, *Dance, Theatre, and Music Quiz, Over 600 Questions and Answers* (London: Danceland Publications, 1943).

Thompson, C. J. S., *Dancing* (London: Collins Publishers, 1942).

Unknown author, *Ballroom Dancing in Youth Clubs* (London: Central Council of Physical Recreation, 1944).

Unknown author, *Bombers over Merseyside: The Authoritative Record of the Blitz, 1940–41* (Liverpool: Daily Post and Echo, 1943).

Unknown author, *Recreation and Physical Fitness for Youths and Men* (London: HM Stationery Office, 1937, 1942).

Unknown author, *Recreation and Physical Fitness for Girls and Women* (London: HM Stationery Office, 1937).

Books, articles, and theses

Abra, Allison, 'Doing the Lambeth Walk: novelty dances and the British nation', *Twentieth-Century British History* 20:3 (2009), 346–69.

Abra, Allison, 'On with the dance: nation, culture, and popular dancing in Britain, 1918–1945' (PhD dissertation, University of Michigan, 2009).

Abra, Allison, 'Dancing in the English style: professionalisation, public preference, and the evolution of popular dance in 1920s Britain', in Brett Bebber (ed.), *Leisure and Cultural Conflict in Twentieth-Century Britain* (Manchester: Manchester University Press, 2012), pp. 41–62.

Abravanel, Genevieve, *Americanising Britain: The Rise of Modernism in the Age of the Entertainment Empire* (Oxford: Oxford University Press, 2012).

Abreu, Christina D., *Rhythms of Race: Cuban Musicians and the Making of Latino New York City and Miami, 1940–1960* (Chapel Hill, NC: University of North Carolina Press, 2015).

Addison, Paul, *The Road to 1945* (London: Cape, 1994).

Adorno, Theodor, *The Culture Industry: Selected Essays on Mass Culture* (London: Routledge, 2004).

Albright, Ann Cooper, *Choreographing Difference: The Body and Identity in Contemporary Dance* (Middletown, CT: Wesleyan University Press, 1997).

Aldgate, Anthony and Jeffrey Richards, *Britain Can Take It: The British Cinema in the Second World War* (Oxford: Basil Blackwell, 1986).

Anderson, Benedict, *Imagined Communities: Reflections on the Origins and Spread of Nationalism,* (London: Verso, 1991).

Bailey, Peter, *Popular Culture and Performance in the Victorian City* (Cambridge: Cambridge University Press, 1998).

Bailey, Peter, 'Fats Waller meets Harry Champion: Americanisation, national identity, and sexual politics in inter-war British Music Hall', *Cultural and Social History* 4 (2007), 495–509.

Bailey, Peter, '"Hullo, Ragtime" West End revue and the Americanisation of popular culture in pre-1914 London', in Len Platt, Tobias Becker and David Linton (eds), *Popular Musical Theatre in London and Berlin, 1890–1939* (Cambridge: Cambridge University Press, 2014).

Baim, Jo, *Tango: Creation of a Cultural Icon* (Bloomington, IN: Indiana University Press, 2007).

Barlow, William. *Looking Up at Down: The Emergence of Blues Culture.* (Philadelphia, PA: Temple University Press, 1989).

Bebber, Brett (ed.), *Leisure and Cultural Conflict in Twentieth-Century Britain* (Manchester: Manchester University Press, 2012).

Berlin, Edward A., *Ragtime: A Musical and Cultural History* (Berkeley, CA: University of California Press, 1980).

Bingham, Adrian, *Gender, Modernity, and the Popular Press in Interwar Britain* (Oxford: Clarendon, 2004).

Bland, Lucy, *Modern Women on Trial: Sexual Transgression in the Age of the Flapper* (Manchester: Manchester University Press, 2012).

Bourke, Joanna, *Dismembering the Male: Men's Bodies, Britain, and the Great War* (Chicago, IL: University of Chicago Press, 1993).

Briggs, Asa, *A History of Broadcasting in the United Kingdom* (London: Oxford University Press, 1961).

Buckland, Theresa Jill, 'Edward Scott: The Last of the English Dancing Masters', *Dance Research* 21 (2003), 3–35.

Buckland, Theresa Jill, 'Crompton's Campaign: The Professionalisation of Dance Pedagogy in Late Victorian England', *Dance Research* 25 (2007), 1–34.

Buckland, Theresa Jill, *Society Dancing: Fashionable Bodies in England, 1870–1920*, (Basingstoke: Palgrave Macmillan, 2011).

Calder, Angus, *The People's War: Britain, 1939–1945* (London: Pimlico, 1969, 1992).

Calder, Angus, *The Myth of the Blitz* (London: Jonathan Cape, 1991).

Carter, Alexandra (ed.), *The Routledge Dance Studies Reader* (London: Routledge, 1998).

Carter, Alexandra (ed.), *Rethinking Dance History: A Reader* (London: Routledge, 2004).

Casciani, Elizabeth, *Oh, How we Danced! The History of Ballroom Dancing in Scotland* (Edinburgh: Mercat Press, 1994).

Caunce, Stephen, Ewa Mazierska, Susan Sydney-Smith and John K. Walton (eds), *Relocating Britishness* (Manchester: Manchester University Press, 2004).

Chapman, James, *Cinema, State and Propaganda, 1939–1945* (London: I.B. Tauris, 1998).

Conekin, Becky, Frank Mort and Chris Waters (eds), *Moments of Modernity: Reconstructing Britain, 1945–1964* (London: Rivers Oram Press, 1999).

Cook, James, Lawrence Glickman and Michael O'Malley (eds.), *The Cultural Turn in U.S. History: Past, Present, and Future* (Chicago, IL: University of Chicago Press, 2008): 291–317.

Daly, Ann, *Done Into Dance: Isadora Duncan in America* (Middletown, CT: Wesleyan University Press, 1995).

Daunton, Martin and Bernhard Reiger (eds), *Meanings of Modernity: Britain From the Late-Victorian Era to World War II* (Oxford: Berg, 2001).

Davies, Andrew, *Leisure, Gender, and Poverty: Working-Class Culture in Salford and Manchester, 1900–1939* (Buckingham: Open University Press, 1992).

Dawson, Sandra Trugden, *Holiday Camps in Twentieth-Century Britain: Packaging Pleasure* (Manchester: Manchester University Press, 2011).

DeGrazia, Victoria, *Irresistible Empire: America's Advance through Twentieth-Century Europe* (Cambridge, MA: Harvard University Press, 2006).

Denniston, Christine, *The Meaning of Tango: The Story of the Argentinian Dance* (London: Portico Books, 2007).

Desmond, Jane (ed.), *Meaning in Motion: New Cultural Studies of Dance* (Durham, NC: Duke University Press, 1997).

Doan, Laura. *Disturbing Practices: History, Sexuality, and Women's Experience of Modern War.* (Chicago: University of Chicago Press, 2013).

Driver, Ian, *A Century of Dance: A Hundred Years of Musical Movement, from Waltz to Hip Hop* (London: Hamlyn, 2000).

Enstad, Nan, *Ladies of Labor, Girls of Adventure: Working Women, Popular Culture, and Labor Politics at the Turn of the Twentieth Century* (New York: Columbia University Press, 1999).

Erenberg, Lewis, *Steppin' Out: New York Nightlife and the Transformation of American Culture, 1890–1930* (Westport, CT: Greenwood Press, 1981).

Erenberg, Lewis, 'Things to come: swing bands, bebop, and the rise of a postwar jazz scene', in Larry May (ed.), *Recasting America* (Chicago, IL: University of Chicago Press, 1989), pp. 221–45.

Faulk, Barry J., *Music Hall & Modernity: The Late Victorian Discovery of Popular Culture* (Athens, OH: Ohio University Press, 2004).

Fowler, David, *The First Teenagers: The Lifestyle of Young Wage-earners in Interwar Britain* (London: Woburn Press, 1995).

Franchi, Francesca, 'Mecca Comes to Covent Garden', *About the House: The Magazine of the Friends of Covent Garden* (Spring 1991), 12–20.

Franks, A. H., *Social Dance: A Short History* (London: Routledge & Kegan Paul, 1963).

Freedman, Jean R., *Whistling in the Dark: Memory and Culture in Wartime London* (Lexington, KT: University of Kentucky Press, 1999).

Frith, Simon, 'Music and identity', in Stuart Hall and Paul du Gay (eds), *Questions of Cultural Identity* (London: SAGE, 1996), pp. 108–127.

Gardiner, Juliet, *'Over Here:' The GIs in Wartime Britain* (London: Collins & Brown, 1992).

Gardiner, Juliet, *Wartime: Britain, 1939–1945* (London: Headline Publishing, 2004).

Gardiner, Juliet, *The Blitz: The British Under Attack* (London: Harper Press, 2010).

Genné, Beth, 'Openly English: Phyllis Bedells and the birth of British ballet', *Dance Chronicle* 18 (1995), 437–51.

Genné, Beth, 'Creating a canon: creating the "classics" in twentieth century British ballet', *Dance Research: The Journal of the Society for Dance Research* 18 (Winter 2000), 132–62.

Genné, Beth, ' "Freedom incarnate:" Jerome Robbins, Gene Kelly, and the dancing sailor as an icon of American values in World War II', *Dance Chronicle* 24 (2001), 83–103.

Giles, Judy, ' "Playing hard to get:" working-class women, sexuality, and respectability in Britain, 1918–1940', *Women's History Review* 1 (Spring 1992), 239–55.

Gilroy, Paul, *Black Atlantic: Modernity and Double Consciousness* (Cambridge, CT: Harvard University Press, 1993).

Glancy, Mark, *Hollywood and the Americanisation of Britain: From the 1920s to the Present* (London: I.B. Tauris, 2013).

Glucksmann, Miriam, *Women Assemble: Women Workers and the New Industries in Inter-War Britain* (London: Routledge, 1990).

Godbolt, Jim, *A History of Jazz in Britain, 1919–1950* (London: Northway Publications, 2010).

Golden, Eve, *Vernon and Irene Castle's Ragtime Revolution* (Lexington, KT: University of Kentucky Press, 2007).

Goodman, Philomena, *Women, Sexuality and War* (Basingstoke: Palgrave, 2002).

Grayzel, Susan R., *Women's Identities at War: Gender, Motherhood and Politics in Britain and France during the First World War* (Chapel Hill, NC: University of North Carolina Press, 1999).

Grayzel, Susan R., *At Home and Under Fire: Air Raids and Culture in Britain from the Great War to the Blitz* (Cambridge: Cambridge University Press, 2012).

Grimley, Matthew, 'The religion of Englishness: puritanism, providentialism, and "national character," 1918–1940', *Journal of British Studies* 46 (October 2007), 884–906.

Gullace, Nicoletta F., *'The Blood of our Sons:' Men, Women, and the Renegotiation of British Citizenship during the Great War* (New York: Palgrave Macmillan, 2002).

Guy, Stephen, 'Calling all stars: musical films in a musical decade', in Jeffrey Richards (ed.), *The Unknown 1930s: An Alternative History of the British Cinema, 1929–1939* (London: I.B. Tauris, 1998), pp. 99–120.

Hall, Stuart, 'Notes on deconstructing "the popular" ', in Raphael Samuel (ed.), *People's History and Socialist Theory* (London: Routledge & Kegan Paul, 1981).

Hall, Stuart, 'The question of cultural identity', in Stuart Hall, David Held and Tony McGrew (eds), *Modernity and its Futures* (Cambridge: Cambridge University Press, 1992), pp. 273–326.

Hall, Stuart, 'What is "black" in black popular culture?', in Gina Dent (ed.), *Black Popular Culture* (Seattle, WA: Bay Press, 1992), pp. 21–37.

Higson, Andrew, *Waving the Flag: Constructing a National Cinema in Britain* (Oxford: Clarendon Press, 1995).

Hinton, James, *The Mass Observers: A History, 1937–1949* (Oxford: Oxford University Press, 2013).

Hobsbawm, Eric, *Uncommon People: Resistance, Rebellion, and Jazz* (New York: Norton, 1998).

Hobsbawm, Eric, *Interesting Times: A Twentieth-Century Life* (London: Penguin Books, 2002).

Horn, Adrian, *Juke Box Britain: Americanisation and Youth Culture, 1945–1960* (Manchester: Manchester University Press, 2010).

Horrall, Andrew, *Popular Culture in London, c. 1890–1918: The Transformation of Entertainment* (Manchester: Manchester University Press, 2001).

Horwood, Catherine, *Keeping Up Appearances: Fashion and Class Between the Wars* (Stroud: Sutton, 2005).

Howkins, Alun, 'Greensleeves and the idea of national music', in Raphael Samuel (ed.), *Patriotism: The Making and Unmaking of British National Identity*, Vol. III (New York: Routledge, 1989), pp. 89–98.

Hubble, Nick, *Mass Observation and Everyday Life: Culture, History, Theory* (London: Palgrave Macmillan, 2006).

Jackson, Jeffrey H., *Making Jazz French: Music and Modern Life in Interwar Paris* (Durham, NC: Duke University Press, 2003).

Jones, Gareth Stedman, 'The "cockney" and the nation, 1780–1988', in David Feldman and Gareth Stedman Jones (eds), *Metropolis-London: Histories and Representations Since 1800* (London: Routledge, 1989), pp. 272–324.

Jones, Stephen G., *Workers at Play: A Social and Economic History of Leisure* (London: Routledge & Kegan Paul, 1986).

Kelley, Robin D. G., *Africa Speaks, America Answers: Modern Jazz in Revolutionary Times* (Cambridge, MA: Harvard University Press, 2012).

Kent, Susan Kingsley, *Making Peace: the Reconstruction of Gender in Interwar Britain* (Princeton, NJ: Princeton University Press, 1993).

Knowles, Mark, *The Wicked Waltz and Other Scandalous Dances: Outrage at Couple Dancing in the 19th and Early 20th Centuries* (Jefferson, NC: McFarland, 2009).

Kroes, Rob, R. W. Rydell and D. F. J Bosscher (eds), *Cultural Transmissions and Receptions: American Mass Culture in Europe* (Amsterdam: VU University Press, 1993).

Kumar, Krishan, *The Making of English National Identity* (Cambridge: Cambridge University Press, 2003).

Langhamer, Claire, *Women's Leisure in England, 1920–60* (Manchester: Manchester University Press, 2000).

Laughey, Dan, *Music and Youth Culture* (Edinburgh: Edinburgh University Press, 2006).

Lawrence, Jon, 'Forging a peaceable kingdom: war, violence, and fear of brutalisation in post-First World War Britain', *The Journal of Modern History* 75 (September 2003), 557–89.

Levine, Lawrence, 'Folklore of industrial society: popular culture and its audiences', *American Historical Review* 97 (December 1992), 1369–99.

Light, Alison, *Forever England: Femininity, Literature and Conservatism Between the Wars* (London: Routledge, 1991).

Lipsitz, George, *Dangerous Crossroads: Popular Music, Postmodernism and the Politics of Place* (London: Verso, 1994).

Longmate, Norman, *How We Lived Then* (London: Hutchinson, 1971).

Lunn, Kenneth, 'Reconsidering "Britishness:" the construction and significance of national identity in twentieth-century Britain', in Brian Jenkins and Spyros A. Sofos (eds), *Nation & Identity in Contemporary Europe* (London: Routledge, 1997), pp. 77–94.

Mack, Joanna and Steve Humphries, *The Making of Modern London: London at War* (London: Sidgwick & Jackson, 1985).

Mackay, Robert, *Half the Battle: Civilian Morale in Britain during the Second World War* (Manchester: Manchester University Press, 2002).

Malnig, Julie (ed.), *Ballroom Boogie, Shimmy Sham, Shake: A Social and Popular Dance Reader* (Urbana, IL: University of Illinois Press, 2009).

Mandler, Peter, *The English National Character: The History of an Idea from Edmund Burke to Tony Blair* (New Haven, CT: Yale University Press, 2006).

Maples, Holly, 'Embodying resistance: gendering public space in ragtime social dance', *New Theatre Quarterly* 28:3 (August 2012), 243–59.

Martin, Carol, *Dance Marathons: Performing American Culture in the 1920s and 1930s* (Jackson, MS: University of Mississippi Press, 1994).

Matera, Marc, *Black London: The Imperial Metropolis and Decolonisation in the Twentieth Century* (Berkeley, CA: University of California Press, 2015).

McKibbin, Ross, *Classes and Cultures: England, 1918–1951* (Oxford: Oxford University Press, 1998).

McMains, Juliet, *Glamour Addiction: Inside the American Ballroom Dance Industry* (Middletown, CT: Wesleyan University Press, 2006).

McMillan, James, *The Way it Was, 1914–1934* (London: Kimber, 1979).

Melman, Billie, *Women and the Popular Imagination in the Twenties: Flappers and Nymphs* (Basingstoke: Macmillan, 1988).

The Modern Girl around the World Research Group, *The Modern Girl Around the World: Consumption, Modernity and Globalisation* (Durham, NC: Duke University Press, 2008).

Nava, Mica, *Visceral Cosmopolitanism: Gender, Culture, and the Normalisation of Difference* (Oxford: Berg, 2007).

Nead, Lynda, *Victorian Babylon: People, Streets and Images in Nineteenth-Century London* (New Haven, CT: Yale University Press, 2000).

Nicholas, Siân, *The Echo of War: Home Front Propaganda and the Wartime BBC, 1939–45* (Manchester: Manchester University Press, 1994).

Nicolson, Juliet, *The Great Silence, 1918–1920: Living in the Shadow of the Great War* (Toronto: McArthur & Company, 2009).

Nott, James, *Music for the People: Popular Music and Dance in Interwar Britain* (Oxford: Oxford University Press, 2002).

Nott, James, *Going to the Palais: A Social and Cultural History of Dancing and Dance Halls in Britain, 1918–1960* (Oxford: Oxford University Press, 2015).

Paul, Kathleen, *Whitewashing Britain: Race and Citizenship in the Postwar Era* (Ithaca, NY: Cornell University Press, 1997).

Peiss, Kathy, *Cheap Amusements: Working Women and Leisure in Turn-of-the-Century New York* (Philadelphia, PA: Temple University Press, 1986).

Potts, Alex, 'Constable country between the wars', in Raphael Samuel (ed.), *Patriotism: The Making and Unmaking of British National Identity*, Vol. III (New York: Routledge, 1989), pp. 160–86.

Pugh, Martin, *'We Danced All Night:' A Social History of Britain Between the Wars* (London: Bodley Head, 2008).

Putnam, Lara, *Radical Moves: Caribbean Migrants and the Politics of Race in the Jazz Age* (Chapel Hill, NC: University of North Carolina Press, 2013).

Quirey, Belinda, *May I Have the Pleasure? The Story of Popular Dancing* (London: Dance Books, 1976).

Radway, Janice, *Reading the Romance: Women, Patriarchy, and Popular Literature* (Chapel Hill, NC: University of North Carolina Press, 1984).

Raphael-Hernandez, Heike, *Blackening Europe: The African American Presence* (London: Routledge, 2004).

Rappaport, Erika, and Sandra Trudgen Dawson and Mark J. Crowley (eds), *Consuming Behaviours: Identity, Politics and Pleasure in Twentieth-Century Britain* (London: Bloomsbury Academic, 2015).

Reynolds, David, *Rich Relations: The American Occupation of Britain, 1942–1945* (New York: Random House, 1995).

Richards, Jeffrey, *The Age of the Dream Palace: Cinema and Society in Britain, 1930–1939* (London: Routledge, 1984).

Richards, Jeffrey, *Films and British National Identity: From Dickens to Dad's Army* (Manchester: Manchester University Press, 1997).

Richards, Jeffrey, *Imperialism and Music: Britain, 1876–1953* (Manchester: Manchester University Press, 2001).

Riley, Kathleen, *The Astaires: Fred and Adele* (Oxford: Oxford University Press, 2012).

Roberts, Mary Louise, *Civilisation without Sexes: Reconstructing Gender in Postwar France, 1917–1927* (Chicago, IL: University of Chicago Press, 1994).

Robinson, Danielle, *Modern Moves: Dancing Race during the Ragtime and Jazz Eras* (New York: Oxford University Press, 2015).

Rose, Sonya, *Which People's War? National Identity and Citizenship in Britain, 1939–1945* (Oxford: Oxford University Press, 2003).

Rust, Frances, *Dance in Society* (London: Routledge & Kegan Paul, 1969).

Rydell, Robert and Rob Kroes, *Buffalo Bill in Bologna: The Americanisation of the World, 1869–1922* (Chicago, IL: Chicago University Press, 2005).

Samuel, Raphael and Alison Light, 'Doing the Lambeth Walk', in Raphael Samuel (ed.), *Patriotism: The Making and Unmaking of British National Identity*, Vol. III (New York: Routledge, 1989), pp. 263–71.

Savigliano, Marta E., *Tango and the Political Economy of Passion* (Boulder, CO: Westview Press, 1995).

Schwarz, Bill, 'Black metropolis, white England', in Mica Nava and Alan O'Shea (eds), *Modern Times: Reflections on a Century of English Modernity* (London: Routledge, 1996), pp. 176–207.

Shack, William A., *Harlem in Montmartre* (Berkeley, CA: University of California Press, 2001).

Smith, Graham A., *When Jim Crow Met John Bull: Black American Soldiers in World War II Britain* (London: I.B. Tauris, 1987).

Stearns, Marshall and Jean Stearns, *Jazz Dance: The Story of American Vernacular Dance* (New York: Macmillan, 1968).

Stowe, David, *Swing Changes: Big-Band Jazz in New Deal America* (Cambridge, CT: Harvard University Press, 1994).

Summerfield, Penny, 'Mass-Observation: social research or social movement', *Journal of Contemporary History* 20:3 (July 1985), 439–52.

Tabili, Laura, *We Ask for British Justice: Workers and Racial Difference in Late Imperial Britain* (Ithaca, NY: Cornell University Press, 1994).

Tabili, Laura, 'A homogeneous society? Britain's internal "Others," 1800–Present', in Catherine Hall and Sonya Rose (eds), *At Home With the Empire: Metropolitan Culture and the Imperial World* (Cambridge: Cambridge University Press, 2006), pp. 53–76.

Taylor, Philip M. (ed.), *Britain and the Cinema in the Second World War* (Basingstoke: Macmillan, 1988).

Tebbutt, Melanie, *Being Boys: Youth, Leisure and Identity in the Inter-War Years* (Manchester: Manchester University Press, 2012).

Thomas, Helen (ed.), *Dance in the City* (New York: St. Martin's Press, 1997).

Thompson, Andrew, *The Empire Strikes Back? The Impact of Imperialism on Britain from the Mid-Nineteenth Century* (Harlow: Pearson Educational, 2005).

Todd, Selina, *Young Women, Work, and Family in England, 1918–1950* (Oxford: Oxford University Press, 2005).

Tucker, Sherrie, *Dance Floor Democracy: The Social Geography of Memory at the Hollywood Canteen* (Durham, NC: Duke University Press, 2014).

Wagner, Ann, *Adversaries of Dance* (Urbana, IL: University of Illinois Press, 1997).

Walkowitz, Judith R., 'The "vision of Salome:" cosmopolitanism and erotic dancing in Central London, 1908–1918', *American Historical Review* 108 (April 2003), 337–76.

Walkowitz, Judith R., *Nights Out: Life in Cosmopolitan London* (New Haven, CT: Yale University Press, 2012).

Ware, Vron and Les Back (eds), *Out of Whiteness: Color, Politics, and Culture* (Chicago, IL: University of Chicago Press, 2002).

Warner, Michael, *Publics and Counterpublics* (Cambridge: MIT Press, 2002).

Waters, Chris, ' "Dark strangers in our midst:" discourses of race and nation in Britain, 1947–1963', *Journal of British Studies* 36 (April 1997), 207–38.

Webster, Wendy, *Englishness and Empire, 1939–1965* (Oxford: Oxford University Press, 2007).

Ziegler, Philip, *London at War, 1939–1945* (London: Pimlico, 2002).

Zimring, Rishona, *Social Dance and the Modernist Imagination in Interwar Britain* (Farnham: Ashgate, 2013).

Zweiniger-Bargielowska, Ina, *Managing the Body: Beauty, Health, and Fitness in Britain, 1880–1939* (Oxford: Oxford University Press, 2011).

Index

Lightning Source UK Ltd.
Milton Keynes UK
UKHW021435170919
349942UK00004B/174/P